CHILDREN'S FICTION 1900–1950

For the other members of our family:
Renée, Margaret, Peter, Mark and Jennifer.

.

CHILDREN'S FICTION
1900–1950

John Cooper
and
Jonathan Cooper

Ashgate

Aldershot • Brookfield USA • Singapore • Sydney

Published by
Ashgate Publishing Limited
Gower House
Croft Road
Aldershot
Hants GU11 3HR
England

Ashgate Publishing Company
Old Post Road
Brookfield
Vermont 05036–9704
USA

British Library Cataloguing-in-Publication data

Cooper, John
    Children's fiction 1900–1950
    1. Children's stories, English – Bibliography 2. Children's
  stories, American – Bibliography
    I. Title II. Cooper, Jonathan
    016.8'23'008'09282

Library of Congress Cataloging-in-Publication data

Cooper, John
    Children's fiction, 1900–1950 / John Cooper and Jonathan Cooper.
    ISBN 1–85928–289–X
    1. Children's stories, English—Bibliography. 2. Children's
  stories, American—Bibliography. 3. English fiction—20th century—
  Bibliography. 4. American fiction—20th century—Bibliography.
    I. Cooper, Jonathan. II. Title.
    Z1037.C768   1997
    [PR888.C513]
    016.823'9120809282—dc21   97–19547
                            CIP

ISBN 1 85928 289 X

Printed on acid-free paper

Typeset in Bembo by Bournemouth Colour Press, Poole and printed in Great Britain by The University Press, Cambridge.

CONTENTS

ACKNOWLEDGEMENTS

We wish to thank Margaret Cooper, Peter Cooper and Jennifer Cooper, who all helped in many ways to bring this book to fruition. We acknowledge gratefully the collections from which some of the illustrations derive.

The published sources we have tapped include works by Peter Newbolt (*G.A. Henty, 1832–1902, a biographical study*. Aldershot, Scolar Press, 1996); David Bathurst (*Six of the Best!* Chichester, Romansmead Publications, 1994); David Schutte (*William–The Immortal: An illustrated Bibliography*. Privately published by David Schutte, 1993); Patricia Craig and Mary Cadogan (*You're a Brick, Angela*. London, Gollancz, 1976); Eric Quayle (*The Collector's Book of Boys' Stories*. London, Studio Vista, 1973). A continual resource has been *Twentieth-Century Children's Writers*, initially edited by David Kirkpatrick, and most recently by Laura Standley Berger. London, St James Press, 1996.

INTRODUCTION

This book, covering the works of two hundred and six celebrated writers of children's fiction between 1900 and 1950, is intended for readers, librarians, parents, scholars, collectors (especially of first editions), bookdealers and those interested in artwork produced during this period.

The book has been deliberately set out into five different decades to help the reader locate writers of the same period. This design also helps to show more clearly the changes in fashion of reading material available for children over the years.

All featured authors are listed after this introduction with their pseudonyms. If an author is more well known under a pseudonym, the real name or names is given at the beginning of each article and/or checklist. A list of the author's children's fiction written each year in the relevant decade follows.

We have made the common assumption that books by British authors were first published in Britain, and that books by American authors first appeared in the US, except where we know this to be untrue. We have given the place of publication in checklists and the year of publication which, in the vast majority of cases, corresponds to the date printed in the books themselves, but in a few instances books were published the year preceding the date in them. Publishers are named in full when they appear in the checklists.

All books illustrated are the British first editions except where stated, when they are the American first editions.

There is much interest now in the dust wrappers of books and this is especially the case in children's fiction. Many authors, if not fine artists in their own right, have been blessed with brilliant illustrators. In the course of this book both the terms 'dust wrapper' and 'dust jacket' have been used to describe the protective paper around the book's binding. Readers, librarians and many collectors generally discarded dust wrappers in the early decades of the twentieth century, making any surviving wrappers rare. We are very pleased to be able to illustrate many exceptional dust wrappers, which the general public have little chance to see. Wherever possible, the artists of illustrations shown in this book have been credited. The checklist also gives, when known to us, the name of the artist responsible for any book's internal illustrations.

We have tried to present a wide variety of artwork including examples from S. van Abbé, Edward Ardizzone, Honor C. Appleton, Mabel Lucie Attwell, Cicely Mary Barker, S.G. Hulme Beaman, Alfred Bestall, Anne Bullen, Marguerite de Angeli, Ellen Edwards, Frank R. Grey, Rowland Hilder, S. Walter Hodges, Isobel Morton-Sale, Arthur Rackham, W. Heath Robinson, Ronald Searle, E.H. Shepard, C.E. Tunnicliffe and Denys Watkins-Pitchford.

This book also illustrates some of the many different categories children's fiction can be grouped into:

Boys' school stories such as those by Harold Avery, R.A.H. Goodyear, Walter C. Rhoades, Frank Richards and P.G. Wodehouse.

Girls' school stories such as those by Angela Brazil, Elinor M. Brent-Dyer, Dorita Fairlie Bruce, Antonia Forest and Elsie Oxenham.

Adventure stories such as those by M.E. Atkinson, Enid Blyton, W.E. Johns, Violet Needham and Arthur Ransome.

Fantasy stories such as those by G.E. Farrow, C.S. Lewis, Mervyn Peake, J.R.R. Tolkien and P.L. Travers.

Historical stories such as those by Capt. F.S. Brereton, G.A. Henty, Frank Knight, Naomi Mitchison and Philip Rush.

Animal stories such as those by C.W. Anderson, Primrose Cumming, Monica Edwards, Charles G.D. Roberts and Henry Williamson.

Stories for young children such as those by S.G. Hulme Beaman, Mrs H.C. Cradock, A.A. Milne, Beatrix Potter and Alison Uttley.

Whether the reader is involved in scholastic research, reliving happy childhood memories, trying to locate authors whose works are suitable for their own children's interests or a collector seeking information, we hope you have as much pleasure in using this book as we have had in putting it together.

AUTHORS INCLUDED FROM 1900 TO 1950

Ruth Ainsworth
C.W. Anderson
Edward Ardizzone
Richard Armstrong
Ruth Arthur
M.E. Atkinson
Harold Avery
The Rev. W. Awdry
'BB'
Enid Bagnold
Margaret J. Baker
Helen Bannerman
Cicely Mary Barker
J.M. Barrie
L. Frank Baum/Floyd Akers/Laura
    Bancroft/Hugh Fitzgerald/Suzanne
    Metcalf/Edith van Dyne
S.G. Hulme Beaman
E.F. Benson
Alfred Bestall
Val Biro
Enid Blyton/Mary Pollock
Helen Dore Boylston
Christianna Brand
Angela Brazil
Elinor M. Brent-Dyer/ E.M. Brent-
    Dyer
Capt. F.S. Brereton/ Lt.-Col F.S.
    Brereton/Lt.-Col. F.S. Brereton,
    CBE
Molly Brett
Joyce Lankester Brisley
Dorita Fairlie Bruce
Anthony Buckeridge
Frances Hodgson Burnett
Virginia Lee Burton
J. Williams Butcher
Arthur Catherall/A.R. Channel
Christine Chaundler
Joseph E. Chipperfield
Arthur Bowie Chrisman
Catherine Christian/Catherine Mary
    Christian
Richard Church

Mavis Thorpe Clark
Beverly Cleary
Dorothy Clewes
Elizabeth Coatsworth
Harry Collingwood
Padraic Colum
Florence Coombe
Mrs H.C. Cradock
Samuel Rutherford Crockett
Richmal Crompton
Primrose Cumming
Roald Dahl
Maureen Daly
Winifred Darch
Peter Dawlish/Lennox Kerr
C. Day Lewis
Mabel Dearmer
Marguerite de Angeli
Jean de Brunhoff
Olive Dehn
Meindert De Jong
Walter de la Mare
Elizabeth Borton de Trevino
V.H. Drummond
William Pène du Bois
Norman Duncan
Monica Edwards
Elizabeth Enright
Evelyn Everett-Green/E. Everett-
    Green/Cecil Adair
Eleanor Farjeon
Walter Farley
G.E. Farrow
G. Manville Fenn/George Manville
    Fenn
Kathleen Fidler
Charles J. Finger
Dorothy Canfield Fisher/Dorothy
    Canfield
Marjorie Flack
Esther Forbes
Antonia Forest
Roy Fuller
Rose Fyleman

Wanda Gág
Eve Garnett
Doris Gates
Charles Gilson/C.L. Gilson/Captain
    Charles Gilson/Major Charles Gilson
Rumer Godden
R.A.H. Goodyear
Elizabeth Goudge
Eleanor Graham
Kenneth Grahame
Hardie Gramatky
Graham Greene
Roderick Haig-Brown/R.L. Haig-
    Brown
J.B.S. Haldane
Kathleen Hale
Cynthia Harnett
Mary K. Harris
Charles Boardman Hawes
Robert A. Heinlein
Racey Helps
Margeurite Henry
G.A. Henty
Constance Heward
Lorna Hill
C. Walter Hodges
Andrew Home
Edith Howes
Richard Hughes
Katharine Hull & Pamela Whitlock
Norman Hunter
M.R. James
Tove Jansson
W.E Johns/William Earle/Captain W.E.
    Johns
Erich Kästner
James W. Kenyon
Rudyard Kipling
Eric Knight
Frank Knight
Elizabeth Kyle
Robert Lawson
Munro Leaf/John Calvert/Mun
Amy Le Feuvre/Mary Thurston Dodge
Robert Leighton
C.S. Lewis
Elizabeth Foreman Lewis

Hilda Lewis
Norman Lindsay
Eric Linklater
Hugh Lofting
Jack London
Patricia Lynch
Robert McCloskey
Angus MacVicar
Ruth Manning-Sanders
Bessie Marchant
John Masefield
L.T. Meade
Stephen W. Meader
Florence Crannell Means
Cornelia Meigs/Adair Aldon
Annette Mills
A.A. Milne
Naomi Mitchison
Mrs Molesworth
L.M. Montgomery
Rutherford Montgomery/
    A.L.Avery/Everitt Proctor
Dorothea Moore
Ursula Moray Williams
Bill Naughton
Violet Needham
E. Nesbit
Mary Norton
Mary O'Hara
Elsie J. Oxenham/Elsie Oxenham/Elsie
    Jeanette Oxenham
M. Pardoe
Richard Parker
Mervyn Peake
Eleanor H. Porter/Eleanor Stuart
Gene Stratton Porter
Beatrix Potter/Beatrix Heelis
Rhoda Power
Evadne Price
Willard Price
Christine Pullein-Thompson
Diana Pullein-Thompson
Josephine Pullein-Thompson
Virginia Pye
Gwynedd Rae
Arthur Ransome
Walter C. Rhoades/Walter Rhoades

1900–1909

AUTHORS INCLUDED FROM 1900 TO 1909

Harold Avery
Helen Bannerman
J.M. Barrie
L. Frank Baum/Floyd Akers/Laura Bancroft/Hugh Fitzgerald/Suzanne Metcalf/Edith Van Dyne
Angela Brazil
Capt. F.S. Brereton/ Lt. Col. F.S. Brereton/Lt. Col. F.S. Brereton, CBE
Frances Hodgson Burnett
J. Williams Butcher
Harry Collingwood
Florence Coombe
Mrs H.C. Cradock
Samuel Rutherford Crockett
Mabel Dearmer
Norman Duncan
Evelyn Everett-Green/E. Everett-Green/Cecil Adair
G.E. Farrow
G. Manville Fenn/George Manville Fenn
Charles Gilson/C.L. Gilson/Captain Charles Gilson/Major Charles Gilson
Kenneth Grahame
G.A. Henty
Andrew Home
Rudyard Kipling
Amy Le Feuvre/Mary Thurston Dodge
Robert Leighton
Jack London
Bessie Marchant
L.T. Meade
Mrs Molesworth
L.M. Montgomery
Dorothea Moore
E. Nesbit
Elsie J. Oxenham/Elsie Oxenham/Elsie Jeanette Oxenham
Eleanor H. Porter/Eleanor Stuart
Gene Stratton Porter
Beatrix Potter/Beatrix Heelis
Walter C. Rhoades/Walter Rhoades
Charles G.D. Roberts
Gordon Stables/Gordon Stables RN/Gordon Stables MD RN/Dr Gordon Stables RN
Herbert Strang
Mary Tourtel
Jean Webster
Percy F. Westerman/P.F. Westerman/P. Westerman
F. Cowley Whitehouse
Kate Douglas Wiggin
P.G.Wodehouse
May Wynne

Many of the children's books published in this decade are some of the most handsome looking volumes that have ever been produced and make a magnificent display in any book collection. The books often have richly coloured pictorial spines and front covers. The lettering and part of the design are often in gilt while the boards may have bevelled edges and the page edges could be gilt or olivine. There are usually several internal illustrations, including a tissue-covered frontispiece.

Some of the notable artists illustrating children's books during this period are Mabel Lucie Attwell, C.E. Brock, Gordon Browne, Harold Copping, Cyrus Cuneo, H.R. Millar, Wal Paget, Arthur Rackham, William Rainey, Charles Sheldon, Stanley L. Wood and Alan Wright.

To whet the appetite of readers, several pages of advertisements, sometimes illustrated, giving details of similar publications are often located at the back of the books.

Boys' adventure and school stories formed a large part of the children's fiction published in the first decade of the twentieth century. Authors Harold Avery, Harry Collingwood (pseudonym for William Joseph Cozens Lancaster), G. Manville Fenn, G.A. Henty, Andrew Home, Robert Leighton and Gordon Stables continued to write books of a similar style to that which had been popular towards the end of the nineteenth century. Newcomers such as Captain F.S. Brereton, Captain Charles Gilson, Herbert Strang (pseudonym for George Herbert Ely and C. James L'Estrange), Percy F. Westerman and P.G. Wodehouse quickly established themselves in these fields.

The adventure yarns often had an historical basis and our hero or heroes shared in exploits with the likes of Robert Henry Buller, Oliver Cromwell, Francis Drake, Giuseppe Garibaldi, Horatio Nelson, Frederick Sleigh Roberts, Garnet Joseph Wolseley and Arthur Wellington. War played an important part in many of the stories, be it Afghan, Boer, Carlist, Crimean, Franco-Prussian, Russo-Japanese or Zulu; which reflected the turbulent history of the second half of the nineteenth century.

These books were popular with the middle and upper classes and helped to establish the patriotic and heroic values held by a generation of readers, many of whom would die in the First World War.

Boys' school fiction was by no means a new genre in 1900. Indeed its history can be traced back to the last part of the eighteenth century and Maria Edgeworth's *The Barring Out* (1796). It can be said that the formula of dorm feasts, cricket matches and wallopings for misdemeanours real or alleged that constituted the archetypal school story was set down as early as Thomas Hughes's *Tom Brown's Schooldays* (1857) and F.W. Farrar's *Eric, or Little by Little – A Tale of Roslyn School* (1858). However, it took the fifty years following the publication of these two didactic volumes to popularise and universalise school fiction. This was achieved by splicing together the moral fibre advocated by Hughes and Farrar with the thrills of the original 'Penny Dreadfuls'. This resulted in publications like the *Boy's Own Paper* published, among others, by Talbot Baines Reed. The advantages of submitting to a closely defined moral code – inevitable victory over less auspicious foes and resultant fame and glory within the school (which should, of course, be greeted modestly) – are evident but do not override the actual narrative of schoolboy heroics. Those authors writing in the first decade of this century are Baines Reed's direct successors and, although each developed his own style, it was the *Boy's Own Paper* that first provided school fiction in a form that was universally accessible and affordable. For instance, many of Wodehouse's school stories were first published in the boys' paper *The Captain* and the latter half of this decade saw the inception of the hugely popular and influential *Magnet* and *Gem*. Although the Billy Bunter books only just fit into the scheme of the present survey, the influence of Charles Hamilton's creation of an academic idyll can be seen through many a description of golden summer days, cricket and wrongs righted. These are characteristics that will constantly emerge durng the following study of Wodehouse, Harold Avery, J. Williams Butcher, F. Cowley Whitehouse and all those other writers who gave such pleasure through their tales of life in imaginary public schools during the first years of this century.

The stories written for girls in the early and middle nineteenth century furnished suitable reading material for young ladies who had outgrown fairy tales and were to be prepared to take their place in a male-dominated society. Early writers such as Catherine Sinclair and Charlotte M. Yonge produced sentimental stories with a high moral tone that were often presented as Sunday School prizes and are not much read now. The heroines were docile and well mannered and educated by a governess. A book that has stood the test of time is Louisa May Alcott's *Little Women* (1868), which reflects the bravery of mother and daughters coping while Mr March is away at war and is genuinely moving. Susan Coolidge's 'Katy' books in the last quarter of the century introduced a tomboy who went on to feature in some of the first girls' school stories, such as *What Katy Did At School* (1874). Girls' stories became far more exciting towards the end of the nineteenth century and beginning of the twentieth century when writers such as Evelyn Everett Green, Bessie Marchant, L.T. Meade and Kate Douglas Wiggin created red-blooded heroines who had adventures, sometimes in far-flung loations. Important new writers then started to challenge their position, such as Angela Brazil, L.M. Montgomery, Dorothea Moore and Elsie J. Oxenham.

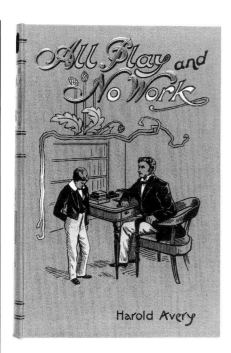

Harold Avery

Harold Avery (1867–1943). British.

Harold Avery wrote over sixty books and was the doyen of writers in the first few decades of the twentieth century who set their stories around life at a boys' school. Although the books set a high moral tone in which honesty and fidelity are encouraged, at no time does the reader think that life at a boarding school is dull or unpleasant. His characters are firmly bound by class and tend to be rather stereotypic but the stories, particularly the early ones, are enjoyable.

An early example of Harold Avery's work is *All Play and No Work* (1901) in which Bob Crossley, who is in the Third Form at Rudwick Grammar School, is having real problems learning his Latin irregular verbs. Bob is caught cribbing during a test and sent to Mr Bruce, the headmaster. It is this scene, that Harold Copping has drawn, which is shown on the book cover against a red background. Mr Bruce gives Bob '500 lines as a punishment. If it were not for the fact that this is the first offence, I should have felt it my duty to give you a caning.'

Gunpowder Treason and Plot, and Other Stories for Boys, with Fred Whishaw and R.B. Townshend. London, Nelson, 1900.

Heads or Tails. London, Nelson, 1900.
A Toast-Fag and Other Stories. London, Nelson, 1900.
All Play and No Work, illustrated by Harold Copping. London, Partridge, 1901.
With Wellington to Waterloo, illustrated by J. Finnemore. London, Wells Gardner, 1901.
Sale's Sharpshooters, illustrated by Rosa C. Petherick. London, Nelson, 1902.
An Armchair Adventurer. London, Simpkin Marshall, 1903.
The House on the Moor. London, Nelson, 1903.
Manor Pool Island. London, Collins, 1903.
Highway Pirates. London, Nelson, 1904.
Out of the Running. London, Collins, 1904.
Under Padlock and Seal. London, Nelson, 1905.
Firelock and Steel. London, Nelson, 1906.
The Magic Beads. London, Nelson, 1906.
Play the Game! London, Nelson, 1906.
Captain Swing. London, Nelson, 1907.
Through the Wood, illustrated by John Hassall. London, Nelson, 1907.
True to His Nickname. London, Nelson, 1907.
The Enchanted Egg. London, Nelson, 1908.
The Little Robinson Crusoes; or, Ronald and Betty's Adventures on an Uninhabited Island, illustrated by Harry Rountree. London, Nelson, 1908.
The Wizard's Wand, illustrated by P.B. Hickling. London, Nelson, 1908.
In the Days of Danger, illustrated by A.T. Smith. London, Nelson, 1909.

Helen Bannerman (1862–1946). British.

The seven books written and illustrated by Helen Bannerman in this decade were not published under her name, but anonymously. They were very popular with young children who appreciated the many brightly coloured drawings, easy language and light-hearted approach.

Her first book, *The Story of Little Black Sambo*, was published in 1899 by Grant Richards in a very small format 13cm. x 8cm. and dated on the front of the title page. The book has green cloth with nine vertical black lines on the front cover, plus the title and

THE STORY OF

LITTLE BLACK MINGO

author's name in a rectangle (contrary to the widely held belief that this volume, too, was published anonymously).

Little Black Mingo is drawn on the black and white front cover of *The Story of Little Black Mingo* (1901). She has no father or mother and has to live with a horrid cross old woman called Black Noggy, who ends up being eaten by a crocodile, along with a tin of kerosene and a box of matches. Inside the crocodile's stomach it is dark and Black Noggy lights a match to see where she is. The resulting explosion blows the crocodile and Black Noggy into little bits. Little Black Mingo then gets the nice little house for her own and the head of the crocodile as a seat.

Illustrated by the author.

The Story of Little Black Mingo. London, Nisbet, 1901; New York, Stokes, 1902.
The Story of Little Black Quibba. London, Nisbet, 1902; New York, Stokes, 1903.
Little Degchie-Head: An Awful Warning to Bad Babas. London, Nisbet, 1903; as *The Story of Little Kettle-Head*, New York, Stokes, 1904.
Pat and the Spider: The Biter Bit. London, Nisbet, 1904; New York, Stokes, 1905.
The Story of the Teasing Monkey. London, Nisbet, 1906; New York, Stokes, 1907.

The Story of Little Black Quasha. London, Nisbet and New York, Stokes, 1908.
The Story of Little Black Bobtail. London, Nisbet, and New York, Stokes, 1909.

J(ames) M(atthew) Barrie (1860–1937). British.

J.M. Barrie is correctly famous for Peter Pan, who made his debut in the world in the book *The Little White Bird* (1902), which was written for adults. Peter then became immortalised in the magical play *Peter Pan*, which was first performed at the Duke of York's theatre in London during 1904. J.M. Barrie later received a knighthood.

The book *Peter Pan in Kensington Gardens* consists of the chapters concerned with Peter Pan that were included in *The Little White Bird*. It tells us that Peter 'escaped from being a human when he was seven days old; he escaped by the window and flew back to the Kensington Gardens.' This book has fifty outstanding illustrations drawn by Arthur Rackham and was published in 1906. The first edition, in reddish-brown cloth with gilt lettering and front cover illustration of Peter

riding a goat, was issued with a frontispiece, but all other illustrations are found at the back of the book, set on brown paper. The tissue guard covering each illustration has a brief appropriate quotation from the text printed on it. Arthur Rackham's drawings, especially of the fairies, are now world renowned. The fairies 'hold their great balls in the open air, in what is called a fairy ring... these tricky fairies sometimes slyly change the board on a ball night, so that it says the Gardens are to close at six-thirty, for instance, instead of seven. This enables them to get begun half an hour earlier.'

Peter Pan in Kensington Gardens, illustrated by Arthur Rackham, London, Hodder & Stoughton, 1906.

L(yman) Frank Baum (1856–1919). American.
a.k.a. Floyd Akers.
a.k.a. Laura Bancroft.
a.k.a. Hugh Fitzgerald.
a.k.a. Suzanne Metcalf.
a.k.a. Edith Van Dyne.

L. Frank Baum is well known for his long series of books about that memorable and fascinating place Oz, where Dorothy has her adventures. The green, black and orange front cover of the UK first edition of *The Wizard of Oz* shows W.W. Denslow's drawing of a depressed looking scarecrow being told, 'Any crow of sense would see that you are only stuffed with straw.' Life becomes much more exciting when he meets Dorothy and travels to Oz with the Lion and the Tin Woodman. The head of the Lion appears on the book's spine, whilst the Tin Woodman is depicted sitting on a wall on the back cover. The title page of the book states *The New Wizard of Oz* in yellow and orange with the Scarecrow and Tin Woodman drawn in blue and white, superimposed against an orange circle. The book was published by Hodder & Stoughton in 1906 with green and orange endpapers showing the Scarecrow, Lion and Tin Woodman, with seven poppies in the foreground.

Another of L. Frank Baum's celebrated books which deserves special mention is his delightful fairy story *Queen Zixi of Ix* (1905), a story about a magic cloak. For the front cover of the first edition, Frederick Richardson's charming internal illustration is reproduced showing the moment when Queen Zixi throws off the magic cloak, which had been woven by fairies, and runs to the crystal spring, 'but glaring up at her from the glassy surface of the water was the same fearful hag she had always seen as the reflection of her likeness.' She had hoped to see a lovely image of herself but the magic cloak would grant no wish to a person who had stolen it.

A New Wonderland, illustrated by Frank Berbeck. New York, Russell, 1900; as *The Surprising Adventures of the Magical Monarch of Mo*, Indianapolis, Bobbs Merrill, 1903.

The Wonderful Wizard of Oz, illustrated by W.W. Denslow. Chicago, Hill, 1900; as *The New Wizard of Oz*, Indianapolis, Bobbs Merrill, 1903; as *The (New) Wizard of Oz*. London, Hodder & Stoughton, 1906.

Dot and Tot of Merryland, illustrated by W.W. Denslow. Chicago, Hill, 1901.

The Life and Adventures of Santa Claus, illustrated by Mary Cowles Clark. Indianapolis, Bowen Merrill, and London, Stevens and Brown, 1902.

The Master Key: An Electrical Fairy Tale, illustrated by Fanny Cory. Indianapolis, Bowen Merrill, 1901; London, Stevens and Brown, 1902.

The Enchanted Island of Yew, illustrated by Fanny Cory. Indianapolis, Bobbs Merrill, 1903.

The Marvelous Land of Oz, illustrated by John R. Neill. Chicago, Reilly and Britton, and London, Revell, 1904.

Queen Zixi of Ix, illustrated by Frederick Richardson. New York, Century, 1905; London, Hodder & Stoughton, 1906.

The Woggle-Bug Book, illustrated by Ike Morgan. Chicago, Reilly and Britton, 1905.

John Dough and the Cherub, illustrated by John R. Neill. Chicago, Reilly and Britton, 1906; London, Constable, 1974.

Annabel (as Suzanne Metcalf). Chicago, Reilly and Britton, 1906.

Sam Steele's Adventures on Land and Sea (as Hugh Fitzgerald). Chicago, Reilly and Britton, 1906; as *The Boy Fortune Hunters in Alaska* (as Floyd Akers), 1908.

Twinkle Tales (as Laura Bancroft); *Bandit Jim Crow, Mr Woodchuck, Prairie-Dog Town, Prince Mud-Turtle, Sugar-Loaf Mountain, Twinkle's Enchantment*, illustrated by Maginel Wright Enright. Chicago, Reilly and Britton, 6 vols, 1906; as *Twinkle and Chubbins*, 1911.

Ozma of Oz, illustrated by John R. Neill. Chicago, Reilly and Britton, 1907; as *Princess Ozma of Oz*, London, Hutchinson, 1942.

Sam Steele's Adventures in Panama (as Hugh Fitzgerald). Chicago, Reilly and Britton, 1907; as *The Boy Fortune Hunters in Panama* (as Floyd Akers), 1908.

Policeman Bluejay (as Laura Bancroft), illustrated by Maginel Wright Enright. Chicago, Reilly and Britton, 1907; as Babes in Birdland, 1911.

Dorothy and the Wizard in Oz, illustrated by John R. Neill. Chicago, Reilly and Britton, 1908.

The Boy Fortune Hunters in Egypt (as Floyd Akers). Chicago, Reilly and Britton, 1908.

The Road to Oz, illustrated by John R. Neill. Chicago, Reilly and Britton, 1909.

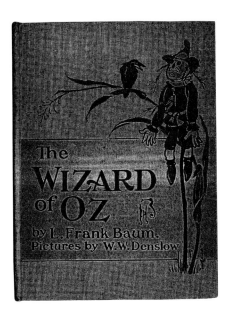

Angela Brazil (1869–1947). British.

For main author article see 1910 to 1919.

A Terrible Tomboy, illustrated by the author and Amy Brazil. London, Gay and Bird, 1904.

The Fortunes of Philippa. London, Blackie, 1906.

The Third Class at Miss Kaye's, illustrated by Arthur A. Dixon. London, Blackie, 1908.

The Nicest Girl in the School, illustrated by Arthur A. Dixon. London, Blackie, 1909; Boston, Caldwell, 1911.

Captain F(rederick) S(adleir) Brereton (1872–1957). British.
a.k.a. Lt. Col. F.S. Brereton.
a.k.a. Lt. Col. F.S. Brereton, CBE.

Captain F.S. Brereton, who served with the Scots Guards until his retirement in 1902, seemed to take up the mantle from G.A. Henty with stories set amidst Cromwell's invasion of Ireland, the French Revolution and the Zulu, Boer, Crimean and Franco-Prussian wars. He eventually wrote over forty titles and these books, with their strong emphasis on moral values, although considered old-fashioned today, are still very enjoyable to read.

With Shield and Assegai: A Tale of the Zulu War (1900) is Captain F.S. Brereton's first book and the style is typical of most of those that were written subsequently. The story follows the fortunes of Donald Stewart, who had been born in Zululand, the son of a Scottish medical missionary. He attends boarding school in England. Afterwards he enlists in the 60th Rifles where his knowledge of horsemanship and the Zulu language are to be a great advantage in exploits at Rorke's Drift. Later he successfully transforms himself into 'a fine, tall, upstanding Zulu, armed with a huge ox shield and a bundle of deadly assegais'. The red, black and white front cover shows such a Zulu warrior in full cry.

Stanley L. Wood, who is responsible for the internal illustrations, is especially noted for his fine action-packed drawings, which certainly helped to bring the printed page alive for boys and girls of this era. The black and white frontispiece for *With Shield and Assegai* is typical of this great artist's work and depicts the scene where 'Donald lifted his empty rifle above his head with both hands and dashed it in the face of the nearest man. The stock struck him full on the side of the head, giving Donald just sufficient time to draw a revolver and put a bullet through his brain' Another illustration shows the Zulu attack on Rorke's Drift, as 'they made assault after assault on the slender wall of mealie bags, defended by its heroic garrison.'

With Shield and Assegai: A Tale of The Zulu War, illustrated by Stanley L. Wood. London, Blackie, 1900.

In the King's Service: A tale of Cromwell's invasion of Ireland, illustrated by Stanley L. Wood. London, Blackie, 1900.

With Rifle and Bayonet: A story of the Boer War, illustrated by Wal Paget. London, Blackie, 1900.

A Gallant Grenadier: A tale of the Crimean War, illustrated by Wal Paget. London, Blackie, 1901.

The Dragon of Pekin: A tale of the Boxer Revolt, illustrated by William Rainey. London, Blackie, 1902.

One of the Fighting Scouts: A tale of Guerrilla Warfare in South Africa, illustrated by Stanley L. Wood. London, Blackie, 1902.

Under the Spangled Banner: A tale of the Spanish-American War, illustrated by Paul Hardy. London, Blackie, 1902.

Foes of the Red Cockade: A story of the French Revolution, illustrated by William Rainey. London, Blackie, 1903.

In the Grip of the Mullah: A tale of Adventures in Somaliland, illustrated by Charles M. Sheldon. London, Blackie, 1903.

A Hero of Lucknow: A tale of the Indian Mutiny, illustrated by William Rainey, London, Blackie, 1904.

With the Dyaks of Borneo: A tale of Head Hunters, illustrated by Fritz Bergen. London, Blackie, 1904.

A Soldier of Japan: A tale of the Russo-Japanese War, illustrated by Stanley L. Wood. London, Blackie, 1905.

A Knight of St. John: A tale of the siege of Malta, illustrated by William Rainey. London, Blackie, 1905.

Roger the Bold: A tale of the conquest of Mexico, illustrated by Stanley L. Wood. London, Blackie, 1906.

With Roberts to Candahar: A tale of the Third Afghan War, illustrated by William Rainey. London, Blackie 1906.

Jones of the 64th: A tale of the battle of Assaye and Laswaree, illustrated by William Rainey. London, Blackie, 1907.

With Wolseley to Kumasi, illustrated by Gordon Browne. London, Blackie, 1907.

How Canada Was Won: A tale of Wolfe and Quebec, illustrated by William Rainey. London, Blackie, 1908.

Rough Riders of the Pampas: A tale of Rand Life in South America, illustrated by Stanley L. Wood. London, Blackie, 1908.

A Hero of Sedan: A tale of the Franco-Prussian War, illustrated by Stanley L. Wood. London, Blackie, 1909.

John Bargreave's Gold: A tale of adventures in the Caribbean, illustrated by Charles M. Sheldon. London, Blackie, 1909.

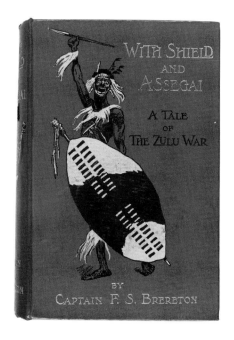

Frances Hodgson Burnett (1849–1924).
American.

Frances Hodgson Burnett's *Little Lord Fauntleroy* was published in 1886, whilst *A Little Princess, Being the Whole Story of Sara Crewe Now Told for the First Time* was put out in 1905, illustrated by Harold Piffard. Both books have a similar theme; the character of an individual is far more important than the amount of money or social position he or she may have. Both Cedric Errol and Sara Crewe were from loving homes but were then transported from their original environment. They face adversity, make firm friends beyond their social classes and ultimately achieve happiness.

Frances Hodgson Burnett also produced a series of four books for young children, which although extremely popular at the time, are now sadly almost unknown. The stories were told by Queen Crosspatch, but spelled by Frances Hodgson Burnett. The preface to *Racketty-Packetty House* (UK 1907), informs the young reader that 'If you think dolls never do anything you don't see them do, you are very much mistaken. When people are not looking at them they can do anything they choose.' *Racketty-Packetty House* was a doll's house, frequented by fairies, that had been pushed into a corner of Cynthia's nursery and been replaced in popularity by Tidy Castle. The book, published by Warne in a similar style to the Beatrix Potter titles, has many delightful illustrations by Harrison Cady. The scene on the front cover is of Cock Sparrow and the doll Meg sitting in a nest named Home Sweet Home; she is knitting and he is reading a paper. A mirror, bag, hat, umbrella and candle hang from the boughs of a tree. The frontispiece for the book shows the frightened dolls, Meg and Peg, who have been awoken in Racketty-Packetty House, by the shouting and screaming coming from Tidy Castle, as the dolls there are all sick with scarlet fever and raving in delirium.

A Little Princess, Being the Whole Story of Sara Crewe Now Told for the First Time. New York, Scribner, and London, Warne, 1905.
Racketty Packetty House. New York, Century, 1905; London, Warne, 1907.

" ' Do you hear a noise?' said Meg."

The Troubles of Queen Silver-Bell. New York, Century, 1906; London, Warne, 1907.
The Cozy Lion, as Told by Queen Crosspatch. New York, Century, 1907; London, Stacey, 1972.
The Spring Cleaning, as Told by Queen Crosspatch. New York, Century, 1908; London, Stacey, 1973.
The Good Wolf, New York, Moffat, 1908.
Barty Crusoe and His Man Saturday. New York, Moffat, 1909.
The Land of the Blue Flower. New York, Moffat, 1909; London, Putnam, 1912.

J(ames) Williams Butcher (b. 1857). British.

For main author article see 1910 to 1919.

Ray: The Boy Who Lost and Won, illustrated by Arthur Twidle. London, Robert Culley, 1908.

Harry Collingwood (1851–1922). British. Pseudonym for William Joseph Cosens Lancaster.

Harry Collingwood was the pseudonym used by William Joseph Cosens Lancaster, an ex-naval officer, therefore it is not surprising that many of his spiritedly written adventure stories have a nautical theme. *A Middy in Command: a tale of the Slave Squadron* (1908) is a typical example of his work. The midshipman aboard the schooner *Francesca* is a Mr Grenville, 'one of the rare young men who carry an old head upon young shoulders, and of possessing the courage to act upon his own responsibility.' He is promoted to the rank of lieutenant and given a roving commission to hunt down and destroy a pirate ship. The blue, cream, pink and black scene on the book cover depicts Mr Grenville leading the boarders helter-skelter over their own bulwarks and those of the brig *Barracouta* to face the pirates, only to find themselves outnumbered two to one. Edward S. Hodgson's illustration for the book's frontispiece depicts the scene on the deck of the *Barracouta*, when 'for ten long minutes the fight raged most furiously'.

Across the Spanish Main: A tale of the sea in the days of Queen Bess, illustrated by William Rainey. London, Blackie, 1906.
Dick Leslie's Luck: A story of shipwreck and adventure, illustrated by Harold Piffard. London, SPCK (Society for Promoting Christian Knowledge), 1906.
Geoffrey Harrington's Adventures, illustrated by Harold Piffard. London, SPCK, 1907.
With Airship and Submarine: A tale of

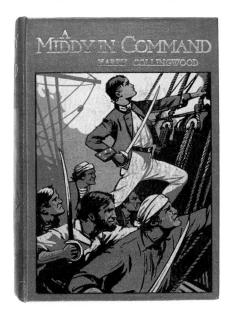

adventure, illustrated by Edward S. Hodgson. London, Blackie, 1907.
Blue and Grey: A story of the American Civil War, illustrated by E.S. Hardy. London, Blackie, 1908.
A Middy In Command: A tale of the Slave Squadron, illustrated by Edward S. Hodgson. London, Blackie, 1908.
Under The Chilian Flag: A tale of war between Chili and Peru 1879–1881, illustrated by William Rainey. London, Blackie, 1908.

Florence Coombe. British.

Florence Coombe wrote school stories for boys, a type of book traditionally a male preserve. In *For the Old School* (1901), Mr Henschel, the headmaster of Amberley School, an academy for the sons of gentlemen, finds he has competition from a new school that has opened nearby. The number of boys has fallen to twelve and the boys work together to find different ways to save the old school. Ted Swift, for example, tries to publicize the school by adding its name onto a local signpost. This act is captured in one of the stylish illustrations by Paul Hardy. Eventually a flood caused by the River Amber solves their problem.

The first edition of *Jack of Both Sides: The Story of a School War* (1900) has the same format as G.A. Henty's *Do Your Duty*, issued in the same year. The front cover for both books has an illustration of a boy reading to a girl and contains a coloured frontispiece by H.M. Brock, whilst a different artist provided the black and white illustrations.

Jack of Both Sides: The Story of a School War, illustrated by S.B. Pearse (coloured frontispiece by H.M. Brock). London, Blackie, 1900.
For The Old School, illustrated by Paul Hardy. London, Blackie, 1901.
Comrades All, illustrated by D. Chamberlain. London, Blackie, 1902.
Two to One: The Tale of a Holiday, illustrated by Audrey J. Watson (coloured frontispiece by H.M. Brock). London, Blackie, 1902.

Mrs H(enry) C. Cradock. British.

For main author article see 1910 to 1919.

The Care Of Babies: A Reading Book for Girls.
London, Bell, 1908.

Samuel Rutherford Crockett
(1860–1914). British.

For main author article see 1910 to 1919.

Sir Toady Crusoe, illustrated by Gordon
Browne. London, Wells Gardner Darton,
and New York, Stokes, 1905.

Mabel Dearmer (1872–1915). British.

Altogether Mabel Dearmer wrote six
charming books for children, five of which
she illustrated. The dull-coloured illustration
of the Ark on the cover of the first edition of
A Noah's Ark Geography (1900) belies the
stylish and sensitively coloured internal
illustrations by the author.

Featured in *A Noah's Ark Geography* is Kit,
a little boy who takes a Cockyolly Bird to bed
on Mondays, Wednesdays and Fridays and a
black doll called Jum-Jum on Tuesdays,

Thursdays and Saturdays. Miss Brown is his
governess, who teaches him geography from a
little red book, as is shown in a delightful
illustration by the author. 'Kit had counted
the flowers on Miss Brown's white dress up to
thirty-nine, and had stretched his left leg, and
he had stretched his right leg and he had
rubbed the hairs out of his eyes, until Miss
Brown had been obliged to give him a black
mark.' Kit's Noah's Ark, which he plays with
on Sundays, lived in the schoolroom and Kit,
instead of learning his lessons, wondered what
the animals were playing at underneath the
lid.

The Noah's Ark Geography, illustrated by the
author. London, Macmillan, 1900.
The Child's Life of Christ, illustrated by
Eleanor Fortescue-Brickdale. London,
Methuen, 1906.

Norman Duncan (1871–1916). Canadian.

Norman Duncan was a Canadian who wrote
three books specifically for children, all
featuring Billy Topsail; from his early years in
The Adventures of Billy Topsail (1906) until
young adulthood in *Billy Topsail, M.D.*
(1916). Each book contains several action

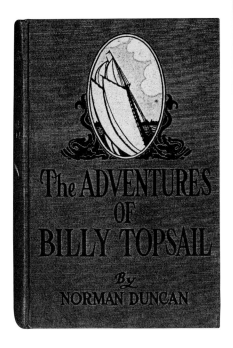

packed episodes involving Billy, who is a fisherman's son from Ruddy Cove, Newfoundland, and his dog, Skipper. Besides being exciting and realistic, the stories propound good values such as kindness, courage and helpfulness to other people.

The first edition of *The Adventures of Billy Topsail* is bound in green cloth, lettered in black, with the white sail of a boat as though reflected in an oval mirror.

The Adventures of Billy Topsail. New York, Revell, and London, Hodder & Stoughton, 1906.

Evelyn Everett-Green (1856–1932). British.
a.k.a. E. Everett-Green.
a.k.a. Cecil Adair.

Evelyn Everett-Green wrote what was considered at the time to be exemplary fiction for children. The bulk of her output was produced during the nineteenth century but she continued to write novels of a similar style, whether school stories, kith and kin adventures or historical novels, well into the twentieth century. Her stories upheld the strict morals of the Victorian age.

Greyfriars (1908) is a grand house owned by Esther Egerton's sister and brother-in-law. Esther is looking after the house and family in their absence. The book's frontispiece shows the moment when Esther, having disturbed a burglar standing next to the open safe in her sister's room during a house party, is grabbed by the man's accomplice. 'A man sprang upon Esther out of another room, grasping her fiercely by the wrist, and laying his disengaged hand upon her mouth to deaden the sound of the cry which she had begun to utter.' The scene on the book's cover drawn by Ernest Prater, is of moments later when Esther's nephew, Dacre, intervenes and becomes locked in a desperate struggle with the intruder, 'whose distorted and furious face Esther was certain she recognised as the groom, Miller.' Dacre is shot and nearly dies.

Bruno and Bimbo: the story of some little people. London, E. Nister, 1900.

Eleanor's Hero: a tale. London, Sunday School Union, 1900.

A Fiery Chariot. London, Hutchinson, 1900.

A Gordon Highlander: A Tale. London, Nelson, 1900.

In Cloister and Court; or, the white flower of a blameless life. The story of Bishop Ken: a tale. London, J.F. Shaw, 1900.

The King's Butterfly. London, E. Nister, 1900.

The Little Match-Girl. London, J.F. Shaw, 1900.

The Master of Fernhurst. London, J.F Shaw, 1900.

Odeyne's Marriage, London, J.F. Shaw, 1900.

The Silver Axe: The narrative of Rupert, Earl of Herondate. London, Hutchinson, 1900.

The Wooing of Val. The Story of six days. London, Hutchinson, 1900.

After Worcester: The Story of a Royal Fugitive. London, Nelson, 1901.

Bob and Bill. London, Religious Tract Society, 1901.

For the Faith: A story of the Young Pioneers of Reformation in Oxford. London, Nelson, 1901.

In Fair Granada: A tale of Moors and Christians. London, Nelson, 1901.

Princess Fairstar: A story of the days of Charles I. London, Ernest Nister, 1901.

The Secret of Maxshelling. London, J.F. Shaw, 1901.

Tregg's Triumph: A story of stormy days. London, Religious Tract Society, 1901.

True Stories of Girl Heroines. London, Hutchinson, 1901.

Alwyn Ravendale, London, Religious Tract Society, 1902.

The Boys of the Red House, illustrated by E.T. Pope. London, Andrew Melrose, 1902.

Fallen Fortunes: Being the adventures of a gentleman of quality in the days of Queen Anne. London, Thomas Nelson. 1902.

Gabriel Garth, Chartist. London, Andrew Melrose, 1902.

A Hero of the Highlands; or, The Romance of a Rebellion, as related by One who Looked on. London, Nelson, 1902.

My Lady Joanna: being a chronicle concerning the King's children. Rendered into model English from the Records by the Lady Edeline. London, James Nisbet, 1902.

A Princess's Token. London, Ernest Nister, 1902.

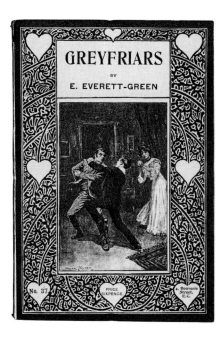

Short Tales from Storyland: a volume of thirty
   stories. London, Ernest Nister, 1902.
Tiny and her Grandfather. London, Ward
   Lock, 1902.
To the Rescue: a tale of a London prentice boy.
   London, Ernest Nister, 1902.
White Wyvill and Red Ruthven: a story of the
   strife of the Roses. London, Ernest Nister,
   1902.
Called of her Country: The story of Joan of Arc,
   illustrated by E.F. Sherie. London, S.H.
   Bousfield, 1903.
Cambria's Chieftain. London, Nelson, 1903.
The Castle of the White Flag: A tale of the
   Franco-German War. London, Nelson,
   1903.
The Conscience of Roger Trehern. London,
   Religious Tract Society, 1903.
The Squire's Heir; or, the Secret of Rochester's
   Will. London, Andrew Melrose, 1903.
Under Two Queens. London, John F Shaw,
   1903.
The Children's Crusade: a story of adventure.
   London, Nelson, 1904.
The Faith of Hilary Lovel: a story of Armada
   days. London, Religious Tract Society,
   1904.
The Jilting of Bruce Heriot. London, Religious
   Tract Society, 1904.
Little Lady Val: A tale of the days of good Queen

Bess, illustrated by Arthur A. Dixon.
   London, E. Nister, 1904.
Ringed by Fire: A story of the Franco-Prussian
   War. London, Nelson, 1904.
The Sisters of Silver Sands. London, Sunday
   School Union, 1904.
The Three Graces. London, Andrew Melrose,
   1904.
In Northern Seas. London, Nelson, 1905.
Jim Trelawny, illustrated by E.A. Pike.
   London, Sunday School Union, 1905.
Madam of Clyst Peveril, illustrated by C.
   Pearse. London, Andrew Melrose, 1905.
Miss Greyshott's Girls, illustrated by Arthur
   Twidle, London, Andrew Melrose, 1905.
Smouldering Fires; or, the Kinsmen of Kinthorns.
   London, Thomas Nelson, 1905.
Treasure Trove: a tale of Shark's Tooth Rocks.
   London, J.F. Shaw, 1905.
Uncle Boo: a story for children, illustrated by
   Rosa C. Petherick. London, Nelson,
   1905.
The Defense of the Rock, illustrated by W.B.
   Wollen. London, Nelson, 1906.
Dickie and Dorrie: a tale of Hallowdene Hall,
   illustrated by Gordon Browne. London,
   Wells Gardner, Darton, 1906.
In a Land of Beasts, illustrated by A.A. Dixon.
   London, Collins, 1906.
In the War of the Roses. London, Nelson,
   1906.
The Master of Marshlands, illustrated by Bertha
   Newcombe. London, Ward Lock, 1906.
A Motherless Maid, illustrated by Dorothy
   Travers-Pope. London, Andrew Melrose,
   1906.
Our Great Undertaking: a grandmother's story.
   London, Hodder & Stoughton, 1906.
Percy Vere, illustrated by R. Lillie. London,
   Cassell, 1906.
Carol Carew; or, Was it Imprudent? London,
   S.W. Partridge, 1907.
Clanrickard Court, illustrated by N.C. Bishop-
   Culpeper. London, Andrew Melrose,
   1907.
Knights of the Road. London, Nelson, 1907.
Miss Lorimer of Chard, illustrated by C.
   Pearse. London, Andrew Melrose, 1907.
Ruth Ravelstan, the Puritan's Daughter.
   London, Nelson, 1907.
Gowrie's Vengeance: the romance of a conspiracy.
   London, Nelson, 1908.

Greyfriars, illustrated by Ernest Prater. London, Leisure Hour Monthly Library, 1908.

Hilary Quest, illustrated by Watson Charlton, London, Pilgrim Press, 1908.

Stepsister Stella: a story for girls, illustrated by Gertrude Steel. London, Pilgrim Press, 1908.

The City of the Golden Gate. London, Stanley Paul, 1909.

The Cossart Cousins: a story for girls. London, Religious Tract Society, 1909.

Half-a-dozen sisters. London, Leisure Hour Monthly Library, 1909.

A Lad of London Town: a tale of darkness and light, illustrated by T. Heath Robinson. London, Pilgrim Press, 1909.

A Wilful Maid. A Story for Girls. London, Partridge, 1909.

G(eorge) E(dward) Farrow (1862–1920?). British.

G.E. Farrow, now sadly a neglected author, should be read and collected by all those who enjoy wonderfully absurd and clever fairy tales similar in style to Lewis Carroll's *Alice's Adventures in Wonderland*. His bizarre fantasy lands of Why, Fancy, Nightmare, Zum and His Importance, the Panjandrum, will thoroughly enchant any new reader. The eccentric characters G.E. Farrow concocted are a delight, whether it is the Wallypug, a bedraggled, bullied sort of king, whose clothes and crown are far too large for him, or the Dodo, a rude, egotistical bird, who ought to be extinct.

G.E. Farrow's creative powers were well matched by the artist Alan Wright in many of the books. The first editions, published by Pearson, are beautifully produced, with richly coloured cloth, usually green, with gilt lettering and illustration on the front cover and page edges also in gilt. *In Search of the Wallypug* (1902), one of a series of books about this unusual creature, is typical with its dark green and gilt front cover showing 'A hippopotamus in a uniform and gold braid … energetically ringing a large bell, and shouting at the top of his voice' on the platform of Muddlehead Junction.

The Mandarin's Kite, illustrated by Alan Wright. London, Skeffington, 1900.

Baker Minor and the Dragon, illustrated by Alan Wright. London, Pearson, 1901.

The New Panjandrum, illustrated by Alan Wright. London, Pearson, 1901; New York, Dutton, 1902.

In Search of the Wallypug, illustrated by Alan Wright. London, Pearson, 1902.

All About the Wallypug. London, Tuck, 1903.

Professor Philanderpan. London, Pearson, 1903.

The Cinematograph Train and Other Stories, illustrated by Alan Wright. London, Johnson, 1904.

Pixie Pickles: The Adventures of Pixene and Pixette in Their Woodland Haunts, illustrated by Harry B. Neilson. London, Skeffington, 1904; New York, Warne, 1906.

The Wallypug Birthday Book, illustrated by Alan Wright. London, Routledge, 1904.

The Wallypug in Fog-land, illustrated by Alan Wright. London, Pearson, and Philadelphia, Lippincott, 1904.

The Mysterious "Mr. Punch." London, SPCK, 1905.

The Wallypug Book, illustrated by Harry Furniss. London, Treherne, 1905.

The Wallypug in the Moon; or, His Badjesty, illustrated by Alan Wright. London,

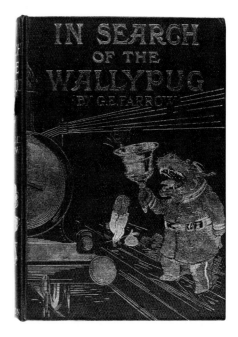

Pearson, and Philadelphia, Lippincott, 1905.

Ruff and Ready: The Fairy Guide, with May Byron, illustrated by John Hassall. London, Cooke, 1905.

Ten Little Jappy Chaps, illustrated by John Hassall. London, Treherne, 1905.

The Adventures of Ji, illustrated by G.C. Tresidder. London, Partridge, 1906.

The Escape of the Mullingong: A Zoological Nightmare, illustrated by Gordon Browne. London, Blackie, 1906.

The Adventures of a Dodo, illustrated by Willy Pogány. London, Unwin, 1907; New York, Wessels, 1908; as *A Mysterious Voyage*, London, Partridge, 1910.

Zoo Babies, illustrated by Cecil Aldin. London, Hodder & Stoughton, 1907; New York, Stokes, 1908.

The Dwindleberry Zoo, illustrated by Gordon Browne. London, Blackie, 1908.

G(eorge) Manville Fenn (1831–1909). British.
a.k.a. George Manville Fenn.

G. Manville Fenn was a former school teacher, newspaper proprietor and journalist who started writing during the 1860s and produced well over a hundred books, mainly read by boys. He wrote well-liked, easy to read adventure stories, usually set in foreign parts but sometimes centred at a school or in a historical period. His heroes are fallible and trustworthy young men who gain assurance through their experiences in their adventures.

The design by Charles Pears for the front cover of *Glyn Severn's School Days* (1904) reveals 'Glyn Severn and his companion of many years, Aziz Singh, a dark English boy in appearance and speech, but maharajah in his own right', wearing their Eton costumes, riding the captured elephant, on its return to the showfield.

'Tention!' A story of boy-life during the Peninsular War (1906) is another typical example of G. Manville Fenn's fine writing for boys. Private Penton Gray (Pen), a sharpshooter in England's rifle-regiment, rescues Punch, the bugler of the company, who has been injured in a skirmish with the French. For the book's green front cover, Charles M. Sheldon pictures Punch being carried by Pen, both wearing their uniforms of black-green, tipped at the collar and cuff with scarlet. After a series of exciting adventures, they assist Sir Arthur Wellesley in the defeat of the French and are presented to the dethroned Spanish monarch. Pen is promoted to Ensign Gray and Punch is rewarded by being made 'the youngest full private in the corps.'

Charge: A story of Briton and Boer, illustrated by W.H.C. Groome. London, Chambers, 1900.

King Robert's Page. London, E. Nister, 1900.

Old Gold; or, the cruise of the "Jason" brig. London, E. Nister, 1900.

Uncle Bart: The tale of a tyrant. London, SPCK, 1900.

Ching, the Chinaman and his Middy friends. London, SPCK, 1901.

A Dash from Diamond City. London, E. Nister, 1901.

The King's Sons. London, E. Nister, 1901.

The Kopje Garrison: A tale of the Boer War, illustrated by W. Boucher. London, Chambers, 1901.

Pulabad; or, the bravery of a boy, London, The Young People's Library, 1901.

Running Amok: A story of adventure. London, Chatto & Windus, 1901.

Something Like A Snake. London, Warwick Bros and Rutter, 1901.

Coastguard Jack. London, E. Nister, 1902.

The Lost Middy: being the secret of the smuggler's gap. London, E. Nister, 1902.

A Meeting of Greeks and the Tug of War, illustrated by C.M. Sheldon. London, S.H. Bousfield, 1902.

The Peril Finders. London, SPCK, 1902.

Stan Lynn: A boy's adventures in China, illustrated by W.H.C. Groome. London, Chambers, 1902.

Two Rough Stones, and a Bad Day's Fishing. London, E. Nister, 1902.

Fitz the Filibuster. London, SPCK, 1903.

The King's Esquires; or, the Jewel of France. London, Grant Richards, 1903.

Walsh the Wonder-Worker, illustrated by W.H.C. Groome, London, Chambers, 1903.

Glyn Severn's Schooldays, illustrated by Charles Pears. London, Chambers, 1904.

The Khedire's Country: The Nile valley and its products. London, Cassell, 1904.

Marcus: the Young Centurion. London, E. Nister, 1904.

The Ocean Cat's-Paw: the story of a strange cruise. London, SPCK, 1904.

The Powder Monkey, illustrated by Ambrose Dudley. London, E. Nister, 1904.

To Win or To Die: a tale of the Klondike gold craze. London, S.W. Partridge, 1904.

Nephew Jack: his cruise for his uncle's craze. London, SPCK, 1905.

Shoulder Arms! A tale of two soldiers' sons, illustrated by W.H.C. Groome. London, Chambers, 1905.

Trapper Dan: a story of the backwoods. London, S.W. Partridge, 1905.

Dead Man's Land: Being the voyage to Zimbambangwe of certain and uncertain Blacks and Whites. London, S.W. Partridge, 1906.

Hunting the Skipper; or, the Cruise of the 'Seafowl' sloop. London, SPCK, 1906.

'Tention!' a story of boy-life during the Peninsular War, illustrated by C.M. Sheldon. London, Chambers, 1906.

The Traitor's Gait, and other stories. London, Digby, Long, 1906.

Trapped by Malays: a tale of bayonet and kris. London, Chambers, 1907.

Jack, the Rascal: a country story. London, Everett, 1909.

Charles Gilson (1878–1943). British.
a.k.a. C(harles) L(ouis) Gilson.
a.k.a. Captain Charles Gilson.
a.k.a. Major Charles Gilson.

For main author article see 1910 to 1919.

The Lost Column: a story of the Boxer Rebellion in China, illustrated by Cyrus Cuneo. London, Henry Frowde; Hodder & Stoughton, 1909.

The Lost Empire: a tale of many lands, illustrated by Cyrus Cuneo. London, Henry Frowde; Hodder & Stoughton, 1909.

Kenneth Grahame (1859–1932). British.

Unlike very many children's authors writing in this decade, who were so prolific, Kenneth Grahame's reputation rests upon the strength of a single book. Both *The Golden Age* (1895) and *Dream Days* (1898) were popular in their time but are now largely forgotten. These two

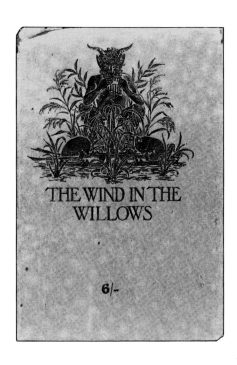

do, however, stress the primacy of innocence: one of the themes that runs throughout Grahame's most famous work *The Wind in the Willows* (1908). This is the tale of Toad, Water Rat, Mole and Badger and their adventures when the influence of such human devices as motor cars and the subversiveness of the Wild Wooders encroach upon their Arcadian landscape. The book was critically lambasted when first published but this did not prevent it being reprinted continually and its popularity soon spread. It may surprise some to learn that the illustrations by Ernest H. Shepard, that are now so closely associated with the book, were added to the text as late as 1931, the year before Grahame's death. The first edition, with its gilt embossed boards, contained only a frontispiece and a dustwrapper illustration by Graham Robertson. The extremely rare wrapper depicts a scene from the book's most mystic, mysterious and frequently excised chapter, *The Piper at the Gates of Dawn*. Rat and Mole are seeking Otter's lost son, Portly, when they are lulled to sleep by some eerie music. The illustration shows Mole and Rat asleep in the latter's rowing boat and towered over by the piper, the god Pan. This design is repeated in gilt on the book's dark green front cover. The spine of the book shows a smiling Toad in gilt wearing a cap and goggles, all set for a motor car ride. The first edition was issued with a gilt top edge to the pages.

The Wind in the Willows, illustrated by Graham Robertson. London, Methuen, and New York, Scribner, 1908.

G(eorge) A(lfred) Henty (1832–1902). British.

G.A. Henty, who wrote over one hundred and twenty books, was an extremely popular author of adventure stories which frequently had a military flavour. Before he could take his degree, Henty left Gonville and Caius College, Cambridge to volunteer to fight in the Crimean War. Later he became a war correspondent and covered the Austro-Italian War.

The hero in his stories was usually from a public school, in his early teens, clean cut, moral, brave, gallant and patriotic, with a middle to upper-class background, who triumphs over adversity. The books are a mine of information on historical battles which had obviously been carefully researched. For example, in *With the British Legion: A Story of the Carlist Wars* (UK, 1902), Arthur Hallett joins the British Legion, which was raised by Sir de Lacy Evans to support the cause of Queen Christina and the infant Queen Isabella, and as soon as he sets foot on Spanish soil his adventures begin. Captain Arthur Hallett is shown on the front cover of the book, wearing a red jacket and brown breeches and carrying the infant Queen Isabella, whom he had rescued after she had been kidnapped by traitors. For his brave deeds, he is created a Knight of Isabella of the first class and a Companion of the Order of San Fernando the Catholic. He also appears on the spine of the book, wiping a blooded sword. The book is illustrated by Wal Paget and the frontispiece depicts Captain Hallett and Major Hawkins dashing forward on horseback through the Carlist lines, but unfortunately the major is shot and dies.

The binding is typical of the books published by Blackie during this period. For collectors of this author's first editions during this decade, the books should all be dated at the base of the title page, except *Do Your Duty* and *In the Hands of the Cave-Dwellers*, which are undated. Because Henty was so popular in his own time, books were reprinted several times shortly after the first edition. As a consequence there are several different bindings. The correct coloured cloth boards for the Blackie first editions are: *Out With Garibaldi, With Buller in Natal, To Herat and Cabul,* blue; *With Roberts in Pretoria, With Kitchener in the Soudan, Through Three Campaigns, In the Hands of the Malays,* red; whilst *At the Point of a Bayonet, In the Irish Brigade, The Treasure of the Incas, With the Allies to Pekin* are green. *Do Your Duty, In the Hands of the Cave Dwellers* and *With the British Legion* are found in blue or green cloth boards; *By Conduct and Courage* is found in red or green; whilst *A Soldier's Daughter* occurs in all three colours.

Chambers first published *Gallant Deeds*

with grey-blue cloth. Their first edition of *At Duty's Call* is undated, with paper covers, whilst *The Sole Survivors* is undated, with red limp cloth. *John Hawke's Fortune* was published by Chapman and Hall in a white paper cover, dated 1901.

With the exception of *In the Hands of the Cave-Dwellers*, all Henty's titles were first published in the UK. The Scribner editions are dated a year earlier than the Blackie editions because Blackie had the habit of dating books with the year after their actual publication.

Harry Lindsay is the hero of *At the Point of a Bayonet: A Tale of the Mahratta War* (UK, 1901). His parents are killed by Mahrattas in India when he is three months old and he is saved by Soyera, his Mahratta ayah, who has served the family for over ten years. She takes him to her own people where he is brought up as a native until he is eventually told of his parentage before he is sent to Bombay to be educated. When he is sixteen he obtains a commission in the British Army, and his knowledge of the Mahratta tongue combined with his ability and bravery enables him to give great service in the Mahratta War. Captain Harry Lindsay is shown on the book's cover, carrying a rifle with a fixed bayonet at the battle of Assaye, which lasted for three hours and in which 'one thousand five hundred and sixty-six of the British force were killed or wounded.'

In the Irish Brigade: A Tale of War in Flanders and Spain, illustrated by Charles M. Sheldon. London, Blackie, 1900; New York, Scribner, 1900.

With Buller in Natal: A Born Leader, illustrated by W. Rainey. London, Blackie, 1900; New York, Scribner, 1900.

Out With Garibaldi: A Story of the Liberation of Italy, illustrated by W. Rainey. London, Blackie, 1900; New York, Scribner, 1900.

Do Your Duty, illustrated by R. Lillie (coloured frontispiece by H.M. Brock). London, Blackie, 1900.

John Hawke's Fortune: A Story of Monmouth's Rebellion, illustrated by Lance Thackeray. London, Chapman and Hall, 1901.

The Sole Survivors, illustrated by W. Boucher. London, Chambers, 1901.

At the Point of a Bayonet: A Tale of the Mahratta War, illustrated by Wal Paget. London, Blackie, 1901; New York, Scribner, 1901.

To Herat and Cabul: A Story of the First Afghan War, illustrated by Charles M. Sheldon. London, Blackie, 1901; New York, Scribner, 1901.

With Roberts to Pretoria: A Tale of the South African War, illustrated by William Rainey. London, Blackie, 1901; New York, Scribner, 1901.

In the Hands of the Cave-Dwellers, illustrated by Wat Miller. New York, Harper, 1900; London, Blackie, 1902.

With Kitchener in the Soudan: A Story of Atbara and Omdurman, illustrated by William Rainey. London, Blackie, 1902; New York, Scribner, 1902.

At Duty's Call. London, Chambers, 1902.

The Treasure of the Incas: A Story of Adventure in Peru, illustrated by Wal Paget. London, Blackie, 1902; New York, Scribner, 1902.

With the British Legion: A Story of the Carlist Wars, illustrated by Wal Paget. London, Blackie, 1902; New York, Scribner, 1902.

Through Three Campaigns: A Story of Chitral, Tirah and Ashantee, illustrated by Wal Paget. London, Blackie, 1903; New York, Scribner, 1903.

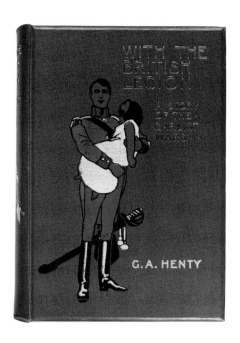

With the Allies to Pekin: A Tale of the Relief of the Legations, illustrated by Wal Paget. London, Blackie, 1903; New York, Scribner, 1903.

By Conduct and Courage: A Story of the Days of Nelson, illustrated by William Rainey. London, Blackie, 1904; New York, Scribner, 1904.

In the Hands of the Malays, illustrated by J. Jellicoe. London, Blackie, 1904.

Gallant Deeds, illustrated by Arthur Rackham and W. Boucher. London, Chambers, 1905.

A Soldier's Daughter, illustrated by Frances Ewan. London, Blackie, 1905.

Andrew Home. British.

The Boys of Badminster (1905) is one of several interesting school stories written by Andrew Home. Benjamin Franklin Prescott, an American from Boston, Massachusetts, and his chum Jack Coverdale are both fifth-form pupils at Badminster School. 'Badminster school is a fine old stone building, part of which is very aged, dating back to medieval times. It stands on the coast, overlooking the sea.'

The book's attractive frontispiece by Charles M. Sheldon, shows Jack Coverdale hitting a boundary in the match against Ravenscroft House: 'He felt the bat spring in his hand as he smote with all his strength.' Jack is not out at the end of the match which is a victory for his house, Strong's. Later Ben and Jack are kidnapped and taken aboard the ship *Clematis*, which collides with a steamer in fog. Jack falls in the collision, hurts his arm and rolls helplessly upon the deck whilst Ben leaps upon the bulwarks and clutches at the anchor-chains in the bows of the other steamer. It is this scene, of Ben climbing up the anchor-chains, that is reproduced in red, blue, black and gilt on the front cover of the book.

The Fellow Who Won: A tale of school life, illustrated by Emily A Cook. London, Nelson, 1900.

The Story Of A School Conspiracy, illustrated by A. Monro. London, Chambers, 1901.

Out of Bounds: A series of school stories,

He felt the bat spring in his hand as he smote with all his strength.

illustrated by Harold Copping. London, Chambers, 1901.

Jack and Black: A tale of school life and adventure, illustrated by Harold Copping. London, Chambers, 1902.

By A Schoolboy's Hand, illustrated by Strickland Brown. London, A. & C. Black, 1904.

The Boys of Badminster: A school tale, illustrated by Charles M. Sheldon. London, Chambers, 1905.

Well Played! Illustrated by Harold Copping. London, Chambers, 1907.

Bravo Bob! A school story, illustrated by Harold Copping. London, Chambers, 1909.

Rudyard Kipling (1865–1936). British.

Rudyard Kipling, who worked as a journalist in India during his early years, is rightly famous for several books written during the nineteenth century. *The Jungle Book* published in 1894 with its many memorable characters such as Shere Khan, the tiger; Bagheera, the panther; Baloo, the brown bear; Kaa, the python; Akela, the wolf and, of course,

Mowgli, the Indian boy, has always been popular with children. The sequel *The Second Jungle Book* is of equal importance and delight. Two books written especially for boys *Captains Courageous*, (1897), a sea story and *Stalky & Co*, (1899), which is set in a Devon boarding school for boys, also deserve special mention.

In 1901 *Kim* was published, following the exploits of Kimball O'Hara in India. The book was illustrated by Kipling's father, John Lockwood Kipling. Rudyard Kipling himself went on to illustrate *Just So Stories for Little Children* (1902), containing humorous tales, including some about the physical features of animals. The front cover of the first edition shows Kipling's illustration from the story *The Elephant's Child* when 'the Elephant's Child sat back on his little haunches, and pulled, and pulled, and pulled, and his nose began to stretch. And the Crocodile floundered into the water, making it all creamy with great sweeps of his tail, and he pulled, and pulled, and pulled. And the Elephant's Child's nose kept on stretching.' The Bi-Coloured-Python-Rock-Snake watches the tussle in the foreground of the scene. Other animals featured on the cover are the Camel from the Story *How the Camel Got His Hump* and the Leopard from *How the Leopard Got His Spots*. The incredibly rare dustwrapper portrays the author's drawing of the Cat that Walked by Himself, walking thorugh the Wet Wild Woods. Underneath is a picture of the Cave that the Man and the Woman live in. During this decade, Rudyard Kipling also wrote *Puck of Pook's Hill*, a series of charmingly planned historical stories which were beautifully illustrated by H.R. Millar for the U.K. edition and Arthur Rackham for the U.S. edition.

Kim, illustrated by J. Lockwood Kipling. New York, Doubleday, and London, Macmillan, 1901.
Just So Stories for Little Children, illustrated by the author. London, Macmillan, and New York, Doubleday, 1902.
Puck of Pook's Hill, illustrated by H.R. Millar. London, Macmillan, 1906. Illustrated by Arthur Rackham, New York, Doubleday, 1906.

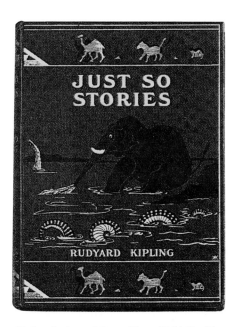

Kipling Stories and Poems Every Child Should Know, edited by Mary E. Burt and W.T. Chapin, illustrated by Charles Livingston Bull and others. New York, Doubleday, 1909.

Amy Le Feuvre (d. 1929). British.
a.k.a. Mary Thurston Dodge.

Amy Le Feuvre specialised in stories based around family life, and the vast majority of her output, over eighty books, was published by the Religious Tract Society, as the Christian message in her tales made them ideally suited for Sunday School prizes. In *Robin's Heritage* (1907), the story revolves around the Harcourt family. Gordon Browne illustrates the book and the front cover shows Ellen Harcourt reading a letter to her three daughters, Poppet, Muffet and Twinkles. Her disabled son Robin's crutch rests at her side. The frontispiece presents Poppet putting her head round the schoolroom door to announce to her brother and sisters that their father, Captain Harcourt, has come home from the Navy.

Brownie, illustrated by W.H.C. Groome. London, Hodder & Stoughton, and New York, American Tract Society, 1900.

Olive Tracy. London, Hodder & Stoughton, 1900; New York, Dodd Mead, 1901.

A Cherry Tree. London, Hodder & Stoughton, 1901; as *Cherry, The Cucumber That Bore Fruit*, Chicago, Revell, 1901.

Heather's Mistress. London, Religious Tract Society, and New York, Crowell, 1901.

A Daughter of the Sea. London, Hodder & Stoughton, and New York, Crowell, 1902.

Odd Made Even, illustrated by Harold Copping. London, Religious Tract Society, 1902.

The Making of a Woman. London, Hodder & Stoughton, 1903.

Two Tramps. London, Hodder & Stoughton, and Chicago, Revell, 1903.

Jill's Red Bag, illustrated by Alfred Pearse. London, Religious Tract Society, and Chicago, Revell, 1903.

His Little Daughter. London, Religious Tract Society, 1904.

A Little Maid. London, Religious Tract Society, 1904.

Bridget's Quarter Deck. London, Hodder & Stoughton, 1905.

The Buried Ring, illustrated by Gordon Browne. London, Hodder & Stoughton, 1905.

The Children's Morning Message, illustrated by Jenny Wylie. London, Hodder & Stoughton, 1905.

Christina and the Boys, illustrated by Gordon Browne. London, Hodder & Stoughton, 1906.

The Mender, illustrated by W. Rainey. London, Religious Tract Society, 1906.

Miss Lavender's Boy and Other Sketches. London, Religious Tract Society, 1906.

Robin's Heritage, illustrated by Gordon Browne. London, Hodder & Stoughton, 1907.

Number Twa! London, Religious Tract Society, 1907.

The Chateau by the Lake. London, Hodder & Stoughton, 1907.

A Bit of Rough Road, illustrated by Percy Tarrant. London, Religious Tract Society, 1908.

Me and Nobbles, illustrated by W.H.C. Groome. London, Religious Tract Society, 1908.

Us and Our Donkey, illustrated by W.H.C. Groome. London, Religious Tract Society, 1909.

A Country Corner, illustrated by Steven Spurrier. London, Cassell, 1909.

His Birthday: A Christmas Sketch, illustrated by Eveline Lance. London, Religious Tract Society, 1909.

Robert Leighton (1859–1934). British.

Robert Leighton was another tried and true writer of a long series of adventure stories, set either at sea as in *With Nelson in Command: A story of adventure in the battle of the Baltic* (1905), or on land, *Gildersley's Tenderfoot: A story of Redskin and prairie* (1909).

During *Hurrah for the Spanish Main! A tale of Drake's third voyage to Darien* (1904), Captain Francis Drake, on his mission to destroy the Spanish Plate Fleet, journeys partly by land with a landing party of forty-eight. 'Only eighteen of them were English; the other thirty were Cimeroons. … For days and days they tramped through the gloom and eternal silence of that vast primeval forest.' Eventually Drake climbs a monster tree that grows alone upon a mountain ridge and he stands upon a tiny platform called 'Mountain's Eye'. J. Ayton Symington's illustration on the book cover shows Drake pointing westwards towards 'the fabled golden sea', the great Pacific Ocean. Drake tells Oliver Axten and Anthony Goddard, the two boys who are standing with him, 'There is that which no English eye hath before looked upon!'

The Boys of Waveney. London, Grant Richards, 1902.

Cap'n Nat's Treasure: a tale of Old Liverpool. London, S.W. Partridge, 1902.

Fighting Fearful Odds; or, the Temptations of Jack Rodney. London, Melrose, 1903.

The Haunted Ship: a tale of the Devon Smugglers. London, Melrose, 1903.

In the Land of Ju-Ju: a tale of Benin. London, Melrose, 1903.

The Kidnapping of Peter Kray: A story of the South Seas. London, Grant Richards, 1903.

Hurrah for the Spanish Main! A tale of Drake's third voyage to Darien, illustrated by J. Ayton Symington. London, Melrose, 1904.

The Other Fellow; or, the Heir from the Colonies. London, Melrose, 1904.

The Green-Painted Ship. London, Melrose, 1905.

With Nelson in Command: a story of adventure in the battle of the Baltic. London, Melrose, 1905.

Gipsy Kit; or, the man with the tattooed face. London, Partridge, 1906.

Monitor at Megson's: A master, a schoolboy and a secret, illustrated by Gordon Browne. London, Cassell, 1906.

Gildersley's Tenderfoot: A story of Redskin and prairie. London, Scout Library, 1909.

Jack London (1876–1916). American.

The American Jack London wrote a masterpiece of a wild animal story, *The Call of the Wild* (1903), as well as the popular *White Fang* (1905). The author's knowledge of the Yukon, gained from taking part in the gold rush, was used to great effect in his books.

In *The Call of the Wild*, four-year-old Buck, who is a cross between a St Bernard and a Scotch shepherd dog, is kidnapped and becomes involved in the 1897 Klondike gold rush. He escapes and eventually runs with a wolf pack. This book's UK first edition has internal illustrations by two artists whilst the endpapers and title page were attractively decorated by Charles Edward Hooper. The title page depicts the head of Buck whilst the front cover has three scenes of men and dogs against an arctic landscape.

The UK first edition of *White Fang* shows on its front boards the wild wolf which, during the story, gradually becomes domesticated.

The Call of the Wild, illustrated by Philip R. Goodwin and Charles Livingston Bull. New York. Macmillan. 1903; London, Heinemann, 1903.

Tales of the Fish Patrol, illustrated by George Varian, New York, Macmillan, 1905; London, Heinemann, 1906.

White Fang, New York, Macmillan, 1905; London, Methuen, 1907.

Bessie Marchant (1862–1941). British.

A farmer's daughter, Bessie Marchant was born in Kent where several of her books are set. She later taught at a Baptist school in London, and wrote over one hundred and thirty children's books. She was a pioneer in the field of girls' adventure stories, allowing her readers to travel the world with her heroes and heroines and face challenging scenarios, which would reveal their pluck and initiative. The adventure over, the heroine would find true fulfilment in love and marriage, thus reinforcing traditional values.

Bessie Marchant was an armchair traveller, never leaving the British Isles, but still providing realistic locations ranging from Canada to Tasmania, where *Sally Makes Good* and *The Apple Lady* were set. The attractive front cover of *The Apple Lady* (1908), drawn by George Soper, shows Silver Blair who lives on an apple plantation near Wattle Hill, Tasmania. Although immensely popular in her day, Bessie Marchant's books have not really stood the test of time, possibly as a result of her fondness for coincidence and her firm belief in male supremacy.

The Ghost of Rock Grange. London, SPCK, 1900.

Held at Ransom, illustrated by Sydney Cowell. London, Blackie, 1900.

Cicely Frome. The Captain's Daughter. Edinburgh, Nimmo, 1900.

In the Toils of the Tribesmen. London, Gall and Inglis, 1900.

From the Scourge of the Tongue. London, Melrose, 1900.

Among Hostile Hordes. London, Gall and Inglis, 1901.

The Fun o' the Fair. London, Culley, 1901.

In Perilous Times. London, Gall and Inglis, 1901.

That Dreadful Boy! London, Culley, 1901.

Three Girls on a Ranch, illustrated by William Rainey. London, Blackie, 1901.

Tommy's Trek. London, Blackie, 1901.

The Bertrams of Ladywell, illustrated by John Jellicoe. London, Wells Gardner, 1902.

A Brave Little Cousin. London, SPCK, 1902.

Fleckie. London, Blackie, 1902.

The House at Brambling Minster. London, SPCK, 1902.

Leonard's Temptation. London, Culley, 1902.

The Secret of the Everglades. London, Blackie, 1902; New York, Mershon, 1915.

A Heroine of the Sea. London, Blackie, 1903.

Lost on the Saguenay. London, Collins, 1903.

The Owner of Rushcote. London, Culley 1903.

The Captives of the Kaid. London, Collins, 1904.

Chupsie. London, Culley, 1904.

The Girls of Wakenside. London, Collins, 1904.

Hope's Tryst. London, Blackie, 1904.

Yew Tree Farm. London, SPCK, 1904.

Caspar's Find. London, Culley, 1905.

A Daughter of the Ranges, illustrated by A.A. Dixon. London, Blackie, 1905.

The Debt of the Damerals. London, Clarke, 1905.

The Mysterious City, illustrated by W.S. Stacey, London, SPCK, 1905.

The Queen of Shindy Flat. illustrated by Charles Sheldon. London, Wells Gardner, 1905.

Athabasca Bill, illustrated by Harold Piffard, London, SPCK, 1906.

A Girl of the Fortunate Isles, illustrated by Paul Hardy. London, Blackie, 1906.

Kenealy's Ride. London, Gall and Inglis, 1906.

Maisie's Discovery, illustrated by R. Tod. London, Collins, 1906.

Uncle Greg's Man Hunt. London, Culley, 1906.

Darling of Sandy Point, illustrated by Harold Piffard. London, SPCK, 1907.

Juliette, The Mail Carrier, illustrated by R. Tod. London, Collins, 1907.

The Mystery of the Silver Run. London, Wells Gardner, 1907.

No Ordinary Girl, illustrated by Frances Ewan. London, Blackie, 1907; New York, Caldwell, 1911.

Sisters of Silver Creek, illustrated by Robert Hope. London, Blackie, 1907.

The Apple Lady, illustrated by G. Soper. London, Collins, 1908.

A Courageous Girl, illustrated by William Rainey. London, Blackie, 1908.

Daughters of the Dominion. London, Blackie, 1908.

Rolf the Rebel, illustrated by W.S. Stacey. London, SPCK, 1908.

As Island Heroine, illustrated by W.H. Margetson. London, Collins, 1909.

Jenny's Adventure. London, Butcher, 1909.

L(Elizabeth) T(homasina) Meade
(1854–1914). Irish.

L.T. Meade's first books were published in the 1870s. She was a very productive author writing over two hundred and twenty books for children. Her plots were typical of this period, with their plucky and trustworthy heroes and heroines overcoming all obstacles. She is best remembered as one of the originators of girls' school stories, that were to become so popular in the early decades of the twentieth century.

The front cover of the first edition of L.T. Meade's *The Scamp Family* (1907) was illustrated by the artist A. Talbot Smith, showing Dandy, Roger, Snowball (Victoria) and Nora Scamp sitting on their garden wall, the boundary of their mischievous dominion. The family dynamics are unusual since it is the youngest child, Snowball, who rules the roost. Matters are complicated when the two girls become lost in the East End of London but normality eventually ensues and Snowball is crowned queen of the East End children.

Three Girls from School (1907), another title of L.T. Meade's from this period, has the interior illustrations for the first edition by Percy Tarrant, but it is A. Talbot Smith who draws the three girls in brown, blue and grey for the book's front cover. Priscilla Weir, Mabel Lushington and Annie Brook are the three girls being educated at Mrs Lyttelton's school, 'no school in the whole of England produced such girls: so well-bred, so thoroughly educated, so truly taught those things which make for honour, for purity, for a life of good report.'

Wages. London, Nisbet, 1900.

A Plucky Girl. Philadelphia, Jacobs, 1900.

The Beauforts. London, Griffith and Farran, 1900.

A Brave Poor Thing. London, Isbister, 1900.

Daddy's Girl. London, Newnes, 1900: Philadelphia, Lippincott, 1901.

Miss Nonentity, illustrated by William Rainey. London, Chambers, 1900.

Seven Maids, illustrated by Percy Tarrant. London, Chambers, 1900.

A Sister of the Red Cross: A Tale of the South African War. London, Nelson, 1900.

The Time of Roses. London, Nister, 1900.

Wheels of Iron. London, Nisbet, 1901.

Cosey Corner; or, How They Kept a Farm, illustrated by Percy Tarrant. London, Chambers, 1901.

The Blue Diamond. London, Chatto and Windus, 1901.

Girls of the True Blue, illustrated by Percy Tarrant. London, Chambers and New York, Dutton, 1901.

The New Mrs. Lascelles. London, Clarke, 1901.

A Stumble by the Way. London, Chatto & Windus, 1901.

A Very Naughty Girl, illustrated by William Rainey. London, Chambers, 1901.

Drift. London, Methuen, 1902.

The Princess Who gave Away All, and The Naughty One of the Family, illustrated by Kate Street. London, Nister, 1902.

Girls of the Forest, illustrated by Percy Tarrant. London, Chambers, 1902.

Margaret. London, White, 1902.

The Pursuit of Penelope. London, Digby, 1902.

Queen Rose. London, Chambers, 1902.

The Rebel of the School. London, Chambers, 1902.

The Squire's Little Girl. London, Chambers, 1902.

Through Peril for a Wife. London, Digby, 1902.

The Witch Maid. London, Nisbet, 1903.

The Burden of Her Youth. London, Long, 1903.

By Mutual Consent. London, Digby Long, 1903.

A Gay Charmer, illustrated by W.H.C. Groome. London, Chambers, 1903.

The Manor School, illustrated by Lewis Baumer. London, Chambers and New York, Mershon, 1903.

Peter the Pilgrim, illustrated by Harold Copping. London, Chambers, 1903.

Resurgam. London, Methuen, 1903.

Rosebury. London, Chatto & Windus, 1903.

That Brilliant Peggy. London, Hodder & Stoughton, 1903.

A Maid of Mystery. London, White, 1904.

At the Back of the World. London, Hurst and Blackett, 1904.

Castle Poverty. London, Nisbet, 1904.

The Adventures of Miranda. London, John Long, 1904.

The Girls of Mrs Pritchard's School, illustrated by Lewis Baumer. London, Chambers, 1904.

Love Triumphant. London, T. Fisher Unwin, 1904.

A Madcap. London, Cassell, and New York, Mershon, 1904.

A Modern Tomboy, illustrated by Percy Tarrant. London, Chambers, 1904.

Nurse Charlotte. London, Long, 1904.

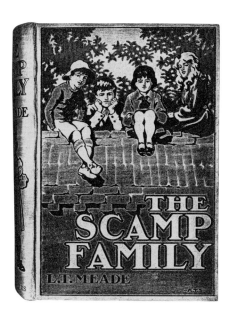

Petronella, and the Coming of Polly, illustrated by William Rainey. London, Chambers, 1904.

Wilful Cousin Kate, illustrated by William Rainey. London, Chambers, 1905.

Bess of Delaney's. London, Digby Long, 1905.

A Bevy of Girls, illustrated by Lewis Baumer. London, Chambers, 1905.

Dumps: A Plain Girl, illustrated by R. Lillie. London, Chambers, and New York, Dutton, 1905.

His Mascot. London, Long, 1905.

Little Wife Hester. London, Long, 1905.

Loveday: The Story of an Heiress. London, Hodder & Stoughton, 1905.

Old Readymoney's Daughter. London, Partridge, 1905.

Virginia. London, Digdy, 1905.

The Colonel and the Boy. London, Hodder & Stoughton, 1906.

The Face of Juliet. London, Long, 1906.

The Girl and Her Fortune. London, Hodder & Stoughton. 1906.

The Heart of Helen. London, Long, 1906.

The Hill-Top Girl. London, Chambers, 1906.

The Home of Sweet Content. London, White, 1906.

In the Flower of Her Youth. London, Nisbet, 1906.

The Maid with the Goggles. London, Digby, 1906.

Sue. London, Chambers, 1906.

Turquoise and Ruby. London, Chambers, and New York, Chatterton Peck, 1906.

Victory. London, Methuen, 1906.

The Home of Silence. London, Sisley's, 1907.

The Red Ruth. London, T. Werner Laurie, 1907.

The Colonel's Conquest. Philadelphia, Jacobs, 1907.

The Curse of the Feverals. London, Long, 1907.

A Girl from America. London, Chambers, 1907.

Kindred Spirits. London, Long, 1907.

The Lady of Delight. London, Hodder & Stoughton, 1907.

Little Josephine. London, Long, 1907.

The Little School-Mothers. London, Cassell, and Philadelphia, McKay, 1907.

The Love of Susan Cardigan. London, Digby Long, 1907.

The Red Cap of Liberty. London, Nisbet, 1907.

The Scamp Family, illustrated by A. Talbot Smith. London, Chambers, 1907.

Three Girls from School, illustrated by Percy Tarrant. London, Chambers, 1907.

The Aim of Her Life. London, Long, 1908.

The Court-Harman Girls. London, Chambers, 1908.

The Courtship of Sybil, London, Long, 1908.

Hetty Beresford. London, Hodder & Stoughton, 1908.

Sarah's Mother. London, Hodder & Stoughton, 1908.

The School Favourite, illustrated by Percy Tarrant. London, Chambers, 1908.

The School Queens. London, Chambers, 1908; New York, New York Book Company, 1910.

Oceana's Girlhood. New York, Hurst, 1909.

Aylwyn's Friends. London, Chambers, 1909.

Betty Vivian: A Story of Haddo Court School. London, Chambers, 1909.

Blue of the Sea. London, Nisbet, 1909.

Brother or Husband. London, White, 1909.

The Fountain of Beauty. London, Long, 1909.

I Will Sing a New Song. London, Hodder & Stoughton, 1909.

The Princess of the Revels. London, Chambers, 1909; New York, New York Book Company, 1910.

The Stormy Petrel. London, Hurst and Blackett, 1909.

Mrs Molesworth (Mary Louisa)
(1839–1921). British.

Mrs Molesworth wrote over eighty children's books, many of which now seem old-fashioned, but some are still quite enchanting. In *The February Boys* (1909), Rolf is four and is upset as a new brother is born on his birthday, when he really wanted a pony. On the frontispiece of the first edition, the magnificent artist Mabel Lucie Attwell depicts him seated on an old rustic seat, sobbing, 'It's spoiled my brufday – kite, kite spoiled it.' The book's front cover also depicts Rolf, this time holding his new brother. Rolf has two older sisters, Fay and Beryl, and the book tells of their exploits.

In another title, *Jasper* (1906), illustrated by Gertrude Demain Hammond, the appealing

'It's spoiled my brufday – kite, kite spoiled it,' he wailed.
F. B.—*Front*. PAGE 1.

frontispiece features Chrissie Fortescue watching as her seven-year-old brother, Jasper, puts on her stockings for her, '"You'd better be a boy at a boot-shop, Jap" she remarked "You're so clever."'

The Three Witches, illustrated by Lewis Baumer. London, Chambers, 1900.

The House That Grew, illustrated by Alice B. Woodward, London, Macmillan, 1900.

The Wood-Pigeons and Mary, illustrated by H.R. Millar. London, Macmillan, 1901.

'My Pretty' And Her Little Brother 'Too' and Other Stories, illustrated by Lewis Baumer, London, Chambers, 1901.

The Blue Baby and Other Stories, illustrated by Maud C. Foster. London, Unwin, 1901.

Peterkin, illustrated by H.R. Millar. London, Macmillan, 1902.

The Mystery of Pinewood And Hollow Tree House, illustrated by A.A. Dixon. London, Nister, 1903.

The Ruby Ring, illustrated by Rosie Pitman. London, Macmillan, 1904.

The Bolted Door and Other Stories, illustrated by L. Baumer. London, Chambers, 1906.

Jasper: A Story for Children, illustrated by Gertrude Demain Hammond. London, Macmillan, 1906.

The Little Guest: A Story for Children, illustrated by Gertrude Demain Hammond. London, Macmillan, 1907.

Fairies-Of-Sorts, illustrated by Gertrude Demain Hammond. London, Macmillan, 1908.

The February Boys, illustrated by Mabel Lucie Attwell. London, Chambers, 1909.

L(ucy) M(aud) Montgomery (1874–1942). Canadian.

L.M. Montgomery was a Canadian novelist who achieved an international reputation and put beautiful, rural Prince Edward Island, the smallest of Canadian provinces, firmly on the world literary map. Her best known book, *Anne of Green Gables* (1908), was the first of an extended series of books following the life of Anne Shirley. Anne, with her flame-red hair, is portrayed in a head and shoulders study on the front cover of the first edition. Anne

" 'THERE'S SOMETHING SO STYLISH ABOUT YOU, ANNE,' SAID DIANA." *(See page 372.)*

arrives at Green Gables as an orphan and turns the world of Merille and Matthew Cuthbert upside down; an enriching experience for all. L.M. Montgomery's lasting popularity probably owes much to her realistic portrayal of growing up and all the emotional turmoil that that process creates. She conveys feelings with which readers, wherever they may live, can identify.

The frontispiece of the first edition of *Anne of Green Gables*, drawn by M.A. and W.A. Claus, shows Anne Shirley dressing for a concert, at which she is to recite. The concert is to be held at the White Sands Hotel in aid of the Charlottetown hospital. Diana Barry, who was beginning to have a reputation for notable taste in dressing, is assisting Anne. 'Pull out that frill a little more-so; here, let me tie your sash; now for your slippers. I'm going to braid your hair in two thick braids, and tie them half-way up with big white bows.'

Anne of Green Gables, illustrated by M.A. and W.A. Claus. Boston, Page, and London, Pitman, 1908.

Anne of Avonlea. Boston, Page, and London, Pitman, 1909.

Dorothea Moore (1881–1933). British.

Although Dorothea Moore wrote several historical novels in her output of over sixty books, it is her stories that carefully describe life in girls' boarding schools that are still nostalgically popular. She also used her practical knowledge of Guiding with great authority in various books, notably *Terry the Girl-Guide* and *Greta of the Guides*.

A Plucky School-Girl (1908), set at the Manor School, is an archetypal example of Dorothea Moore's early work. The scene shown on the front cover, by the artist A.A. Dixon, is the moment when Terry (Theresa Vaughan) 'landed in triumph on the top' of the wall leading to Miss Mervyn's garden. She has reached her goal via Tip's shoulders (properly known as Alicia Georgina Carrington de Montmorency Fitzhugh). Later in the book it is Terry who hits the winning four for the Manor School cricket team against Gorringe's.

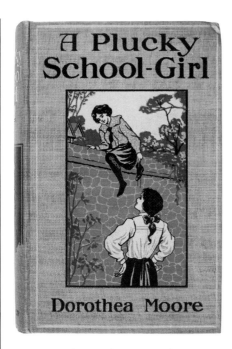

Mistress Dorothy. London, National Society, 1902.

Evelyn. London, Nelson, 1904.

God's Bairn. London, Blackie, 1904; as *Marlowe of the Fens*, 1934.

Brown. London, Nisbet, 1905; New York, Eaton and Mains, 1907; as *Three Feet of Valour*, Nisbet, 1921.

Sydney Lisle, illustrated by Wal Paget. London, Partridge, 1905; Philadelphia, McKay, 1910.

Jepthah's Lass, illustrated by P.H. London, Partridge, 1907.

Elizabeth's Angel and Other Stories. London, National Society, 1907.

Knights of the Red Cross. London, Nelson, 1907.

Pamela's Hero, illustrated by A.A. Dixon. London, Blackie, 1907.

A Plucky School-Girl, illustrated by A.A. Dixon. London, Nisbet, 1908.

The Christmas Children, illustrated by C.T. Howard. London, Partridge, 1909.

The Luck of Ledge Point, illustrated by C. Horrell. London, Blackie, 1909.

E(dith) Nesbit (1858–1924). British.

The children in the books of E. Nesbit are usually poor, middle-class, brave, kind, well-mannered – real characters who leap from the page. The books are as readable today as when they were originally written.

The trilogy about the Bastable children is the best example of E. Nesbit's work. The first book in the series, *The Story of the Treasure Seekers*, was published in 1899; its sequel, *The Wouldbegoods*, in 1901, and the final book, *New Treasure Seekers*, in 1904. The attractive looking first edition of *New Treasure Seekers* is bound in deep red cloth and the lettering on the front cover plus the Gordon Browne illustration is in gilt. The Bastable children, Alice, Oswald, Horace Octavious (H.O.), Noel, Dicky and Dora, have walked through Greenwich Hospital grounds and down to the terrace by the river, looking for their lost fox-terrier, Pincher. The scene, drawn by Gordon Browne, records the consequences when they disturb a sailor, who unknown to them was asleep, to ask him if he has seen their dog. The sailor is very angry at being disturbed and swears at them.

Another famous book features three children, Phyllis, Bobbie (Roberta) and Peter, better known as *The Railway Children* (1906). C.E. Brock's illustrations for the first edition reflect the rural adventures of the three and capture the world of Edwardian England. The first edition is bound in deep red cloth, lettered in gilt. On the front cover are the three children drawn in gilt, holding red flags; Peter has two. 'Stand firm,' said Peter, 'and wave like mad!'

Three fantasy titles, *The Phoenix and the Carpet, Five Children and It* and *The Story of the Amulet*, star five children, Robert, Jane, Anthea, Cyril and their young baby brother, Lamb, 'because the first thing he ever said was "Baa"!' In *The Phoenix and the Carpet*, an egg-shaped object, 'very yellow and shiny, half-transparent' with 'an odd sort of light in it' rolls out from a carpet which is being put down in their nursery. The egg falls into the fire grate, becomes red-hot, cracks into two and from it emerges a flame-coloured bird, the Phoenix. This book, like the two other fantasy tales, is attractively illustrated by H.R.

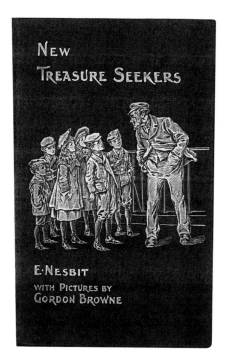

Millar, who draws the Phoenix emerging from the grate with the four older children goggle-eyed as it states, 'Be careful; I am not nearly cool yet'. The Phoenix reveals that their new carpet is magic and this ancient bird joins the children on a series of enthralling adventures.

The Book of Dragons, illustrated by H.R. Millar. London and New York, Harper, 1900.

Nine Unlikely Tales for Children, illustrated by H.R. Millar and Claude Shepperson. London, Unwin, and New York, Dutton, 1901.

The Wouldbegoods, Being the Further Adventures of the Treasure Seekers, illustrated by Arthur H. Buckland and John Hassell. London, Unwin, 1901; New York, Harper, 1902.

Five Children and It, illustrated by H.R. Millar. London, Unwin, 1902; New York, Dodd Mead, 1905.

The Revolt of the Toys and What Comes of Quarrelling, illustrated by Ambrose Dudley. London, Nister, and New York, Dutton, 1902.

Playtime Stories. London, Tuck, 1903.

The Rainbow Queen and Other Stories. London, Tuck, 1903.

The Phoenix and the Carpet, illustrated by H.R. Millar. London, Newnes and, New York, Macmillan, 1904.

The Story of the Five Rebellious Dolls. London, Nister, 1904.

New Treasure Seekers, illustrated by Gordon Browne and Lewis Baumer. London, Unwin, and New York, Stokes, 1904.

Cat Tales, with Rosamund Bland, illustrated by Isabel Watkin. London, Nister, and New York, Dutton, 1904.

Pug Peter: King of Mouseland, Marquis of Barkshire, D.O.G., P.C. 1906, Knight of the Order of the Gold Dog Collar, Author of Doggerel Lays and Days ..., illustrated by Harry Rountree. Leeds, Alf Cooke, 1905.

Oswald Bastable and Others, illustrated by C.E. Brock and H.R. Millar. London, Wells Gardner, 1905; New York, Coward McCann, 1906.

The Story of the Amulet, illustrated by H.R. Millar. London, Unwin, 1906; New York, Dutton, 1907.

The Railway Children, illustrated by C.E. Brock. London, Wells Gardner, and New York, Macmillan, 1906.

The Enchanted Castle, illustrated by H.R. Millar. London, Unwin, 1907; New York, Harper, 1908.

The House of Arden, illustrated by H.R. Millar. London, Unwin, 1908; New York, Dutton, 1909.

Harding's Luck, illustrated by H.R. Millar. London, Hodder & Stoughton, 1909; New York, Stokes, 1910.

Elsie J. Oxenham (1880–1960). British. Pseudonym for Elsie Jeanette Dunkerley.
a.k.a. Elsie Oxenham.
a.k.a. Elsie Jeanette Oxenham.

For main author article see 1910 to 1919.

Goblin Island, illustrated by T. Heath Robinson. London, Collins, 1907.

A Princess in Tatters, illustrated by Frank Adams. London, Collins, 1908.

The Conquest of Christina, illustrated by G.B. Foyster. London, Collins, 1909.

The Girl Who Wouldn't Make Friends,
illustrated by P.B. Hickling. London,
Nelson, 1909.
Mistress Nanciebel, illustrated by James
Durden. London, Hodder & Stoughton,
1909.

Eleanor H(odgman) Porter (1868–1920).
American.
a.k.a. Eleanor Stuart.

For main author article see 1910 to 1919.

Cross Currents, illustrated by William Stecher.
Boston, Wilde, 1907; London, Harrap,
1928.
The Turn of the Tide, illustrated by Frank
Merrill. Chicago, Wilde, 1908; London,
Harrap, 1928.

Gene Stratton Porter (1863–1924).
American.

Gene Stratton Porter was an American with a
great interest in natural history. She used her
knowledge of the American countryside and
its flora and fauna to create authentic
backdrops for her famous children's novels, *A
Girl of Limberlost* (1909) and *Freckles*. The 1904
Doubleday first US edition of *Freckles* has a
fawn cloth bearing a small brown and cream
illustration of trees and clouds. The lettering is
also brown and cream. Freckles, the hero of
the story, is a nineteen-year-old Irish lad who
lost his right hand when a baby but does not
expect any favours. In E. Stetson Crawford's
illustration for the frontispiece he is shown
asking Mr McLean, the firm but kindly boss of
a logging camp near Grand Rapids, Michigan,
for a job. The boss is impressed by Freckles'
honesty and determination to work hard
despite his handicap. The most attractive
characters in Gene Stratton Porter's books live
close to nature, are in harmony with their
surroundings and inherently decent.

Freckles, illustrated by E. Stetson Crawford.
New York, Doubleday, 1904; London,
Murray, 1905.
A Girl of the Limberlost, illustrated by
Wladyslaw T. Benda. New York,

" 'I'll do pracisely what you tell me or die trying.' "

Doubleday, 1909; London, Hodder &
Stoughton, 1911.

Beatrix Potter (1866–1943). British.
a.k.a. Beatrix Heelis.

Beatrix Potter wrote a series of animal stories
which have continued to capture the
imagination of children through nine decades.
She was a wonderful illustrator taking great
care that her drawings of animals and plants
were accurate. Beatrix Potter created many
endearing characters, like Peter Rabbit,
Jemima Puddleduck, Squirrel Nutkin, Mrs
Tiggy Winkle, Jeremy Fisher and Pigling
Bland.

The small format used by her publisher,
Warne, for most of the books, made them ideal
for youngsters to hold, and their presentation,
with a picture seen each time a page is turned
and the few sentences of text, immediately
held the attention of the majority of children.
Three titles, *The Pie and the Patty-Pan*, *The
Roly Poly Pudding* and *Ginger and Pickles*, were
originally produced in a larger format, whilst
two other books, *The Story of Miss Moppet* and

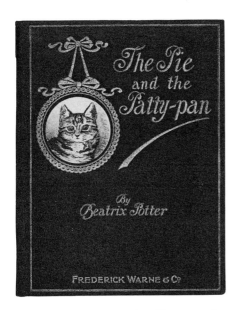

The Story of a Fierce Bad Rabbit, were first published in a wider, panoramic style.

The brown front cover of the first edition of *The Pie and the Patty-Pan* (1905) shows a portrait of a cat called Ribby looking glamorous in a blue bow. She invites a small dog called Duchess to tea and bakes a pie especially for her. Duchess, worried about it being mouse and bacon pie, bakes her own with a tin patty-pan to hold up the crust. She is served Ribby's pie and thinks she has swallowed the patty-pan when she cannot find it, but Ribby has not used one and Duchess realises she has indeed eaten mouse.

Illustrated by the author.

The Tale of Peter Rabbit. Privately printed, 1900; revised edition, London and New York, Warne, 1902.
The Tailor of Gloucester. Privately printed, 1902; revised edition, London and New York, Warne, 1903.
The Tale of Squirrel Nutkin. London and New York, Warne, 1903.
The Tale of Benjamin Bunny. London and New York, Warne, 1904.
The Tale of Two Bad Mice. London and New York, Warne, 1904.
The Tale of Mrs. Tiggy-Winkle. London and New York. Warne, 1905.
The Pie and the Patty-Pan. London and New York, Warne, 1905.

The Tale of Mr. Jeremy Fisher. London and New York, Warne, 1906.
The Story of a Fierce Bad Rabbit. London and New York, Warne, 1906.
The Story of Miss Moppet. London and New York, Warne, 1906.
The Tale of Tom Kitten. London and New York, Warne, 1907.
The Tale of Jemima Puddle-Duck. London and New York, Warne, 1908.
The Roly-Poly Pudding. London and New York, Warne, 1908; as *The Tale of Samuel Whiskers; or, The Roly-Poly Pudding*, London, Warne, 1926.
The Tale of the Flopsy Bunnies. London and New York, Warne, 1909.
Ginger and Pickles. London and New York, Warne, 1909.

Walter C. Rhoades. British.
a.k.a. Walter Rhoades.

During this period, J. Williams Butcher, Florence Coombe and Walter C. Rhoades all produced competently written school stories for boys. *The Boy From Cuba* (1900), written by Walter C. Rhoades, tells of the arrival, from Cuba, of Beltran René Gilbert at

Redcliff House School, and his subsequent friendship with fifteen-year-old Colin Bathurst and Frank Holland. Gilbert is kidnapped by two Spaniards and locked in a boathouse, but is eventually rescued by his two new friends. For the book's front cover, J.R. Burgess has drawn Colin Bathurst winning the mile race closely followed by Jordan from the rival school St Nicholas. 'Sheer will-power carried him along, and with open mouth and head thrown back, Colin forced himself along blindly.' Colin becomes the hero of the day and is carried round the course, seated in a chair, by two seniors. When Colin is presented with his prize, Dr Borthwick, the headmaster, states, 'A cool head and a stout heart are two qualities that go far in life. ... Pluck and that dogged perseverance which Englishmen regard as their heritage have been fully recognised.'

The Boy From Cuba: a school story, illustrated by J.R. Burgess, London, S.W. Partridge, 1900. a.k.a. *The Boys of Redcliff: The Story of a Boy From Cuba*. London, S.W. Partridge, 1927.

The Hidden City: A Story of Central America, illustrated by S.L.W. London, S.W. Partridge, 1907.

For The Sake of His Chum: a school story, illustrated by N. Tenison. London, Blackie, 1909.

Charles G(eorge) D(ouglas) Roberts (1860–1943). Canadian.

The Canadian poet Charles G.D. Roberts, who was later knighted, was an important writer of nature stories, who brought the thrilling world of the wild into the comfort of a child's home. The books fully describe the predator/prey relationship and are written with a reverence for the animals involved but with a lack of sentimentality.

The majority of Charles G.D. Roberts' books were stunningly illustrated by either Paul Branson or Charles Livingston Bull. The central character of *Kings in Exile* (1909), 'The Grey Master', the great grey Alaskan timber-wolf, is featured on the grey and green cover

of the book. The wolf is captured in a trap and presented to a zoo by Arthur Kane who later regrets his action.

The Kindred of the Wild: A Book of Animal Life, illustrated by Charles Livingston Bull. Boston, Page, 1902; London, Duckworth, 1903.

The Watchers of the Trails: A Book of Animal Life, illustrated by Charles Livingston Bull. Boston, Page, and London, Duckworth, 1904.

Red Fox: The Story of His Adventurous Career in the Ringwaak Wilds, and of His Final Triumph over the Enemies of his Kind, illustrated by Charles Livingston Bull. Boston, Page, and London, Duckworth, 1905.

The Haunters of the Silences: A Book of Animal Life, illustrated by Charles Livingston Bull. Boston, Page, and London, Duckworth, 1907.

In the Deep of the Snow, illustrated by Denman Fink. New York, Crowell, 1907.

The House in the Water: A Book of Animal Life, illustrated by Charles Livingston Bull and Frank Vining Smith. Boston, Page, 1908; London, Ward Lock, 1909.

The Backwoodsmen. New York, Macmillan, and London, Ward Lock, 1909.

Kings in Exile, illustrated by Paul Branson and Charles Livingston Bull. London, Ward Lock, 1909; New York. Macmillan, 1910.

Gordon Stables (1840–1910). British.
a.k.a. Gordon Stables RN.
a.k.a. Gordon Stables MD RN.
a.k.a. Dr Gordon Stables RN.

Gordon Stables had been a surgeon in the Royal Navy who on retiring turned to writing adventure stories, many with a nautical flavour, based on his own former journeys, especially to the Arctic regions.

In *Chris Cunningham* (1903), which is a tale of adventure on the high seas, the hero of the title has recently contributed to the Spanish defeat at the battle of St. Vincent. The scene in orange and brown on the book's cover shows the captain of the Spanish flag ship, the *San Joseph*, dropping to his knees and presenting his sword to Nelson as a sign of surrender.

Allan Adair, or Here and There In Many Lands. London, Religious Tract Society, 1900.
Prince: A story of the Black Prince. London, J.F. Shaw, 1900.
Old England On The Sea: The Story of Admiral Drake. London, J.F. Shaw, 1900.
On War's Red Tide: A tale of the Boer War. London, J. Nisbet, 1900.
Crusoes of the Frozen North, illustrated by S.B. Pearse. London, Blackie, 1901.
In Far Bolivia: A story of a strange wild land, illustrated by J. Finnemore. London, Blackie, 1901.
In Quest of the Giant Sloth: A tale of adventure in South America. London, Blackie, 1901.
With Cutlass and Torch: A story of the Great Slave Coast, illustrated by Henry Austin. London, J. Nisbet, 1901.
The Cruise of the "Vengeful". A story of the Royal Navy. London, J.F. Shaw, 1902.
In Forest lands: a story of pluck and endurance. London, J. Nisbet, 1902.
In Ships of Steel: A tale of the navy of to-day. London, J.F. Shaw, 1902.
In The Great White Land: A tale of the Antarctic Ocean, illustrated by Ambrose de Walton. London, Blackie, 1902.

Rob Roy MacGregor: Highland chief and outlaw. London, E. Nister, 1902.
Sweeping The Seas: A tale of the Alabama. London, E. Nister, 1902.
Chris Cunningham: A story of the stirring days of Nelson, illustrated by H.E. Butler. London, J.F. Shaw, 1903.
The Cruise of the "Arctic Fox" in icy seas around the Pole. London, S.H. Bousfield, 1903.
The Shell Hunters. London, Religious Tract Society, 1903.
Young Peggy McQueen, illustrated by Warwick Goble. London, Collins, 1903.
In Regions of Perpetual Snow: A story of wild adventures, illustrated by Henry Austin. London, Ward Lock, 1904.
As We Sweep Through The Deep. London, Nelson, 1905.
The Meteor Flag of England: The story of a coming conflict. London, J. Nisbet, 1905.
The Sauciest Boy In The Service, illustrated by Henry Austin. London, Ward Lock, 1905.
The City At The Pole. London, J. Nisbet, 1906.
War On The World's Roof. London, J.F. Shaw, 1906.
Wild Life In Sunny Lands: A romance of butterfly hunting, illustrated by Alfred Pearse. London, Religious Tract Society, 1906.

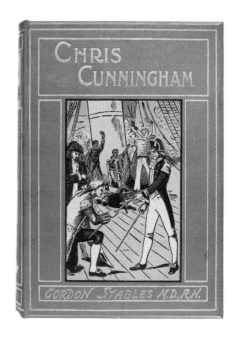

A Little Gipsy Lass, illustrated by William
    Rainey. London, Chambers, 1907.
The Voyage of The "Blue Vega". London,
    Religious Tract Society, 1907.
From Slum To Quarterdeck, illustrated by
    Alfred Pearse. London, Religious Tract
    Society, 1908.
*The Cruise of The Snowbird: A story of Arctic
    adventure*, illustrated by W.B. Handforth.
    London, Hodder & Stoughton, 1909.
*The Ivory Hunters: A story of wild adventure by
    land and sea*. London, Ward Lock, 1909.

Herbert Strang. Pseudonym for George
Herbert Ely (1866–1958), British, and C.
James L'Estrange (1867–1947). British.

Herbert Strang was the pseudonym used by
two writers, George Herbert Ely and C. James
L'Estrange, who together wrote over sixty
boys' adventure stories. The dauntless young
heroes of their stories always win through and
prosper. *Rob the Ranger* (1907) is a tale of Rob
Somer's part in Wolfe's Canadian victories of
1757 against the French. White man is set
against white man and Indian against Indian.
The front cover of the first edition shows
Somer's Mohawk comrade Deerfoot, 'His
skin was red with the redness of nature; his
high cheekbones, arched nose, and black
scalp-tuft decorated with plumes proclaimed
him an Indian', leading the Rangers over the
ice against the savage Hurons, who are hostile
to Mohawak and Englishman alike. The
coloured illustrations by W.H. Margetson
certainly capture the mood of the book.

In Herbert Strang's *Boys of the Light Brigade*
(1904), William Rainey has drawn the
frontispiece of the 95th charging home, when
Jack Lumsden with fellow comrades Bates and
Plunket break through the barricade but are
soon surrounded by French dragoons during
the battle of Corunna. However, with typical
British pluck, the three smash their way
through the enemy and facilitate their side's
victory in this crucial stage of the Peninsular
War that raged during the early years of the
nineteeth century.

The two authors also wrote, with the
assistance of other writers, a very popular
Historical Series including titles such as *With

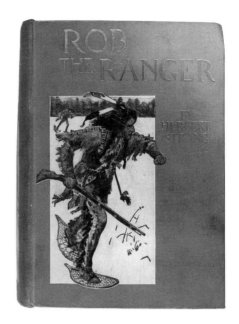

Marlborough to Malplaquet and *Claud the Archer*,
which were used in many schools.

The books which are of special interest to
many readers, however, are their tales of
fantastic voyages which were influenced by
H.G. Wells and Jules Verne; examples are *King
of the Air*, *The Cruise of the Gyro-Car* and
Round the World in Seven Days.

Tom Burnaby, illustrated by Charles M.
    Sheldon. London, Blackie, 1904; as *Young
    Tom Burnaby*, New York, Street and
    Smith, 1904.
Boys of the Light Brigade, illustrated by
    William Rainey. London, Blackie, 1904;
    as *The Light Brigade in Spain*, New York,
    Putnam, 1904.
Kobo, illustrated by William Rainey. London,
    Blackie, 1904; New York, Putnam, 1905.
Brown of Moukden, illustrated by William
    Rainey. London, Blackie, 1905; New
    York, Putnam, 1906; as *Jack Brown, The
    Hero*, New York, Street and Smith; as *Jack
    Brown in China*, London, Oxford
    University Press, 1923.
The Adventures of Harry Rochester, illustrated
    by William Rainey. London, Blackie, and
    New York, Putnam, 1905.
Jack Hardy, illustrated by William Rainey.
    London, Hodder & Stoughton, 1906;
    Indianapolis, Bobbs Merrill, 1907.

One of Clive's Heroes, illustrated by William Rainey. London, Hodder & Stoughton, 1906; as *In Clive's Command*, Indianapolis, Bobbs Merrill, 1906.

Samba, illustrated by William Rainey. London, Hodder & Stoughton, 1906; as *Fighting on the Congo*, Indianapolis, Bobbs Merrill, 1906.

Rob the Ranger, illustrated by W.H. Margetson. London, Hodder & Stoughton, and Indianapolis, Bobbs Merrill, 1907.

With Drake on the Spanish Main, illustrated by Archibald Webb. London, Hodder & Stoughton, 1907; as *On the Spanish Main*, Indianapolis, Bobbs Merrill, 1909.

King of the Air, illustrated by W.E. Webster. London, Hodder & Stoughton, and Indianapolis, Bobbs Merrill, 1907.

On the Trail of the Arabs, illustrated by Charles Sheldon. Indianapolis, Bobbs Merrill, 1907.

Herbert Strang's Historical Series (With Marlborough to Malplaquet, With the Black Prince, A Mariner of England, One of Rupert's Horse, and *Lion-Heart*, all with Richard Stead; *Claud the Archer* and *In the New Forest*, both with John Aston; *Roger the Scout* and *For the White Rose*, both with George Lawrence). London, Hodder & Stoughton, 9 vols. 1907–9.

Humphrey Bold, illustrated by W.H. Margetson, London, Hodder & Stoughton, 1908; Indianapolis, Bobbs merrill, 1909.

Barclay of the Guides, illustrated by H.W. Koekkoek. London, Hodder & Stoughton, 1908; New York, Doran, 1909.

Lord of the Seas, illustrated by C. Fleming Williams. London, Hodder & Stoughton, 1908; New York, Doran, 1910.

Palm Tree Island, illustrated by Archibald Webb and Alan Wright. London, Hodder & Stoughton, 1909; New York, Doran, 1910.

Settlers and Scouts, illustrated by T.C. Dugdale. London, Hodder & Stoughton, 1909; New York, Doran, 1910.

Swift and Sure, illustrated by J. Finnemore. London, Hodder & Stoughton, 1909; New York, Doran, 1910.

Mary Tourtel (1874–1948). British.

For main author article see 1920 to 1929.

Illustrated by the author.

A Horse Book. London, Richards, 1901; New York, Stokes, 1902.
The Three Little Foxes. London, Richards, 1903.

Jean Webster (1876–1916). American.

For main author article see 1910 to 1919.

When Patty Went to College. New York, Century, 1903; as *Patty and Priscilla*, London, Hodder & Stoughton, 1915.

Percy F(rancis) Westerman (1876–1959). British.
a.k.a. P.F. Westerman.
a.k.a. P. Westerman.

For main author article see 1910 to 1919.

A Lad of Grit, illustrated by E.S. Hodgson. London, Blackie, 1908.

F(rancis) Cowley Whitehouse. British.

F. Cowley Whitehouse usually wrote school stories for boys, such as *The Sniper*, but in *Mark Maturin, Parson* (1906) the hero is a minister of religion. Joe Blencowe, a London hansom cab driver by profession, is having a fist fight with the Reverend Mark Maturin. Joe thought he would be an easy opponent to beat and planned to 'close up 'is peepers, and loosen 'is ivories.' The scene on the front cover, by the artist B. E. Minns, shows the parson hitting Joe Blencowe: 'E stopped me prompt with a left smash full on the beak,' Joe was to say afterwards. The fight occurs at the 'Young Men's Club', held in the St Hegbert's Mission. Joe and his friends had decided to break up the club but got more than they bargained for from this exponent of muscular Christianity.

Mark Maturin, Parson, illustrated by B.E. Minns. London, Ward Lock, 1906.

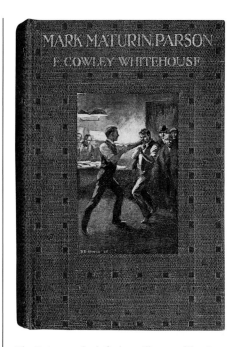

The Sniper – a book for boys, illustrated by A. Pearse. London, J. Nisbet, 1907.

Kate Douglas Wiggin (1856–1923). American.

Kate Douglas Wiggin, an American, had been head of a kindergarten and author of several volumes before she wrote the two books which have kept her name alive, *Rebecca of Sunnybrook Farm* and *New Chronicles of Rebecca*.

Lively, intelligent and kind, Rebecca Rowena Randall lives in Maine at Randall's Farm, which she calls Sunnybrook Farm. Rebecca, who is one of seven children, goes to live at the brick house with her two aunts, Miranda and Jane Sawyer, who undertake to pay for her education to make life a little easier financially for her widowed mother. All adults in the book dote on Rebecca, except for her Aunt Miranda, even though Rebecca herself makes every effort to like her aunt. Obviously Rebecca eventually made a deep impression on Aunt Miranda because Rebecca inherits the brick house from her. The house is shown on the green front cover of the first edition of *Rebecca of Sunnybrook Farm* (1903). The book

closes with 'God bless the brick house that was; God bless the brick house that is to be!'.

Penelope's Irish Experiences. Boston, Houghton Mifflin, and London, Gay and Bird, 1901.
The Diary of a Goosegirl, illustrated by Claude Shepperson. Boston, Houghton Mifflin, and London, Gay and Bird, 1902.
Rebecca of Sunnybrook Farm. Boston, Houghton Mifflin, and London, Gay and Bird, 1903.
Half-a Dozen Housekeepers, illustrated by Mills Thompson. Philadelphia, Altemus, and London, Gay and Bird, 1903.
A Village Stradivarius, London, Gay and Bird, 1904.
Rose o' the River, illustrated by George Wright. Boston, Houghton Mifflin, and London, Constable, 1905.
New Chronicles of Rebecca. Boston, Houghton Mifflin, and London, Constable, 1907; as *More about Rebecca of Sunnybrook Farm*, London, A & C. Black, 1930.
Finding A Home, Boston, Houghton Mifflin, 1907.

P(elham) G(renville) Wodehouse (1881–1975). British.

The effect of P.G. Wodehouse's foray into school fiction was the revolutionisation of the genre. He produced only seven such books, in addition to the adventure yarn *William Tell Told Again*, published between 1902 and 1909. His bright and breezy tone helped to dispel the often gloomy and overtly moralistic air that pervaded the work of earlier writers of schoolboy literature (who owed much to the evangelising tales of F.W. Farrar, Talbot Baines Reed and their Religious Tract Society successors).

Wodehouse wrote about five fictional schools: Beckford College (*A Prefect's Uncle*), St Kay's (*The Head of St Kay's*), St Austin's (*The Pothunters* and *Tales of St Austin's*), Wrykyn (*The Gold Bat, The White Feather* and *Mike*) and Sedleigh (the setting for the second half of *Mike*). Those novels set at Wrykyn are considered to be the most autobiographical, although the school is different in numerous ways from Wodehouse's Dulwich. An instance of the author's own obsessions being foisted upon his young creations is evident in the boys' universal passion for sport, and cricket in particular. Cricket matches are the characters' foremost formulative arenas. It is one such scene that is illustrated on the olive green boards of *Mike* (1909) by T.M.R. Whitwell. It depicts, perhaps surprisingly, a less than auspicious moment in the cricketing career of the book's hero, Mike Jackson. He has been run out by the arrogant prefect Firby-Smith (shown wearing glasses on the right of the illustration) in the heat of a House match. This action provokes Mike to call the senior boy a 'grinning ape', a remark which results in his temporary expulsion from the team. Needless to say, 'Achilles leaves his tent' later in the book and, among other feats of derring-do, scores 277 not out in spectacular fashion in another match.

The Pothunters, illustrated by R. Noel Pocock. London, A. & C. Black, 1902; New York, Macmillan, 1924.
A Prefect's Uncle, illustrated by R. Noel Pocock. London, A. & C. Black, 1903; New York, Macmillan, 1924.
Tales of St. Austin's, illustrated by R. Noel Pocock, E.F. Skinner & T.M.R. Whitwell. London, A. & C. Black, 1903; New York, Macmillan, 1923.

The Gold Bat, illustrated by T.M.R. Whitwell. London, A. & C. Black, 1904; New York, Macmillan, 1923.
William Tell Told Again, with J.W. Houghton; illustrated by Philip Dadd. London, A. & C. Black, 1904.
The Head Of Kay's, illustrated by T.M.R. Whitwell. London, A. & C. Black, 1905; New York, Macmillan, 1922.
The White Feather, illustrated by W. Townend. London, A. & C. Black, 1907; New York, Macmillan, 1922.
Mike, illustrated by T.M.R. Whitwell. London, A. & C. Black, 1909; New York, Macmillan, 1924.

May Wynne (1875–1949). British. Pseudonym for Mabel Winifred Knowles.

For main author article see 1910 to 1919.

Mollie's Adventures. London, Russell, 1903.

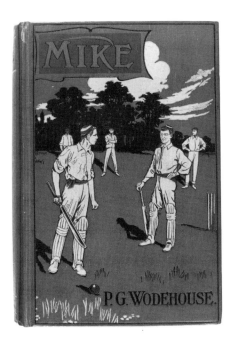

1910–1919

AUTHORS INCLUDED FROM 1910 TO 1919

Harold Avery
J.M. Barrie
L. Frank Baum/Floyd Akers/Laura
    Bancroft/Hugh Fitzgerald/Suzanne
    Metcalf/Edith Van Dyne
E.F. Benson
Angela Brazil
Capt. F.S. Brereton/ Lt.-Col. F.S.
    Brereton/Lt.-Col. F.S. Brereton,
    CBE
Frances Hodgson Burnett
J. Williams Butcher
Christine Chaundler
Harry Collingwood
Padraic Colum
Mrs H.C. Cradock
Samuel Rutherford Crockett
Mabel Dearmer
Walter de la Mare
Norman Duncan
Evelyn Everett-Green/E. Everett-
    Green/Cecil Adair
G.E. Farrow
G. Manville Fenn/George Manville
    Fenn
Dorothy Canfield Fisher/Dorothy
    Canfield
Charles Gilson/C.L. Gilson/Captain
    Charles Gilson/Major Charles Gilson

Edith Howes
Rudyard Kipling
Amy Le Feuvre/Mary Thurston Dodge
Robert Leighton
Norman Lindsay
Bessie Marchant
John Masefield
L.T. Meade
Cornelia Meigs/Adair Aldon
A.A. Milne
Mrs Molesworth
L.M. Montgomery
Dorothea Moore
E. Nesbit
Elsie J. Oxenham/Elsie Oxenham/Elsie
    Jeanette Oxenham
Eleanor H. Porter/Eleanor Stuart
Beatrix Potter/Beatrix Heelis
Walter C. Rhoades/Walter Rhoades
Charles G.D. Roberts
Caroline Dale Snedeker
Herbert Strang
Ethel Talbot
Jean Webster
Percy F. Westerman/P.F. Westerman/P.
    Westerman
F. Cowley Whitehouse
Kate Douglas Wiggin
May Wynne

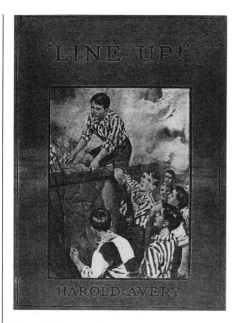

Harold Avery (1867–1943). British.

Harold Earnshaw's dust wrapper illustration for *Line Up!* by Harold Avery (1918) reveals that football practice has been curtailed by smoke drifting on to the pitch from outside the school. Moreton climbs the wall to report that the gorse common adjacent to the school has been set on fire by the rough Curly and his gang.

Off the Wicket, illustrated by A.T. Smith. London, Nelson, 1910.
Not Cricket!, illustrated by Ernest Prater. London, Partidge, 1911.
The Forbidden Room. London, Nelson, 1911.
Head of the School. London, Partridge, 1912.
Talford's Last Term. London, Partridge, 1912.
The Chartered Company. London, Nelson, 1915.
Line up!, illustrated by Harold Earnshaw. London, Collins, 1918.
Caught Out, illustrated by G.S. London, Collins, 1919.

J(ames) M(atthew) Barrie (1860–1937). British.

J.M. Barrie's Peter Pan had been a literary figure for some years when *Peter and Wendy* was published in 1911. However, this was the first telling in book form of his now familiar adventures with the Darling children, John, Michael and Wendy, in Never-Never Land. Here, in one of F.D. Bedford's internal line drawings, Peter follows the fairy Tinkerbell through the Nursery window in search of his lost shadow, 'the window of the nursery blew open, and a boy did drop on the floor. He was accompanied by a strange light, no bigger than your fist, which darted about the room like a living thing.' It is just the beginning of a series of adventures that will ultimately set Peter against a motley crew of pirates and his arch enemy, Captain Hook.

Peter and Wendy, illustrated by F.D. Bedford. London and New York, Hodder & Stoughton, 1911; as *Peter Pan and Wendy*, illustrated by Mabel Lucie Attwell. London, Hodder & Stoughton, 1921.

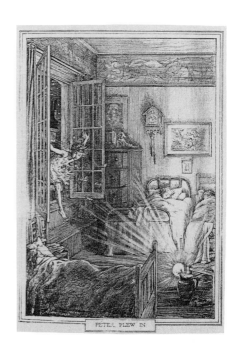

PETER FLEW IN

L(yman) Frank Baum (1856–1919).
American.
a.k.a. Floyd Akers.
a.k.a. Laura Bancroft.
a.k.a. Hugh Fitzgerald.
a.k.a. Suzanne Metcalf.
a.k.a. Edith Van Dyne.

The Emerald City of Oz, illustrated by John
R. Neill. Chicago, Reilly and Britton,
1910.
The Sea Fairies, illustrated by John R. Neill.
Chicago, Reilly and Britton, 1911.
The Daring Twins, illustrated by Pauline
Batchelder. Chicago, Reilly and Britton,
1911.
The Flying Girl [and Her Chum] (as Edith Van
Dyne). Chicago, Reilly and Britton, 2
vols., 1911–12.
Sky Island, illustrated by John R. Neill.
Chicago, Reilly and Britton, 1912.
Phoebe Daring, illustrated by Joseph Pierre
Nuyttens. Chicago, Reilly and Britton,
1912.
The Patchwork Girl of Oz, illustrated by John R.
Neill. Chicago, Reilly and Britton, 1913.
*The Little Wizard Series (Jack Pumpkinhead and
the Sawhorse, Little Dorothy and Toto,
Ozma and the Little Wizard, The Cowardly
Lion and the Hungry Tiger, The Scarecrow
and the Tin Woodman, Tik-Tok and the
Nome King)*. Chicago, Reilly and Britton,
6 vols, 1913; as *Little Wizard Stories of Oz*,
Reilly and Britton, 1914; London,
Simpkin, 1939.
Tik-Tok of Oz, illustrated by John R. Neill.
Chicago, Reilly and Britton, 1914.
The Scarecrow of Oz, illustrated by John R.
Neill. Chicago, Reilly and Britton, 1915.
Rinkitink in Oz, illustrated by John R. Neill.
Chicago, Reilly and Britton, 1916.
*The Snuggle Tales (Little Bun Rabbit, Once
upon a Time, The Yellow Hen, The Magic
Cloak, The Ginger-Bread Man, Jack
Pumpkinhead)*, illustrated by John R. Neill.
Chicago, Reilly and Britton, 6 vols.,
1916–17; as *Oz-Man Tales*, 6 vols, 1920.
*Mary Louise [in the Country, Solves a Mystery,
and the Liberty Girl, Adopts a Soldier]* (as
Edith Van Dyne). Chicago, Reilly and
Britton, 4 vols., and Reilly and Lee, 1
vol., 1916–19 .

The Lost Princess of Oz, illustrated by John R.
Neill. Chicago, Reilly and Britton, 1917.
The Tin Woodman of Oz, illustrated by John
R. Neill. Chicago, Reilly and Britton,
1918.
The Magic of Oz, illustrated by John R. Neill.
Chicago, Reilly and Lee, 1919; London,
Armada, 1974.

E(dward) F(rederic) Benson (1867–1940).
British.

Between 1909 and 1939 E.F. Benson wrote
over seventy novels, as well as many short
story collections and works of non-fiction.
However, from this great output came only
three children's books. Two, *David Blaize*
(1916) and *David of King's* (1924) follow in the
tradition of Thomas Hughes' Tom Brown and
chart the progress of the author's young hero
through public school and university. The
third, *David Blaize and the Blue Door* (1918) is
entirely different. More Wonderland than
Rugby, it tells how nine-year-old David, who
had always believed that there was a door to
another world, 'pushed his pillow aside, and
there, in the middle of his bolster, was a
beautiful shining blue door with a gold
handle.' This scene is reproduced on the
book's dust wrapper by Henry J. Ford. When

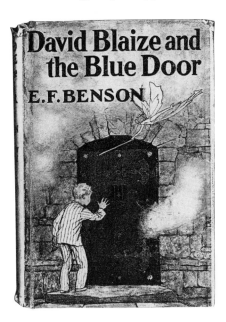

through the door, David meets dancing rats, the animals from his Noah's Ark and characters from nursery rhymes. He also takes a flying test and is examined by a committee of birds.

David Blaize. London, Hodder & Stoughton, 1916.
David Blaize and the Blue Door, illustrated by H.J. Ford. London, Hodder & Stoughton, 1918.

Angela Brazil (1869–1947). British.

Angela Brazil's school yarns were, from their inception, a hit with the author's schoolgirl audience, if not with their headmistresses, who objected to her liberal use of slang. This popularity with the young was almost certainly due to the attractive and lively nature of Brazil's characterisations and the charm and excitement of the situations she portrayed. These characteristics, along with the books' colourful boards, made her stories more desirable to the young reader than the rather staid and moralising tales that made up the fare previously available to girls. All the first editions published up to 1914 were dated and have gilt spine lettering.

A typical example of Brazil's work is *The Luckiest Girl in the School* (1916). The 'luckiest girl' is Winowa Woodward, a bright, impulsive girl, who is better at games than at her books. To the surprise of her family, she gains one of only two scholarships to Seaton High School. It later turns out that there had been a mix-up of marks and that Winowa should never have won the scholarship. However, she overcomes adversity and becomes Games Captain, leading from the front. Before Seaton's important cricket match against Binsworth, Winowa exhorts her troops with the rallying cry, 'Look here, my hearties!' She proceeds to open the batting and, as Balliol Salmon's dust wrapper illustration shows, dispatches her first ball to the off-side boundary. Salmon was also responsible for the portrait of Raymonde Armitage on the dustwrapper of *The Madcap of the School* (1917) reproduced on the jacket of the present study.

Bosom Friends: A Seaside Story, illustrated by Jenny Wylie. London, Nelson, 1910.
The Manor House School, illustrated by F. Moorsom. London, Blackie, 1910; Boston, Caldwell, 1911.
A Fourth Form Friendship, illustrated by Frank E. Wiles. London, Blackie, 1911.
The New Girl at St. Chad's, illustrated by John Campbell. London, Blackie, 1911.
A Pair of Schoolgirls, illustrated by John Campbell. London, Blackie, 1912.
The Leader of the School, illustrated by John Campbell. London, Blackie, 1913.
The Youngest Girl in the Fifth, illustrated by Stanley Davis. London, Blackie, 1913.
The Girls of St Cyprian's, illustrated by Stanley Davis. London, Blackie, 1914.
The School by the Sea, illustrated by John Campbell. London, Blackie, 1914.
The Jolliest Term on Record, illustrated by Balliol Salmon. London, Blackie, 1915.
For the Sake of the School. London, Blackie, 1915.
The Luckiest Girl in the School, illustrated by Balliol Salmon. London, Blackie, and New York, Stokes, 1916.
The Madcap of the School, illustrated by Balliol Salmon. London, Blackie, 1917; New York, Stokes, 1922.

The Slap-Bang Boys, illustrated by George Morrow. London, Nelson, 1917.

A Patriotic Schoolgirl, illustrated by Balliol Salmon. London, Blackie, 1918.

For the School Colours, illustrated by Balliol Salmon. Londn, Blackie, 1918.

A Harum-Scarum Schoolgirl, illustrated by John Campbell. London, Blackie, 1919; New York, Stokes, 1920.

The Head Girl at The Gables, illustrated by Balliol Salmon. London, Blackie, 1919; New York, Stokes, 1920.

Two Little Scamps and a Puppy, illustrated by E. Blampied. London, Nelson, 1919.

Captain F(rederick) S(adlier) Brereton
(1872–1957). British.
a.k.a. Lt. Col. F.S. Brereton.
a.k.a. Lt. Col. F.S. Brereton, CBE

Throughout the history of boys' adventure fiction there was always a strong core of books that dealt with contemporary events. Indeed, it often seemed that the latest British victory had just been reported in the newspapers when G.A. Henty produced his latest, highly detailed, adventure yarn around that very campaign. The First World War, a conflict where, more than ever before, young readers were likely to know people participating, provided much for the adventure writer. *With Joffre at Verdun* (1916) by Brereton is an archetypal instance of recent history fictionalised. The wider story is of the struggle for supremacy between the French and Germans before Verdun. The scene, illustrated by Archibald Webb on the novel's dust wrapper, portrays the advance of the French (identifiable by their prominent moustaches!) from their trenches against the foe. Within this framework lies the tale of two young French friends, Henri de Farquissare and Jules Epain, who find themselves in Berlin at the outbreak of war and become interned as alien enemies. Along with an Englishman, they escape through a subterranean tunnel. After thrilling adventures and hair's-breadth escapes they succeed in reaching Belgium. They then join the French Army and, as greater and smaller themes coalesce, take part in the months of fighting before Verdun.

Indian and Scout. A tale of the Gold Rush to California, illustrated by Cyrus Cuneo. London, Blackie, 1910.

The Great Aeroplane. A thrilling tale of adventure, illustrated by Edward S. Hodgson. London, Blackie, 1910.

Tom Stapleton, the Boy Scout, illustrated by Gordon Brown. London, Blackie, 1911.

The Hero of Panama. A tale of the great canal, illustrated by William Rainey. London, Blackie, 1912.

Under the Chinese Dragon. A tale of Mongolia, illustrated by Charles M. Sheldon. London, Blackie, 1912.

Kidnapped by Moors. A story of Morocco, illustrated by Edward S. Hodgson, London, Blackie, 1912.

A Boy of the Dominion. A tale of the Canadian immigration, illustrated by William Rainey. London, Blackie, 1912.

King of Ranleigh. A school story, illustrated by Ernest Prater. London, S.W. Partridge, 1913.

The Great Airship. A tale of adventure, illustrated by C.M. Padday. London, Blackie, 1913.

With Wellington to Spain. A story of the Peninsula, illustrated by William Rainey. London, Blackie, 1913.

On the Field of Waterloo, illustrated by John De Walton, London, Blackie, 1914.

A Sturdy Young Canadian, illustrated by
Charles M. Sheldon. London, Blackie,
1914.

*Under French's Command. A story of the
Western Front from Neuve Chapelle to Loos*,
illustrated by Archibald Webb. London,
Blackie, 1915.

*With French at the Front. A story of the Great
European War down to the battle of the Aisne*,
illustrated by Archibald Webb. London,
Blackie, 1915.

With our Russian Allies, illustrated by Wal
Paget. London, Blackie, 1915.

*At Grips with the Turk. A story of the
Dardanelles campaign*, illustrated by Wal
Paget. London, Blackie, 1915.

*With Joffre at Verdun. A story of the Western
Front*, illustrated by Archibald Webb.
London, Blackie, 1916.

*On the Road to Bagdad. A story of the British
Expeditionary Force in Mesopotamia*,
illustrated by Wal Paget. London, Blackie,
1916.

*Under Haig in Flanders. A story of Vimy,
Messines and Ypres*, illustrated by J.E.
Sutcliffe. London, Blackie, 1917.

*Under Foch's Command. A tale of the Americans
in France*, illustrated by Wal Paget.
London, Blackie, 1918.

*From the Nile to the Tigris. A story of
campaigning from Western Egypt to
Mesopotamia*, illustrated by Frank Gillett.
London, Blackie, 1918.

*The Armoured-Car Scouts. A tale of the
campaign in the Caucasus*, illustrated by
Archibald Webb. London, Blackie, 1918.

*With the Allies to the Rhine. A story of the
finish of the War*, illustrated by Frank
Gillett. London, Blackie, 1919.

*With Allenby in Palestine. A story of the latest
Crusade*, illustrated by Frank Gillett.
London, Blackie, 1919.

Frances Hodgson Burnett (1849–1924).
American.

Frances Hodgson Burnett's *The Secret Garden*
(1911) tells the story of spoilt orphan, Mary
Lennox, and the way she rejuvenates her own
existence and that of her sickly cousin, Colin.
She achieves this with the aid of her friend

F.H. Burnett – *The Secret Garden*
1911 Illustrated by Charles Robinson
He would lie on the grass watching things grow

Dickon by replanting an enclosed garden that
had lain neglected for many years. This corner
of Eden in the grounds of her uncle's bleak
Yorkshire mansion bestows a peace of mind
that will help all three children adjust to adult
life. Charles Robinson furnished the first
edition with eight lovely colour plates. The
one reproduced here depicts the scene in
which Colin, who is usually confined to bed
in his gloomy room, is brought into the
garden for the first time. The magical
atmosphere has an immediate effect and he
professes that all he wants to do now is to 'lie
on the grass watching things grow'.

The Secret Garden, illustrated by Charles
Robinson. New York, Stokes, and
London, Heinemann, 1911.

The Lost Prince. New York, Century, and
London, Hodder & Stoughton, 1915.

*The Way to the House of Santa Claus: A
Christmas Story.* New York and London,
Harper, 1916.

Little Hunchback Zia. New York, Stokes, and
London, Heinemann, 1916.

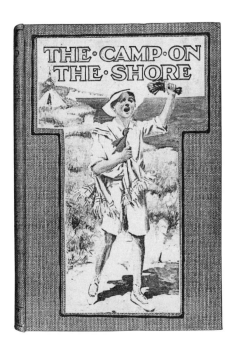

J(ames) Williams Butcher. British.

J. Williams Butcher wrote public school stories that focused on triumph over adversity and the importance of loyalty to friends and alma mater. *The Camp on the Shore* (1913) is atypical because it is set outside the confines of the school and during the summer holidays. Three brothers, Norman, John and Francis, known as 'The Prikles', go on a camping holiday with their cousin Harold. Norman is illustrated on the front cover as he goes off to bathe. He is soon involved in the rescue of a younger boy from drowning. Other vacation activities for the four include rock climbing and singing as minstrels.

The Making of Treherne, illustrated by Arthur Twidle. London, Charles H. Kelly, 1911.

The Senior Prefect and Other Chronicles of Rossiter, illustrated by B. Hutchinson. London, Charles H. Kelly, 1913.

The Camp on the Shore, illustrated by J.D. Mills. London, Hodder & Stoughton, 1913.

Christine Chaundler (1887–1972). British.

Best known in later decades for her 'school' and 'guide' stories, which were marked by a greater degree of realism than found in the work of many other exponents of this type of fiction, Christine Chaundler's initial literary output consisted of fairy stories. The front cover of her first, *The Magic Kiss* (1916), shows Princess Elva hiding in a toadstool ring during a game of hide and seek on her seventh birthday. The children fail to find her and, whilst she sleeps, the evil Goblin King squeezes toadstool juice on to her beautiful visage to transform her into the most horrendously ugly princess ever. Her royal parents search for a cure but, in true Fairy Tale fashion, all it takes is a kiss from the page Pierrot to restore Elva to her former beauty.

The Magic Kiss, illustrated by Florence Mary Anderson. London, Cassell, 1916.

Little Squirrel Tickletail, illustrated by Harry Rountree. London, Cassell, 1917; New York, Stokes, 1918.

Ronald's Burglar, illustrated by Helen Stratton. London, Nelson, 1919; New York, Nelson, 1921.

The Reputation of the Upper Fourth. London, Nisbet, 1919.

Pat's Third Term, illustrated by Harold Earnshaw. London, Oxford University Press, 1919.

Harry Collingwood (1851–1922). British. Pseudonym for William Joseph Cosens Lancaster.

The Cruise of the Thetis: A tale of the Cuban insurrection, illustrated by Cyrus Cuneo. London, Blackie, 1910.

Harry Escombe: A tale of adventure In Peru, illustrated by Victor Prout. London, Blackie, 1910.

A Middy of the Slave Squadron: A West African Story, illustrated by William Rainey. London, Blackie, 1911.

Overdue; or, the Strange Story of a Missing Ship, illustrated by W.H. Holloway. London Blackie, 1911.

The Adventures of Dick Maitland: A tale of unknown Africa, illustrated by Alec Ball. London, Blackie, 1912.

A Middy of the King: A romance of the old British Navy, illustrated by Edward S. Hodgson. London, Blackie, 1912.

A Strange Cruise: A tale of piracy on the high seas, illustrated by Archibald Webb. London, Blackie, 1912.

Two Gallant Sons of Devon: A tale of the days of Queen Bess, illustrated by Edward S. Hodgson. London, Blackie, 1912.

Turned Adrift: An adventurous voyage, illustrated by Edward S. Hodgson. London, Blackie, 1913.

Through Veld and Forest: An African story, illustrated by Archibald Webb. London, Blackie, 1913.

The Cruise of the "Nonsuch" Buccaneer, illustrated by John Williamson. London, SPCK, 1914.

The First Mate: The story of a strange cruise, illustrated by Edward S. Hodgson. London, Blackie, 1914.

A Chinese Command: A story of adventure in eastern seas, illustrated by Archibald Webb. London, Blackie, 1914.

A Pair of Adventurers in Search of El Dorado, illustrated by Oscar Wilson. London, Sampson Low, 1915.

Under the Ensign of the Rising Star: A story of the Russo-Japanese War. London, Sampson Low, 1916.

Padraic Colum (1881–1972). Irish.

Padraic Colum's children's fiction, like that of many of his writing contemporaries, formed only a small part of his literary productivity. He writes with passion and in detail about his Irish homeland and its traditions. His first, semi-autobiographical, novel, *A Boy in Eirinn* (1915), was thus an ideal choice of book to be included in Dent's 'Children of the Nations' series. As the blurb that replaces a dustwrapper illustration on the first edition informs the reader, the series' intention was to educate English children about the ways of life in foreign parts. The story traces the childhood experiences and travels of Finn O'Donnell. The book is rather thin on plot, but the emphasis is on creating a suggestion of Irish life. This is brought about through detailed descriptions of such institutions as a country market, illustrated on the frontispiece, where Finn would spend his pocket money and meet many eccentric rustic 'characters'.

FINN GENERALLY BOUGHT TWO PIECES OF GINGERBREAD.

Jack B. Yeats depicts Finn O'Donnell buying two gingerbreads.

A Boy in Eirinn, illustrated by Jack B. Yeats. London, Dent, and New York, Dutton, 1915.

Mrs H(enry) C. Cradock. British.

Mrs Henry Cradock's major contribution to children's fiction was her 'Josephine' series of books, written over a period of twenty-five years with younger children in mind. They relate Josephine's adventures with her animate toys. Typical of the series' tales is the second book, *Josephine's Happy Family* (1917), illustrated, like so many of the 'Josephine' series, by the delicate artwork of Honor C. Appleton. The design on the front boards reveals Josephine watching some of her sixteen dolls dancing. Her closest associates, Big Teddy, resplendent in a bright new pink bow, and Quacky-Jack, sit close to her, with Charlie and Dorothy on Josephine's left.

Josephine And Her Dolls, illustrated by Honor C. Appleton. London, Blackie, 1916.
Josephine's Happy Family, illustrated by Honor C. Appleton. London, Blackie, 1917.
Josephine is Busy, illustrated by Honor C. Appleton. London, Blackie, 1918.
Everyday Stories to Tell Children. London, Harrap, 1919.

Where The Dolls Lived, illustrated by Honor C. Appleton. London, SPCK, 1919.

Samuel Rutherford Crockett
(1860–1914). British.

Samuel Rutherford Crockett's sentimental nursery tales are now largely, and some would say thankfully, forgotten. His last children's novel, *Sweethearts At Home* (1912), is probably his most mawkish and reviled volume. The book's chapters represent the reminiscences of 'Sweetheart', the nineteen-year-old heroine. Her favourite colour is purple and her ultimate desire is to possess 'a purple nursery' and a baby to consume 'beautiful purple jelly'; a noble, if slightly limited, ambition. The illustration on the book's cover shows Sweetheart with a purple trim to her hat and a purple bodice. Her partners in purpleness include Hugh John, Sir Toady Lion and Elizabeth Fortinbras.

Sweethearts at Home: Assisted by Sweetheart Herself, and with Additions and Corrections by Hugh John, Sir Toady Lion, Maid Margaret, and Miss Elizabeth Fortinbras, illustrated by C.E. Brock. London and New York, Hodder & Stoughton, 1912.

Mabel Dearmer (1872–1915). British.

The Cockyolly Bird, illustrated by the author. London, Hodder & Stoughton, 1914.
Brer Rabbit And Mr. Fox. London, Joseph Williams, 1914.

Walter de la Mare (1873–1956). British.

A prolific poet, critic and fiction writer specialising in the unusual and supernatural, Walter de la Mare also produced ten children's books, published between 1910 and 1960 (four years after his death). These books are often allegorical and reflect the author's interest in the fantastic. The beginning of his first, and most collectable, children's book, *The Three Mulla Mulgars* (1910), introduces the sort of thing the reader is to expect from this and later works: 'On the borders of the Forest of Munza-mulgar lived once an old grey fruit monkey of the name of Mutta-matutta. She had three sons, the eldest Thumma, the next Thimbulla, and the youngest, who was a Nizzo-neela, Ummanodda. And they called each other for short: Thumb, Thimble and Nod.'

The green cover of this book, that tells of the monkeys' (or mulgars') journey to paradise (the land of Tishnar), depicts the three protagonists in black with the title in gilt.

The first edition's coloured frontispiece by E.A. Monsell pictures the scene when 'From every peak the eagles swooped upon the Mulgars ... And with sticks and stones and flaming torches they turned on the fierce birds that came sweeping and swirling out of the dark upon them on bristling feathers, with ravening beaks and talons'

The Three Mulla-Mulgars, illustrated by E.A. Monsell. London, Duckworth, 1910; New York, Knopf, 1919; as *The Three Royal Monkeys*; or, *The Three Mulla-Mulgars*, London, Faber, 1935.

Norman Duncan (1871–1916). Canadian.

Norman Duncan's *Billy Topsail, M.D.* (1916) is the last of his three books about his young hero from the eastern coast of Canada. This novel is a gripping tale of medical adventure in the icy plains of Newfoundland. It traces the harrowing experiences of Billy, now a young adult, as he aids the inspirational Doctor Luke. Billy fights weaknesses in the human condition as well as the area's wild elements as he achieves the self-esteem and know-how that will eventually send him to medical college.

Billy Topsail and Company. New York, Revell, 1910.
Billy Topsail, M.D.: A Tale of Adventure With Doctor Luke of the Labrador. New York, Revell, 1916; London, Hodder & Stoughton, 1917.

Evelyn Everett-Green (1856–1932). British.
a.k.a. E. Everett-Green.
a.k.a. Cecil Adair.

Evelyn Everett-Green's tales of (usually female) heroism against the odds continued to

"The air was aflock with eagles."

appear at regular intervals during this decade, if not with the spectacular frequency that was such a prominent feature of her earlier output. *Sweepie* (1918), one of her last books, is a narration of the adventures of a seven-year-old girl of that name: so called after her father's favourite flower, the Sweet Pea. Sweepie lives at Greyshott Hall with her parents, sisters and dog, Toddie. The dust wrapper of this book, which has a frontispiece as its only other illustration, pictures Sweepie attempting to rescue her playmate, Jock, who has been thrown off his pony and into a gravel pit. At this stage the future for poor Jock does not look rosy: 'his face [was] quite white, except where it was marked by blood … his body [was] all limp.'

The Family Next Door: a story for girls, illustrated by Lancell Speck. London, Religious Tract Society, 1910.
General John: A story for boy scouts and others, illustrated by H.R. Millar. London, S.W. Partridge, 1910.
In Grandfather's Garden. London, Nelson, 1910.
Ursula Tempest, illustrated by Victor Prout. London, Religious Tract Society, 1910.
Dickie and Dorrie at School, illustrated by Gordon Browne. London, Wells Gardner, Darton, 1911.

A Disputed Heritage, illustrated by Savile Lumley. London, Pilgrim Press, 1911.
Aunt Patience: A story for girls. London, Religious Tract Society, 1912.
Miss Mallory of Mote. London, Hutchinson, 1912.
Tommy and the Owl. London, S.W. Partridge, 1912.
The Yellow Pup: A story for boys, illustrated by C. Fleming Williams. London, Partridge, 1912.
Inchfallen, London, Ward Lock, 1913.
The House on the Cliff. London, Ward Lock, 1914.
The Heronstroke Mystery. London, Religious Tract Society, 1915.
Adventurous Anne. London, Stanley Paul, 1916.
Sweepie. London, Religious Tract Society, 1918.

G(eorge) E(dward) Farrow (1862–1920?). British.

The Mysterious Shin Shira (1914) tells of exotic travel and adventure; sometimes, as W.G. Easton's cover design indicates, in very bizarre circumstances. The bird is the Roc, 'His pinions were strong and mighty', and the narrator and his slave have only some ropes

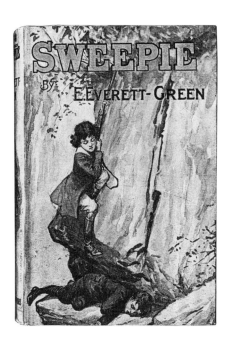

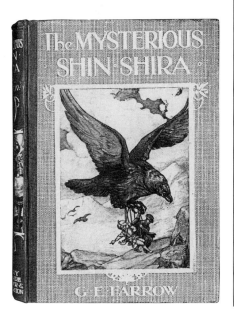

and straps between them and a very nasty fall indeed.

The Mysterious Shin Shira, illustrated by W.G. Easton. London, Hodder & Stoughton, 1914.

G(eorge) Manville Fenn (1831–1909). British.

Cutlass and Cudgel, illustrated by James Durden. London, Hodder & Stoughton, 1910.

Dorothy Canfield Fisher (1879–1958). American.
a.k.a. Dorothy Canfield.

Dorothy Canfield Fisher was brought up in academic surroundings in New England and her cultural preferences are reflected in her work. Her first children's novel was *Understood Betsy* (1917). Betsy, who has endured a somewhat stifling upbringing in a midwestern city, goes to stay with her Uncle Harry and two aunts, Ann and Abigail, at their home in the New England countryside. Here Betsy is allowed to develop into a self-confident and

UNDERSTOOD BETSY

DOROTHY CANFIELD

AUTHOR OF
THE BENT TWIG

more loving young lady. The illustration on the book's cover is framed by the cream and brown dust wrapper and shows Aunt Abigail looking on as Betsy receives the doll Deborah for the first time.

Understood Betsy, illustrated by Ada C. Williamson. New York, Holt, 1917; London, Constable, 1922.

Charles Gilson (1878–1943). British.
a.k.a. C(harles) L(ouis) Gilson.
a.k.a Captain Charles Gilson.
a.k.a Major Charles Gilson.

Captain Charles Gilson, one of numerous military gentlemen who found the pen more profitable than the sword, spun adventure yarns for boys over a period of three decades. He wrote both historical and contemporary tales and an archetypal example of the former is *The Mystery of Ah Jim* (1919). The book's dust wrapper shows Fred Barrington, boatswain of the *Mary Ann Rutland*, fighting off the scheming Sun Wing and his fellow pirates. Fred is aided by the excitable Mr Wong and 'Ah Jim' (who actually turns out to be Richard Lyndsay Lynne, the long lost son of the politician Sir Robert Lynne).

The Lost Island: a strange tale of the Far East, illustrated by Cyrus Cuneo. London, Henry Frowde; Hodder & Stoughton, 1910.

The Spy: A tale of the Peninsula War, illustrated by Cyrus Cuneo. London, Hodder & Stoughton. 1910.

The Sword of Freedom: a tale of the English Revolution, illustrated by Frank Gillett. London, Hodder & Stoughton, 1912.

The Pirate Aeroplane, illustrated by Christopher Clark. London, Hodder & Stoughton, 1913.

Scenes from a Subaltern's Life. London, William Blackwood, 1913.

The Sword of Deliverance: A story of the Balkan War, the Battle of Lule Burgas and the Siege of Adrianople, illustrated by H.C. Seppings Wright. London, James Nisbet, 1913.

The Race Round the World, illustrated by Cyrus Cuneo. London, Hodder & Stoughton, 1914.

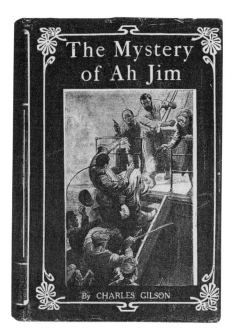

By CHARLES GILSON

*A Motor-Scout In Flanders; or, Held By the
    Enemy*. London, Blackie, 1915.
*Across the Cameroons: a story of War and
    Adventure*. London, Blackie, 1916.
Submarine U93: a tale of the Great War.
    London, Boy's Own Paper, 1916.
In Arms For Russia, illustrated by C.F. Brock.
    London, Humphrey Milford, 1918.
In the Power of the Pigmies, illustrated by
    Archibald Webb. London, Humphrey
    Milford, 1918.
The Pirate Yacht: a tale of the Southern Seas,
    illustrated by P. Hard. London, Collins,
    1918.
*The Captain of the Caves, and other stories of
    adventure*, illustrated by Leo Bates.
    London, Cassell, 1919.
*The Mystery of Ah Jim: a story of the Chinese
    under-world, and of piracy and adventures in
    Eastern Seas*, illustrated by George Soper.
    London, Boy's Own Paper, 1919.
On Secret Service, illustrated by John De
    Walteon. London, Humphrey Milford,
    1919.

Edith Howes (1874–1954). New Zealander.

Edith Howes' children books, undoubtedly
diverting as they are, reveal this school
teacher's incessant desire to instruct her
young audience. *The Cradle Ship* (1916) is
(in)famously her attempt to teach the 'Facts
of Life' via a child's observations of various
young animals and their mothers. Her first
book, *The Sun's Babies* (1910), is a collection
of short stories and poems that feature such
sprites as Rain Fairy, Leaf Fairy and May
Fairy; plants Willy Wallflower, Daffodil Baby
and Milly Mushroom and also Sally Snail,
Bobby Barnacle and Kitty Crayfish. All the
illustrations are by Frank Watkins whose
Rain Fairy features on the book's front
cover. She has woken in a pink poppy and
now wants to 'go up to the blue sky and play
with the sunbeams and clouds.'
Unfortunately for the fairy, these incumbents
of the ether turn out to be party-poopers: the
sunbeams feel it their duty to ripen
strawberries, whilst the clouds have a shower
and rainbow to prepare. The Rain Fairy has
to learn the lesson that there is 'no time for
play till the day's work is done.'

The Sun's Babies, illustrated by Frank
    Watkins. London, Cassell, 1910.
Fairy Rings, illustrated by Frank Watkins.
    London, Cassell, 1911.

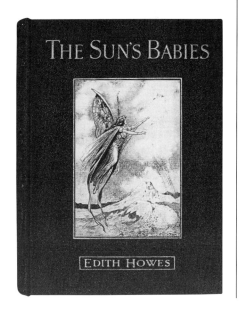

THE SUN'S BABIES

EDITH HOWES

Rainbow Children, illustrated by Alice B. Woodward. London, Cassell, 1912.

Where Bell-Birds Chime. Christchurch, Whitcombe and Tombs, 1912.

The Cradle Ship, illustrated by Florence Mary Anderson. London, Cassell, 1916.

Wonderwings and Other Fairy Stories, illustrated by Alice Polson. Auckland, Whitcombe and Tombs, 1918.

Little Make-Believe, illustrated by Alice Polson. Auckland, Whitcombe and Tombs, 1919.

Rudyard Kipling (1865–1936). British.

Rewards and Fairies, illustrated by Frank Craig. London. Macmillan, and New York, Doubleday, 1910.

Amy Le Feuvre (d. 1929). British.
a.k.a. Mary Thurston Dodge.

The dust wrapper of Amy Le Feuvre's *Terrie's Moorland Home* (1918) reflects this romance's evocative moorland setting and it is something of a pity that J.F. Campbell's frontispiece is the only other piece of artwork included in it. Terrie Deverell's 'Horse literally threw her into Mr Benerton's outstretched arms.' A sign of things to come?

Joyce and the Rambler. London, Hodder & Stoughton, 1910.

A Little Listener, illustrated by W.H.C. Groome. London, Religious Tract Society, 1910.

Us, and Our Empire, illustrated by W.H.C. Groome. London, Religious Tract Society, 1911.

Tested! Philadelphia, Heidelberg Press, 1911; London, Partridge, 1912.

Four Gates. London and New York, Cassell, 1912.

Laddie's Choice, illustrated by W.H.C. Groome. London. Religious Tract Society, 1912; as Mary Thurston Dodge, New York, Dodd Mead, 1912.

Some Builders. London, Cassell, 1913.

Her Husband's Property. London, Religious Tract Society, 1913.

Herself and Her Boy. London, Cassell, 1913.

Harebell's Friend. London, Religious Tract Society, 1914.

Daddy's Sword. London, Hodder & Stoughton, 1915.

Joan's Handful. London, Cassell, 1915.

Dudley Napier's Daughters. London, Morgan and Scott, 1916.

A Madcap Family; or, Sybil's Home. London, Partridge, 1916.

Us, and Our Charge. London, Religious Tract Society, 1916.

Tomina in Retreat. London, Religious Tract Society, 1917.

Joy Cometh in the Morning, illustrated by Harold Copping. London, Religious Tract Society, 1917.

Dreamikins. London, Religious Tract Society, 1918.

A Happy Woman. London, Religious Tract Society, 1918.

Terrie's Moorland Home, illustrated by J.F. Campbell. London, Morgan and Scott, 1918.

Little Miss Moth. London, Partridge, 1919.

The Chisel. London, Religious Tract Society, 1919.

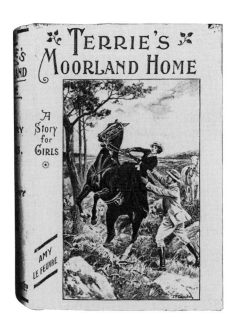

Robert Leighton (1859–1934). British.

Mark Redisham and the skipper of the trawler *Dainty* watch HMS *Carlisle* arrive in pursuit of the German submarine U15, which had been trailing a British convoy of dreadnoughts and cruisers through a newly cleared mine area. A well-aimed shell sinks the submarine in the climactic scene from Robert Leighton's *Dreadnoughts of the Dogger* (1916), illustrated on the book's wrapper by Watson Charlton.

The Cleverest Chap in the School, illustrated by P.A. Staynes. London, Jarrold, 1910.
Kiddie of the Camp: A story of the Western prairies. London, Scout Library, 1910.
Coo-ee! A story of peril and adventure in the South Seas. London, Scout Library, 1911.
The Kidnapped Regiment: A story of 1745, illustrated by Watson Charlton. London, Pilgrim Press, 1911.
The Perils of Peterkin: A story of adventure in North-West Canada, illustrated by Arthur Twidle. London, Jarrold, 1911.
The Bravest Boy in the Camp: A story of adventure on the Western prairies, illustrated by Charles Norman. London, Jarrold, 1912.
Rattlesnake Ranch: A story of adventure in the great North West. London, Scout Library, 1912.

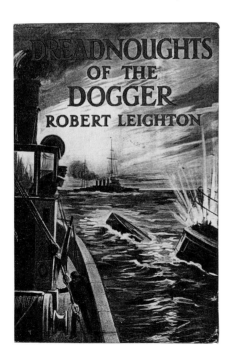

Sergeant Silk, the prairie scout, illustrated by Charles Norman, London, Jarrold 1913.
The Red Patrol: A story of the North-West mounted police, illustrated by Frank Alcock. London, Jarrold, 1915.
Dreadnoughts of the Dogger: A story of the war on the North Sea, illustrated by Watson Charlton. London, Ward Lock, 1916.
Wooly of the Wilds, a story. London, Ward Lock, 1917.

Norman Lindsay (1879–1969). Australian.

Norman Lindsay was primarily a cartoonist in his native Australia and his wonderfully evocative illustrations bring to life *The Magic Pudding* (1918), probably one of the best children's books to emanate from Australia. It is the uproarious tale of Bunyip Bluegum (a Koala) and his friends Bill Barnacle (a sailor) and Sam Sawnoff (a 'penguin bold') as they consume and protect from kidnap a never-ending pudding. This pudding is no dumb beast: it is called Albert and has long spindly legs. It dispenses witty and useful advice to its 'protectors', whilst retaining the sprinting ability to counter personally all unwelcome attempts upon it. This is one of only two children's books Lindsay wrote, his other was a comparative failure. Hailed as the next *Alice in Wonderland* when first published, *The Magic Pudding* has perhaps received less attention on these shores than it deserves.

Illustrated by the author.

The Magic Pudding, Being, the Adventures of Bunyip Blueglum and His Friends Bill Barnacle and Sam Sawnoff. Sydney, Angus and Robertson, 1918; London, Hamish Hamilton, and New York, Farrar and Rinehart, 1936.

Bessie Marchant (1862–1941). British.

The bedraggled figure of Cynthia Beauchamp is shown by John E. Sutcliffe on his dust wrapper for Bessie Marchant's 1918 novel *Cynthia Wins*. The heroine is holding a lantern aloft near the mouth of a railway tunnel in the Rockies: a foreign setting typical for this author. She is trying to warn an approaching train that it is in danger of derailment at the hands of German agents in this First World War thriller. Of course, as the book's title predicts, ultimately Cynthia wins.

The Adventures of Phyllis, illustrated by F. Whiting. London, Cassell, 1910.

The Black Cockatoo, illustrated by Lancelot Speed. London, Religious Tract Society, 1910.

A Countess from Canada, illustrated by Cyrus Cuneo. London, Blackie, 1910.

Greta's Domain, illustrated by William Rainey. London, Blackie, 1910.

Molly of One Tree Bend. London, Butcher, 1910.

The Deputy Boss, illustrated by Oscar Wilson. London, SPCK, 1910.

The Ferry House Girls, illustrated by W.R.S. Stott. London, Blackie, 1911.

A Girl of Distinction, illustrated by William Rainey. London, Blackie, 1911.

Redwood Ranch, illustrated by Harold Piffard. London, SPCK, 1911.

Three Girls in Mexico, illustrated by William Rainey. London, Blackie, 1911.

A Girl of the Northland, illustrated by N. Tenison. London, Hodder & Stoughton, 1912.

His Great Surrender, illustrated by Gordon Browne. London, SPCK, 1912.

A Princess of Servia, illustrated by William Rainey. London, Blackie, 1912.

Sibyl of St. Pierre, illustrated by William Rainey. London, Wells Gardner, 1912.

The Western Scout, illustrated by W.S. Stacey. London, SPCK, 1912.

The Youngest Sister, illustrated by William Rainey. London, Blackie, 1912.

The Adventurous Seven, illustrated by W.R.S. Stott. London, Blackie, 1913.

The Heroine of the Ranch, illustrated by Cyrus Cuneo. London, Blackie, 1913.

Denver Wilson's Double, illustrated by W. Douglas Almond. London, Blackie, 1914.

Helen of the Black Mountain. London, Blackie, 1914.

The Loyalty of Hester Hope, illustrated by William Rainey. London, Blackie, 1914.

A Mysterious Inheritance. London, Blackie, 1914.

A Girl and a Caravan. London, Blackie, 1915.

Joyce Harrington's Trust. London, Blackie, 1915.

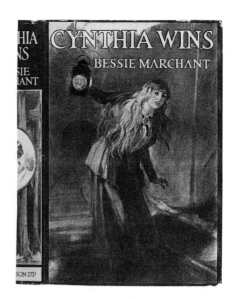

Molly Angel's Adventures. London, Blackie, 1915.

A Canadian Farm Mystery; or, Pam the Pioneer. London, Blackie, 1916.

A Girl Munition Worker, illustrated by John E. Sutcliffe. London, Blackie, 1916.

The Unknown Island. London, Blackie, 1916.

The Gold-Marked Charm. London, Blackie, 1917.

Lois in Charge;or, A Girl of Grit. illustrated by Cyrus Cuneo. London, Blackie, 1917.

A V.A.D. in Salonika. London, Blackie, 1917.

Cynthia Wins, illustrated by John E. Sutcliffe. London, Blackie, 1918.

A Dangerous Mission, illustrated by Wal Paget. London, Blackie, 1918.

Norah to the Rescue, illustrated by W.R.S. Stott. London, Blackie, 1919.

A Transport Girl in France. London, Blackie, 1919.

John Masefield (1878–1967). British.

Poet Laureate, playwright, author and scholar; John Masefield's juvenilia contains the complexity one would automatically associate with a man of such diverse talent. In the early part of his career he wrote two historical adventures, which were injected with a rare degree of realism: *Martin Hyde, the Duke's*

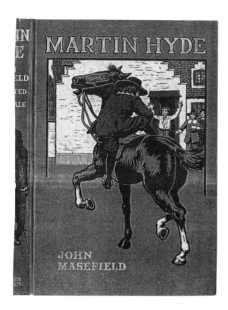

Messenger (1910) and *Jim Davis; or the Captive of the Smugglers* (1911). Whilst the latter is set during the Napoleonic Wars, the former tells of the adventures of the recently orphaned Martin Hyde in the aftermath of Charles II's death. The Duke of Monmouth tries to wrestle James II from the throne. Martin acts as a messenger for the Duke and is shown on the cover of the book mounting his horse. Although initially risking life and limb for the Duke, Martin, in true Masefield style, becomes disillusioned. The adventure has turned sour and Martin is only just rescued from a firing squad in the book's final pages.

A Book of Discoveries, illustrated by Gordon Browne. London, Wells Gardner, and New York, Stokes, 1910.

Lost Endeavour. London, Nelson, 1910; New York, Macmillan, 1917.

Martin Hyde, The Duke's Messenger, illustrated by T.C. Dugdale. London, Wells Gardner, and Boston, Little Brown, 1910.

Jim Davis; or, The Captive of the Smugglers, illustrated by Mead Schaeffer. London, Wells Gardner, 1911; New York, Stokes, 1912.

L(Elizabeth) T(homasina) Meade
(1854–1914). Irish.

L.T. Meade's prolific output of girls' school stories continued through this decade. *The Maid Indomitable* (1916) of the title is called Antigone. Her sisters nickname her 'the Greek goddess'. This is not merely for her good looks, of which she is quite aware (witness the narcissistic way in which she brushes her hair whilst transfixed by her own image in the looking-glass on the book's wrapper), but also for her pride. Antigone was the notoriously stubborn principal character in the Sophoclean tragedy of that name. A maid indomitable indeed, she opposed the tyrannical state and buried her traitorous brother illegally.

The A.B.C. Girl. London, White, 1910.
Belinda Treherne. London, Long, 1910.
A Girl of Today. London, Long, 1910.
Lady Anne. London, Nisbet, 1910.
Miss Gwendoline. London, Long, 1910.
Nance Kennedy. London, Partridge, 1910.
Pretty-Girl and the Others. London, Chambers, 1910.
Rose Regina. London, Chambers, 1910.
A Wild Irish Girl, illustrated by Lewis Baumer. London, Chambers and New York, Hurst, 1910.
A Bunch of Cousins, and The Barn "Boys." London, Chambers, 1911.
Desborough's Wife. London, Digby Long, 1911.
The Doctor's Children. London, Chambers and Philadelphia, Lippincott, 1911.
For Dear Dad. London, Chambers, 1911.
The Girl from Spain. London, Digby Long, 1911.
The Girls of Merton College. London, Chambers and New York, Hurst, 1911.
Mother and Son. London, Ward Lock, 1911.
Ruffles. London, Stanley Paul, 1911.
The Soul of Margaret Rand. London, Ward Lock, 1911.
Corporal Violet. London, Hodder & Stoughton, 1912.
A Girl of the People. London, Everitt, 1912.
Kitty O'Donovan. London, Chambers, and New York, Hurst, 1912.
Lord and Lady Kitty. London, White, 1912.

Love's Cross Roads. London, Stanley Paul, 1912.

Peggy from Kerry. London, Chambers, and New York, Hurst, 1912.

The Chesterton Girl Graduates, illustrated by Harold Earnshaw. New York, Hurst, 1913; London, Chambers, 1914.

The Girls of Abinger Close. London, Chambers, 1913.

The Girl's of King's Royal, illustrated by Gordon Browne. New York, Hurst, 1913; London, Chambers, 1914.

The Passion of Kathleen Duveen. London, Stanley Paul, 1913.

A Band of Mirth. London, Chambers, 1914.

Col. Tracy's Wife. London, Aldine, 1914.

Elizabeth's Prisoner. London, Stanley Paul, 1914.

A Girl of High Adventure. London, Chambers, 1914.

Her Happy Face. London, Ward Lock, 1914.

The Queen of Joy. London, Chambers, and New York, Hurst, 1914.

The Wooing of Monica. London, Long, 1914.

The Darling of the School. London, Chambers, 1915.

The Daughter of a Soldier, illustrated by Charles L. Wrenn. London, Chambers and New York, Hurst, 1915.

Greater Than Gold. London, Ward Lock, 1915.

Jill the Irresistible, illustrated by William Rainey. London, Chambers and New York, Hurst, 1915.

Hollyhock, London, Chambers, 1916.

Madge Mostyn's Nieces. London, Chambers, 1916.

The Maid Indomitable. London, Ward Lock, 1916.

Mother Mary. London, Chambers, 1916.

Daughters of Today. London, Hodder & Stoughton, 1916.

Better Than Riches. London, Chambers, 1917.

The Fairy Godmother. London, Chambers, 1917.

Cornelia Meigs (1884–1973). American. **a.k.a. Adair Aldon.**

Her most lasting work in the field of children's literature may be as a critic, but Cornelia Meigs produced a sizeable canon of fiction tracing the historical development of America. Meigs' first book, the fairy tale *The Kingdom of the Winding Road* (1915), does not reveal her interest in her country's past but does betray another passion, that for horticulture. One of Frances White's coloured internal illustrations depicts the mysterious beggar, who plays a

"COME, PRINCESS, DRY YOUR EYES"

silver pipe and gives helpful advice to those who need cheering up, dressed in ragged clothes of fantastic colours and sitting with an unhappy princess Priscilla on a garden bench. She is upset because her garden will not grow as she wishes. The beggar, responding like an expert from *Gardeners' Question Time*, suggests that many of the plants should be moved to better positions: for instance those requiring shade and dampness should be placed near a wall. Later, in more serious circumstances, the beggar suggests an effective way of raising the ransom money to free the captured father of the princess. The book's green cover shows the beggar drawn in blue.

The Kingdom of the Winding Road, illustrated by Frances White. New York, Macmillan, 1915.
Master Simon's Garden. New York, Macmillan, 1916.
The Pool of Stars. New York, Macmillan, 1919.

A(lan) A(lexander) Milne (1882–1956). British.

A.A. Milne is, of course, most famous for his creation of a bear of very little brain. However, a decade before Pooh was born, he had written a book, *Once on a Time* (1917),

which demonstrates Milne's inimitable creative talent. This story of war, magic, romance and adventure centres around the often stormy relationship between two fairy tale Kingdoms, Euralia and Barodia. The tone is set by the very first chapter, a scene from which is illustrated by H.M. Brock on the book's wrapper. The King of Euralia's breakfast, which he is sharing with his daughter Hyacinth, is disturbed by the winging overhead of the King of Barodia, who is making his way home after an all-night flight, wearing his magic boots.

Once on a Time, illustrated by H.M. Brock. London, Hodder & Stoughton, 1917; New York, Putnam, 1922.

Mrs Molesworth (Mary Louisa).
(1839–1921). British.

The Story of A Year, illustrated by Gertrude Demain Hammond. London, Macmillan, 1910.
Fairies Afield, illustrated by Gertrude Demain Hammond. London, Macmillan, 1911.

L(ucy) M(aud) Montgomery (1874–1942). Canadian.

M.G. Hook's elegant wrapper for L.M. Montgomery's *Rainbow Valley* (1919) shows Anne Shirley, now Mrs Gilbert Blythe, walking through the beautiful Ingleside countryside at sunset. She is glad to have come back to her children and the familiar landscape after returning from a medical conference in England with her husband. Anne is framed by a kaleidoscopic collection of flowers on the dust wrapper: 'The sun was setting over Rainbow Valley. The pond was wearing a wonderful tissue of purple and gold and green and crimson.'

Kilmeny of the Orchard, illustrated by George Gibbs. Boston, Page, and London, Pitman, 1910.
The Story Girl. Boston, Page, and London, Pitman, 1911.
Chronicles of Avonlea. Boston, Page, and London, Sampson Low, 1912.

The Golden Road. Boston, Page, 1913; London, Cassell, 1914.

Anne of the Island. Boston, Page, and London, Pitman, 1915.

Anne's House of Dreams. New York, Stokes, and London, Constable, 1917.

Rainbow Valley. Toronto, McClelland and Stewart, and New York, Stokes, 1919; London, Constable, 1920.

Dorothea Moore (1881–1933). British.

C.E. Brock's dust wrapper design for Dorothea Moore's *The Head Girl's Sister* (1918) captures a particularly hectic moment in this schoolgirl adventure. During the dress rehearsal for a school production of *A Midsummer Night's Dream* the fairy Moonshine's lantern is dropped and sets the scenery on fire: 'Venance made one wild dash to the chair, and caught the blazing flat as it was falling, holding it up with all her strength away from the little ones.' Venance Trethuen, the Head Girl's sister, is badly burned but recovers and is later enrolled in St Cyprion's School Red Roll of Honour.

A Lady of Mettle. London, Partridge, 1910.
The Making of Ursula. London, Partridge, 1910.

The Lucas Girls, illustrated by Tom Peddie, London, Partridge, 1911.

Under the Wolf's Fell. London, Partridge, 1911.

Nadia to the Rescue. London, Nisbet, 1912.

A Runaway Princess. London, Partridge, 1912.

Terry the Girl-Guide, illustrated by A.A. Dixon, London, Nisbet, 1912.

A Brave Little Royalist, illustrated by John Campbell. London, Nisbet, 1913.

Only a Girl! London, Partridge, 1913.

Rosemary the Rebel. London, Partridge, 1913.

Captain Nancy. London, Nisbet, 1914.

Cecily's Highwayman, illustrated by John Campbell. London, Nisbet, 1914.

Septima, Schoolgirl. London, Cassell, 1915.

Wanted, An English Girl: The Adventures of an English Schoolgirl in Germany. London, Partridge, 1916.

The New Girl, illustrated by Elizabeth Earnshaw. London, Nisbet, 1917.

The Head Girl's Sister, illustrated by C.E. Brock. London, Nisbet, 1918.

Tam of Tiffany's. London, Partridge, 1918.

Her Schoolgirl Majesty. London, Partridge, 1918.

Head of the Lower School, illustrated by C.E. Brock. London, Nisbet, 1919; New York, Putnam, 1920.

A Nest of Malignants. London, SPCK, 1919; New York, Macmillan, 1920.

E(dith) Nesbit (1858–1924). British.

The Magic City, illustrated by H.R. Millar. London, Macmillan, 1910; New York, Coward McCann, 1958.
The Wonderful Garden; or, The Three C's, illustrated by H.R. Millar. London, Macmillan, 1911; New York, Coward McCann, 1935.
The Magic World, illustrated by H.R. Millar and Spencer Pryse. London and New York, Macmillan, 1912.
Wet Magic, illustrated by H.R. Millar. London, Laurie, 1913; New York, Coward McCann, 1937.
Our New Story Book, with others, illustrated by Elsie Wood and Louis Wain. London, Nister, and New York, Dutton, 1913.

Elsie J. Oxenham (1880–1960). British. Pseudonym for Elsie Jeanette Dunkerley.
a.k.a. Elsie Oxenham.
a.k.a. Elsie Jeanette Oxenham.

Elsie J. Oxenham wrote stories for and featuring schoolgirls, but they cannot be classified as straightforward 'school stories'. Each of her series, the most famous of which is set around Abbey School in Wycombe, has school life as a background, but the greater part of the action occurs outside school hours and walls. The character of the books changed little during Oxenham's fifty years as an author and this has resulted in some of her later books being renounced as anachronistic. The content of the stories reflected Oxenham's personal interest in the Camp Fire Association, Girl Guiding and English folk dancing. A typical example of Oxenham's work is *A Go-Ahead Schoolgirl* (1919). Rena, a blond sixteen year old, and Nancy, six months younger and brunette, are best friends at their boarding school and spend a summer holiday together at a cottage in Derbyshire. They are pictured at the edge where moor meets valley but they 'had no suspicion of boy-eyes watching them from among the tumbled boulders.' Brothers Rex and Rufus, both wearing red caps, are shown on the spine of the dust wrapper as they observe the two girls new to the neighbourhood, 'I say, who can

they be?' Eventually the four, and the boys' sister, Tessa, become chums.

A Holiday Queen, illustrated by E.A. Overnell. London, Colllins, 1910.
Rosaly's New School, illustrated by T.J. Overnell. Edinburgh, Chambers, 1913.
Girls of the Hamlet Club, illustrated by Harold C. Earnshaw. Edinburgh, Chambers, 1914.
Schoolgirls and Scouts, illustrated by A.A. Dixon. London, Collins, 1914.
At School with the Roundheads, illustrated by H.C. Earnshaw. Edinburgh, Chambers, 1915.
Finding Her Family, illustrated by W.S. Stacey. London, SPCK, 1915.
The Tuck-Shop Girl, illustrated by H.C. Earnshaw. Edinburgh, Chambers, 1916.
A School Camp Fire, illustrated by Percy Tarrant. Edinburgh, Chambers, 1917.
The School of Ups and Downs, illustrated by H.C. Earnshaw. Edinburgh, Chambers, 1918.
A Go-Ahead Schoolgirl, illustrated by H.C. Earnshaw. Edinburgh, Chambers, 1919.
Expelled from School, illustrated by Victor Prout. London, Collins, 1919.

"'OH, I KNOW JUST THE PLACE FOR YOU,' SHE CRIED."

Eleanor H(odgman) Porter (1868–1920). American.
a.k.a. Eleanor Stuart.

Eleanor H. Porter wrote five children's books but it is for the creation of one charismatic little girl that she will always be remembered. The orphaned Pollyanna, in the book of the same name (1913), enters the house of her aunt as an unwanted guest but soon spreads cheer and hope to all those in the local community. One of Stockton Mulford's internal illustrations for the first edition shows Pollyanna promising Jimmy Bean, who has quit the orphanage, new accommodation: her Aunt Polly's house.

The Sunbridge Girls at Six Star Ranch (as Eleanor Stuart), illustrated by Frank Murch. Boston, Page, 1913; as *Six Star Ranch*, Boston, Page, and London, Stanley Paul, 1916.
Pollyanna, illustrated by Stockton Mulford. Boston, Page, and London, Pitman, 1913.
Pollyanna Grows Up, illustrated by H. Weston Taylor. Boston, Page, and London, Pitman, 1915.

Beatrix Potter (1866–1943). British.
a.k.a. Beatrix Heelis.

The Tale of Pigling Bland (1913) is one of Beatrix Potter's ever-popular books about the life and (mis)adventures of various animal characters. Potter's own delicate watercolour paintings grace every other page, as always, in this account of Pigling Bland's fortunes. He and his brother Alexander are sent off to seek their fortunes when their mother cannot cope with her large family any more. He is separated from his brother and gets lost. However, he meets the glamorous black pig Pig-Wig who runs away with him: but is he nevertheless doomed to the sausage factory?

Illustrated by the author.

The Tale of Mrs. Tittlemouse. London and New York, Warne, 1910.
The Tale of Timmy Tiptoes. London and New York, Warne, 1911.
The Tale of Mr. Tod. London and New York, Warne, 1912.
The Tale of Pigling Bland. London and New York, Warne, 1913.
The Tale of Johnny Town-Mouse. London and New York, Warne, 1918.

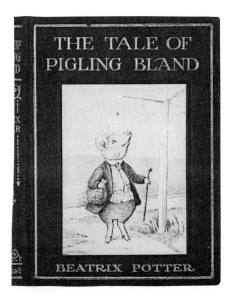

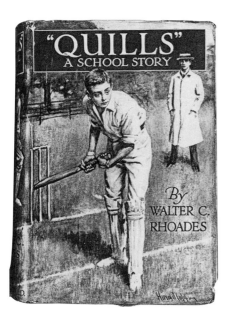

Walter C. Rhoades. British.
a.k.a. Walter Rhoades.

"*Quills*" (1918) is Walter Rhoades's tale of school life at Bedinghurst. It revolves around the chequered but finally triumphant career of Ronald Aveling (whose nickname is 'Quills'). Harold Copping's beautiful dust wrapper design portrays 'Quills' batting for the 'Classics' team in a particularly exciting cricket match, which will decide once and for all how his time at the school will be remembered.

"Quills": A Tale of Schoolboys at Bedinghurst, illustrated by Harold Copping. London, Blackie, 1918.

Charles G(eorge) D(ouglas) Roberts (1860–1943). Canadian.

Neighbours Unknown, illustrated by Paul Bransom. London, Ward Lock, 1910; New York, Macmillan, 1911.
More Kindred of the Wild, illustrated by Paul Bransom. London, Ward Lock, and New York, Macmillan, 1911.
Babes of the Wild, illustrated by Warwick Reynolds. London and New York, Cassell, 1912; as *Children of the Wild*, New York, Macmillan, 1913.

The Feet of the Furtive, illustrated by Paul Bransom. London, Ward Lock, 1912; New York, Macmillan, 1913.
Hoof and Claw, illustrated by Paul Bransom. London, Ward Lock, 1913; New York, Macmillan, 1914.
The Secret Trails, illustrated by Paul Bransom and Warwick Reynolds. New York, Macmillan, and London, Ward Lock, 1916.
The Ledge on Bald Face, illustrated by Paul Bransom. London, Ward Lock, 1918; as *Jim: The Story of a Backwoods Police Dog*, New York, Macmillan, 1919.

Caroline Dale Snedeker (1871–1956). American.

Caroline Dale Snedeker's writing was much affected by her personal experiences and education. *The Coward of Thermopylae* (1911), for instance, focusing as it does on a particular Spartan and his involvement with the fateful battle of 479BC, reflects her lifelong love of the classics. Her childhood home in Indiana was decorated with pictures of Greek gods which caught her imagination and later inspired her story telling. Snedeker researched the background for her books carefully and created sympathetic characters with genuine appeal.

The Coward of Thermopylae. New York, Doubleday, 1911; as *The Spartan*, Doubleday, 1912; London, Hodder & Stoughton, 1913.

Herbert Strang. Pseudonym for George Herbert Ely (1866–1958), British, and C. James L'Estrange (1867–1947). British.

Two books by Herbert Strang reflect the two very different types of adventure story that pervaded the children's book market in this century's second decade. *Through the Enemy Lines* (1916) concentrates on a nail-biting episode of subterfuge during the real-life conflict that dominated this period – the First World War. *The Blue Raider* (1919), on the other hand, is an adventure yarn of the old, but ever-popular, school. It relates the hair-raising experiences of a group of Britons in a hostile environment. Hoole and Gerthan (the two gentlemen explorer types who lead the expedition), followed by the rough and ready Grinsow and the timorous and well-named Meek, boatswain and first mate of their ship, are led through the jungle to the natives' settlement on C.E. Brock's dust-wrapper picture. At least one aspect of this is familiar to the four, it is called 'Oxford'.

The Cruise of the Gyro-Car, illustrated by A.C. Michael. London, Hodder & Stoughton, 1910.

The Adventures of Dick Trevanion, illustrated by William Rainey. London, Hodder & Stoughton, 1910.

Round the World in Seven Days, illustrated by A.C. Michael. London, Hodder & Stoughton, and New York, Doran, 1910.

The Flying Boat, illustrated by T.C. Dugdale. London, Hodder & Stoughton, 1911.

The Air Scout, illustrated by W.R.S. Stott. London, Hodder & Stoughton, 1911.

The Motor Scout, illustrated by Cyrus Cuneo. London, Hodder & Stoughton, 1912.

The Air Patrol, illustrated by Cyrus Cuneo. London, Hodder & Stoughton, 1912.

Cerdic the Saxon, with L.L. Weedon. London, Hodder & Stoughton, 1913.

A Little Norman Maid. London, Hodder & Stoughton, 1913.

Sultan Jim, Empire Builder. London, Hodder & Stoughton, 1913.

A Gentleman-at-Arms. London, Hodder & Stoughton, 1914.

A Hero of Liège. London, Hodder & Stoughton, 1914.

Fighting with French. London, Hodder & Stoughton, 1915.

The Boy Who Would Not Learn. London, Oxford University Press, 1915; New York, Oxford University Press, 1921.

The Silver Shot. London, Oxford University Press, 1915; New York, Oxford University Press, 1921.

In Trafalgar's Bay. London, Oxford University Press, 1915; New York, Oxford University Press, 1921.

Burton of the Flying Corps, illustrated by C.E. Brock. London, Hodder & Stoughton, 1916.

Frank Forester. London, Hodder & Stoughton, 1916.

The Old Man of the Mountain, illustrated by René Bull. London, Hodder & Stoughton, 1916.

Through the Enemy's Lines, illustrated by H.E. Elcock. London, Hodder & Stoughton, 1916.

Carry On!, illustrated by H.E. Elcock and H. Evison. London, Hodder & Stoughton, 1917.

With Haig on the Somme. London, Oxford University Press, 1917.

Steady, Boys, Steady. London, Hodder & Stoughton, 1917.

The Long Trail. London, Oxford University Press, 1918.

Tom Willoughby's Scouts. London, Oxford University Press, 1919.

The Blue Raider, illustrated by C.E. Brock. London, Oxford University Press, 1919.

Ethel Talbot. British.

Ethel Talbot was primarily a writer of 'girls' stories' in the Brazil mould. During the third and fourth decades of the century in particular her output was considerable: ten books in a single year at her peak in the late 1920s. She set her stories around school life and guide

BILLY THE SCOUT
HIS ADVENTURES

packs. Her first book, although one of very few 'boys' books', reflects this interest in scouting matters. The twelve-year-old eponymous hero of *Billy the Scout and His Day of Adventures* (1918) has passed his Second Class test in the scouts and has gone camping with the Eagle patrol to Craigside. He is entrusted with the task of conveying a dispatch to camp whilst all the other scouts 'would do their level best to seize the dispatch from the carrier'. Billy's activities during his 'day of adventures' include rescuing a little terrier puppy from a cliff edge, assisting an old lady up some steps, helping some lost children, stopping a runaway horse, outwitting the other scouts and returning the dispatch. The scenes of everyday scouting life are illustrated in full colour plates by Harold Earnshaw.

Billy the Scout and His Day of Adventures,
    illustrated by Harold Earnshaw. London,
    Nelson, 1918.
The School on the Moor, illustrated by Noel
    Harrold. London, Cassell, 1919.

Jean Webster (1876–1916). American.

Jean Webster had been deeply affected by several visits to the grim orphanages of New York during her student days. These experiences influenced her literary output and two of the children's books she produced before her early death are set in orphanages. They call for drastic reforms to the system that dealt with parentless children and stress the equal importance of every child, whatever his status. Her most well-known book was *Daddy-Long-Legs* (1912). It tells of Jerusha (known as Judy) Abbott, an orphan who, although seventeen, can see no way by which she could ever quit the orphanage in which she now works. However, an anonymous gentleman trustee, who Jerusha only remembers as being very tall and whose shadow looked 'like a huge, wavering daddy-long-legs', pays for the girl's board and tuition through college and in addition bestows upon her an allowance of thirty-five dollars a month. He wants no thanks but letters telling of the progress in her studies and the details of her daily life, 'Just such a letter as you would write to your parents if they were living.' The identity of this benefactor and his motivation are gradually revealed but the ultimate outcome of his action is only discovered in the book's final letter. On the blue front cover of the first edition is a portrait in black of Jerusha at her desk with a stream of letters cascading from it to the floor.

Just Patty. New York, Century, 1911;
    London, Hodder & Stoughton, 1915.
Daddy-Long-Legs, illustrated by the author.
    New York, Century, 1912; London,
    Hodder & Stoughton, 1913.
Dear Enemy, illustrated by the author. New
    York, Century, and London, Hodder &
    Stoughton, 1915.

Percy F(rancis) Westerman (1876–1959).
British.
a.k.a. P.F. Westerman.
a.k.a P. Westerman.

Percy Westerman's longevity as a writer of adventures for boys was such that he was able to boost morale through two World Wars and live to see Sputnik I and II in orbit. His stories tended to be set in the air or at sea and a criticism of Westerman has been that his narrative technique mirrored his choice of setting: vague, distant and out of his depth. Such carping is possibly rather unfair at a man whose enormous output gave pleasure and an air of excitement to generations of young Britons.

Westerman's very first stories were period adventures such as *The Young Cavalier – a story of the Civil War* (1911). The cover of this paperback, which has magenta edges and white lettering, depicts Humphrey Markham, recently recovered from a serious bullet wound, examining the sword he had believed lost in battle, 'Almost reverently he drew the blade, and, marvellous to behold, it still glittered like a ray of light.' Mary Widdicombe, Markham's nurse, looks on as the young hero prepares to rejoin the King's men in the civil war.

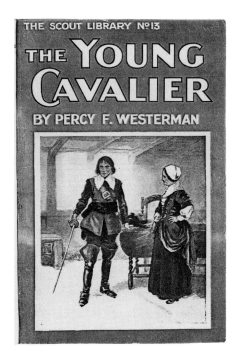

The Winning of Golden Spurs. London, Nisbet, 1911.

The Young Cavalier, illustrated by Gordon Browne. London, Pearson, 1911.

The Quest of the "Golden Hope," illustrated by Frank Wiles. London, Blackie, 1911.

The Flying Submarine. London, Nisbet, 1912.

Captured at Tripoli, illustrated by Charles Sheldon. London, Blackie, 1912.

The Sea Monarch, illustrated by E.S. Hodgson. London, A. & C. Black, 1912.

The Scouts of Seal Island, illustrated by Ernest Prater. London, A. & C. Black, 1913; New York, Macmillan, 1922.

The Rival Submarines, illustrated by C. Fleming Williams. London, Partridge, 1913.

The Stolen Cruiser. London, Jarrolds, 1913.

When East Meets West, illustrated by C.M. Padday. London, Blackie, 1913.

Under King Henry's Banners, illustrated by John Campbell. London, Pilgrim Press, 1913.

The Sea-Girt Fortress, illustrated by W.E. Wigfull. London, Blackie, 1914.

The Sea Scouts of the "Petrel", illustrated by Ernest Prater. London, A. & C. Black, 1914.

The Log of a Snob, illustrated by W.E. Wigfull. London, Chapman and Hall, 1914.

'Gainst the Might of Spain: A story of the Days of the Great Armada, illustrated by Saville Lumley. London, Pilgrim Press, 1914.

Building the Empire. London, Jarrolds, 1914.

The Dreadnought of the Air. London, Partridge, 1914.

The Dispatch-Riders. London, Blackie, 1915.

The Fight for Constantinople. London, Blackie, 1915.

The Nameless Island. London, Pearson, 1915.

A Sub. of the R.N.R. London, Partridge, 1915.

Rounding Up the Raider, illustrated by E.S. Hodgson. London, Blackie, 1916.

The Secret Battleplane. London, Blackie, 1916.

The Treasures of the "San Philipo." London, Religious Tract Society, 1916.

A Watch-Dog of the North Sea. London, Partridge, 1916.

Deeds of Pluck and Daring in the Great War. London, Blackie, 1917.

To the Fore with the Tanks!. illustrated by Dudley Tennant, London, Partridge, 1917.

Under the White Ensign. London, Blackie, 1917.

The Fritz Strafers. London, Partridge, 1918.

Billy Barcroft, R.N.A.S. London, Partridge, 1918.

A Lively Bit of the Front, illustrated by Wal Paget. London, Blackie, 1918.

The Secret Channel and Other Stories. London,
A. & C. Black, 1918; New York,
Macmillan, 1919.

The Submarine Hunters. London, Blackie,
1918.

A Sub and a Submarine, illustrated by E.S.
Hodgson. London, Blackie, 1918.

With Beatty off Jutland. London, Blackie,
1918.

Wilmshurst of the Frontier Force. London,
Partridge, 1919.

Winning His Wings, illustrated by E.S.
Hodgson. London, Blackie, 1919.

The Thick of the Fray at Zeebruge, April 1918,
illustrated by W.E. Wigfull. London,
Blackie, 1919.

Midst Arctic Perils, illustrated by W. Edward
Wigfull. London, Pearson, 1919.

F(rancis) Cowley Whitehouse. British.

Meltonians All! (1911) by F. Cowley
Whitehouse is a typical example of the genre
of early twentieth-century school fiction and
is set at the fictional public school 'Melton'.
The pupils' lives seem centred around games
and there are detailed descriptions of gripping
soccer, rowing and cricket matches (and even
a snowball fight between 'school' and

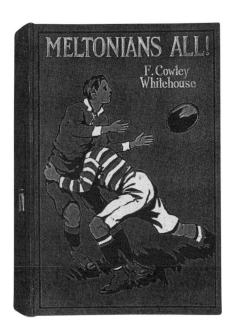

'college'). Interestingly, there is no mention of
rugby and so the mandate of the cover artist
(who is not responsible for the three colour
plates inside) must have been to give a 'taste'
of what is inside rather than depicting any
particular scene. He must not have known
much about rugby either: for the tackler's
method is dubious to say the least!

Meltonians All! illustrated by J. Finnemore.
London, Religious Tract Society, 1911.

*Rob Wylie of Jordan's – a story of public school
life*, illustrated by T.M.R. Whitwell.
London, Blackie, 1914.

Kate Douglas Wiggin (1856–1923).
American.

Mother Carey's Chickens. Boston, Houghton
Mifflin, 1911; as *Mother Carey* London,
Hodder & Stoughton, 1911.

A Child's Journey with Dickens. Boston,
Houghton Mifflin, and London, Hodder
& Stoughton, 1912.

*Penelope's Postscripts: Switzerland, Venice,
Wales, Devon, Home*. Boston, Houghton
Mifflin, and London, Hodder &
Stoughton, 1915.

The Romance of a Christmas Card, illustrated
by Alice Hunt. Boston, Houghton
Mifflin, and London, Hodder &
Stoughton, 1916.

May Wynne (1875–1949). British.
Pseudonym for Mabel Winifred Knowles.

May Wynne was a Christian missionary in the
East End of London and her interest in social
matters is evident in *Mollie's Adventures* (1903),
which is partly an attack on unpleasant
working conditions for young people.
Evangelical fervour and the desire to debunk
unfairness are not as apparent in her later
work. She became best known for her
thrilling school stories but had an intervening
period during which she developed several
narratives for younger children. The first of
these, *Jimmy: The Tale Of A Little Black Bear*
(1910), is a whimsical piece about a small
bear's adventures. A notable aspect of the

book is that the narrative voice is the bear's. This sometimes subverts expectations. For instance, the book's cover by George Soper presents the bear being disturbed by a young boy. Our own human expectation anticipates that the focus of observation should be the boy. However, such assumptions are confounded when it is the bear, not the boy, who recalls, 'I opened my eyes, and as I did so I heard the queerest little chuckling noise close beside me.'

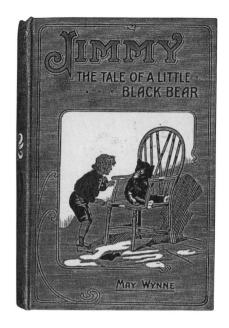

Jimmy: The Tales of a Little Black Bear, illustrated by George Soper. London, Partridge, 1910.

Phil's Cousins, illustrated by Paul Hardy. London, Blackie, 1911.

Crackers: The Tale of a Mischievous Monkey. London, Partridge, 1911.

The Story of Heather. London, Nelson, 1912; New York, Sully, 1913.

Tony's Chums, illustrated by A.A. Dixon. London, Blackie, 1914.

Murray Finds a Chum. London, Stanley Paul, 1914.

When Auntie Lil Took Charge, illustrated by A.A. Dixon. Londn, Blackie, 1915.

An English Girl in Serbia. London, Collins, 1916.

Three's Company. London, Blackie, 1917.

Stranded in Belgium. London, Blackie, 1918.

A Cousin from Canada, illustrated by John Campbell. London, Blackie, 1918.

The Honour of the School, illustrated by C.E. Brock. London, Nisbet, 1918.

Dick, London, Religious Tract Society, 1919.

Phyllis in France, illustrated by Frank Gillett. London, Blackie, 1919.

The Little Girl Beautiful, illustrated by Gordon Browne. London, Religious Tract Society, 1919.

Nan and Ken. London, Nelson, 1919.

Nipper & Co., illustrated by Harry Riley. London, Stanley Paul, 1919.

Scouts for Serbia, illustrated by Archibald Webb. London, Nelson, 1919.

Comrades from Canada, illustrated by John Campbell. London, Blackie,1919.

1920–1929

Harold Avery
L. Frank Baum/Floyd Akers/Laura
    Bancroft/Hugh Fitzgerald/Suzanne
    Metcalf/Edith Van Dyne
S.G. Hulme Beaman
E.F. Benson
Enid Blyton/Mary Pollock
Angela Brazil
Elinor M. Brent-Dyer/ E.M. Brent-
    Dyer
Capt. F.S. Brereton/ Lt. Col. F.S.
    Brereton/Lt. Col. F.S. Brereton,
    CBE
Joyce Lankester Brisley
Dorita Fairlie Bruce
Christine Chaundler
Arthur Bowie Chrisman
Catherine Christian/Catherine Mary
    Christian
Dorothy Clewes
Elizabeth Coatsworth
Harry Collingwood
Padraic Colum
Mrs H.C. Cradock
Richmal Crompton
Winifred Darch
Walter de la Mare
Evelyn Everett-Green/E. Everett-
    Green/Cecil Adair
Eleanor Farjeon
G. Manville Fenn/George Manville
    Fenn
Charles J. Finger
Dorothy Canfield Fisher/Dorothy
    Canfield
Marjorie Flack
Rose Fyleman
Wanda Gág
Charles Gilson/C.L. Gilson/Captain
    Charles Gilson/Major Charles Gilson
R.A.H.Goodyear
Elizabeth Goudge

Eleanor Graham
Charles Boardman Hawes
Constance Heward
Edith Howes
M.R. James
Rudyard Kipling
Amy Le Feuvre/Mary Thurston Dodge
Robert Leighton
Hugh Lofting
Patricia Lynch
Bessie Marchant
John Masefield
L.T. Meade
Stephen W. Meader
Florence Crannell Means
Cornelia Meigs/Adair Aldon
A.A. Milne
L.M. Montgomery
Dorothea Moore
E. Nesbit
Elsie J. Oxenham/Elsie Oxenham/Elsie
    Jeanette Oxenham
Gene Stratton Porter
Beatrix Potter/Beatrix Heelis
Rhoda Power
Evadne Price
Walter C. Rhoades/Walter Rhoades
Charles G.D. Roberts
Ruth Sawyer
Caroline Dale Snedeker
Herbert Strang
L.A.G Strong
Ethel Talbot
Barbara Euphan Todd/Euphan
Mary Tourtel
Alison Uttley
H.G.Wells
Percy F. Westerman/P.F. Westerman/P.
    Westerman
Kate Douglas Wiggin
Henry Williamson
May Wynne

Harold Avery (1867–1943). British.

Jack and the Redskins. London, Nelson, 1920.
The Runaways, illustrated by Gordon
    Browne. London, Collins, 1920.
Schoolboy Pluck. London, Nisbet, 1921.
A Choice of Chums. London, Nelson, 1922.
The Prefects' Patrol. London, Nisbet, 1922.
Between Two Schools, illustrated by Albert
    Morrow, London, Nelson, 1923.
A Fifth Form Mystery. London, Boy's Own
    Paper, 1923.
The Spoilt-Sport, and Double Dummy. London,
    Nelson, 1923.
The Adventures of Woodeny and Other Stories,
    with Ethel Talbot and Ada Holman.
    London, Nelson, 1923.
Pocket Thunder and Other Stories, with others.
    London, Nelson, 1926.
A Sixth-Form Feud. London, Ward Lock,
    1926.
Who Goes There?, illustrated by Roy.
    London, Nelson, 1927.
Won for the School, illustrated by Archibald
    Webb. London, Collins, 1927.
Any Port in a Storm and Other Stories, with
    others. London, Nelson, 1928.
Day Boy Colours, illustrated by J. Phillips
    Paterson. London, Nelson, 1928.
Cock-House of Claverhill, London, Collins,
    1929.

L(yman) Frank Baum (1856–1919).
American.
a.k.a. Floyd Akers.
a.k.a. Laura Bancroft.
a.k.a. Hugh Fitzgerald.
a.k.a. Suzanne Metcalf.
a.k.a. Edith Van Dyne.

Glinda of Oz, illustrated by John R. Neill.
    Chicago, Reilly and Lee, 1920.

S(ydney) G(eorge) Hulme Beaman
(1886–1932). British.

S.G. Hulme Beaman died in 1932, but the
popularity of BBC radio's *Children's Hour* and
a television series of the 1970s ensured that his
Toytown characters have outlived their
creator by many years. The success of Larry
the Lamb, Dennis the Dachshund and the
other Toytown personalities in alternative
media should not detract from the attention
the original books deserve. Illustrated in
Beaman's distinctive style, created by drawing
all pictures from various assembled wooden
models, these stories are entertaining classics in
their own right. The red, blue and white
design on the boards of the initial book, *The
Road to Toytown* (1925), is of Tom and his dog
Trot. They are on their way to Toytown:
'Tom had heard that Toytown was a very
wonderful place, and he was so anxious to see
it that one day he determined to set out to
find it. "Trot", he said to his dog, "how
would you like to come with me and have
some adventures?"' Of course, the dog cannot
refuse such an invitation and so the two make
their way to Toytown: sometimes in
unconventional ways, as their ride on a
broomstick bears witness.

Illustrated by the author.

The Road to Toytown. London, Oxford
    University Press, 1925.
Jerry and Joe. London, Oxford University
    Press, 1925.
Trouble in Toyland. London, Oxford
    University Press, 1925.
The Wooden Knight. London, Oxford
    University Press, 1925.

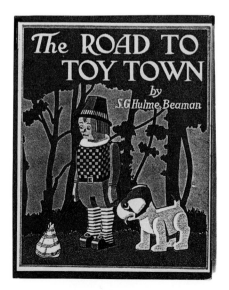

Out of the Ark Books (*Teddy's New Job, Wally the Kangaroo, Grunty the Pig, Jimmy the Baby Elephant, Ham and the Egg, Jenny the Giraffe*). London and New York, Warne, 6 vols., 1927.
The Tale of the Magician. London, Oxford University Press, 1928.
The Tales of the Inventor. London, Oxford University Press, 1928.
The Tale of Captain Brass, The Pirate. London, Oxford University Press, 1928.
Tales of Toytown. London, Oxford University Press, 1928; as *Ernest the Policeman*, New York, Oxford University Press, 1930.
John Trusty. London, Collins, 1929.

E(dward) F(rederic) Benson (1867–1940). British.

David of King's. London, Hodder & Stoughton, 1924.

Enid Blyton (1897–1968). British.
a.k.a. Mary Pollock.

Enid Blyton was, and still is, a phenomenon like none other in the field of children's fiction. In over forty years of writing she published more than seven hundred books, differently aimed at all ages from infanthood to teenage years. The output of her first decade was, in comparison with her later incredible record, slim. At the beginning of the 1920s she was much involved in teaching and writing was just a hobby. She contributed stories to some of the leading magazines of the time and was so popular that in 1926 she was the founder editor of a children's paper *Sunny Stories*. It was in this magazine that she was later to create some of her most popular series. Blyton's first writings were for the very young, for she perceived that there was little suitable in existence for this age range. The result was a couple of volumes of verse and her first story book, *The Enid Blyton Book of Fairies* (1924). She was evidently well-known enough at this early stage to have her name as part of the title. *The Fairies* were followed by *The Enid Blyton Book of Bunnies* (1925). This tells the tale of Flip and Binkle, the 'Bad

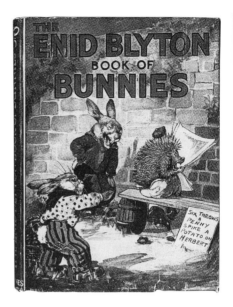

Bunnies', who live in Heather Cottage. In the dust wrapper illustration by K. Nixon, the two mischief makers hurl potatoes at Herbert Hedgehog, for whom the chips really are down. In our bibliography, we have tried to keep to the original works of Enid Blyton and have excluded her re-workings of old stories.

The Enid Blyton Book of Fairies, illustrated by Horace J. Knowles. London, Newnes, 1924.
The Enid Blyton Book of Bunnies, illustrated by K. Nixon. London, Newnes, 1925.
Pinkity's Pranks, illustrated by A.E. Jackson and Phyllis Chase. London, Nelson, 1925.
The Book of Brownies, illustrated by Ernest Aris. London, Newnes, 1926.
Tarrydiddle Town, illustrated by Rosa C. Petherick. London, Nelson, 1926.
Tales Half Told, illustrated by Rosa C. Petherick. London, Nelson, 1926.
The Wonderful Adventure, illustrated by K.M. Waterson. London, Birn, 1927.
Let's Pretend, illustrated by I. Bennington Angrave. London, Nelson, 1928.

Angela Brazil (1869–1947). British.

Queen of the Dormitory (1926), because it is a set of short stories, is unlike Angela Brazil's other work. The Queen of the Dormitory is Daisy Davenport, who attends Seaton House School. The portrait on the book's jacket, showing Daisy before a backdrop of the dormitory, is by P.B. Hickling. The petulant expression on Daisy's face is reminiscent of Hickling's most famous work, the study of Mrs Manderson on the dust wrapper of E.C. Bentley's *Trent's Last Case* (1913), one of the first true detective stories.

A Gift From the Sea, illustrated by A.E. Jackson. London, Nelson, 1920.

A Popular Schoolgirl, illustrated by Balliol Salmon. London, Blackie, 1920; New York, Stokes, 1921.

The Princess of the School, illustrated by Frank Wiles. London, Blackie, 1920; New York, Stokes, 1921; as *A Princess at the School*, London, Armada, 1970.

Loyal to the School, illustrated by Treyer Evans. London, Blackie, 1921.

A Fortunate Term, illustrated by Treyer Evans. London, Blackie, 1921; as *Marjorie's Best Year*, New York, Stokes, 1923.

Monitress Merle, illustrated by Treyer Evans. London, Blackie, 1922.

The School in the South, illustrated by W. Smithson Broadhead. London, Blackie, 1922; as *The Jolliest School of All*, New York, Stokes, 1923.

The Khaki Boys and Other Stories. London, Nelson, 1923.

Schoolgirl Kitty, illustrated by W.E. Wightman. London, Blackie, 1923; New York, Stokes, 1924.

Captain Peggie, illustrated by W.E. Wightman. London, Blackie, and New York, Stokes, 1924.

Joan's Best Chum, illustrated by W.E. Wightman. London, Blackie, 1926; New York, Stokes, 1927.

Queen of the Dormitory and Other Stories, illustrated by P.B. Hickling. London, Cassell, 1926.

Ruth of St. Ronan's, illustrated by F. Oldham. London, Blackie, 1927.

At School with Rachel, illustrated by W.E. Wightman. London, Blackie, 1928.

St. Catherine's College, illustrated by Frank Wiles. London, Blackie, 1929.

Elinor M(ay) Brent-Dyer (1894–1969). British.
a.k.a. E.M. Brent-Dyer.

Unlike her rival Angela Brazil, Elinor Brent-Dyer's school stories for girls were a continuous saga. Consequently, her principal heroine, Jo, is twelve in *The School at the Châlet* (1925) and nearly sixty when the fifty-eighth and final book in the series, *Prefects of the Chalet School*, was published in 1970. It is believed that Brent-Dyer first conceived of her multi-cultural, ultra-modern international school whilst holidaying in the Austrian Tyrol. This was to be the first of five settings for the school which is continually beset by difficulties (most famously Hitler's advance on Austria) until it settles down, and thereafter stagnates, according to several unkindly critics, in Switzerland. The stories are action packed and Jo (or Joey as she is also called) is required to save the lives of six girls (and a dog!) during the course of the first five books. It does seem that the Tyrol was a dangerous place to send one's daughter to school. The books also contain a strong religious streak, with an unusual degree of acceptance of other faiths. This element has been dismissed as mawkish by some, but it is another indication of the author's interest in narrowing the divide

between different nations and peoples. The dust wrapper of the first book was designed by Nina K. Brisley, sister of the creator of Milly-Molly-Mandy, and portrays twenty-four-year-old Madge Bettany, the school's founder, reading a letter from her twin brother Dick in India to Jo. It wishes them well in their new life, which has been made necessary by their parents' death. The sisters are by the Thiern See Lake near Innsbrück, the location Madge has chosen as the site for her new school. At the moment, Jo is her only pupil!

Gerry Goes to School, illustrated by Gordon Browne. Edinburgh, Chambers, 1922; Philadelphia, Lippincott, 1923.
A Head Girl's Difficulties, illustrated by Nina K. Brisley. Edinburgh, Chambers, 1923.
The Maids of La Rochelle, illustrated by Nina K. Brisley. Edinburgh, Chambers, 1924.
The School at the Châlet, illustrated by Nina K. Brisley. Edinburgh, Chambers, 1925.
Jo of the Châlet School, illustrated by Nina K. Brisley. Edinburgh, Chambers, 1926.
A Thrilling Term at Janeways, illustrated by F.M. Anderson. London, Nelson, 1927.
Seven Scamps Who Are Not All Boys, illustrated by Percy Tarrant. Edinburgh, Chambers, 1927.
The Princess of the Châlet School, illustrated by Nina K. Brisley. Edinburgh, Chambers, 1927.

The Head Girl of the Châlet School, illustrated by Nina K. Brisley. Edinburgh, Chambers, 1928.
Judy the Guide, illustrated by L.A. Govey. London, Nelson, 1928.
The New House Mistress, illustrated by Florence Mary Anderson. London, Nelson, 1928.
Heather Leaves School, illustrated by Percy Tarrant. Edinburgh, Chambers, 1929.
The Rivals of the Châlet School, illustrated by Nina K. Brisley. Edinburgh, Chambers, 1929.

Captain F(rederick) S(adleir) Brereton (1872–1957). British.
a.k.a. Lt.-Col. F.S. Brereton.
a.k.a. Lt.-Col. F.S. Brereton, CBE.

Scouts of the Baghdad Patrols (1921) was one of F.S. Brereton's last books. Seventeen-year-old Mick Dent comes to Arabia to work for his uncle. He forms a Boy Scout troop in Baghdad, which helps to suppress a revolt against the British by some Arab bandits under the villainous Mahmut. Mick's older friend and assistant Jack Frazer shows the way on the book's dust wrapper, designed by Stanley L. Wood. He puts a fiendish Arab in his place by means of a hefty right hook.

Scouts of the Baghdad Patrols, illustrated by
  Stanley L. Wood. London, Cassell, 1921.
Colin the Scout, illustrated by Cyril Holloway.
  London, Blackie, 1925.

Joyce Lankester Brisley (1896–1978).
British.

Joyce Lankester Brisley is most famous for her
'Milly-Molly-Mandy' books which, by
spanning a period of almost exactly half a
century, proved to be one of the most long-
lived series in the history of children's
literature. Brisley created an idealised view of
childhood set amidst the almost Arcadian
surroundings of the English countryside. She
has been criticised for being 'unrealistic', but,
in these days of uncertainty, anything that
provides a child with comfort and hope
should surely be given some credit. Milly-
Molly-Mandy is actually Millicent Margaret
Amanda who lives with her father, mother,
grandpa, grandma, uncle and aunty as well as
Toby the dog and Topsy the cat. The wrapper
of the second book in the series, *More of Milly-
Molly-Mandy* (1929), shows the young
heroine, wearing her red and white striped
dress and accompanied by her dog, Toby. The
image is repeated several times against a cream
background. Unlike some children's book

characters, Milly-Molly-Mandy's escapades
are hardly fantastic. In this volume, for
instance, the narrative focuses upon such
exploits as climbing a tree, enjoying a picnic,
having her photograph taken, going to the
pictures and discovering a bird's nest.

Illustrated by the author.

Milly-Molly-Mandy Stories. London, Harrap,
  1928; New York, McKay, 1977.
More of Milly-Molly-Mandy. London, Harrap,
  1929; New York, McKay, 1977.

Dorita Fairlie Bruce (1885–1970). British.

Dorita Fairlie Bruce wrote uncomplicated and
enjoyable public school sagas for girls. These
lacked the more fantastic or moralising
elements of some of her rivals' work and
instead concentrated on the everyday
elements of a girl's education. She would
often follow her characters' progress from
fresh-faced juniors to battle-hardened sports
captains in the Sixth. Consequently, her books
tend to be divided into different series. The
best known and most popular of these are
undoubtedly the 'Dimsie' and the 'Nancy'
books. Dimsie proved to be one of the most
popular schoolgirl heroines of the 1920s. In
The Senior Prefect (1921), the ten-year-old
Dimsie begins her time at her new school,
watched over by her own cousin Daphne.
Dimsie's full name is Daphne Isabel Maitland,
but she is rarely referred to in this way. At first
this was presumably to avoid confusion with
her elder cousin of the same name. The scarce
dust wrapper by Wal Paget for *The Senior
Prefect* shows Daphne, accompanied by Dimsie
and their friend Nancy, surprised at seeing a
mysterious pale face peering at her from the
bushes. Henry Coller's illustration on the dust
wrapper of the first 'Nancy' book, *The Girls of
St. Brides* (1923), captures an even more
dramatic scene. Cynthia, Charlotte and
Christine put themselves in some danger as
they attempt to rescue old Rory's Scotch
terrier from being swept off some rocks
during a storm. On the whole, however,
Bruce did not wallow in melodrama. She was
also vitriolically hostile to overtly sentimental

and romantic relationships between girls. At a time when the portrayal of such relationships was common in school stories, Bruce has Dimsie found the 'Anti-Soppists', a group that boycotted drippy behaviour.

The Senior Prefect, illustrated by Wal Paget. London, Oxford University Press, 1921; as *Dimsie Goes to School*, 1933.
Dimsie Moves Up, illustrated by Wal Paget. London, Oxford University Press, 1921.
Dimsie Moves Up Again, illustrated by Gertrude D. Hammond. London, Oxford University Press, 1922.
Dimsie among the Prefects, illustrated by Gertrude D. Hammond. London, Oxford University Press, 1923.
The Girls of St. Bride's, illustrated by Henry Coller. London, Oxford University Press, 1923.
Dimsie Grows Up, illustrated by Henry Coller. London, Oxford University Press, 1924.
Dimsie, Head-Girl, illustrated by M.S. Reeve. London, Oxford University Press, 1925.
That Boarding School Girl, illustrated by Roy. London, Oxford University Press, 1925.
The New Girl and Nancy, illustrated by Mary Strange Reeve. London, Oxford University Press, 1926.
Nancy to the Rescue. London, Oxford University Press, 1927.

THE·SENIOR ∷ PREFECT ∷

DORITA·FAIRLIE·BRUCE

Dimsie Goes Back, illustrated by M.S. Reeve. London, Oxford University Press, 1927.
The New House-Captain, illustrated by M.S. Reeve. London, Oxford University Press, 1928.

Christine Chaundler (1887–1972). British.

Christine Chaundler's *The Thirteenth Orphan* (1920), although written in a period that heralded the author's emergence as a leading composer of girls' school stories, goes to show that once a fairy fan always a fairy fan. The story juxtaposes Chaundler's interest in sprites, already made apparent by *The Magic Kiss*, with the attention she was later to give to the development of young girls. Honor Appleton's evocative illustration for the book's dust wrapper shows young orphan Jane darning a sock. Her rather drab life is enlivened by the intervention of three friendly fairies which protect Jane as she has a fairy luck-mark on her arm. Gleam O'Gold, a boy fairy, and Silverdew, a girl fairy, are depicted on the front cover of the wrapper whilst the other boy fairy, Thistledown, is shown on the base of the spine. Jane is the oldest and biggest of the motherless children at Salem House and eventually leaves to become the playmate of Cecilia at Castle Lethbridge, where there are also fairies. Jane is taken in a Cradle-boat to Fairyland and, needless to say, the book has a very happy ending. The first edition is bound in blue cloth with gilt spine lettering and a small gilt illustration of a fairy inside a circle on the front cover. The book's attractive endpapers have fourteen fairies drawn in blue against a cream background.

The Thirteenth Orphan, illustrated by Honor Appleton. London, Nisbet, 1920; New York, Stokes, 1921.
Just Gerry, illustrated by H. Coller. London, Nisbet, 1920.
The Right St. John's, illustrated by Savile Lumley. London, Oxford University Press, 1920.
The Binky Books (The Motor Bandits, The Circus Lion), illustrated by Will Owen. London, Nisbet, 2 vols, 1920.

Snuffles for Short, illustrated by Honor Appleton. London, Nisbet, 1921.

The Fourth Form Detectives. London, Nisbet, 1921.

The Reformation of Dormitory Five. London, Nisbet, 1921.

A Fourth Form Rebel. London, Nisbet, 1922.

Captain Cara, London, Nisbet, 1923.

Jan of the Fourth. London, Nisbet, 1923.

Tomboy Toby. London, Partridge, 1923.

Dickie's Day. London, Nelson, 1924.

Winning Her Colours. London, Nisbet, 1924.

Sally Sticks it Out. London, Partridge, 1924.

Judy the Tramp. London, Nisbet, 1924.

Princess Carroty-Top and Timothy. London, Warne, 1924.

Jill the Outsider, illustrated by Elizabeth Earnshaw. London, Cassell, 1924.

An Unofficial Schoolgirl. London, Nisbet, 1925.

Bunty of the Blackbirds. London, Nisbet, 1925.

The Adopting of Mickie, illustrated by T. Peddie. London, Religious Tract Society, 1925.

A Credit to Her House. London, Ward Lock, 1926.

Twenty-Six Christine Chaundler School Stories for Girls, illustrated by Arthur Twidle. London, Religious Tract Society, 1926.

The Exploits of Evangeline. London, Nisbet, 1926.

Reforming the Fourth. London, Ward Lock, 1927.

The Chivalrous Fifth, illustrated by Anne Rochester. London, Nelson, 1927.

Philippa's Family. London, Nisbet, 1927.

Meggy Makes Her Mark, illustrated by M. Lane Foster. London, Nisbet, 1928.

The Games Captain, illustrated by J. Dewar Mills. London, Ward Lock, 1928.

Friends in the Fourth, illustrated by J. Dewar Mills. London, Ward Lock, 1929.

Arthur Bowie Chrisman (1889–1953). American.

Arthur Bowie Chrisman was an American with an intense interest in Chinese folklore. His two books for children, *Shen of the Sea* (1925) and *The Wind that Wouldn't Blow* (1927), are collections of short stories that bring out certain truths about human existence through the goings-on in a topsy-turvy Chinese world. For instance, the title story of *Shen of the Sea* concentrates on the struggle for supremacy of good (in the form of the first King of Wa Tien) over evil (the shen, or sea demons, who threaten to overwhelm his kingdom with water). Each of the books

was illustrated with copious silhouette drawings by Else Hasselriis. The lack of distinct features in these enhances the creation of a mystic world. The blue and cream dust wrapper of *Shen of the Sea* reveals three portly mandarins hiding behind a single rose tree. For all the underlying moral points, the principal aim of the stories was, as the flap of the dustwrapper of *The Wind that Wouldn't Blow* puts it, to present 'Fun for Fun's sake in a setting of originality and beauty.'

Shen of the Sea, illustrated by Else Hasselriis. New York, Dutton, 1925; London, Dent, 1926.
The Wind that Wouldn't Blow: Stories of the Merry Middle Kingdom, illustrated by Else Hasselriis. New York. Dutton, and London, Dent, 1927.

Catherine Christian. British.
a.k.a. Catherine Mary Christian.

For main author article see 1940 to 1950.

Greenie and the Pink'Un. London, Every Girl's Paper Office, 1928.
The Luck of the Scallop Shell. Glasgow, Brown, Son and Ferguson, 1929.

Dorothy Clewes (b. 1907). British.

For main author article see 1940 to 1950.

The Rivals of Maidenhurst. London, Nelson, 1925.

Elizabeth Coatsworth (1893–1986). American.

For main author article see 1930 to 1939.

The Cat and the Captain, illustrated by Gertrude Kaye. New York, Macmillan, 1927.
Toutou in Bondage, illustrated by Thomas Handforth. New York, Macmillan, 1929.

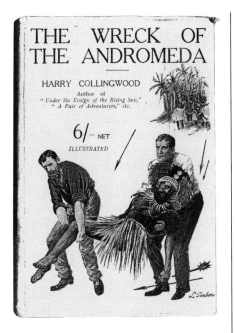

Harry Collingwood (1851–1922). British. Pseudonym for William Joseph Cosens Lancaster.

Dust wrappers for the first editions of Harry Collingwood's work are extraordinarily scarce. Consequently, L. Parker's design for *The Wreck of the Andromeda* (1923) is a very rare item. It portrays Massey and Wilkinson carrying the wounded Kilau Minga, while spears hurtle about their ears.

The Strange Adventures of Eric Blackburn, illustrated by C.M. Padday. London, Blackie, 1922.
The Wreck of the Andromeda, illustrated by L. Parker. London, Sampson Low, 1923.
The Cruise of the "Flying Fish", the airship submarine, illustrated by M.L.P. London, Sampson Low, 1924.
In the Power of the Enemy (with Percival Lancaster), illustrated by M.L.P. London, Marston, 1925.

Padraic Colum (1881–1972). Irish.

The Boy Apprenticed to an Enchanter, illustrated by Dugald Stuart Walker. New York, Macmillan, 1920.

The Peep-Show Man, illustrated by Lois Lenski. New York, Macmillan, 1924; London, Macmillan, 1932.

Mrs H(enry) C. Cradock. British.

Josephine's Birthday, illustrated by Honor C. Appleton. London, Blackie, 1920.
Josephine, John And The Puppy, illustrated by Honor C. Appleton. London, Blackie, 1920.
Peggy's Twins, illustrated by Honor C. Appleton. London, SPCK, 1920.
The House Of Fancy, illustrated by Honor C. Appleton. London, O'Connor, 1922.
Peggy and Joan, illustrated by Honor C. Appleton. London, Blackie, 1922.
The Story Of Pat. London, SPCK, 1923.
Josephine Keeps School, illustrated by Honor C. Appleton. London, Blackie, 1925.
Josephine Goes Shopping, illustrated by Honor C. Appleton. London, Blackie, 1926.
The Best Teddy Bear In The World, illustrated by Honor C. Appleton. London, Nelson, 1926.
Pamela's Teddy Bears, illustrated by Honor C. Appleton, London, Jack, 1927.
Josephine's Christmas Party, illustrated by Honor C. Appleton. London, Blackie, 1927.

Richmal Crompton (1890–1969). British.

Richmal Crompton has achieved something approaching superstar status as an author but, as happens so often with a writer who becomes inextricably associated with a single character, the way this occurred was rather accidental. Crompton's utmost desire was to write quality works for adults. Instead she will always be remembered as the creator of the greatest anti-hero in the history of children's literature, William Brown. William is forever a dirty, scruffy eleven-year-old anarchist who causes well-meaning mayhem wherever he goes and through whatever time he happens to be living in. Whether he is imitating the film stars of the early silent era, helping the A.R.P. or hobnobbing with pop-stars in the space age, the result is the same: trouble for

unsuspecting adults or unsympathetic peers. William is leader of the 'Outlaws' (other members Ginger, Douglas, Henry and, of course, Jumble the dog), a band of young adventurers (or hooligans, depending on your point of view) whose aim is to have fun, entertain and right wrongs, especially if there is some pecuniary advantage in doing so. They are loath to aid damsels in distress (although William has a distinct soft spot for dark-haired Joan); especially when the damsel in question is often the lisping bundle of curls, Violet Elizabeth Bott. It is naturally William's family who suffers most from his never-ending capacity for provoking catastrophe. His placid mother despairs at her youngest son's unkempt state, his father is continually bearing the brunt of the latest domestic disaster and vain Ethel and sporty Robert are always having their latest romantic relationship ruined by their younger brother's interference. William made his first appearance in *Home Magazine* in February 1919 and transferred to the *Happy Mag* in December 1922. The 'William' books were for most of the character's career made up of pieces reprinted from these and other periodicals. This is why the books, with one exception, consist of unrelated short stories. The name of the artist, Thomas Henry, is almost as closely associated with the name of William Brown as Richmal Crompton herself is. Henry provided the wonderful illustrations for all of the 'William' books, except the last four (for which Henry Ford took over), and it is his interpretation of William that has influenced the imaginations of generations of readers. The first nine 'William' books were bound in the now familiar red boards with black lettering but the tenth, *William* (1929), was issued in blue cloth with gold lettering. The dust wrapper for the first edition of this book is so rare that it would be no exaggeration to suppose that the copy reproduced here and on the jacket of this study is the only example in existence. It shows William, in an (unusually smart!) red blazer and a blue and white cap, which is in its usual precarious position atop his tousled mane, volunteering to photograph a bathing belle, in a green cap and suit, with his Brownie box camera. The wrapper is essentially in the characteristic red and yellow William colour scheme. The picture had been previously reproduced on the cover of the *Tit-Bits* Summer Annual 1924 with the caption 'Peep Bo!'. However, this scene does not appear in the book *William* at all. Nevertheless the cover illustration for *William* is a delightful work of art which captures William's unique brand of mischievous and rough and ready innocence. First editions of the next three 'William' books also have blue cloth, but *William the Pirate* has brown, *William the Rebel* buff, *William the Gangster* blue, *William the Detective* brown, whilst the next twenty titles have green cloth and the last title, *William the Lawless* (1970), is red.

All illustrated by Thomas Henry.

Just William. London, Newnes, 1922.
More William. London, Newnes, 1922.
Wiliam Again. London, Newnes, 1923.
William the Fourth. London, Newnes, 1924.
Still William. London, Newnes, 1925.
William the Conqueror. London, Newnes, 1926.
William the Outlaw. London, Newnes, 1927.
William in Trouble. London, Newnes, 1927.
William the Good. London, Newnes, 1928.
William. London, Newnes, 1929.

Winifred Darch. British.

Winifred Darch was a passionate exponent of the 'play up and play the game' sort of school fiction for girls. Indeed one of her books is entitled *Margaret Plays the Game* (1931). Her characters become involved in every kind of schoolgirl antic but never abandon their code of honour. *Jean of the Fifth* (1923) is classic Darch. It revolves around the experiences of two sisters, Bride and Jean Galbraith, as they join Haysbrook House School in different capacities. Whilst Jean is to enrol as a new pupil, Bride is to start teaching at the school. M.D. Johnston's illustration for the dust wrapper shows both sisters at Victoria Station *en route* to the school. Jean, holding her cricket bat like a veteran, at least is ready for the fray.

Chris and Some Others, illustrated by Savile Lumley. London, Oxford University Press, 1920.
Poppies and Prefects, illustrated by Charles E. Brock. London, Oxford University Press, 1923.
Jean of the Fifth, illustrated by M.D. Johnston. London, Oxford University Press, 1923.
Heather at the High School, illustrated by Charles E. Brock. London, Oxford University Press, 1924.

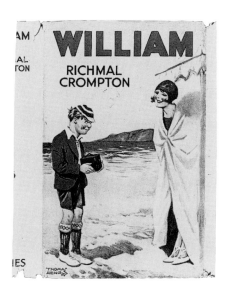

Cecil of the Carnations, illustrated by Mary
    Strange Reeve. London, Oxford
    University Press, 1924.
Gillian of the Guides, illustrated by M.D.
    Johnston. London, Oxford University
    Press, 1925.
Katharine Goes to School, illustrated by M.D.
    Johnston. London, Oxford University
    Press, 1925.
The New School and Hilary, illustrated by
    Mary Strange Reeve. London, Oxford
    University Press, 1926.
Cicely Bassett–Patrol Leader, illustrated by
    M.D. Johnston. London, Oxford
    University Press, 1927.
Varvara Comes to England, illustrated by M.D.
    Johnston. London, Oxford University
    Press, 1927.
The Upper Fifth In Command, illustrated by
    M.D. Johnston. London, Oxford
    University Press,1928.
For the Honour of the House, illustrated by
    M.D. Johnston. London, Oxford
    University Press, 1929.

Walter de la Mare (1873–1956). British.

Broomsticks and Other Tales, illustrated by
    Bold. London, Constable, and New York,
    Knopf, 1925.
Miss Jemima, illustrated by Alec Buckels.
    Oxford, Blackwell, 1925.
Lucy, illustrated by Hilda T. Miller, Oxford,
    Blackwell, 1927.
Old Joe, illustrated by C.T. Nightingale.
    Oxford, Blackwell, 1927.

Evelyn Everett-Green (1856–1932). British.
a.k.a. E. Everett-Green.
a.k.a. Cecil Adair.

Crystal's Victory; or, The House of the Ghost (as
    Cecil Adair), illustrated by C. Fitz-Gerald.
    London, Stanley Paul, 1921.
Daddy's Ducklings. London, Religious Tract
    Society, 1921.
Queen's Manor School. London, Stanley Paul,
    1921.
The Tyrant of Tylecourt. London, Stanley Paul,
    1922.

Twins at Tachbury. London, Wells Gardner,
    Darton, 1924.
Uncle Quayle. London, Stanley Paul, 1928.

Eleanor Farjeon (1881–1965). British.

Eleanor Farjeon traced her own ability to write
without restraint about fantastic people and
places to her lack of formal education. This, she
believed, allowed her imagination to flow free.
Martin Pippin in the Apple Orchard (1921) was
originally intended for an adult audience but was
so popular amongst younger readers that it has
always been considered a children's book. It is a
collection of six fairy stories based on the
children's game 'The Emperor's Daughter' and
linked by the character Martin Pippin, a
wandering minstrel. Farjeon employed the
device of a connecting figure so successfully here
and in later books that it became something of a
trademark. The dust wrapper of the first book
shows the young mediaeval minstrel dressed in
red, sitting on the green gate which leads to the
apple orchard and playing his lute.

Martin Pippin in the Apple Orchard, illustrated
    by C.E. Brock. London, Collins, 1921;
    New York, Stokes, 1922.

Tom Cobble, illustrated by M. Dobson. Oxford, Blackwell, 1925.

Nuts and May: A Medley for Children, illustrated by Rosalind Thornycroft. London, Collins, 1926.

Italian Peepshow and Other Tales, illustrated by Rosalind Thornycroft. New York, Stokes, 1926; as *Italian Peepshow and Other Stories*, Oxford, Blackwell, 1934.

The Wonderful Knight, illustrated by Doris Pailthorpe. Oxford, Blackwell, 1927.

The King's Barn; or, Joan's Tale. London, Collins, 1927.

The Mill of Dreams; or, Jennifer's Tale. London, Collins, 1927.

Young Gerard; or, Joyce's Tale. London, Collins, 1927.

A Bad Day for Martha, illustrated by Eugenie Richards. Oxford, Blackwell, 1928.

Kaleidoscope. London, Collins, 1928; New York, Stokes, 1929.

The Perfect Zoo. London, Harrap, and Philadelphia, McKay, 1929.

The King's Daughter Cries for the Moon, illustrated by May Smith. Oxford, Blackwell, 1929.

The Tale of Tom Tiddler, illustrated by Norman Tealby. London, Collins, 1929; New York, Stokes, 1930.

G(eorge) Manville Fenn (1831–1909). British.
a.k.a. George Manville Fenn.

In Mid-Air: A tale of 1870. London, Sheldon, 1924.

In Marine Armour. London, Sheldon, 1927.

Staunch as Steel. London, Sheldon, 1927.

Charles J(oseph) Finger (1869–1941). American.

Charles J. Finger was an adventurer in his own right and some of his experiences on the high seas and in the jungles of Africa and South America could rival those of many a fictional hero. He wrote lusty adventure tales and also collections of folk stories compiled from those he had heard in the far corners of the Earth during his travels. *Courageous Companions*

(1929) is a typical example of Finger fare. This work, which according to the introduction is based on historical documents, tells of a young English lad called Osborne who, as Finger himself had done, escapes to sea whilst still a teenager. He joins the Portuguese Magellan on his first voyage round the world. The characterful illustrations by James H. Daugherty that adorn the book vivify this tale of life before the mast: including mutiny at sea, famine, bold rescues and struggles with hostile natives.

The Spreading Stain, illustrated by Paul Honoré. New York, Doubleday, and London, Heinemann, 1927.

Courageous Companions, illustrated by James Daugherty. New York, Longman, 1929.

Dorothy Canfield Fisher (1879–1958). American.
a.k.a. Dorothy Canfield.

Made-to-Order Stories, illustrated by Dorothy P. Lathrop. New York, Harcourt Brace, 1925; London, Cape, 1926.

Marjorie Flack (1897–1958). American.

For main author article see 1930 to 1939.

Illustrated by the author.

Taktuk, An Arctic Boy, with Helen Lomen.
   New York. Doubleday, 1928; London,
   Lane, 1956.
All Around the Town. New York, Doubleday,
   1929.

Rose Fyleman (1877–1957). British.

Rose Fyleman wrote for very young children
and did a lot to popularise the more beautiful
and delicate type of fairy through her verse
writing. She also specialised in taking themes
from European folk stories and creating
something distinctly her own (although she
was also a prolific translator). Two short story
collections are typical of this aspect of her
work. *Forty Good-Night Tales* (1923) and *Forty
Good-Morning Tales* (1926) are, as their titles
suggest, little volumes full of self-contained
stories that are ideal for reading aloud to
infants. The dust wrapper illustrations for
these two books give a good indication of the
whimsy within. Eugenie Richards' cover for
Forty Good-Night Tales reveals Mrs Moddle
and her dog Troddle who, whilst out for a
stroll, are caught up by a whirlwind and enjoy
an airborne trip over their home town, kept in
the air by Mrs Moddle's open umbrella.
Richards' illustration for *Forty Good-Morning
Tales* (disappointingly the only picture in this
book) shows the Little Old Woman following
the baker's cart as the back of the vehicle
becomes unfastened. The loaves drop on to
the road one by one, much to the delight of
the local birds!

The Rainbow Cat and Other Stories, illustrated
   by Thelma Cudlipp Grosvenor. London,
   Methuen, 1922; New York, Doran, 1923.
Forty Good-Night Tales, illustrated by Thelma
   Cudlipp Grosvenor. London, Methuen,
   1923; New York, Doran, 1924.
The Adventure Club, illustrated by A.H.
   Watson. London, Methuen, 1925; New
   York, Doran, 1926.
Letty: A Study of a Child, illustrated by Lisl

Hummel. London, Methuen, 1926; New
   York, Doran, 1927.
Forty Good-Morning Tales. London, Methuen,
   1926; New York, Doran, 1929.
Twenty Tea-Time Tales. London, Methuen,
   1929; as *Tea Time Tales*, New York,
   Doubleday, 1930.

Wanda Gág (1893–1946). American.

Wanda Gág, besides producing her
children's fantasies, translated the tales of the
brothers Grimm. The macabre influence of
those two gentlemen is detectable in her
own work. Gág's *Millions of Cats* (1928) is
deceptively tame at first. This impression is
aided by the simple woodcut illustrations
and the homespun handwritten text. It tells
of a very elderly couple who, through
loneliness, desire to own a cat for company.
The old man departs in search of a feline
friend and eventually discovers 'a hill which
was quite covered with cats … millions and
billions and trillions of cats.' He chooses
several favourite kittens to take home but, as
Gág's own design for the dust wrapper
shows, the rest of the cats follow him. The
objects which were supposed to bring

MILLIONS OF CATS

BY WANDA GAG

comfort to the couple's dotage inflict misery upon them and the neighbouring countryside. The problem is eventually resolved in a way that is original, if not designed to please cat fans.

Illustrated by the author.

Millions of Cats. New York, Coward McCann, 1928; London, Faber, 1929.
The Funny Thing. New York, Coward McCann, 1929; London, Faber, 1962.

Charles Gilson (1878–1943). British.
a.k.a. C(harles) L(ouis) Gilson.
a.k.a. Captain Charles Gilson.
a.k.a. Major Charles Gilson.

Major Charles Gilson's *The Lost City* (1923) is a rather unusual thriller, and the reader is warned of the fact by R. Caton Woodville's striking artwork for the dust wrapper. Depicted are men dressed as Anubis, the Egyptian jackal god and Lord of Death, Thot, the ibis-headed deity, and Horus, the hawk headed god, standing on the banks of the Nile. They were somehow involved with a cursed scarab and the twentieth-century death of Josephus MacAndrew. This intriguing story is told by Miles Bowater Unthank, a professor of Ancient History and Egyptology.

The Fire-Gods: a tale of the Congo. London, Boy's Own Paper, 1920.
The Scarlet Hand. London, Boy's Own Paper, 1920.
Held By Chinese Brigands. London, Humphrey Milford, 1921.

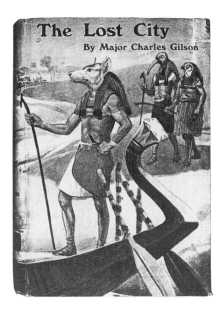

The Lost City
By Major Charles Gilson

The Society of the Tortoise Mask, illustrated by
H. Gale. London, Cassell, 1921.

The Realm of the Wizard King. London, Boy's
Own Paper, 1922.

Red Lynx. London, Collins, 1922.

Treasure of Kings. London, Boy's Own Paper,
1922.

Jack Without a Roof. London, Boy's Own
Paper, 1923.

The Lost City, illustrated by R. Caton
Woodville. London, Boy's Own Paper,
1923.

In the Land of Shame. London, Boy's Own
Paper, 1924.

The Silver Shoe. London, Boy's Own Paper,
1924.

The Treasure of the Red Tribe. London,
Cassell, 1926.

Mystery Island, illustrated by G.W. Goss.
London, Partridge, 1928.

R(obert) A(rthur) H(anson) Goodyear
(1877–1948). British.

R.A.H Goodyear wrote many exciting and
atmospheric school stories for boys. He focused
upon the importance of schoolboy honour and
the necessity to play all the googlies life delivers
with a straight bat. It is thus interesting to
speculate upon his reaction to the stance the
dust-wrapper artist of *Boys of the Mystery School*
(1926) has given to the young hero facing the
fast bowling – more baseball than MCC
coaching manual. Goodyear's vision of public
school life was not distorted by overt
sentimentality. He did not ignore the many
difficulties and potential sources of disharmony
that existed within the school system. The dust
wrapper of *The Luck of the Fifth* (1928) shows
Chip and Scar (both colourful Goodyear
nicknames) exchanging angry words after a
Castle Keep House cricket match. The game
that is so often portrayed as character-building
can prove to be divisive and bring out the more
base characteristics in individuals.

Forge of Foxenby. London, Blackie, 1920.

The Boys of Castle Cliff School. London,
Blackie, 1921.

The Boys of Tudorville. London, Lloyd's
School Yarns, 1921.

Luckless Leo's Schooldays. London, Lloyd's
School Yarns, 1921.

Newspaper Ned. London, Lloyd's Boys'
Adventure Series, 1921.

Tom and Tim at School. London, Lloyd's
School Yarns, 1921.

Two Terms at Linglands. London, Lloyd's
School Yarns, 1921.

The White House Boys. London, G.G. Harrap,
1921.

The Far Schools. London, Blackie, 1922.

Further Adventures of Newspaper Ned. London,
Lloyd's Boys Adventure Stories, 1922.

The Greenway Heathens. London, Nisbet, 1922.

Topsy-Turvy Academy. London, G.G. Harrap,
1922.

The Worst Boy in Town. London, Lloyd's
School Yarns, 1922.

*The Captain and the Kings: A public school
story*. London, A. & C. Black, 1923.

Jack o' Langsett: A public school story. London,
Nelson, 1923.

The Life of the School. London, Jarrolds, 1923.

Tom at Tollbar School. London, Blackie, 1923.

The Fifth Form at Bech House. London, Black's
Boys' Library, 1924.

The Sporting Fifth at Ripley's, illustrated by
M.L.P. London, Sampson Low, 1924.

Young Rookwood at School. London, Ward
Lock, 1924.

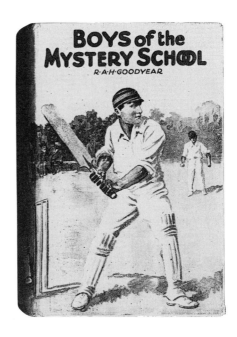

The Boys of Ringing Rook. London, Ward
 Lock, 1925.
Boys of the Valley School. London, John
 Castle, 1925.
The School's Best Man. London, Jarrolds,
 1925.
Three Joskins at St. Jude's, illustrated by J.H.
 Hartley. London, Black's Boys' Library,
 1925.
Blake of the Modern Fifth. London, Ward
 Lock, 1926.
Boys of the Mystery School, illustrated by
 M.L.P. London, Sampson Low, 1926.
The Hope of His House. London, Nelson,
 1926.
The New Boy at Baxtergate. London, Black's
 Boys' Library, 1926.
The Fellows of Ten Trees School. London,
 Sampson Low, 1927.
His Brother at St. Concord's. London, Jarrolds,
 1927.
Up Against the School. London, Black's Boys'
 Library, 1927.
Rival Schools At Schooner Bay. London, Ward
 Lock, 1928.
Strickland of the Sixth. London, Sampson Low,
 1928.
With Wat at Winterglean. London, Black's
 Boys' and Girls' Library, 1928.
The Luck of the Lower Fifth, illustrated by
 G.W.G. London, J.F. Shaw, 1928.
Clare of Glen House. London, Nelson, 1929.
The Hardy Brockdale Boys. London, Sampson
 Low, 1929.
Too Big for the Fifth. London, Ward Lock,
 1929.

Elizabeth Goudge (1900–1984). British.

For main author article see 1940 to 1950.

The Fairies' Baby and Other Stories.
 Amersham, Buckinghamshire, and
 London, Morland-Foyle, 1920.

Eleanor Graham (1896–1984). British.

For main author article see 1930 to 1939.

The Night Adventures of Alexis, illustrated by
 Winifred Langlands. London, Faber, 1925.

Charles Boardman Hawes (1889–1923).
American.

Charles Boardman Hawes, who produced
only three adventure yarns before his untimely
death at the age of thirty-four has been
compared with that greatest of boys' authors
who wrote of the sea, Robert Louis
Stevenson. Hawes' two pirate stories, *The
Mutineers* (1920) and *The Dark Frigate* (1923),
owe much to Stevenson in terms of plot and
description. His third novel, *The Great Quest*
(1921), revolves around a perilous expedition
to the Peruvian jungle and has more in
common with the boys' books produced in
the decades after Stevenson. The dust wrapper
illustration for *The Dark Frigate*, set before and
during the Cromwellian period of the
seventeenth century, shows Philip Marsham
leading his band of English pirates from the
Rose of Dreams (otherwise known as 'The
Dark Frigate') as they engage in battle in the
Caribbean. Marsham later returns to England
and fights for King Charles at the fateful Battle
of Newbury.

The Mutineers. Boston, Atlantic Monthly
 Press, 1920; London, Heinemann, 1923.

CHARLES BOARDMAN HAWES

The Great Quest, illustrated by George
   Varian. Boston, Atlantic Monthly Press,
   1921; London, Heinemann, 1922.
The Dark Frigate, Boston, Atlantic Monthly
   Press, 1923; illustrated by D.A. Ripley,
   London, Heinemann, 1924.

Constance Heward (1884–1968). British.

Constance Heward was nearly forty when she
first wrote for children but made up for this
late entrance by contributing stories for
another forty-eight years. Her most famous
creation is a virtuous but endearing little girl
called Ameliaranne. The front boards of
Ameliaranne and the Green Umbrella (1920)
reveal Heward's heroine with her back to her
adoring audience. The tousled tot shows off
the famous curl rags that adorn her hair. She
balances on her head the open green umbrella
in which she tries to smuggle out cakes for her
poorly younger brothers and sisters, who have
been too ill to attend the Squire's tea party. A
shower of sweet items seems to restore
Ameliaranne's five brothers and sisters, also
shown on the cover, to the pink of health.
Further Ameliaranne adventures were
composed by Heward and other writers (most
notably Eleanor Farjeon, who was responsible
for the 'Martin Pippin' books) and they were
all illustrated by S.B. Pearse, whose children
are all charmingly cherubic.

Ameliaranne and the Green Umbrella, illustrated
   by Susan Beatrice Pearse. London,
   Harrap, and Philadelphia, Jacobs, 1920.
*Cheery Tales [and More Cheery Tales] for Little
   People*. London, SPCK, 2 vols., 1920;
   New York, Macmillan, 2 vols 1921.
The Twins and Tabiffa, illustrated by S.B.
   Pearse. London, Harrap, and Philadelphia,
   Jacobs, 1923.
Sunshiny Stories. London, Sheldon Press,
   1924.
Grandpa and the Tiger, illustrated by Lilian
   Govey. London, Harrap, and Philadelphia,
   Jacobs, 1924.
The Story Book, edited by Isa M. Jackson.
   London, Collins, 1924.
Chappie and the Others, illustrated by Savile
   Lumley. London, Warne, 1926.

A Handful of Happiness, illustrated by Patience
   Arnold. London, Sheldon Press, 1926.
Kitty's Tea Party. London, Sheldon Press,
   1926.
Mr. Pickles and the Party, illustrated by Anne
   Anderson. London, Warne, 1926.
Fairy Circle series (*Fairy [Gnome, Laughter,
   Story, Nonsense, Magic] Circle*). London,
   Collins, 6 vols., 1927.
Faithful Teddy. London, Sheldon Press, 1927.
The Fortune Finders. Leeds, Arnold, 1928.
An Eventful Holiday. Leeds, Arnold, 1928.
Ameliaranne Keeps Shop, illustrated by S.B.
   Pearse. London, Harrap, and Philadelphia,
   McKay, 1928.
A Tale of Two Mysteries. Leeds, Arnold, 1928.
Ameliaranne, Cinema Star, illustrated by S.B.
   Pearse. London, Harrap, 1929.
Ameliaranne and the Monkey, illustrated by
   S.B. Pearse. Philadelphia, McKay, 1929.
Rolf's First Earnings and Other Stories,
   illustrated by G. Robinson. London,
   Sheldon Press, 1929.

Edith Howes (1874–1954). New Zealander.

Silver Island (1928) is rather different from
Edith Howe's gentle fairy stories. Silver Island

is a small uninhabited island off the south west coast of New Zealand. It was so called after the discovery of silver in Threefold Creek. The Lester children, Wuffles (nine), Jim (eleven) and Enid (twelve), spend their holidays at Home Bay with Aunt Kathleen and Uncle Jack. The youngsters beach their dinghy on Silver Island and Wuffles is shown on Kathleen W. Coales' dust wrapper trying to light a camp fire. Enid kneels up with Home Bay in the background and Jim is on the spine of the wrapper. They camp out on Silver Island and have adventures which lead to a valuable discovery.

The Singing Fish, illustrated by Florence Mary Anderson. London, Cassell, 1921.
Snowdrop. Auckland, Whitcombe and Tombs, 1923.
The Dream Girl's Garden, illustrated by P. Osborne. London, Ward Lock, 1923.
The Enchanted Road, illustrated by Janet Smalley. New York, Morrow, 1927.
Silver Island, illustrated by Kathleen Coales. Auckland, Whitcombe and Tombs, and London, Oxford University Press, 1928.
Sandals of Pearl, illustrated by Audrey Chalmers. New York, Morrow, 1928; London, Dent, 1929.

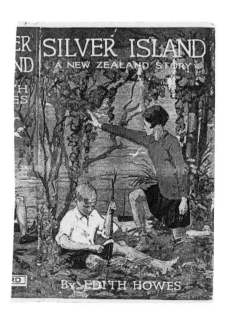

M(ontogue) R(hodes) James (1862–1936). British.

M.R. James is now best remembered for his spine-chilling ghost stories, but was also a highly respected scholar and held the position of Provost of King's College, Cambridge for thirteen years. His interest in children's literature is borne out by an admirable translation of Hans Christian Andersen's tales and his single children's book, *The Five Jars* (1922), which James described as 'more or less a fairy tale.' It was illustrated by the unrelated Gilbert James and the title page shows the mysterious Five Jars with a Latin inscription above, meaning 'Join eyes, ears, tongues, features, hearts.'

The Five Jars, illustrated by Gilbert James. London, Arnold, 1922.

Rudyard Kipling (1865–1936). British.

Land and Sea Tales for Scouts and Guides. London. Macmillan, and New York, Doubleday, 1923.

Amy Le Feuvre (d. 1929). British.
a.k.a. Mary Thurston Dodge

My Heart's in the Highlands (1924) is one of Amy le Feuvre's last books, but it demonstrates that she was still more than capable of composing stories that touched her audience's feelings. It is an emotive piece set before the backdrop of the beautiful Highlands of Scotland. The book tells of a family's response to social upheaval and illness. Norman Sutcliffe's dust-wrapper illustration depicts the excitable Mysie 'Flora' MacDonald, who has come to visit her granny but is surprised to find Rowena in the house instead.

The Discovery of Damaris. London, Religious Tract Society, 1920.
Martin and Margot, illustrated by Gordon Browne. London, Religious Tract Society, 1921.
Oliver and the Twins, illustrated by Gordon Browne. London, Religious Tract Society, 1922.

The Children of the Crescent, illustrated by
Arthur Twidle. London, Religious Tract
Society, 1923.

The Little Discoverers, illustrated by M.D.
Johnston. London and New York, Oxford
Unviersity Press, 1924.

My Heart's in the Highlands, illustrated by
Norman Sutcliffe. London, Ward Lock,
1924.

A Girl and Her Ways. London, Ward Lock,
1925.

Granny's Fairyland. London, Sheldon Press,
1925.

Noel's Christmas Tree. London, Ward Lock,
1926.

Three Little Girls. London, Shaw, 1926.

Andy Man: A Story of Two Simple Souls.
London, Pickering and Inglis, 1927.

Jock's Inheritance. London, Ward Lock, 1927.

Cousins in Devon. London, Religious Tract
Society, 1928.

Adrienne. London, Ward Lock, 1928.

Alick's Corner. London, Religious Tract
Society, 1929.

Around a Sundial, and Dicky's Brother.
London, Pickering and Inglis, 1929.

Her Kingdom: A Story of the Westmorland Fells.
London, Ward Lock, 1929.

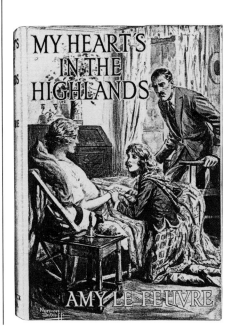

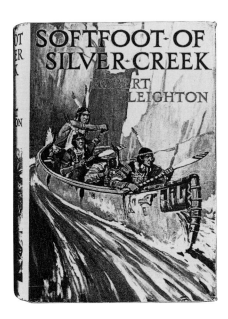

Robert Leighton (1859–1934). British.

Robert Leighton's literary output was
diminished in this decade, but many of the
stories he did produce reflected his interest in
North American life and history. *Softfoot of
Silver Creek* (1926) involves the massacre of
General Custer by the Sioux Indians, but that
is incidental to the adventures of the book's
Redskin hero. The dust wrapper illustration
shows Softfoot with fellow Pawnees as they
brave the rapids.

Kiddie the Scout, London, Pearson, 1920.

The White Man's Trail, illustrated by Thomas
Somerfield. London, Pearson, 1922.

Sea Scout and Savage. London, Ward Lock,
1923.

Kiddie the Prairie Rider. London, Pearson,
1924.

Softfoot of Silver Creek. London, Ward Lock,
1926.

Hugh Lofting (1886–1947). British.

Hugh Lofting's view of animals and humans
was moulded to a considerable extent by his
experiences in the trenches of Flanders
during the First World War. He there
witnessed the inhumanity of man both to
man and also to beast, in the cruel treatment

of the Regimental Horses. It is consequently tempting to superimpose a lot of Lofting on to his most famous creation, Doctor Dolittle. *The Story of Doctor Dolittle* (1920) tells of how Dr John Dolittle, a medical doctor who is abandoned by his patients and family because of his obvious preference for the company of other species, is taught the language of animals by Polynesia the parrot. He soon becomes an accomplished animal doctor, the only one who is not reliant on guesswork but able to receive information literally from the horse's mouth. Doctor Dolittle's new-found skills take him to Africa in this book (Lofting's liberal use of such words as 'savages', 'niggers' and 'coons' to describe the natives of this fair continent has provoked considerable criticism from persons who fail to appreciate the overriding innocence of these expressions in the 1920s) and as far afield as the moon in later stories. Each volume is illustrated by Lofting's own distinctive drawings. A typical example of Lofting's work can be seen on the dust wrapper of *Doctor Dolittle's Circus* (1924). This story follows the fortunes of Dolittle and his animal entourage as they join a circus to pay off debts incurred by the Doctor's latest sea voyage. Initially involvement goes no further than displaying the two-headed Pushmi-Pullyu to visitors but, eventually, a complete Dolittle's circus is established. The book, in an act of what would now be termed political correctness, stresses that all animals were treated kindly and enjoyed performing. This is borne out in the wrapper illustration which shows the Doctor and his animal chums sitting down to tea together. The arresting white, black and pastel blue endpapers display scenes of animals working (and singing!) in harmony with humans.

Illustrated by the author.

The Story of Doctor Dolittle, Being the History of His Peculiar Life and Astonishing Adventures in Foreign Parts. New York, Stokes, 1920; as Doctor Dolittle, London, Cape, 1922.
The Voyages of Doctor Dolittle. New York, Stokes, 1922; London, Cape, 1923.
Doctor Dolittle's Post Office. New York, Stokes, 1923; London, Cape, 1924.

The Story of Mrs. Tubbs. New York, Stokes, 1923; London, Cape, 1924.
Doctor Dolittle's Circus. New York, Stokes, 1924; London, Cape, 1925.
Doctor Dolittle's Zoo. New York, Stokes, 1925; London, Cape, 1926.
Doctor Dolittle's Caravan. New York, Stokes, 1926; London, Cape, 1927.
Doctor Dolittle's Garden. New York, Stokes, 1927; London, Cape, 1928.
Doctor Dolittle in the Moon. New York, Stokes, 1928; London, Cape, 1929.
Noisy Nora. New York, Stokes, and London, Cape, 1929.

Patricia Lynch (1898–1972). Irish.

Patricia Lynch's close affinity with her Irish roots influenced her work greatly. She told entertaining and ardent tales of her homeland which almost always contained an element of the supernatural. Her stories interweave down-to-earth, lively characters with folklore and fantasy. Tinkers, children and leprechauns combine to produce a series of modern Irish fairy stories often with a moral. Good triumphs over evil and kindness is rewarded.

The Green Dragon, illustrated by Dorothy Hardy. London, Harrap, 1925.

Bessie Marchant (1862–1941). British.

Sally Makes Good, illustrated by Leo Bates. London, Blackie, 1920.
The Girl of the Pampas. London, Blackie, 1921.
Island Born, illustrated by Leo Bates. London, Blackie, 1921.
The Mistress of Purity Gap. London, Cassell, 1921; New York, Funk and Wagnalls, 1922.
Harriet Goes a-Roaming. London, Blackie, 1922.
The Fortunes of Prue, illustrated by J. Dewar Mills. London, Ward Lock, 1923.
Rachel Out West, illustrated by Henry Coller. London, Blackie, 1923.
A Bid for Safety. London, Ward Lock, 1924.
Diana Carries On. London, Nelson, 1924.
The Most Popular Girl in the School. London, Partridge, 1924.
Sylvia's Secret, illustrated by W.E. Wightman. London, Blackie, 1924.
By Honour Bound. London, Nelson, 1925.
Her Own Kin. London, Blackie, 1925.
To Save Her School, illustrated by H.L. Bacon. London, Partridge, 1925.
Delmayne's Adventures. London, Collins, 1925.
Cousin Peter's Money. London, Sheldon, 1926.
Di the Dauntless, illustrated by W.E. Wightman. London, Blackie, 1926.
Millicent Gwent, Schoolgirl. London, Warne, 1926.
Molly in the West, illustrated by F.E. Hiley. London, Blackie, 1927.
The Two New Girls. London, Warne, 1927.
Glenallan's Daughters. London, Nelson, 1928.
Lucie's Luck, illustrated by F.E. Hiley. London, Blackie, 1928.
The Bannister Twins, illustrated by E. Brier. London, Nelson, 1929.
Hilda Holds On, illustrated by F.E. Hiley. London, Blackie, 1929.
How Nell Scored. London, Nelson, 1929.

John Masefield (1878–1967). British.

The Midnight Folk. London, Heinemann, and New York, Macmillan, 1927.

L(Elizabeth) T(homasina) Meade (1854–1914). Irish.

Miss Patricia. London, Long, 1925.
Roses and Thorns. London, Long, 1928.

Stephen W(arren) Meader (1892–1977). American.

For main author article see 1930 to 1939.

The Black Buccaneer, illustrated by the author. New York, Harcourt Brace, 1920.
Down the Big River, illustrated by the author. New York, Harcourt Brace, 1924.
Longshanks, illustrated by Edward Caswell. New York, Harcourt Brace, 1928.

Florence Crannell Means (1891–1980). American.

For main author article see 1930 to 1939.

Rafael and Consuelo, with Harriet Louise Fullen. New York, Friendship Press, 1929.

Cornelia Meigs (1884–1973). American. **a.k.a. Adair Aldon.**

The Windy Hill. New York, Macmillan, 1921.
The New Moon, illustrated by Marguerite de Angeli. New York, Macmillan, 1924.
Rain on the Roof, illustrated by Edith Ballinger Price. New York, Macmillan, 1925.
The Trade Wind, illustrated by Henry Pitz. Boston, Little Brown, 1927; London, Hodder & Stoughton, 1928.
As the Crow Flies. New York, Macmillan, 1927.
Clearing Weather, illustrated by Frank Dobias. Boston, Little Brown, 1928.
The Wonderful Locomotive, illustrated by Berta and Elmer Hader. New York, Macmillan, 1928.
The Crooked Apple Tree, illustrated by Helen Mason Grose. Boston, Little Brown, 1929.

A(lan) A(lexander) Milne (1882–1956).
British.

A.A. Milne's *Winnie-the-Pooh* (1926) has been considered a classic of children's literature almost since its publication. Milne based the character of Christopher Robin on his own son and the rotund, slow but crafty Pooh Bear, squeaky Piglet and gloomy Eeyore on toys in his son's nursery. Their adventures in and around the Hundred Acre Wood have enchanted readers, both young and not so young, for seventy years. The first edition is bound in green cloth with Pooh and Christopher Robin stamped in gold on the front boards. The dust wrapper is orange with black lettering and is decorated by E.H. Shepard's elegant line drawings, which grace the text throughout. Two scenes from Pooh's adventures are illustrated. In the top right corner, the industrious bear is attempting to reach some elusive honey in a lofty bee hive. In a commendable attempt at subterfuge, Pooh is trying to avoid hostile bees by disguising himself as a little black rain cloud. However, his best efforts do not appear to be enough to deter the bees from taking an interest. The picture in the bottom left-hand corner bears witness to Pooh's over indulgence at a tea party with Rabbit. He has become too fat to leave and is stuck in the opening of Rabbit's front door. After putting the bear on a diet, Christopher Robin is organising the new slim-line Pooh's extraction from Rabbit's home:

> So he took hold of Pooh's front paws and Rabbit took hold of Christopher Robin, and all Rabbit's friends and relations took hold of Rabbit, and they all pulled together. …
> And for a long time Pooh only said "Ow!" …
> And "Oh!" …
> And then, all of a sudden, he said "Pop!" just as if a cork were coming out of a bottle.

The House at Pooh Corner (1928), although introducing the irrepressibly bouncy Tigger, is

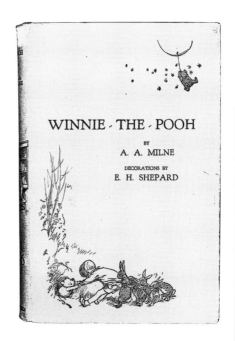

in some ways a valediction to childhood and ultimately a little melancholy. The first edition has salmon-coloured cloth with Christopher, Pooh and Piglet in gilt on the front cover. The dust wrapper is peach, printed in blue. Milne's two other related titles, *When We Were Very Young* (1924) and *Now We Are Six* (1927), are both delightful collections of short poems, some of which contain further details of the life and adventures of Pooh.

A Gallery of Children, illustrated by Saida (Pseudonym of H. Willebeek le Mair). London, Stanley Paul, and Philadelphia, Mckay, 1925.
Winne-the-Pooh, illustrated by Ernest Shepard. London, Methuen, and New York, Dutton, 1926.
The House at Pooh Corner, illustrated by Ernest Shepard. London, Methuen, and New York, Dutton, 1928.

L(ucy) M(aud) Montgomery (1874–1942).
Canadian.

L.M. Montgomery made her name as a children's author in the first two decades of the century by writing about one orphaned

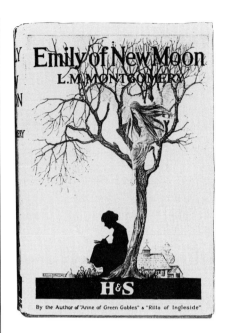

By the Author of "Anne of Green Gables" & "Rilla of Ingleside"

little girl. Her success continued in this decade through the creation of a second, Emily Byrd Starr. Montgomery's 'Emily' books are thought to be more autobiographical than the stories about Anne Shirley. Emily is, like her author, deeply creative and aspires to be a writer. Ellen Edwards's dust wrapper for *Emily of New Moon* (1923), the first of the trilogy, shows Emily, who seems to have a clear sense of the supernatural, writing under a tree with the house of New Moon in the background.

Further Chronicles of Avonlea ..., illustrated by John Goss. Boston, Page, 1920; London, Harrap, 1953.

Rilla of Ingleside. Toronto, McClelland and Stewart, New York, Stokes, and London, Hodder & Stoughton, 1921.

Emily of New Moon. New York, Stokes, and London, Hodder & Stoughton, 1923.

Emily Climbs. New York, Stokes, and London, Hodder & Stoughton, 1925.

The Blue Castle. Toronto, McClelland and Stewart, New York, Stokes, and London, Hodder & Stoughton, 1926.

Emily's Quest. New York, Stokes, and London, Hodder & Stoughton, 1927.

Magic for Marigold. Toronto, McClelland and Stewart, New York, Stokes, and London, Hodder & Stoughton, 1929.

Dorothea Moore (1881–1933). British.

The Right Kind of Girl. London, Nisbet, 1920.

The New Prefect. London, Nisbet, 1921.

An Adventurous Schoolgirl, illustrated by Archibald Webb. London, Cassell, 1921; New York, Funk and Wagnalls, 1922.

Greta of the Guides. London, Partridge, 1921.

Guide Gilly, Adventurer. London, Nisbet, 1922.

The New Girl at Pen-y-Gant. London, Nisbet, 1922.

The Only Day-Girl. London, Nisbet, 1923.

A Young Pretender. London, Nisbet, 1924.

Fen's First Term, illustrated by P.B. Hickling. London, Cassell, 1924.

In the Reign of the Red Cap, illustrated by Archibald Webb. London, Sheldon Press, 1924.

Smuggler's Way, illustrated by H.M. Brock. London, Cassell, 1924.

A Rough Night. London, Partridge, 1925.

"Z" House. London, Nisbet, 1925.

My Lady Venturesome. London, Sheldon Press, 1926.

Perdita, Prisoner of War. London, Cassell, 1926.

A Schoolgirl Adventurer. London, A. & C. Black, 1927.

Tenth at Trinder's. London, Cassell, 1927.

Adventurers All!, illustrated by P. Walford. London, Partridge, 1927.

Brenda of Beech House. London, Nisbet, 1927.

Seraphine-Di Goes to School. London, Religious Tract Society, 1927.

Darry the Dauntless. London, Cassell, 1928.

A Rebel of the Third. London, Nisbet, 1929.

Adventurers Two. London, Sheldon Press, 1929.

The Wrenford Tradition. London, Nisbet, 1929.

E(dith) Nesbit (1858–1924). British.

Five of Us – And Madeline, edited by Mrs Clifford Sharp, illustrated by Nora S. Unwin. London, Unwin, 1925; New York, Adelphi, 1926.

Elsie J. Oxenham (1880–1960). British. Pseudonym for Elsie Jeanette Dunkerley.
a.k.a. Elsie Oxenham.
a.k.a. Elsie Jeanette Oxenham.

This was a highly successful decade for Elsie J. Oxenham, who often produced two or three popular school stories for every year of it. Oxenham's interest in, among other activities, country dancing has already been noted and it is reflected in the subject matter of *Jen of the Abbey School* (1927). Elsie Ann Wood's dust wrapper depicts seventeen-year-old Jen Robins, on the left in a blue dress, looking on in some trepidation as the morris dancers, whom she has been coaching, perform. This book was later split up to form three separate titles about Rocklands School.

The School Without a Name (1924), the dust wrapper of which is reproduced on the jacket of the present study, is one of Oxenham's non-Abbey stories. Monica Hayward, Beryl Blaydon, Elizabeth McCrae, Rita Tompkins and Moll Sanderson comprise 'The Gang', a group of girls who become firm friends when they start simultaneously at Miss Angel's newly founded school. The story follows the fortunes of 'The Gang' as they find their feet in their new environment. Nina K. Brisley's dust wrapper illustration shows Beryl Blaydon, known to her family and friends as Blackberry, dropping a cricket ball in surprise at the sight of two girls materialising over the wall in front of her.

The Abbey Girls, illustrated by A.A. Dixon. London, Collins, 1920.
The School Torment, illustrated by H.C. Earnshaw. Edinburgh, Chambers, 1920.
The Twins of Castle Charming, illustrated by Harold C. Earnshaw. London, Swarthmore Press, 1920.
The Girls of the Abbey School, illustrated by Elsie Wood. London, Collins, 1921.
The Two Form-Captains, illustrated by Percy Tarrant. Edinburgh, Chambers, 1921.
The Abbey Girls Go Back to School, illustrated by Elsie Wood. London, Collins, 1922.
The Captain of the Fifth, illustrated by Percy Tarrant. Edinburgh, Chambers, 1922.
Patience Joan, Outsider. London, Cassell, 1922; New York, Funk and Wagnalls, 1923.

The Junior Captain, illustrated by Percy Tarrant. Edinburgh, Chambers, 1923.
The New Abbey Girls, illustrated by Elsie Anna Wood. Edinburgh, Chambers, 1923.
The Abbey Girls Again, illustrated by Elsie Anna Wood. London, Collins, 1924.
The Girls of Gwynfa, illustrated by Elsie Anna Wood. London and New York, Warne, 1924.
The School Without a Name, illustrated by Nina K. Brisley. Edinburgh, Chambers, 1924.
"Tickles"; or, The School That Was Different. London, Partridge, 1924.
The Testing of the Torment, illustrated by P.B. Hickling. London, Cassell, 1925.
Ven at Gregory's, illustrated by Nina K. Brisley. Edinburgh, Chambers, 1925.
The Abbey Girls in Town, illustrated by Rosa Petherick. London, Collins, 1926.
The Camp Fire Torment, illustrated by Nina Browne. Edinburgh, Chambers, 1926.
Queen of the Abbey Girls, illustrated by E.J. Kealey. London, Collins, 1926.
The Troubles of Tazy, illustrated by Percy Tarrant. Edinburgh, Chambers, 1926.
Jen of the Abbey School, illustrated by F. Meyerheim. London, Collins, 1927.
Patience and Her Problems, illustrated by Molly Benatar. Edinburgh, Chambers, 1927.
Peggy Makes Good!, illustrated by H.L. Bacon. London, Partridge, 1927.

JEN OF THE ABBEY SCHOOL
A SCHOOL STORY FOR GIRLS
Elsie J. Oxenham
Author of "The New Abbey Girls." "Queen of the Abbey Girls."
COLLINS

The Abbey Girls Win Through. London, Collins, 1928.

The Abbey School, illustrated by Elsie Anna Wood. London, Collins, 1928.

The Crisis in Camp Keema, illustrated by Percy Tarrant. Edinburgh, Chambers, 1928.

Deb at School, illustrated by Nina K. Brisley. Edinburgh, Chambers, 1929.

Gene Stratton Porter (1863–1924). American.

The Magic Garden, illustrated by Lee Thayer. New York, Doubleday, and London, Hutchinson, 1927.

Beatrix Potter (1866–1943). British. **a.k.a. Beatrix Heelis.**

Illustrated by the author.

The Fairy Caravan (as Beatrix Heelis). London, privately printed, and Philadelphia, McKay, 1929.

Rhoda Power (1890–1957). British.

Rhoda Power's historical stories have probably had a greater impact in educational circles than in the field of children's fiction. She and her sister Eileen, with whom she collaborated, were expert historians and Rhoda was Director of Children's Broadcasting at the BBC during this and the next decade. *Her Boys and Girls of History* (1926) and its companion volume *More Boys and Girls of History* (1928) present the adventures of mainly fictional children who become involved in well-known events in British history. The stories are so well informed that they were used by both teacher and pupil in the classroom. However, Power's style was neither turgid nor patronising and brought the past vividly alive to her readers, whatever their ages.

Boys and Girls of History, with Eileen Power. London, Cambridge University Press, 1926; New York, Macmillan, 1927;

revised edition, London, Dobson, 1968; New York, Roy, 1970.

More Boys and Girls of History, with Eileen Power. London, Cambridge University Press, and New York, Macmillan, 1928.

Evadne Price (1896–1985). British. Pseudonym for Helen Zenna Smith.

For all their similarities with the 'William' stories (including the titles of the first and fourth volumes in the series), Evadne Price's 'Jane' books were unrelated to those of her more famous forebear. Indeed, the author insisted that she had never heard of, let alone read about, William until the comparisons were later brought to her attention by a critic. Jane is the self-appointed leader of the Council of Three. The other two members, Charles (Chaw) and Perceval (Pug), are, pointedly, boys. They disturb through their well-meaning interference the otherwise placid rural village of Little Duppery and its varied inhabitants: love-sick young men, small-minded mothers and nosey elderly spinsters among them. No village institution is sacrosanct when Jane & Co. take an interest. M. Crichton's full-length portrait of Jane against a red background on the dust wrapper of *Just Jane* (1928) presents a foretaste of the character we are to meet inside. Jane's blue and white check dress is tied untidily, her socks need pulling up, her hair is tousled and she is in possession of the sort of mischievous grin that ought to strike fear into any adult's heart. After this disconcerting image of Jane Turpin (her very surname is that of the infamous Highwayman!), the front flap of the jacket provides a more formal, if less intriguing, introduction to her character:

> Jane is dreadfully truthful, fearless, ingenious, an enemy to false sentiment and ultra refinement, enjoys amazing adventures and helps to unmask one villain and his accomplice. She is determined to gratify her desires by lawful means if possible and has a strong sense of justice.

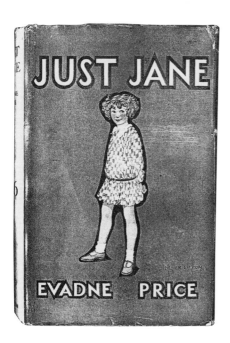

Just Jane. London, John Hamilton, 1928.

Walter C. Rhoades. British.
a.k.a. Walter Rhoades.

In the Scrum: A School Story, illustrated by
  Gordon Browne. London, Humphrey
  Milford, 1922.
*In Stirring Times: A Story of the English
  Revolution*, illustrated by Howard K.
  Elcock. London, Humphrey Milford, 1922.
The Last Lap: A School Story, illustrated by
  G.W. Goss. London, Humphrey Milford,
  1923.
The Whip Hand: A School Story, illustrated by
  G.W. Goss. London, Blackie, 1925.
Jimmy Cranston's Crony, illustrated by Frank
  Wright. London, Blackie, 1927.

Charles G(eorge) D(ouglas) Roberts
(1860–1943). Canadian.

Wisdom of the Wilderness. London, Dent, and
  New York, Dutton, 1922.
They Who Walk in the Wild, illustrated by
  Charles Livingston Bull. New York,
  Macmillan, 1924; as *They That Walk in the
  Wild*, London, Dent, 1924.

Ruth Sawyer (1880–1970). American.

Ruth Sawyer was interested in folk stories and
history throughout her long life. It was a
fascination that had its roots in the stories of
Sawyer's Irish nurse, whose influence can be
felt in many of the Gaelic associations in the
novels. *The Tale of the Enchanted Bunnies*
(1923) is her first book and has its origins in
European mythology. The dust wrapper for
the US first edition shows the Faery-man, a
Pied Piper figure, playing an alluring tune on
his pipe. He is listened to attentively by the
Bunnies who seem to be signalling their
approbation of the sprite's performance by
applauding.

The Tale of the Enchanted Bunnies. New York,
  Harper, 1923.

Caroline Dale Snedeker (1871–1956).
American.

The Perilous Seat. New York, Doubleday, and
  London, Methuen, 1923.
Theras and His Town, illustrated by Mary
  Haring. New York, Doubleday, and
  London, Heinemann, 1924.
Downright Dencey, illustrated by Maginel
  Wright Barney. New York, Doubleday,
  and London, Heinemann, 1927.

The Beckoning Road, illustrated by Manning Lee. New York, Doubleday, 1929.

Herbert Strang. Pseudonym for George Herbert Ely (1866–1958), British, and C. James L'Estrange (1867–1947). British.

No Man's Island (1921) is something of a break from Herbert Strang's usual militaristic adventures. Jack Armstrong and Phil Warrender spend their summer holidays in the West Country. They are accompanied by a schoolfriend, Percy Pratt, whose uncle owns a large property near Southampton. The boys sense that all is not as it should be in the uncle's mansion and they discover that the house is the base for a den of forgers. C.E. Brock's illustration for the dust wrapper shows Jack and Phil entering the supposedly empty cottage in the mansion's grounds. It actually contains the opening of a secret passage which is the forgers' entrance and exit from the larger building.

Bright Ideas, illustrated by C.E. Brock. London, Oxford University Press, 1920.
No Man's Island, illustrated by C.E. Brock. London, Oxford University Press, 1921.
The Cave in the Hills. London, Oxford University Press, 1922.
Bastable Cove. London, Oxford University Press, 1922.
Winning His Name, illustrated by C.E. Brock. London, Oxford University Press, 1922.
Honour First, illustrated by W.E. Wightman. London, Oxford University Press, 1923.
True as Steel, illustrated by C.E. Brock. London, Oxford University Press, 1923.
A Thousand Miles an Hour, illustrated by Howard K. Elcock. London, Oxford University Press, 1924.
The Heir of a Hundred Kings, illustrated by D.C. Eyles. London, Oxford University Press, 1924.
Young Jack: A Story of Road and Moor, illustrated by H.M. Brock. London, Oxford University Press, 1924.
Martin of Old London, illustrated by C.E. Brock. London, Oxford University Press, 1925.
Olwyn's Secret. London, Oxford University Press, 1925.

Dan Bolton's Discovery, illustrated by C.E. Brock. London, Oxford University Press, 1926.
Strang's Penny Books (Three Boys at the Fair, Kitty's Kitten, The Cinema Dog, Bill Sawyer's V.C., The Game of Brownies, Jenny's Ark, Baa-Baa and the Wide World, Tom Leaves School, The Mischief-Making Magpie. A Ride with Robin Hood, Pete's Elephant, Ten Pound Reward, Adolf's Dog, The Adventures of a Penny Stamp, Don't Be Too Sure, Jack and Jocko, The Princess and the Robbers, The Christmas Fairy, The Seven Sons, The Red Candle, The Miller's Daughter, The Grey Goose Feathers, The Birthday Present, There Was a Little Pig, The Magic Smoke, The Children of the Ferry, Sugar Candy Town, Little Mr. Pixie, The Little Sea Horse, The Little Blue-Grey Hare). London, Oxford University Press, 30 vols., 1926–27.
Lost in London. London, Oxford University Press, 1927.
The River Pirates. London, Oxford University Press, 1927.
The Riders: A Story of the Smuggling Days, illustrated by Terence Cuneo. London, Oxford University Press, 1928.
On London River: A Story of the Days of Queen Elizabeth, illustrated by Terence Cuneo. London, Oxford University Press, 1929.

L(eonard) A(lfred) G(eorge) Strong
(1896–1958). British.

The diversity of L.A.G. Strong's children's fiction reflects the man's wide range of interests. He was also a poet, playwright and purveyor of adult novels, including some notable detective stories. He only wrote eleven children's books over a period of sixteen years but they included several historical tales, an Arthur Ransome-like sailing story, a contribution to juvenile detective fiction and possibly the last school story which followed the precepts of the nineteenth-century *Boy's Own Paper* (Strong was a school master until 1930). His first work for children, *Patricia Comes Home* (1929) relates the sometimes mysterious experiences of a young girl in the Highlands.

Patricia Comes Home, illustrated by Ruth Cobb. Oxford, Blackwell, 1929.

Ethel Talbot. British.

Ethel Talbot wrote an amazing number of spirited girls' school stories during the decade. *The New Girl at the Priory* (1923) reflects the pluck, determination and sporting attitude which Talbot bestowed upon her girls. The viewer of Norman Sutcliffe's dust-wrapper illustration finds Pippa Curtis being dragged out of a rock pool by her teacher, Miss Warwick. The impetuous girl had fallen in whilst hunting for treasure. She emerges 'soaked through to the very skin'.

The Cosy-Comfy book, illustrated by Anne Anderson. London, Collins, 1920.
Peggy's Last Term, illustrated by C.E. Brock. London, Nelson, 1920.
Farmyard Fun, illustrated by M. Morris. London, Collins, 1922.
Holiday Chums. London, Sheldon Press, 1923.
The Island Camp. London, Sheldon Press, 1923.
The Adventures of Woodeny and Other Stories, with Harold Avery and Ada Holman. London, Nelson, 1923.
Neighbours at School. London, Nelson, 1923.
The New Girl at the Priory, illustrated by Norman Sutcliffe. London, Ward Lock, 1923.
The Sport of the School, illustrated by J.R. Burgess. London, Chambers, 1923.
Two on an Island and Other Stories. London, Nelson, 1923.
Betty at St. Benedick's [Holds the Reins]. London, Nelson, 2 vols., 1924–29.
Billy at St. Bede's. London, Nelson, 1924.
The Bravest Girl in the School. London, Cassell, 1924.
The Luck of the School, illustrated by Molly Benatar. London, Chambers, 1924.
Sally at School. London, Nelson, 1924.
Scout Island. London, Nelson, 1924.
While Mother Was Away. London, Sheldon Press, 1924.
The Best of All Schools. London, Jarrolds, 1924.
Between Two Terms, illustrated by J. Dewar Mills. London, Ward Lock, 1925.
Fellow Fags, illustrated by P. Walford. London, Sheldon Press, 1925.
The Girls of the Rookery School. London, Nelson, 1925.
Patricia, Prefect. London, Nelson, 1925.
The Stranger in the Train and Other Stories, illustrated by R.H. Brock. London, Sheldon Press, 1925.
That Wild Australian School-girl. London, South, 1925.

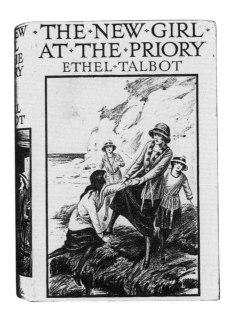

An Unexpected Schoolgirl. London, Cassell, 1925.

Bringing Back the Frasers and Other Stories. London, Nelson, 1926.

The Camp in the Wood. London, Epworth Press, 1926.

Jane and the Beanstalks, illustrated by R.B. Ogle. London, Pearson, 1926.

Little Black Tumgo's Tale and Other Stories. London, Epworth Press, 1926.

The Luckiest Girl at St. Chad's. London, Jarrolds, 1926.

The Magic Island. London, Children's Companion, 1926.

Rags: The Pranks of a Little Doggie. London, Epworth Press, 1926.

The School of None-Go-By, illustrated by Margaret Forbes. London, Ward Lock, 1926.

Aunt Mary. London, Sheldon Press, 1927.

Bunch at Boarding-School, illustrated by T. Heath Robinson. London, Warne, 1927.

The Family Next Door. London, Sheldon Press, 1927.

Jan at Island School, illustrated by E. Brier. London, Nelson, 1927.

Jill, Lone Guide, illustrated by R.B. Ogle. London, Pearson, 1927.

Just the Girl for St. Jude's. London, Cassell, 1927.

Let's Pretend Tales. London, Epworth Press, 1927.

Priscilla the Prefect. London, Sheldon Press, 1927.

Twenty-Six Ethel Talbot Tales for Girls, illustrated by R.H. Stone. London, Religious Tract Society, 1927.

Listening-in and Other Stories for Girls, with others. London, Nelson, 1927.

Adventures of Skurry the Scout. London, Epworth Press, 1928.

At School with Morag. London, Warne, 1928.

Baby Animals, illustrated by A.E. Kennedy. London, Nelson, 1928.

Brownies at St. Bride's. London, Warne, 1928.

Carol's Second Term, illustrated by W.B. Hamilton. London, Nelson, 1928.

The Half-and-Half Schoolgirl, illustrated by R.F.C. Waudby. London, Nelson, 1928.

Ranger Rose. London, Nelson, 1928.

Schoolgirl Rose. London, Cassell, 1928.

The New Centre-Forward, illustrated by R.H. Brock. London, Collins, 1929; as *Meta, The New Girl; Meta, Centre-Forward*; and *Meta's Last Term*. 3 vols., 1930–31.

The Peppercorn Patrol. London, Cassell, 1929.

Ranger Jo. London, Pearson, 1929.

Rhona Runs Away. London, Pilgrim Press, 1929.

Skipper & Co. London, Warne, 1929.

The Smiths of Silver Lane, illustrated by R.F.C. Waudby. London, Nelson, 1929.

Barbara Euphan Todd (1897–1976). British.

a.k.a. Euphan.

Barbara Euphan Todd's name will always be associated with the cantankerous animate scarecrow Worzel Gummidge and his straw-stuffed chums. Todd's earliest and final titles are devoid of Worzel but possess the same combination of magic and commonplace settings that makes the Gummidge books so alluring. One of her first children's books was *Mr Blossom's Shop* (1929), which propounds a view of adult humans that, in contrast with the overwhelming picture in later books, is remarkably sympathetic. Mr Blossom is a

kindly old gentleman whose slightly ramshackle grocery store exerts a particular fascination over a small group of young girls. E.S. Duffin's dust wrapper illustration has Jennifer Wild being fitted for sand-shoes by Mr Blossom.

The 'normous Saturday Fairy Book, with Marjory Royce and Moira Meighn, illustrated by G.L. Stampa and Mary Stella Edwards. London, Stanley Paul, 1924.
The 'normous Sunday Story Book, with Marjory Royce and Mora Meighn, illustrated by G.L. Stampa and Mary Stella Edwards. London, Stanley Paul, 1925.
The Very Good Walkers, with Marjory Royce, illustrated by H.R. Millar. London, Methuen, 1925.
Mr. Blossom's Shop, illustrated by E.S. Duffin. London, Nelson, 1929.

Mary Tourtel (1874–1948). British.

Mary Tourtel had been illustrating children's books featuring animals since the turn of the century. However, it was not until her creation of Rupert Bear for the *Daily Express* in 1920 that she found the character that would bestow lasting fame upon her. Rupert was Tourtel's third attempt at inventing a character for the newspaper whose success could rival or exceed that of Teddy Tail in the *Daily Mail*. Rupert's popularity was immediate and a sizeable collection of minor characters from friends like Edward Trunk the elephant, Podgy Pig, Algy Pug and Bill Badger to the mystic Wise Old Goat, came into being. The very first Rupert tale 'Little Lost Bear', presents the now familiar timeless world of near–Arthurian magic and landscape mingled with more contemporary intrusions (Rupert flies in an airship, reflecting Tourtel's passion for all aircraft). The illustration on the cover of the book version of this first story, *The Adventures of Rupert the Little Lost Bear* (1921), depicts a transitive stage in the ursine hero's Odyssey: 'Rupert enters the Unknown Place'. A citation of the text beneath this illustration will give an indication of Tourtel's appropriately balladic pattern of verse writing (the present rhyming couplets were introduced by Tourtel's Rupert successor, Alfred Bestall):

> He ventures in, and sees his hoop;
> "Ah! here it is", he cries.
> He picks it up and gazes round,
> His eyes big with surprise.
>
> "This is a lovely place", he says,
> "And no one is in sight;
> I think I'll walk along this road –
> I wonder if I might?"

Illustrated by the author.

The Adventures of Rupert the Little Lost Bear. London, Nelson, 1921.
The Little Bear and the Fairy Child. London, Nelson, 1921.
Margot the Midget; The Little Bear's Christmas. London, Nelson, 1922.
The Little Bear and the Ogres. London, Nelson, 1922.
Rupert Little Bear's Adventures:
1. *Rupert and the Magic Toy Man, Rupert and the Princess, Rupert at School, Rupert and the Old Miser.* London, Sampson Low, 1924.
2. *Rupert and the Magic Key, Rupert and the Brigands, Rupert and Reynard Fox, Rupert in Dreamland.* London, Sampson Low, 1924.
3. *Rupert and the Robber Wolf, Rupert and the Dragon, Rupert and the Snowman, Rupert at the Seaside.* London, Sampson Low, 1925.

Rupert and the Enchanted Princess. London, Sampson Low, 1928.

Rupert and the Black Dwarf. London, Sampson Low, 1928.

Rupert and His Pet Monkey. London, Sampson Low, 1928.

Rupert and His Friend Margot; Rupert, Margot and the Fairies. London, Sampson Low, 1928.

Rupert in the Wood of Mystery. London, Sampson Low, 1929.

Further Adventures of Rupert and His Pet Monkey; Rupert and the Stolen Apples. London, Sampson Low, 1929.

Rupert and the Three Robbers. London, Sampson Low, 1929.

Rupert, The Knight and the Lady; Rupert and the Wise Goat's Birthday Cake. London, Sampson Low, 1929.

Rupert and the Circus Clown. London, Sampson Low, 1929.

Rupert and the Magic Hat. London, Sampson Low, 1929.

Alison Uttley (1884–1976). British.

The setting for Alison Uttley's delightful children's books was, by her own admission, inspired by her own childhood experiences in the Derbyshire Peak District. Uttley's most famous creation is Little Grey Rabbit who, along with her friends Hare, Squirrel, Fuzzypeg, Wise Owl and Moldy Warp the Mole, tripped serenely through a whole series of situations dramatic and domestic from 1929 till 1975. Margaret Tempest's pictorial interpretation of Uttley's words brings the author's naturalistic landscape perfectly to life whilst smoothly integrating the partly anthropomorphic animals into it. The green cover of Uttley's first book, *The Squirrel, The Hare and The Little Grey Rabbit* (1929), shows the enterprising bunny bouncing over a stream whilst searching for her lost friends,

> '"Oh , my dear Squirrel, my darling Hare", she cried, with tears running down her cheeks. "Has that bad Weasel got you?".
> She took a pair of scissors, a rope and a stick, and started out to look for her companions.'

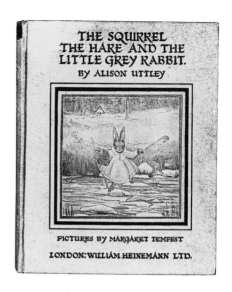

THE SQUIRREL THE HARE AND THE LITTLE GREY RABBIT.
BY ALISON UTTLEY

PICTURES BY MARGARET TEMPEST
LONDON: WILLIAM HEINEMANN LTD.

The Weasel indeed has got them both and sings in a rough voice,

> '"Hare for lunch, and Squirrel for tea,
> With acorn sauce is a feast for me."'

Tragedy is averted, as the rope provided by Little Grey Rabbit assists in the escape of Hare and Squirrel from an upstairs room, whilst Little Grey Rabbit pushes the Weasel into a hot oven and shuts the oven door. The little house on the edge of a wood, where Hare, Squirrel and Little Grey Rabbit live, is depicted on the book's green and cream endpapers.

Alison Uttley was also responsible for another important series, featuring the brave but somewhat conceited Sam Pig. Sam, along with his brothers and sisters, is often in trouble, whilst the paternal figure of Brock the Badger tries to keep the pigs orderly.

Other series characters are Tim Rabbit, plus the two mice, Snug and Serena, who are both found in the Little Brown Mouse series.

The Squirrel, The Hare, and the Little Grey Rabbit, illustrated by Margaret Tempest. London, Hcinemann, 1929.

Now the rich man was very grateful to Tommy for having saved his life and wanted to give him a thousand pounds (£1000) he had in his pocket. But Tommy had been told never to take money from strangers and refused this

"Oh" said the rich man, "I must give you something."

"A good deed is its own Reward" said Tommy.

H(erbert) G(eorge) Wells (1866–1946). British.

H.G. Wells wrote one work for children, although his science fiction epics have always been devoured by boys. *The Adventures of Tommy* (1929) had been written as early as 1898. It is a whimsical story, very different in tone from his more famous heavy works. Illustrated by Wells himself, with the author's manuscript reproduced below each piece of artwork, it tells of how Tommy Bates rescues a rich man from drowning. As the internal illustration and accompanying text reveal, Tommy refuses the rich man's financial offer. He does, however, receive an extraordinary reward.

The Adventures Of Tommy, illustrated by the author. London, Harrap, 1929.

Percy F(rancis) Westerman (1876–1959). British.
a.k.a. P.F. Westerman.
a.k.a. P. Westerman.

Percy F. Westerman's *The Terror of the Seas* (1927) is a good example of this author's interest in maritime adventures. The 'Terror' referred to in the title is the pirate submarine commanded by Klinkor. The dust-wrapper illustration by W. Edward Wigfull depicts the scene in which the submarine shells a ship, the *Frauenlob*, prior to hostages being taken.

The Airship "Golden Hind", illustrated by S.F. Williams. London, Partridge, 1920.

The Mystery Ship, illustrated by A. Morrow. London, Partridge, 1920.

The Salving of the "Fusi Yama," illustrated by E.S. Hodgson. London, Blackie, 1920.

Sea Scouts All, illustrated by Charles Pears. London, Blackie, 1920.

Sea Scouts Abroad, illustrated by Charles Pears. London, Blackie, 1921.

The Third Officer, illustrated by E.S. Hodgson. London, Blackie, 1921.

Sea Scouts Up-Channel, illustrated by C.M. Padday. London, Blackie, 1922.

The Wireless Officer, illustrated by W.E. Wigfull. London, Blackie, 1922.

The War of the Wireless Waves, illustrated by W.E. Wigfull. London, Oxford University Press, 1923.

The Pirate Submarine. London, Nisbet, 1923.

A Cadet of the Mercantile Marine, illustrated by W.E. Wigfull, London, Blackie, 1923.

Clipped Wings, illustrated by E.S. Hodgson. London, Blackie, 1923.

The Mystery of Stockmere School. London, Partridge, 1923.

Sinclair's Luck. London, Partridge, 1923.

Captain Cain. London, Nisbet, 1924.

The Good Ship "Golden Effort", illustrated by W.E. Wigfull. London, Blackie, 1924.

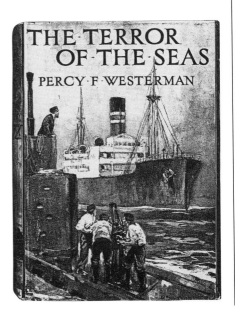

The Treasure of the Sacred Lake. London, Pearson, 1924.

Unconquered Wings, illustrated by E.S. Hodgson. London, Blackie, 1924.

Clinton's Quest, illustrated by R.B. Ogle. London, Pearson, 1925.

East in the "Golden Gain," illustrated by Rowland Hilder. London, Blackie, 1925.

The Boys of the "Puffin", illustrated by G.W. Goss. London, Partridge, 1925.

The Buccaneers of Boya, illustrated by William Rainey. London, Blackie, 1925.

The Sea Scouts of the "Kestrel". London, Seeley, 1925.

Annesley's Double. London, A. & C. Black, and New York, Macmillan, 1926.

King of Kilba. London, Ward Lock, 1926.

The Luck of the "Golden Dawn", illustrated by Rowland Hilder. London, Blackie, 1926.

The Riddle of the Air, illustrated by Rowland Hilder. London, Blackie, 1926.

The Terror of the Seas, illustrated by W. Edward Wigfull. London, Ward Lock, 1927.

Mystery Island. London, Oxford University Press, 1927.

Captain Blundell's Treasure, illustrated by J. Cameron. London, Blackie, 1927.

Chums of the "Golden Vanity", illustrated by Rowland Hilder. London, Blackie, 1927.

In the Clutches of the Dyaks, illustrated by F. Marston. London, Partridge, 1927.

The Junior Cadet, illustrated by Rowland Hilder. London, Blackie, 1928.

On the Wings of the Wind, illustrated by W.E. Wigfull. London, Blackie, 1928.

A Shanghai Adventure, illustrated by Leo Bates. London, Blackie, 1928.

Pat Stobart in the "Golden Dawn", illustrated by Rowland Hilder. London, Blackie, 1929.

Rivals of the Reef, illustrated by Kenneth Inns. London, Blackie, 1929.

Captain Starlight, illustrated by W.E. Wigfull. London, Blackie, 1929.

Kate Douglas Wiggin (1856–1923). American.

The Spirit of Christmas, Boston, Houghton Mifflin, 1927.

Henry Williamson (1895–1977). British.

Henry Williamson's reputation as a writer has unfortunately been marred by the light shone upon certain aspects of his private life. He was interred for a time at the beginning of the Second World War as an alleged Nazi sympathiser. More recently, his association with the local hunt (*Tarka* is dedicated to the Master of the Hunt) has provoked questions about the man who describes the cruel violence of such hunting in his most famous work. On a more positive note, Williamson's evident love for nature and his beloved West Country emanates from the page. Williamson had composed some angst-ridden novels in the early twenties, but *Tarka the Otter* (1927) is his most enduring contribution to fiction. It is a comprehensive and tightly knit narrative of an otter's eventful life in the 'country of the two rivers', which stretches from Dartmoor to the sea. The author's famous attention to the exact detail of river life stretched back to his experiences when searching for his own lost pet otter. Hester Sainsbury's design for the dust jacket consists of a black and white illustration of Tarka surveying his watery domain with some trepidation, set against a pale blue background.

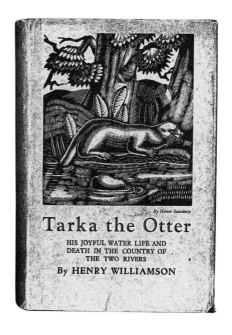

By Hester Sainsbury

Tarka the Otter

HIS JOYFUL WATER LIFE AND
DEATH IN THE COUNTRY OF
THE TWO RIVERS

By HENRY WILLIAMSON

Tarka the Otter, Being His Joyful Water-Life and Death in the Country of the Two Rivers. London, Putnam, 1927; New York, Dutton, 1928.

May Wynne (1875–1949). British.
Pseudonym for Mabel Winifred Knowles.

The Adventures of Dolly Dingle: A Fairy Story, illustrated by Florence Anderson. London, Jarrolds, 1920.

Aventures of Two, illustrated by Henry Coller. London, Blackie, 1920.

The Heroine of Chelton School. London, Stanley Paul, 1920.

The Girls of Beechcroft School, illustrated by C.E. Rhodes. London, Religious Tract Society, 1920.

Roseleen at School. London, Cassell, 1920.

Three Bears and Gwen, illustrated by John Campbell. London, Blackie, 1920.

Little Ladyship, illustrated by Gordon Browne. London, Religious Tract Society, 1921.

Lost in the Jungle. London, Stanley Paul, 1921.

Mervyn, Jock, or Joe, illustrated by Thomas Somerfield. London, Blackie, 1921.

Peggy's First Term. London, Ward Lock, 1922.

Angela Goes to School. London, Jarrolds, 1922; Cleveland, World, 1929.

The Girls of the Veldt Farm, illustrated by A.J. Shackel. London, Pearson, 1922.

The Red Boy's Gratitude. Exeter, Wheaton, 1922.

Christmas at Holford, illustrated by Thomas Somerfield. London, Blackie, 1922.

Two Girls in the Wild. London, Blackie, 1923; abridged edition, as *Sisters Out West,* 1930.

The Best of Chums. London, Ward Lock, 1923.

A Heather Holiday, illustrated by Thomas Somerfield. London, Blackie, 1923.

Blundering Bettina. London, Religious Tract Society, 1924.

The Girl Who Played the Game. London, Ward Lock, 1924.

Bertie, Bobby, and Belle, illustrated by Norman Sutcliffe. London, Blackie, 1924.

The Girls of Clanways Farm, illustrated by Archibald Webb. London, Cassell, 1924.

Kits at Clynton Court School. London, Warne, 1924.

The Sunshine Children. London, Nelson, 1924.

Three and One Over, illustrated by E.P. Kinsella. London, Cassell, 1924.

A Rebel at School. London, Jarrolds, 1924.

Two and a Chum, illustrated by D.C. Eyles. London, Pearson, 1924.

Hootie Toots of Hollow Tree. Philadelphia, Altemus, 1925.

The Girls of Old Grange School. London, Ward Lock, 1925.

Over the Hills and Far Away, illustrated by G.W. Goss. London, Religious Tract Society, 1925.

Dare-All Jack and the Cousins, illustrated by G.W. Goss. London, Religious Tract Society, 1925.

Hazel Asks Why. London, Ward Lock, 1926.

Carol of Hollydene School. London, Sampson Low, 1926.

The Secret of Carrock School. London, Jarrolds, 1926.

Diccon the Impossible. London, Religious Tract Society, 1926.

The Girl over the Wall, illustrated by G.W. Goss. London, Religious Tract Society, 1926.

Jean Plays Her Part, illustrated by Louise Parker. London, Religious Tract Society, 1926.

Dinah's Secret, illustrated by M.L. Parker. London Relegious Tract Society, 1927.

Jean of the Lumber Camp. London, Ward Lock, 1927.

Robin Hood to the Rescue. Exeter, Wheaton, 1927.

Terry the Black Sheep, illustrated by R.B. Ogle. London, Pearson, 1928.

The Girls of Mackland Court, illustrated by J. Dewar Mills. London, Ward Lock, 1928.

Little Sally Mandy's Christmas Present, illustrated by Bess Goe Willis. Philadelphia, Altemus, 1929.

The House of Whispers, illustrated by N. Sutcliffe. London, Ward Lock, 1929.

The Guide's Honour, illustrated by T.H. Robinson. London, Ward Lock, 1929.

1930–1939

Ruth Ainsworth
C.W. Anderson
Edward Ardizzone
Ruth Arthur
M.E. Atkinson
Harold Avery
'BB'
Enid Bagnold
Helen Bannerman
Cicely Mary Barker
S.G. Hulme Beaman
Alfred Bestall
Enid Blyton/Mary Pollock
Helen Dore Boylston
Angela Brazil
Elinor M. Brent-Dyer/ E.M. Brent-Dyer
Molly Brett
Joyce Lankester Brisley
Dorita Fairlie Bruce
Virginia Lee Burton
Arthur Catherall/A.R. Channel
Christine Chaundler
Joseph E. Chipperfield
Catherine Christian/Catherine Mary Christian
Mavis Thorpe Clark
Elizabeth Coatsworth
Padraic Colum
Mrs H. C. Cradock
Richmal Crompton
Primrose Cumming
Winifred Darch
Peter Dawlish/Lennox Kerr
C. Day Lewis
Marguerite de Angeli
Jean de Brunhoff
Olive Dehn
Meindert De Jong
Walter de la Mare
Elizabeth Borton de Trevino
V.H. Drummond
William Pène du Bois
Elizabeth Enright

Evelyn Everett-Green/E. Everett-Green/Cecil Adair
Eleanor Farjeon
Charles J. Finger
Marjorie Flack
Rose Fyleman
Wanda Gág
Eve Garnett
Doris Gates
Charles Gilson/C.L. Gilson/Captain Charles Gilson/Major Charles Gilson
R.A.H. Goodyear
Elizabeth Goudge
Eleanor Graham
Hardie Gramatky
Roderick Haig-Brown/R.L. Haig-Brown
J.B.S. Haldane
Kathleen Hale
Cynthia Harnett
Constance Heward
C. Walter Hodges
Edith Howes
Richard Hughes
Katharine Hull & Pamela Whitlock
Norman Hunter
W.E Johns/William Earle/Captain W.E. Johns
Erich Kästner
Rudyard Kipling
Robert Lawson
Munro Leaf/John Calvert/Mun
Amy Le Feuvre/Mary Thurston Dodge
Robert Leighton
Elizabeth Foreman Lewis
Hilda Lewis
Norman Lindsay
Hugh Lofting
Patricia Lynch
Ruth Manning-Sanders
Bessie Marchant
John Masefield
Stephen W. Meader
Florence Crannell Means

Cornelia Meigs/Adair Aldon
Naomi Mitchison
L.M. Montgomery
Rutherford Montgomery/Al
  Avery/Everitt Proctor
Dorothea Moore
Ursula Moray Williams
Violet Needham
Elsie J. Oxenham/Elsie Oxenham/Elsie
  Jeanette Oxenham
M. Pardoe
Mervyn Peake
Beatrix Potter/Beatrix Heelis
Evadne Price
Gwynedd Rae
Arthur Ransome
Charles G.D. Roberts
Ruth Sawyer
Helen Sewell
C. Fox Smith

Caroline Dale Snedeker
Phil Stong
Herbert Strang
Noel Streatfeild
L.A.G. Strong
Ethel Talbot
Barbara Euphan Todd/Euphan
J.R.R. Tolkien
Mary Tourtel
Katharine Tozer
P.L. Travers
Geoffrey Trease
Alison Uttley
Elfrida Vipont/Charles Vipont
Percy F. Westerman/P.F. Westerman/P.
  Westerman
T.H. White
Laura Ingalls Wilder
Henry Williamson
May Wynne

Ruth Ainsworth (b. 1908). British.

Ruth Ainsworth's writing was aimed at younger children and, as her experience as a script writer for the BBC's *Listen With Mother* programme would suggest, is ideal for reading aloud. Hers is a comforting world where children, adults and animals live together in harmony. *Mr Popcorn's Friends* (1938) reflects this happy outlook and also Ainsworth's love of the British countryside, especially that of her native Suffolk. Phyl E. Webb's illustration for the book's dust wrapper shows Mr Popcorn, Teddy, Jasper and the yellow monkey sharing a meal with some friendly gypsies.

Tales about Tony, illustrated by Cora E.M. Paterson. London, Epworth Press, 1936.
Mr. Popcorn's Friends, illustrated by Phyl E. Webb. London, Epworth Press, 1938.
The Gingerbread House. London, Epworth Press, 1938.
The Ragamuffins. London, Epworth Press, 1939.

C(larence) W(illiam) Anderson
(1891–1971). American.

C.W. Anderson was an expert in all matters equine and put his extensive knowledge to good use by creating a series of informative and exciting stories that revolved around horses. The nature of his work is such that its straightforwardness is capable of encouraging an interest in horses in the uninitiated, whilst the detail contained within the stories should satisfy the most fervent pony-phile. Anderson thought of himself initially as just an artist and his superb charcoal pictures enhance his work. His original reticence when it came to writing meant that his first stories are usually read by a rather younger audience. *Blaze and the Gypsies* (1937) is the second in Anderson's series, which stretched until the 1970s, about the pony Blaze. Anderson's portrayal of gypsies is rather less charitable than Ruth Ainsworth's cosy view of them. Blaze is kidnapped by gypsies but escapes. After a lengthy and hazardous journey through woods and over streams, he finds his way home. The dust wrapper shows Blaze being welcomed by his young master Billy and his dog Rex.

Illustrated by the author.

Billy and Blaze. New York, Macmillan, 1936.
Blaze and the Gypsies. New York, Macmillan, 1937; London, Country Life, 1939.

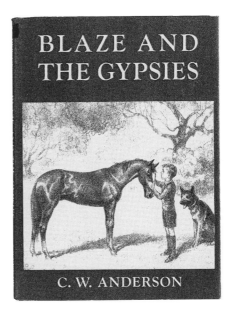

Blaze and the Forest Fire. New York, Macmillan, 1938.

Edward Ardizzone (1900–1979). British.

When his work was first published, during a period when conventional artwork was favoured in children's fiction, Edward Ardizzone's quirky pictures must have been a breath of fresh air. They remain so today and his original, simple but extraordinarily effective style is instantly recognizable. Besides the twenty books he wrote himself, Ardizzone illustrated the works of Dickens and Trollope, as well as the children's stories of C. Day Lewis, Walter de la Mare and Eleanor Farjeon. His own stories generally involve perilous adventures with an ultimate return to a reassuringly safe home. Ardizzone wrote ten tales about Tim and his hazardous life on the high seas. The dust wrapper for the first of these, *Little Tim and The Brave Sea Captain* (1936), contains two illustrations. At the top of the wrapper, Little Tim climbs the rigging whilst the sea captain looks through his telescope. In the other picture, 'The lifeboat came alongside and a life line was thrown to them.'

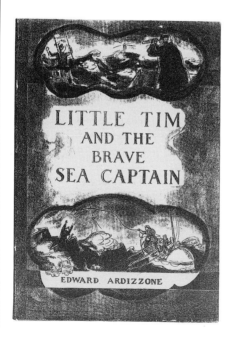

Illustrated by the author.

Little Tim and the Brave Sea Captain. London and New York, Oxford University Press, 1936; revised edition, London, Oxford University Press, and New York, Walck, 1955.
Lucy Brown and Mr. Grimes. London and New York, Oxford University Press, 1937; revised edition, London, Bodley Head, 1970; New York, Walck, 1971.
Tim and Lucy Go to Sea. London and New York, Oxford University Press, 1938; revised edition, London, Oxford University Press, and New York, Walck, 1958.

Ruth Arthur (1905–1979). British.

Ruth Arthur's stories are a journey of self-discovery for both her narrator heroine and her readers. Set before the backdrop of a particularly beautiful part of the British Isles such as Cornwall or Wales, each of her books is a study in solitude and the main character's reaction to psychological problems. Some of Arthur's writing delves into the supernatural and presents an almost cosmic battle between good and evil.

Friendly Stories, illustrated by C.F. Christie. London, Harrap, 1932.
The Crooked Brownie, illustrated by R.M. Turvey. London, Harrap, 1936.
Pumpkin Pie. London, Collins, 1938.

M(ary) E(velyn) Atkinson (1899–1974). British.

M.E. Atkinson is best known for her thirteen books about the Lockett children, Bill, Jane and Oliver, which appeared every year from 1936 to 1949. Hers is a secure, middle-class world, where adventures are always there for the taking. The stories are written in the first person (but apparently with the assistance of Aunt Margaret) and centre around the exciting experiences of the youngsters (whose parents live in India) whilst on their holidays. Harold Jones provided the first book, *August Adventure* (1936), with an enticing rural scene

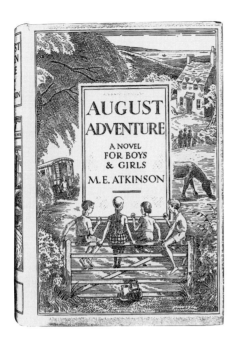

for its dust wrapper, his first work as an artist. It depicts the three Locketts, with Anna Angel, sitting on a five-barred gate and eating apples. Their caravanning adventure is about to begin.

August Adventure, illustrated by Harold Jones. London, Cape, 1936.
Mystery Manor, illustrated by Harold Jones. London, Lane, 1937.
The Compass Points North, illustrated by Harold Jones. London, Lane, 1938.
Smuggler's Gap, illustrated by Harold Jones. London, Lane, 1939.

Harold Avery (1867–1943). British.

A Term on Trial. London, Partridge, 1930.
The Cock-House Cup, illustrated by J. Phillips Paterson. London, Nelson, 1933.
A Close Finish and Other School Stories. London, Partridge, 1934.
The Marlcot Mystery. London, Ward Lock, 1935.
Chums at Charlhurst. London, Nelson, 1936.
Through Thick and Thin, illustrated by J. Phillips Paterson. London, Nelson, 1938.
The Side Line. London, Ward Lock, 1939.

'BB' (1905–90). British. Pseudonym for D(enys) J(ames) Watkins-Pitchford.

D.J. Watkins-Pitchford, or 'BB' as he was known, was a countryman all his life and felt passionately about his rural surroundings. This love is evident in his writings for children, which were very much lesser considerations than his non-fictional country sketches, and the setting of the English countryside is integral to his storytelling. He only produced two children's stories during this decade. *Wild Lone* (1938) is the touching story of a fox and its risk-filled rustic life, whilst *Sky Gipsy* (1939) is a similarly realistic but affectionate tale of a wild goose. The vivid tale of Sky Gipsy starts in the Arctic with the hatching of four goslings, then their short but traumatic journey with the goose and gander from the river to a lake and the sad loss of one of them trapped on its back in a six inch crack in the ground. 'The tiny legs kicked more slowly as though the springs were running down. One leg stopped, then started again, one two, one two … one … two … one …… two. It stopped. The squeaks became feebler then ceased also, for it was a very tired little gosling and this life business was not a nice affair.'. One of the surviving goslings is Manka, The Sky Gipsy, and this beautifully written story describes his first flight 'It was a marvellous sensation, and he gloried in it.' The book traces the flight south to the fens of East Anglia and his subsequent battle for survival against 'Foxy' Fordham, a poacher.

Illustrated by the author.

Wild Lone. London, Eyre & Spottiswoode, and New York, Scribner, 1938.
Sky Gipsy: The Story of a Wild Goose. London, Eyre and Spottiswoode, 1939; as *Manka, The Sky Gipsy*, New York, Scribner, 1939.

Enid Bagnold (1889–1981). British.

Enid Bagnold was a playwright first and foremost, but she wrote two children's books, one of which was an enormous success. *National Velvet* (1935) is the story of a family's

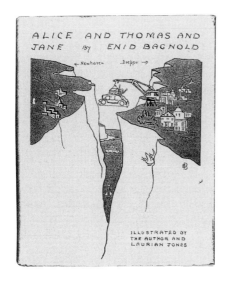

obsession with horses and how a little girl's fondest dream comes true. Young Velvet wins a horse in a raffle and then becomes determined to ride him in the Grand National. However, many hurdles have to be overcome before this wish can be fulfilled. Bagnold's first book, *Alice and Thomas and Jane* (1930), is more whimsical than *National Velvet*, which has great emotional depth. Thomas is eight, Jane seven and Alice five and they live in a village called Rottingdean. One day Thomas finds himself with no one to play with, since his sisters both have whooping cough, and so decides to have an adventure. He sails from Newhaven to Dieppe and then hides in a car. Unfortunately, he discovers himself being lowered by crane on to the dockside at Dieppe. Bagnold's own highly stylized dust wrapper, which is white, green, black and yellow, depicts this last scene.

Alice and Thomas and Jane, illustrated by the author and Laurian Jones. London, Heinemann, 1930; New York, Knopf, 1931.
National Velvet, illustrated by Laurian Jones. London, Heinemann, and New York, Morrow, 1935.

Helen Bannerman (1862–1946). British.

Illustrated by the author.

The Story of Sambo and the Twins. New York, Stokes, 1936; London, Nisbet, 1937.

Cicely Mary Barker (1895–1973). British.

Cicely Mary Barker's six *Flower Fairy* books, which were published between 1923 and 1948, consist of attractive verses and delightful, delicate pictures. The books revolve around the lives of various fairies, who are shown attired in the bright garb of different flowers, and are spiced by a great deal of country wisdom. Barker's passion for nature and her extensive knowledge of botany is evident in the loving detail lavished upon her artwork. She was also deeply religious and illustrated editions of Bible stories and hymn books. Barker's Christian convictions influenced her when writing *The Lord of the Rushie River* (1938), which is, in part, a morality tale. Young Susan is maltreated by Dame Dinnage, with whom she has been left whilst her father is away at sea. The little girl's single solace, and the source of the strength by which faith triumphs over affliction, is the swans. One swan, whose broken leg had been tended to by Susan's father when it was a cygnet, was now

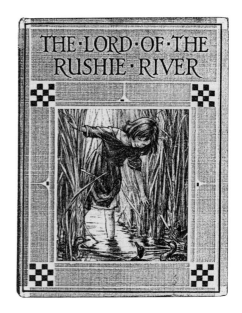

'a splendid swan'. As he sailed along, with his brothers, sisters and parents following behind, he seemed to be saying 'See me! I am the Lord of the Rushie River!' Susan is taken by Dame Dinnage to live in a city, but the girl hates it there. A swan flies over the city and carries Susan back to Rushiebanks, where she is happy. The swans and other birds look after her until a seagull brings news of her father's imminent return. This small book contains exquisite illustrations by the author, a good example of which is that reproduced on the front boards, detailing the scene in which 'Susan discovers where the wild duck had their home.' The attractive blue and white endpapers show John Swan carrying Susan away from the city. Every facet of this captivating book demonstrates this remarkable lady's affinity with all aspects of creation.

Illustrated by the author.

The Lord of the Rushie River. London, Blackie, 1938; New York, Hippocrene, 1977.

S(ydney) G(eorge) Hulme Beaman
(1886–1932). British.

S.G. Hulme Beaman's own dust wrapper illustration for *Wireless in Toytown* (1930)

shows many of the author's famous creations listening to a pronouncement by Ernest the Policeman. Larry the Lamb, Dennis the Dachshund, the Mayor of Toytown, the Inventor and the Magician are all present. The public message involves the mayor's imminent departure on a voyage on *The Mermaid*.

Illustrated by the author.

Wireless in Toytown. London, Collins, 1930.
The Toytown Mystery. London, Collins, 1932.
The Mayor's Sea Voyage. London, Collins, 1938.
Stories from Toytown. London, Oxford University Press, 1938.
The Arkville Dragon. London, Collins, 1938.

Alfred Bestall (1892–1986). British.

Alfred Bestall was entrusted with the daunting task of taking over the 'Rupert' stories from Mary Tourtel, after her retirement because of failing eyesight in 1935. Bestall's name became inseparable from that of Rupert , but he had supplied work for earlier children's works, most notably Enid Blyton's *The Play's the Thing!* (1927). Bestall's first year's work for the *Daily Express* was collated in *The New Adventures of Rupert* (1936), a special Christmas book. This was the beginning of the still

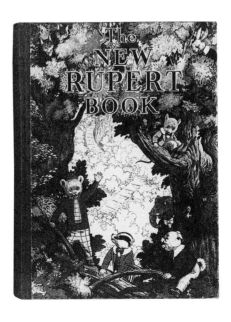

continuing 'Rupert' Annual. New advances in printing meant that red could be included in the book's colour scheme, and the result was Rupert's now familiar red sweater (he had been depicted previously in blue). *The New Rupert Book* (1938) was the third part of a series that was already becoming something of a tradition. The illustration on the front cover is taken from the story 'Rupert and Bill in the Tree Tops'. Rupert Bear, Bill Badger, Algy Pug, Edward Elephant and Willie Mouse are 'amazed to see a flight of steps winding through the upper branches of the trees.' The greatest threat to Rupert's continued existence was the Second World War. Although Rupert was not conscripted to battle with the Hun, paper shortages meant that there was a real threat that, like his arch rivals Teddy Tail and Pip, Squeak and Wilfred, the little bear's adventures would come to an end. However, thanks to the intervention of the *Express's* proprietor, it was decided that the 'Rupert' stories were an aid to the war effort and the bear was reprieved. Bestall removed by request some of the more fantastic elements from the tales, but introduced such fresh characters as Tiger Lily and the Chinese Conjuror, as well as developing Tourtel's original creations. Nutwood and its environs, as well as the many more exotic locations for Rupert's adventures, were in Alfred Bestall's safe hands for some thirty years.

Ilustrated by the author.

Boys and Girls Book (annual). London, Lane Publications, 4 vols., 1935–38.
Daily Express Rupert Annuals. London, Daily Express, 4 vols., 1936–39.

Enid Blyton (1897–1968). British.
a.k.a. Mary Pollock

The Secret Island (1938) is an important Enid Blyton book. It was her very first full length adventure book, and its success paved the way for the later "Famous Five", "Secret Seven" and "Adventure" series. Mike, Peggy, Nora and their friend Jack are shown on the book's dust jacket by I.M. loading their boat with baskets of mushrooms and strawberries to sell at market. The proceeds will allow them to stay on their newly discovered secret island.

Cheerio! A Book for Boys and Girls, illustrated by Molly Benatar. London, Birn, 1933.
Five Minute Tales. London, Methuen, 1933.
The Red Pixie Book, illustrated by Kathleen Nixon. London, Newnes, 1934.
Ten Minutes Tales: Twenty-Nine Varied Stories for Children. London, Methuen, 1934.
The Talking Teapot, illustrated by Peacock and Oxley. London, Johnston, 1934.
Hop, Skip and Jump. London. Johnston, 1934.
The Strange Tale of Mr Wumble, illustrated by MacDowell. London, Johnston, 1934.
The Button Elves. London, Johnston, 1935.
The Adventures of Bobs, illustrated by MacDowell. London, Johnston, 1935.
The Green Goblin Book, illustrated by Gordon Robinson. London, Newnes, 1935; shortened version, as *Feefo, Tuppeny and Jinks*, London, Staples Press 1951.
Hedgerow Tales, illustrated by V. Temple. London, Methuen, 1935.
Fifteen Minute Tales. London, Methuen, 1936.
The Famous Jimmy, illustrated by Benjamin Rabier. London, Muller, 1936; New York, Dutton, 1937.
The Yellow Fairy Book, (coloured frontispiece by H.R. Millar). London, Newnes, 1936.
Adventures of the Wishing Chair, illustrated by Hilda McGavin. London, Newnes, 1937.

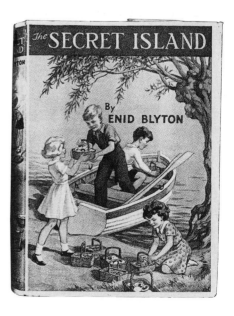

Billy-Bob Tales, illustrated by May Smith. London, Methuen, 1938.

Mr. Galliano's Circus, illustrated by E.H. Davie. London, Newnes, 1938.

The Secret Island, illustrated by E.H. Davie. Oxford, Blackwell, 1938.

Boys' and Girls' Circus Book, illustrated by Hilda McGavin. London, News Chronicle, 1939.

The Enchanted Wood, illustrated by Dorothy M. Wheeler. London, Newnes, 1939.

Hurrah for the Circus! Being Further Adventures of Mr. Galliano and His Famous Circus, illustrated by E.H. Davie. London, Newnes, 1939.

Naughty Amelia Jane!, illustrated by Sylvia I. Venus. London, Newnes, 1939.

All About the Circus, illustrated by D. Cuthill. London, Johnston, 1939.

Helen Dore Boylston (1895–1984). American.

Helen Dore Boylston wrote two series of books, giving an insightful and realistic appraisal of two professions, nursing and acting, which are often perceived as glamorous. In this decade, Boylston traced the career of Sue Barton, during her time as a trainee nurse and through various postings and promotions. The author had been a nurse herself and so the detail of Sue Barton's experiences in hospitals in Boston and New Hampshire came from personal observation. The stories are full of excitement, sometimes verging on melodrama, but also present a level-headed portrayal of nursing. Hookway Cowles' dust wrapper for the 1939 UK first edition of the initial book in the series, *Sue Barton, Student Nurse* (first published in the USA in 1936), shows novice nurse Sue Barton conversing with her future fiancé, Dr Bill Barry, in a busy hospital ward.

Sue Barton, Student Nurse, illustrated by Forrest Orr. Boston, Little Brown, 1936; illustrated by Hookway Cowles, London, Lane, 1939.

Sue Barton, Senior Nurse, illustrated by Forrest Orr. Boston, Little Brown, 1937; London, Lane, 1940.

Sue Barton, Visiting Nurse, illustrated by Forrest Orr. Boston, Little Brown, 1938; London, Lane, 1941.

Sue Barton, Rural Nurse, illustrated by Forrest Orr. Boston, Little Brown, 1939; London, Lane, 1942.

Angela Brazil (1869–1947). British.

The Little Green School, illustrated by Frank Wiles. London, Blackie, 1931.

Nesta's New School, illustrated by J. Dewar Mills. London, Blackie, 1932.

Jean's Golden Term, illustrated by Frank Wiles. London, Blackie, 1934.

The School at The Turrets. London, Blackie, 1935.

An Exciting Term, illustrated by Francis E. Hiley. London, Blackie, 1936.

Jill's Jolliest Term, illustrated by Francis E. Hiley. London, Blackie, 1937.

The School on the Cliff, illustrated by Francis E. Hiley. London, Blackie, 1938.

The School on the Moor, illustrated by Henry Coller. London, Blackie, 1939.

Elinor M(ay) Brent-Dyer (1894–1969). British.
a.k.a. E.M. Brent-Dyer.

The School by the River (1930) is the scarcest of all Elinor Brent-Dyer's books. It is not a 'Châlet School' book, and is one of only two Brent-Dyer volumes to have been published by Burns, Oates and Washbourne. The different publisher may also explain the unusual style of illustration by P.S. for the dust wrapper. Jennifer Craddock is unpacking with her new friends, Yolande and Mollie, at the College Des Musiciens in Mirania. Progress is interrupted by the entrance of unpleasant Emily, who wore 'a fussily-trimmed blue silk frock' and a 'discontented look'.

Eustacia Goes to the Châlet School, illustrated by Nina K. Brisley. Edinburgh, Chambers, 1930.

The School by the River, illustrated by P.S. London, Burns, Oates and Washbourne, 1930.

The Châlet School and Jo, illustrated by Nina K. Brisley. Edinburgh, Chambers, 1931.

The Feud in the Fifth Remove, illustrated by Ellis Silas. London, Religious Tract Society, 1931.

Janie of La Rochelle, illustrated by Percy Tarrant. Edinburgh, Chambers, 1932.

The Little Marie-José. London, Burns, Oates and Washbourne, 1932.

The Châlet Girls in Camp, illustrated by Nina K. Brisley. Edinburgh, Chambers, 1932.

The Exploits of the Châlet Girls, illustrated by Nina K. Brisley. Edinburgh, Chambers, 1933.

Carnation of the Upper Fourth, illustrated by Sutcliffe. London, Religious Tract Society, 1934.

The Châlet School and the Lintons, illustrated by Nina K. Brisley. Edinburgh, Chambers, 1934.

The New House at the Châlet School, illustrated by Nina K. Brisley. Edinburgh, Chambers, 1935.

Jo Returns to the Châlet School, illustrated by Nina K. Brisley. Edinburgh, Chambers, 1936.

Monica Turns Up Trumps, illustrated by L. Otway. London, Religious Tract Society, 1936.

Caroline the Second. London, Religious Tract Society, 1937.

The New Châlet School, illustrated by Nina K. Brisley. Edinburgh, Chambers, 1938.

They Both Liked Dogs. London, Religious Tract Society, 1938.

Molly Brett (1902–90). British.

Molly Brett's children's stories, which she herself attractively illustrated, have given immense pleasure to countless young children, as well as to the young at heart.

Her early books were published in a wide variety of formats. The first two plus Follow Me Round the Farm (1947) were large-sized books, whilst the other four early titles were small. Master Bunny the Baker's Boy (1950) is a strip book, in the Enid Blyton Mary Mouse series.

Molly Brett's first book The Little Garden (1936) is a story about a Japanese Garden with Ping Pong the gardener and Mah Jong who looks after the pets.

The Story of a Toy Car (1938) concerns the adventures of three wooden toys, Plain Jane, a little cat called Jet and the garage man. 'The most unlucky toy in the nursery was Plain Jane. Although small and certainly plain she always seemed to get into trouble.' The garage

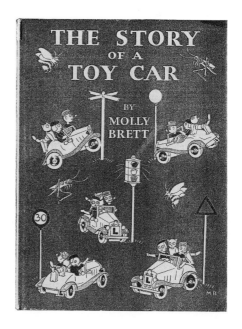

man repairs a battered clockwork motor car, J.O.B. 123. He, Jane and Jet have several adventures involving a collision with Jonah the tortoise, a country drive where they all end up in a pond and then drive down a rabbit hole into the Warren. Eventually Jane and the garage man get married and build a cottage to live in near a big by-pass where they help any small beast that strays among the traffic and gets lost or hurt. The mainly blue dustwrapper with its design is repeated on the book's cover.

Illustrated by the author.

The Little Garden. London, Warne, 1936.
The Story of a Toy Car. London, Warne, 1938.

Joyce Lankester Brisley (1896–1978). British.

Ilustrated by the author.

Further Doings of Milly-Molly-Mandy. London, Harrap, and New York, McKay, 1932.
The Dawn Shops and Other Stories. London, Harrap, and New York, McKay, 1933.
Marigold in Godmother's House. London, Harrap, 1934.
Bunchy. London, Harrap, and New York, McKay, 1937.

Dorita Fairlie Bruce (1885–1970). British.

Dorita Fairlie Bruce was justly famous for her prolific output of girls' school stories. She also wrote four historical novels, of which *The King's Curate* (1930) was the first. The dust wrapper by Iris Brooke depicts Patrick Mellish, the King's Curate, at a very personal moment. After a long enforced delay he proposes to Mistress Anne Carstairs. This is a suspenseful adventure set in seventeenth century Scotland.

The King's Curate. London, Murray, 1930.
The Best House in the School, illustrated by M.S. Reeve. London, Oxford University Press, 1930.

The Best Bat in the School. London, Oxford University Press, 1931.
The School on the Moor, illustrated by M.S. Reeve. London, Oxford University Press, 1931.
Captain of Springdale, illustrated by Henry Coller. London, Oxford University Press, 1932.
Mistress-Mariner. London, Murray, 1932.
Nancy at St. Bride's, illustrated by M.D. Johnston. London, Oxford University Press, 1933.
The New House at Springdale, illustrated by M.D. Johnston. London, Oxford University Press, 1934.
Nancy in the Sixth, illustrated by M.D. Johnston. London, Oxford University Press, 1935.
Dimsie Intervenes, illustrated by M.D. Johnston. London, Oxford University Press, 1937.
Nancy Returns to St. Bride's, illustrated by M.D. Johnston. London, Oxford University Press, 1938.
Prefects at Springdale, illustrated by M.D. Johnston. London, Oxford University Press, 1938.
Captain Anne, illustrated by M.D. Johnston. London, Oxford University Press, 1939.

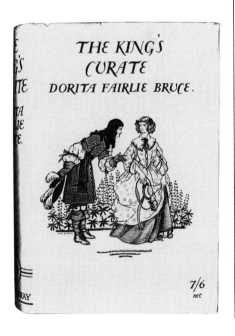

THE KING'S CURATE
DORITA FAIRLIE BRUCE.

7/6 net

Virginia Lee Burton (1909–68). American.

For main author article see 1940 to 1950.

Illustrated by the author.

Choo Choo: Story of a Little Engine Who Ran Away. Boston, Houghton Mifflin, 1937; London, Faber, 1944.
Mike Mulligan and His Steam Shovel. Boston, Houghton Mifflin, 1939; London, Faber, 1941.

Arthur Catherall (1906–80). British.
a.k.a. A.R. Channel.

Arthur Catherall wrote sixty-six stirring adventure books for boys under his real name and a further thirty-four under various pseudonyms between 1936 and his death in 1980. These hundred stories are set in a diverse variety of exotic locations that reflect the author's extensive travels all over the globe. The detail of description demonstrates that Catherall got to know his choice of setting intimately and employed the different places for reasons other than merely providing a glamorous façade for his adventures. Catherall always believed that he had a strong sense of responsibility towards his young audience. Consequently, his heroes are all clean-cut and upright citizens who would be positive rôle models. *Black Gold* (1939) is about rivalry between oil firms; oil is the 'black gold' of the title. The yellow and black dust wrapper by S. Drigin shows the hero Bill Meredith and his friend Val Mathews outside the former's oil-well.

Rod o' the Rail. London, Pearson, 1936.
The Rival Tugboats. London, Partridge, 1937.
Adventurer's Ltd. London, A. & C. Black, 1938.
Black Gold. London, Pearson, 1939.
Vanished Whaler, illustrated by S. Drigin. London, Nelson, 1939.

Christine Chaundler (1887–1972). British.

The principal characters of *Two in Form Four* (1931) by Christine Chaundler, show typical British schoolgirl pluck in the scene

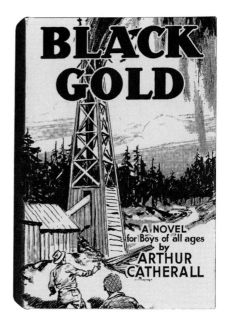

interpreted by P.B. Hickling on the book's wrapper. Marie Randall and Pat Desmond, two pupils at St. Agatha's School, rescue 'the girl in red', who is cut off in Smuggler's Bay. The distressed bathing belle seems made of softer stuff, '"Oh, I can't!" she said, shrinking back against the cliff. "I can never, never swim all that way".'

The Technical Fifth. London, Ward Lock, 1930.
A Disgrace to the Fourth, illustrated by M.D. Swales. London, Nelson, 1930.
The New Girl in Four A. London, Nisbet, 1930.
The Madcap in the School. London, Nelson, 1930.
Two in Form Four, illustrated by P.B. Hickling. London, Cassell, 1931.
The Junior Prefects, illustrated by J. Dewar. London, Ward Lock, 1931.
The Story-Book School, illustrated by V. Mills, London, Oxford University Press, 1931.
Jill of the Guides. London, Nisbet, 1932.
Five B and Evangeline. London, Newnes, 1932.
The Feud with the Sixth. London, Nisbet, 1932.
Cinderella Ann. London, Ward Lock, 1932.
The Amateur Patrol. London, Nisbet, 1933.

The Lonely Garden, and Ronald's Burglar.
London, Nelson, 1934.
Tale of Nicky-Nob. London, Chambers, 4
vols., 1937.
The Children's Story Hour, illustrated by
Alfred E. Kerr. London, Evans, 1938.

Joseph E(ugene) Chipperfield (1912–76).
British.

Joseph E. Chipperfield portrayed the
complete relationship between men and
animals at least as well as any other children's
author. His first book, *Two Dartmoor Interludes*
(1935), concentrated on life in his native West
Country, but his greatest successes came later
and from stories set further afield, such as his
popular narratives of horses and dogs and their
thrilling lives on the plains of North America.

Two Dartmoor Interludes. London, Boswell
Press, 1935.
An Irish Mountain Tragedy. London, Boswell
Press, 1936.
Three Stories (includes *Two Dartmoor Interludes,
An Irish Mountain Tragedy, The Ghosts from
Baylough*). London, Boswell Press, 1936.
*This Earth – My Home: A Tale of Irish
Troubles.* Dublin, Padraic O'Follain, 1937.

Catherine Christian (b. 1901). British.
a.k.a. Catherine Mary Christian.

For main author article see 1940 to 1950.

Cherries in Search of a Captain, illustrated by
Comerford Watson. London, Blackie,
1931.
The Legions Go North. London, Cassell, 1935.
The Wrong Uncle Jim, illustrated by A.J.
Charles. London, Arnold, 1935.
The Marigolds Make Good, illustrated by H.M.
Brock. London, Blackie, 1937.
Sidney Seeks Her Fortune. London, Blackie,
1937.
Baker's Dozen: Thirteen Stories for Girls.
London, Girl's Own Paper Office, 1937.
Bringing Up Nancy Nasturtium. London, Girl's
Own Paper Office, 1938.
A Schoolgirl From Hollywood. London, Blackie,
1939.

Mavis Thorpe Clark (b. 1912?). Australian.

For main author article see 1940 to 1950.

Hatherly's First Fifteen, illustrated by F.E.
Hiley. London, Oxford University Press,
1930.

Elizabeth Coatsworth (1893–1986).
American.

Elizabeth Coatsworth was one of the most
productive writers in the history of American
children's literature. She wrote just over
eighty novels for youngsters, but none of
them has been elevated to classic status.
Although some of her books feature the
supernatural or have a historical slant,
Coatsworth's principal objectives were to
capture successfully human emotions and to
gauge how humankind blends in with the rest
of nature. *Alice-all-by-Herself* (1937) is an early
example of Coatsworth's work. Like many of
Coatsworth's heroines, Alice lives in Maine.
The book tells of Alice's friendship with
Raymond, a young Red Indian, a family
picnic and a trip to Wiscasset, where Alice sits
in a chair which had belonged to Marie
Antoinette. The portrait of Alice carrying a

green book and a bunch of white flowers on the dust wrapper is by Marguerite de Angeli. The book's green front boards have depicted upon them the story's closing scene in which 'Alice took her book and climbed back into the crotch of her favourite apple tree.' The first edition was issued with attractive green and white endpapers showing the town Damariscotta.

The Boy with the Parrot, illustrated by Wilfred Bronson. New York, Macmillan, 1930.
The Cat Who Went to Heaven, illustrated by Lynd Ward. New York, Macmillan, 1930; London, Dent, 1949.
Knock at the Door, illustrated by F.D. Bedford. New York, Macmillan, 1931.
Cricket and the Emperor's Son, illustrated by Weda Yap. New York, Macmillan, 1932; revised edition, Kingswood, Surrey, World's Work, 1962.
Away Goes Sally, illustrated by Helen Sewell. New York, Macmillan, 1934; London, Woodfield, 1955.
The Golden Horseshoe, illustrated by Robert Lawson. New York, Macmillan, 1935; revised edition, as *Tamar's Wager*, London, Blackie, 1971.

Sword of the Wilderness, illustrated by Harve Stein. New York, Macmillan, 1936; London, Blackie, 1972.
Alice-all-by-Herself, illustrated by Marguerite de Angeli. New York, Macmillan, 1937; London, Harrap, 1938.
Dancing Tom, illustrated by Grace Paull. New York, Macmillan, 1938; London, Cambridge, 1939.
Five Bushel Farm, illustrated by Helen Sewell. New York, Macmillan, 1939; London, Woodfield, 1958.

Padraic Colum (1881-1972). Irish.

The White Sparrow, illustrated by Joseph Low. New York, Macmillan, 1933; as *Sparrow Alone*, London, Blackie, 1975.

Mrs H(enry) C. Cradock. British.

Elizabeth, illustrated by Doris Burton. London, Nelson, 1930.
Josephine Keeps House, illustrated by Honor C. Appleton. London, Blackie, 1931.
The Smith Family, illustrated by S.G. Hulme Beaman, London, Nelson, 1931.
Barbara And Peter, illustrated by Doris Burton. London, Nelson, 1931.
Adventures Of A Teddy Bear, illustrated by Joyce L. Brisley. London, Harrap, 1934.
More Adventure Of A Teddy Bear, illustrated by Joyce L. Brisley. London, Harrap, 1935.
In Teddy Bear's House, illustrated by Joyce L. Brisley. London, Harrap, 1936.
Josephine's Pantomine, illustrated by Honor C. Appleton. London, Blackie, 1939.
Teddy Bear's Shop, illustrated by Joyce L. Brisley. London, Harrap, 1939.

Richmal Crompton (1890–1969). British.

The dust wrapper by Thomas Henry for the first edition of Richmal Crompton's *Sweet William* (1936) is as scarce as that of *William* (see previous decade). The scene illustrated on the jacket is taken from the story 'William and the Perfect Child'. William 'borrows' a horse, and soon, as ever, his imagination is working overtime:

He took the reins, said 'Gee up', and – the grey horse began obediently to lumber across the field … A grubby little boy, perched on a saddle from which the stuffing was oozing at all points, on a large clumsy, untended horse of one of the less distinguished breeds, with three other little boys trotting at his heels. … Not so did William see himself. He was a King, surrounded by his bodyguard.

All illustrated by Thomas Henry.

William the Bad. London, Newnes, 1930.
William's Happy Days. London, Newnes, 1930.
William's Crowded Hours. London, Newnes, 1931.
William the Pirate. London, Newnes, 1932.
William the Rebel. London, Newnes, 1933.
William the Gangster. London, Newnes, 1934.
William the Detective. London, Newnes, 1935.
Sweet William. London, Newnes, 1936.
William the Showman. London, Newnes, 1937.
William the Dictator. London, Newnes, 1938.
William and A.R.P. London, Newnes, 1939; as *William's Bad Resolution*, 1956.
Just William: The Story of the Film. London, Newnes, 1939.

Primrose Cumming (b. 1915). British.

Primrose Cumming wrote about what she knew, and she did so very well. All of her books are about horses, but Cumming was a countrywoman to the core. Consequently, her stories cannot be dismissed merely as 'pony books'. They are a microcosm of English rural life from the early 1930s onward. Cumming's first literary work, *Doney, A Borderland Tale* (1934), was published when she was still only nineteen. It thus possesses all the enthusiasm of a genuine teenage horse fanatic. 'Doney', it hardly need be said, is a beast of the equine variety, and the 'Borderland' is not, as one might imagine, the country along the English/Scottish divide, but the area surrounding the border between Sussex and Kent, Cumming's county for her entire life. Allen W. Seaby illustrated Doney's adventures throughout in charcoal and provided a head and shoulders portrait of the noble animal for the book's dust wrapper. Although a notable horsewoman herself, Cumming realised that horses also had an important functional use. *Ben: the Story of a Cart-Horse* (1939) is a detailed examination of a working horse's life on a farm.

Doney, illustrated by Allen W. Seaby. London, Country Life, 1934.
Spider Dog, illustrated by Barbara Turner. London, Country Life, 1936.

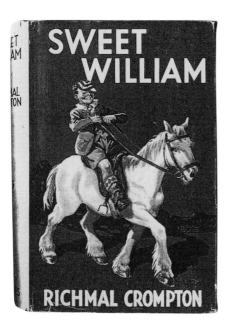

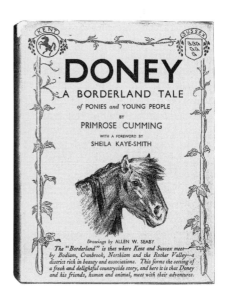

Silver Snaffles, illustrated by Stanley Lloyd. London, Blackie, and New York, Mill, 1937.

The Silver Eagle Riding School, illustrated by Cecil Trew. London, A. & C. Black, 1938.

Rachel of Romney, illustrated by Nina Scott Langley. London, Country Life, 1939; New York, Scribner, 1940.

The Wednesday Pony, illustrated by Stanley Lloyd. London, Blackie, and New York, Mill, 1939.

Ben: The Story of a Cart-Horse, photographs by Harold Burdekin. London, Dent, 1939; New York, Dutton, 1940.

Winifred Darch. British.

The Fifth Form Rivals, illustrated by Mary Strange Reeve. London, Oxford University Press, 1930.

The Lower Fourth and Joan, illustrated by M.D. Johnston. London, Oxford University Press, 1930.

Margaret Plays The Game, illustrated by E. Brier. London, Oxford University Press, 1931.

The Girl of Queen Elizabeth's, illustrated by M.D. Johnston. London, Oxford University Press, 1932.

The School on the Cliff, illustrated by M.D. Johnston. London, Oxford University Press, 1933.

The Head Girl at Wynford, illustrated by Reginald Mills. London, Oxford University Press, 1935.

Susan's Last Term, illustrated by Margaret Horder. London, Oxford University Press, 1936.

Elinor in the Fifth, illustrated by Margaret Horder. London, Oxford University Press, 1937.

The Scholarship and Margery, illustrated by Margaret Horder. London, Oxford University Press, 1938.

Alison Temple-Prefect, illustrated by Gilbert Dunlop. London, Oxford University Press, 1938.

The New Girl at Graychurch, illustrated by Gilbert Dunlop. London, Oxford University Press, 1939.

Peter Dawlish (1899–1963). British. Pseudonym for **James Lennox Kerr**. **a.k.a. Lennox Kerr.**

Peter Dawlish possessed an extensive knowledge of seafaring matters, gained during his time in the Royal Navy during the First World War. His stories are imbued with a love of the sea and a strong sense of the necessity to do one's duty. His first children's book, *The Blackspit Smugglers* (1938), was written as Lennox Kerr (actually closer to his real name, James Lennox Kerr). The well-known landscape artist, Rowland Hilder, furnished this book with an atmospheric dust wrapper. It shows the searchlight of the destroyer *Corinthian* illuminating the *Shark*, on board which are the smugglers of the title. Dawlish's most famous creation is Captain Peg-Leg, a redoubtable sea dog, who featured in four books during the Second World War. In the first, *Peg-Leg and the Fur Pirates* (1939), the captain takes his ship, the *Gleniffer*, into the Arctic ocean to find out why certain valuable cargoes of furs have never reached port.

The Blackspit Smugglers (as Lennox Kerr), illustrated by Rowland Hilder. London, Nelson, 1935.

The Eye of the Earth (as James Lennox Kerr),
   illustrated by F.P. Paterson. London,
   Nelson, 1936.
Peg-Leg and the Fur Pirates, illustrated by
   Norman Hepple. London, Oxford
   University Press, 1939.
Captain Peg-Leg's War, illustrated by J.D. Evans.
   London, Oxford University Press, 1939.

C(ecil) Day Lewis (1904–72). British.

C. Day Lewis is best known as a Poet
Laureate, a rôle he succeeded to after the
death of that other dabbler in children's
fiction, John Masefield, but was also detective
writer Nicholas Blake. However, he did
produce two children's books, the second of
which, *The Otterbury Incident* (1948), became
an undoubted classic of the genre. His first,
Dick Willoughby (1933), is an exciting
adventure yarn set in the sixteenth century.
Dick is the son of Sir Richard Willoughby, a
friend of Drake and Hawkins, who has retired
from the sea, much to the relief of the Spanish
captains who feared him. Dick lives at home
on his father's estate at Lyme Canonicorum,
Dorset, but then decides to pursue the family
trade. H.R. Millar's dust wrapper design
depicts Dick Willoughby, on the right in the

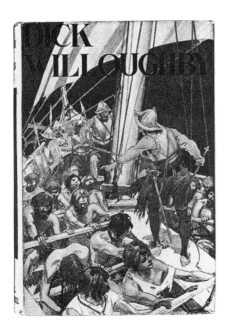

foreground, and his friend Martin plus two
other comrades, chained on a galley after their
capture from the *Retribution*: 'While up and
down the raised platform that bisected the
length of the vessel moved incessantly a
Spanish under officer, slashing at the weary
oarsmen, with a whip.'

Dick Willoughby, Oxford, Blackwell, 1933;
   New York, Random House, 1938.

Marguerite de Angeli (1889–1987). American.

The title of Marguerite de Angeli's first
children's book, *Ted and Nina Go to the Grocery
Store* (1935), may be less than inspirational, but
her particular brand of homespun storytelling
has always proved popular in America. She
portrays life in small town America
realistically, with all its petty interests and
aspirations, but somehow manages to make it
all vaguely attractive. Marguerite de Angeli
was also a fine illustrator of other children's
writers' work, such as that of Cornelia Meigs
and Elizabeth Coatsworth.

Illustrated by the author.

Ted and Nina Go to the Grocery Store. New
   York, Doubleday, 1935.
Ted and Nina Have A Happy Rainy Day. New
   York, Doubleday, 1936.
Henner's Lydia. New York, Doubleday, 1936;
   Kingswood, Surrey, World's Work, 1965.
Petite, Suzanne. New York, Doubleday,
   1937.
Copper-Toed Boots. New York, Doubleday,
   1938; Kingswood, Surrey, World's Work,
   1965.
Skippack School. New York, Doubleday,
   1939; Kingswood, Surrey, World's Work,
   1964.

Jean de Brunhoff (1899–1937). French.

Jean de Brunhoff is just one of a handful of
Continental children's writers who has
achieved success on this side of the Channel.
He introduces his much-loved elephantine
creation with the words, 'In the Great Forest a

little elephant was born. His name was Babar. His mother loved him dearly and used to rock him to sleep with her trunk, singing to him softly the while.' So begins Babar's literary life in *The Story of Babar, The Little Elephant* (1933), and his adventures reach such a height that at the end of the book Babar is crowned King and married to Celeste, 'Then King Babar and Queen Celeste set out on their honeymoon, in a glorious yellow balloon to meet new adventures.' The book is illustrated throughout by de Brunhoff's own jolly pictures, including a bowler hatted Babar for the orange front boards. The author's promise of further adventures was fulfilled by the appearance of a series of sequels to his original story. After his early death in 1937, de Brunhoff's son, Laurent, took over the series but these new stories lacked the original's flair.

Illustrated by the author.

The Story Of Babar, The Little Elephant. New York, Smith & Haas, 1933; London, Methuen, 1934.
The Travels Of Babar. New York, Smith & Haas, 1934; as *Babar's Travels.* London, Methuen, 1935.
Babar The King. New York, Smith & Haas, 1935; London, Methuen, 1936.

ABC Of Babar. New York, Random House, 1936; as *Babar's ABC.* London, Methuen, 1937.
Zephir's Holidays, New York, Random House, 1937; as *Babar's Friend Zephir.* London, Methuen, 1937.
Babar And His Children, New York, Random House, 1938; as *Babar At Home.* London, Methuen, 1938.

Olive Dehn (b. 1914). British.

Olive Dehn wrote a variety of types of children's books, progressing from lively fantasies through countryside adventures to a gruelling depiction of lower-class life in inner-city Manchester. *Tales of Sir Benjamin Bulbous, Bart.* (1935) was her first book and introduces a 'very rich, bad-tempered, mean, narrow-minded old Baronet.' Sir Benjamin is, however, changed for the better by the horse-like Kelpie, the naiad and other inhabitants of fairyland who visit the baronet's Lake District home, as portrayed on Harry Rountree's colourful dust wrapper.

Tales of Sir Benjamin Bulbous, Bart, illustrated by Harry Rountree. Oxford, Blackwell, 1935.
The Basement Bogle, illustrated by Harry Rountree. Oxford, Blackwell, 1935.

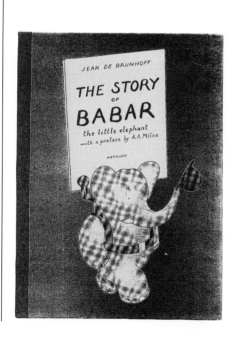

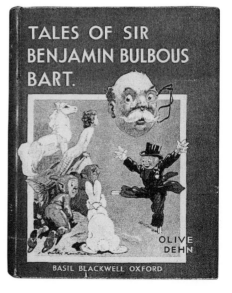

The Nixie from Rotterdam, illustrated by Harry Rountree. Oxford, Blackwell, 1937.

Tales of the Taunus Mountains, illustrated by Charles Folkard. Oxford, Blackwell, 1937.

The Well-Behaved Witch, illustrated by Frances Murray. Oxford, Blackwell, 1937.

Meindert De Jong (1906–91). American.

Meindert De Jong was an expert in portraying young children and their animal friends acutely. *The Big Goose and the Little White Duck* (1938) was her first foray into the literary world. Marguerite Buller's red and white dust wrapper shows the momentous occasion when 'The Little Old Lady and the goose and the duck went to look at the horses.' The goose and the duck are bought by a farmer's son for his father's birthday dinner. The animals survive by helping on the farm (for instance, the goose raises the alarm when the pig tries to escape) and become such institutions that consuming them would be tantamount to cannibalism.

The Big Goose and the Little White Duck, illustrated by Edna Potter and Marguerite Buller. New York, Harper, 1938; London, Heinemann, 1939.

Dirk's Dog Bello, illustrated by Kurt Wiese. New York, Harper, 1939; London, Lutterworth Press, 1960.

Walter de la Mare (1873–1956). British.

The Dutch Cheese and the Lovely Myfanwy, illustrated by Dorothy P. Lathrop. New York, Knopf, 1931.

The Lord Fish and Other Tales, illustrated by Rex Whistler. London, Faber, 1933.

Elizabeth Borton de Trevino (b. 1904). American.

Elizabeth Barton de Trevino's later works were generally set in the historical past, for instance Ancient Greece or seventeenth-century Spain, and contained a serious moral message in which violence and greed were denounced. Her earlier works were more frivolous – most notable was her continuation of the 'Polyanna' series from Eleanor H. Porter.

Pollyanna in Hollywood, illustrated by H. Weston Taylor. Boston, Page, 1931.

Our Little Aztec Cousin of Long Ago, Being the Story of Coyotl and How He Won Honor under His Kings, illustrated by Harold Cue. Boston, Page, 1934.

Pollyanna's Castle in Mexico, illustrated by Harold Cue. Boston, Page, 1934.

Our Little Ethiopian Cousin: Children of the Queen of Sheba. Boston, Page, 1935.

Pollyanna's Door to Happiness, illustrated by Harold Cue. Boston, Page, 1936.

Pollyanna's Golden Horseshoe, illustrated by Griswold Tyng. Boston, Page, 1939.

V(iolet) H(ilda) Drummond (b. 1911). British.

V.H. Drummond illustrated all of her stories for younger children herself and later wrote the 'Little Laura' series of books, which were commissioned for the BBC's *Children's Hour* programme. *Phewtus the Squirrel* (1939) was originally composed for Drummond's own son and is the story of a stuffed squirrel with a large heart. Phewtus is Julian's favourite toy and King of the Nursery until, on one woeful day, Ralph the Rabbit, attired in a natty purple dressing gown, appears on the scene. Unfortunately, the rabbit turns out to be proud, greedy and unkind. He desperately tries to seize power in the Nursery but his tyrannical advances are rebuffed by the other toys, who all preferred the squirrel. Phewtus, the King in exile, teams up with a real squirrel (with chestnuts as his only stuffing) and has an adventure with a little help from a magic sycamore twig.

Illustrated by the author.

Phewtus the Squirrel. London and New York, Oxford University Press, 1939.

William Pène du Bois (1916–93). American.

William Pène du Bois specialised in the surreal. This can possibly best be understood through the citation of the dust wrapper flap for *Giant Otto* (1936), the first of du Bois's five books about the oversize canine.

> Otto was an Otterhound, and he was *so* big that, when he wagged his tail, trees bent to the ground from the wind. So his master, who was called Duke, decided that he would have to find some place that was really big enough for Otto!
>
> That is how they happened to go to the Sahara Desert.
> That is why Duke became a legionnaire, and Otto fought against the Arabs.

And it was there that a handsome medal was awarded Otto for 'extraordinary bravery in the face of danger.'

The book was illustrated by du Bois himself, and the dust jacket illustration finds Otto marching behind a legionnaire in the desert.

Illustrated by the author.

Elizabeth, The Cow Ghost. New York, Nelson, 1936; London, Museum Press, 1944.
Giant Otto. New York, Viking Press, 1936; London, Harrap, 1937.
Otto at Sea. New York, Viking Press, 1936; London, Harrap, 1937.
The Three Policemen; or, Young Bottsford of Farbe Island. New York, Viking Press, 1938.

Elizabeth Enright (1909–68). American.

Elizabeth Enright's work skilfully captures the spirit of America from the time of the great depression until the 1960s. Enright's final books were fairy tales, and there is also the barest whiff of magic in one of her earliest, and seemingly most down-to-earth, stories, *Thimble Summer* (1938). A few hours after

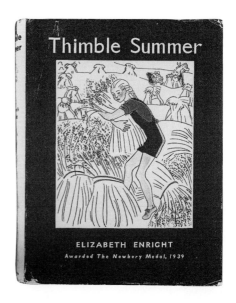

Thimble Summer
ELIZABETH ENRIGHT
Awarded The Newbery Medal, 1939

Garnet Linden finds a silver thimble in a river bed, the rains come to end a long period of drought on the farm. The crops are preserved and much-needed money floods in for Garnet's father. The thimble becomes a talisman. Enright's own dust-wrapper illustration shows Garnet, dressed in red and blue, being a gem and helping Jay and Eric to stack the trussed up yellow oat bundles in shocks.

Illustrated by the author.

Kintu: A Congo Adventure. New York, Farrar & Rinehart, 1935.
Thimble Summer. New York, Farrar & Rinehart, 1938; London, Heinemann, 1939.

Evelyn Everett-Green (1856–1932). British.
a.k.a. E. Everett-Green.
a.k.a. Cecil Adair.

Tall Chimneys. London, Stanley Paul, 1931.
The Squire's Daughter. London, Stanley Paul, 1932.
Under the Old Oaks. London, Pickering & Inglis, 1933.

Eleanor Farjeon (1881–1965). British.

Westwoods, illustrated by May Smith. Oxford, Blackwell, 1930.
The Old Nurse's Stocking Basket, illustrated by E. Herbert Whydale. London, University of London Press, and New York, Stokes, 1931.
Perkin the Pedlar, illustrated by Clare Leighton. London, Faber, 1932.
Katy Kruse at the Seaside; or, The Deserted Islanders. London, Harrap, and Philadelphia, McKay, 1932.
Ameliaranne's Prize Packet, illustrated by S.B. Pearse. London, Harrap, 1933; as *Ameliaranne and the Magic Ring*, Philadelphia, McKay, 1933.
Pannychis, illustrated by Clare Leighton. Shaftesbury, Dorset, High House Press, 1933.

Ameliaranne's Washing Day, illustrated by S.B. Pearse. London, Harrap, and Philadelphia, McKay, 1934.
Jim at the Corner and Other Stories, illustrated by Irene Mountfort. Oxford, Blackwell, 1934; as *The Old Sailor's Yarn Box*, New York, Stokes, 1934.
The Clumber Pup, illustrated by Irene Mountfort. Oxford, Blackwell, 1934.
And I Dance Mine Own Child, illustrated by Irene Mountfort. Oxford, Blackwell, 1935.
Jim and the Pirates, illustrated by Roger Naish. Oxford, Blackwell, 1936.
Martin Pippin in the Daisy-Field, illustrated by Isobel and John Morton-Sale. London, Joseph, 1937; New York, Stokes, 1938.
One Foot in Fairyland: Sixteen Tales, illustrated by Robert Lawson. London, Joseph, and New York, Stokes, 1938.

Charles J(oseph) Finger (1869–1941). American.

The Magic Tower, illustrated by Helen Finger. New York, Kings Arms Press, 1933.
A Dog at His Heel, illustrated by Henry Pitz. Philadelphia, Winston, 1936; London, Harrap, 1937.
When Guns Thundered in Tripoli, illustrated by Henry Pitz. New York, Holt, 1937.
Bobbie and Jock and the Mailman, illustrated by Helen Finger. New York, Holt, 1938.
Give a Man a Horse, illustrated by Henry Pitz. Philadelphia, Winston, 1938; London, Harrap, 1939.
Cape Horn Snorter, illustrated by Henry Pitz. Boston, Houghton Mifflin, 1939.

Marjorie Flack (1897–1958). American.

Marjorie Flack wrote and illustrated simple but enthralling picture books for young children. *Angus and the Ducks* (1930) is the first in a trilogy of stories about a black Scottie dog.

> Once there was a very young little dog whose name was Angus, because his mother and father came from Scotland.

Although the rest of Angus was quite small, his head was very large and so were his feet.

Angus' natural inquisitiveness leads him to investigate curious noises on the other side of a large green hedge. There he finds, as the book's title and dust wrapper foretell, some ducks. Unfortunately for the wee pup, he finds himself outnumbered!

Illustrated by the author unless otherwise stated.

Angus and the Ducks. New York, Doubleday, 1930; London, Lane, 1933.

Angus and the Cat. New York, Doubleday, 1931; London, Lane, 1933.

Angus Lost. New York, Doubleday, 1932; London, Lane, 1933.

Ask Mr. Bear. New York, Macmillan, 1932.

The Story about Ping, illustrated by Kurt Wiese. New York, Viking Press, 1933; London, Lane, 1935.

Wag-Tail Bess. New York, Doubleday, 1933; as *Angus and Wag-Tail Bess,* London, Lane, 1935.

Tim Tadpole and the Great Bullfrog. New York, Doubleday, 1934.

Humphrey: One Hundred Years Along the Wayside with a Box Turtle, New York, Doubleday, 1934.

Christopher. New York, Scribner, 1935.

Topsy. New York, Doubleday, 1935; as *Angus and Topsy,* London, Lane, 1935.

Up in the Air, illustrated by Karl Larsson. New York, Macmillan, 1935.

Wait for William. Boston, Houghton Mifflin, 1935.

What to Do about Molly, illustrated by the author and Karl Larsson. Boston, Houghton Mifflin, 1936; London, Lane, 1938.

Willy Nilly. New York, Macmillan, 1936; London, Lane, 1939.

Lucky Little Lena. New York, Macmillan, 1937.

The Restless Robin. Boston, Houghton Mifflin, 1937.

Walter, The Lazy Mouse. New York, Doubleday, 1937; Edinburgh, Chambers, 1964.

William and His Kitten. Boston, Houghton Mifflin, 1938; London, Lane, 1939.

Angus and the Ducks BY MARJORIE FLACK

Rose Fyleman (1877–1957). British.

The Dolls' House, illustrated by Margaret
Tempest. London, Methuen, 1930; New
York, Doubleday, 1931.
The Katy Kruse Play Book, illustrated by Katy
Kruse. London, Harrap, and Philadelphia,
McKay, 1930.
The Strange Adventures of Captain Marwhopple,
illustrated by Gertrude Lindsay. London,
Methuen, 1931; New York, Doubleday,
1932.
The Easter Hare and Other Stories, illustrated
by Decie Merwin. London, Methuen,
1932.
Jeremy Quince, Lord Mayor of London, illustrated
by Cecil Leslie. London, Cape, 1933.
The Princess Dances, illustrated by Cecil Leslie.
London, Dent, 1933.

Wanda Gág (1893–1946). American.

Illustrated by the author.

Snippy and Snappy. New York, Coward
McCann, 1931; London, Faber, 1932.
The ABC Bunny. New York, Coward
McCann, 1933; London, Faber, 1962.

Eve Garnett (1900–91). British.

Eve Garnett was primarily a professional artist,
but *The Family from One End Street* (1937)
achieved something approaching notoriety in
the world of children's fiction. A passionate
attack on the evils of inner-city existence, it
was rejected by numerous publishers before
Muller accepted it. The struggles of the
Ruggles family still have resonances for
today's society. *The Family from One End Street*
is much more than an attack on slum housing
conditions, however. The family, particularly
the parents, are memorably life-like people
who cope with their very real difficulties
chiefly with love and humour.

Illustrated by the author.

*The Family from One End Street and Some of
Their Adventures*. London, Muller, 1937;
New York, Vanguard Press, 1939.

Doris Gates (1901–87). American.

For main author article see 1940 to 1950.

Sarah's Idea, illustrated by Marjorie Torrey.
New York, Viking Press, 1938; London,
Muller, 1947.

Charles Gilson (1878–1943). British.
a.k.a. C(harles) L(ouis) Gilson.
a.k.a. Major Charles Gilson.
a.k.a. Captain Charles GIlson.

The Substitutes (1935) is an interesting example
of Captain Gilson's work, since it is a change
from his familiar brand of adventure stories.
Although Harold Avery was still going strong,
The Substitutes is one of the few traditional
boys' public school stories produced in this
decade. H.M. Brock's jubilant dust wrapper
design shows Dick Wayne being carried aloft
by his euphoric supporters after cracking a six
into the pavilion. Success is made sweeter by
the fact that it was the odiously over-
confident Ronald Symes who sent down the
fateful 'atrocious long hop'.

The Wizard of the Woods. London, Newnes,
1931.
Forest Treasure, illustrated by T. Cuneo.
London, R. Tuck, 1932.
The Ghost Mountain. London, Newnes, 1932.
The Brigand of the Hills. London, Newnes,
1933.
The Forest King. London, Newnes, 1934.
Raja Dick. London, Oxford University Press,
1934.
Taboo: A story of Mysterious Africa. London,
Warne, 1934.
The Twelfth Man. London, Warne, 1934.
The Cunning of Quang. London, Oxford
University Press, 1935.
The Refugee. London, Warne, 1935.
The Substitutes, illustrated by H.M. Brock.
London, Warne, 1935.
*The War Path and the Creator of Terrors: Two
Adventure Stories*. London, Hutchinson,
1936.
Wolfskin. London, Warne, 1936.
Congo Chains. London, Warne, 1937.
The Adventures of Cornet Michael O'Dare.
London, Boy's Own Paper, 1938.

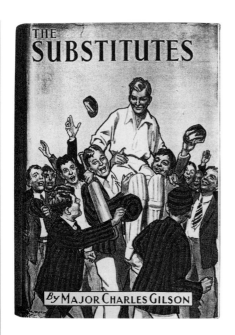

The Bronze Casket: A tale of the air. London, Warne, 1938.

Through the Boxer Lines: A tale of the Boxer Rebellion. London, Arnold, 1938.

The Silent Trail. London, Warne, 1939.

R(obert) A(rthur) H(anson) Goodyear (1877–1948). British.

All Out for the School. London, Sampson Low, 1930.

The Grammar School at Hotspurs. London, J.F. Shaw, 1930.

Tringle of Harlech. London, Ward Lock, 1930.

School Before All. London, J.F. Shaw, 1931.

Something Like a Chum. London, Sampson Low, 1932.

Rivals at St. John's. London, Collins, 1933.

The Old Golds: A romance of football. London, Lincoln Williams, 1934.

The Isle of Sheer Delight. London, J.F. Shaw, 1935.

The Captain of Glendale. London, S.W. Partridge, 1935.

Pulling Templestone Together. London, Sampson Low, 1936.

The School's Airmen. London, Ward Lock, 1936.

Tudorvale Colours. London, Sampson Low, 1936.

The Broom and Heather Boys: A public school story. London, Ward Lock, 1937.

Fenshaven Finds its Feet: A public school story, illustrated by Francis E. Wiley. London, Ward Lock, 1938.

Parry Wins Through. London, Sampson Low, 1938.

Elizabeth Goudge (1900–84). British.

Sister of the Angels: A Christmas Story, illustrated by C. Walter Hodges. London, Duckworth, and New York, Coward McCann, 1939.

Eleanor Graham (1896–1984). British.

Eleanor Graham was a successful editor of children's books for various publishers and founder of Puffin Books. She also wrote a small number of books herself. *The Children Who Lived in a Barn* (1938) concentrated on the self-sufficiency of children when faced with the apparent loss of their parents in an air crash. *Six in a Family* (1935) is a slightly more conventional tale of the Rose children, Dick, Jane, Bill, Marty, John and Lucy, who are avid tobogganists. They, as Alfred Sindall's dust wrapper picture and the

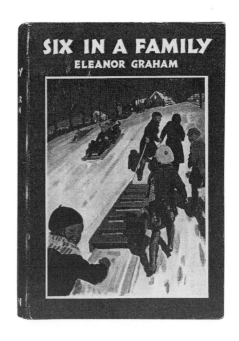

author's description reveal, are not the only locals who are thus inclined: 'the Plain swarmed with families trailing behind them every kind of sledge and toboggan.'

Six in a Family, illustrated by Alfred Sindall. London, Nelson, 1935.
The Children Who Lived in a Barn, illustrated by J.T. Evans. London, Routledge, 1938.

Hardie Gramatky (1907–79). American.

Hardie Gramatky is best known for his creation of a plucky tugboat in *Little Toot* (1939) and its four sequels. Little Toot could be said to represent the little people in society, who battle bravely against adversity and injustice. Besides the portrayal of this universal truth and encouragement, the 'Little Toot' books give an accurately detailed insight into life on the major rivers of the world. An added attraction is the presence of Gramatky's own brightly coloured paintings that punctuate the text at regular intervals.

Illustrated by the author.

Little Toot. New York, Putnam, 1939; London, Dent, 1946.

Roderick Haig-Brown (1908–76). Canadian.
a.k.a. R.L. Haig-Brown.

R. L. Haig-Brown wrote in detail about the waters and wild places of Canada, whither he had emigrated from England in 1926. *Ki-Yu: A Story of Panthers* (1934) is the story of a noble panther and the hostile elements, both animal and human, that threaten him. This struggle for survival and supremacy is played out before the background of the beautiful west coast of Vancouver Island. *Silver: The Life-Story of an Atlantic Salmon* (1931) is a loving recreation of oceanic life. The bright blue, green and cream wrapper by Captain J. P. Moreton shows Silver and fishy friends in the Atlantic.

Silver: The Life-Story of an Atlantic Salmon, illustrated by J.P. Moreton. London, A. & C. Black, 1931.

Ki-yu: A Story of Panthers, illustrated by Kurt Wiese. Boston, Houghton Mifflin, 1934; as *Panther*, London, Cape, 1934.

J(ohn) B(urden) S(anderson) Haldane (1892–1964). Indian.

J. B. S. Haldane was one of the most eminent scientists of this century and his single contribution to children's fiction, *My Friend Mr Leakey* (1937), one of the most brilliant. Mr Leakey is a magician who appears in three of the short stories in this collection: 'A Meal with a Magician', 'A Day in the Life of a Magician' and 'Mr Leakey's Party'. Each story reaches almost Olympic heights of dottiness as Haldane casually introduces all the advantages of wizardry. These include the ability to enjoy strawberries out-of-season (something a modern reader might take for granted) and to metamorphose over-eager party guests. The striking cover design by Leonard H. Roseman is in dark brown, white, yellow and pink, with two-thirds of the wrapper flecked with pink. The illustration is a montage of characters from the nine short stories. These are linked by the common theme of magic, and are bestowed with such enticing titles as 'The Snake with the

135

Golden Teeth'. Mr Leakey is pictured with his magic top hat and wand and Pompey, the fire-breathing dragon. Whispering in the magician's ear is Abdu'l Makkar, a jinn.

My Friend Mr. Leakey, illustrated by Leonard Rosoman. London, Cresset Press, 1937; New York, Harper, 1938.

Kathleen Hale (b. 1898). British.

Kathleen Hale wrote and illustrated nineteen books about a now famous feline. This is how she introduced him in *Orlando, the Marmalade Cat: A Camping Holiday* (1938):

> Orlando was very beautiful, striped like marmalade and the same colour, his eyes reminded you of twin green goose-berries. He and his wife Grace had three kittens: Pansy the tortoiseshell, the white Blanche and coal-black Tinkle.

So begins the book. It is not long before Orlando and his family are off on their camping holiday, and the reader is immersed in Hale's idiosyncratic, humanized pussycat-filled paradise. Hale based her leading player on her own ginger tom called Orlando and the books are ideal for reading aloud to young children. The dust wrapper for the original large sized

'Orlando' book shows the Marmalade Cat strumming a guitar before a green background.

Illustrated by the author.

Orlando, The Marmalade Cat: A Camping Holiday. London, Country Life, and New York, Scribner, 1938.
Orlando, The Marmalade Cat: A Trip Abroad. London, Country Life, 1939.

Cynthia Harnett (1893–1981). British.

Cynthia Harnett enjoyed virtually two different careers as a writer of children's fiction. She began her career composing and illustrating animal stories with her long-standing friend G. Vernon Stokes, with whom she had studied at the Chelsea School of Art. After 1950 Harnett turned to the fashioning of highly detailed and painstakingly researched historical novels in which exciting adventures are blended with authentic period detail.

Velvet Masks, illustrated by G. Vernon Stokes. London, Medici Society, 1937.
The Pennymakers, with G. Vernon Stokes, illustrated by the authors. London, Eyre & Spottiswoode, 1937.

Junk, The Puppy, with G. Vernon Stokes,
  illustrated by the authors. London,
  Blackie, 1937.
Banjo, The Puppy, with G. Vernon Stokes,
  illustrated by the authors. London,
  Blackie, 1938.

Constance Heward (1884–1968). British.

*Tommy's Little Grains of Sand and Other
  Stories*. London, Sheldon Press, 1930.
Benjy Comes. London, Wells Gardner, 1931.
Grandpa Nog and the Nimblies, illustrated by
  Muriel Gill. London, Harrap, and
  Philadelphia, McKay, 1937.
Billety Bill and the Big Brown Bear, illustrated
  by Muriel Gill. London, Harrap, and
  Philadelphia, McKay, 1937.
Ameliaranne at the Farm, illustrated by S.B.
  Pearse. London, Harrap, and Philadelphia,
  McKay, 1937.
Ameliaranne Gives a Christmas Party, illustrated
  by S.B. Pearse. London, Harrap, and
  Philadelphia, McKay, 1938.
Ameliaranne Camps Out, illustrated by S.B.
  Pearse. London, Harrap, and Philadelphia,
  McKay, 1939.

C(yril) Walter Hodges (b. 1909). British.

C. Walter Hodges was a fine illustrator of
many books, including those written by
himself. Examples of his work shown in this
book are *King Richard's Land* by L.A.G. Strong
(1933), *Smoky-House* by Elizabeth Goudge
(1940), and *Flight to Adventure* by Ian Serraillier
(1947). C. Walter Hodges is also a notable
historical novelist writing for children about
the times of King Alfred, Columbus and
Shakespeare. In his first book, *Columbus Sails*
(1939), the different stages of Christopher
Columbus's first voyage to the New World are
told by three different people. The preparation
and departure are described by a monk, Father
Antonio de la Vega; the voyage and arrival by
a sailor, Miguel Pericas; and the triumphant
return of the Admiral by an Indian, Coatta.
The sea-green dust wrapper painted by the
author shows the three caravels, the Santa
Maria, the Pinta and the Nina.

Illustrated by the author.

Columbus Sails. London, Bell, and New
  York, Coward McCann, 1939.

Edith Howes (1874–1954). New Zealander.

The Golden Forest, illustrated by Margaret Lee
  Thompson. London, Dent, 1930.
Mrs. Kind Bush, illustrated by Anne
  Anderson. London, Cassell, 1933.

Richard Hughes (1900–76). British.

Richard Hughes' most famous and lasting
contribution to English literature was *A High
Wind In Jamaica* (1929), which, although
containing a perceptive study of the child's
psyche, was an adult novel. Hughes delighted
in playing with literary and linguistic
conventions (witness his literal interpretation
of some of the English language's dottier
sayings), and the second of his six children's
books, *The Spider's Palace* (1931), is full of the
weird and wonderful. George Charlton's
green and white wrapper depicts numerous
scenes from the twenty short stories that
comprise the collection. Among other figures

on the montage are the little girl from Liverpool who was never seen again, the gardener who encounters a white elephant, the dark child and the china spaniel.

Burial, and The Dark Child (verse and story). Privately printed, 1930.
The Spider's Palace and Other Stories, illustrated by George Charlton. London, Chatto & Windus, 1931; New York, Harper, 1932.

Katharine Hull (1921–77) & Pamela Whitlock (1920–82). British.

Katharine Hull's first book, *The Far-Distant Oxus* (1937), caused something of a commotion when it was first published. This was mainly because its author was a sixteen-year-old schoolgirl and her collaborator, on this and all other books, Pamela Whitlock, was only a year older. *The Far-Distant Oxus* tells of six children's adventures on Exmoor and their momentous journey down the 'Oxus' by raft. It employs the still fresh formula of gripping hols without adults that would become Enid Blyton's stock in trade.

Illustrated by Pamela Whitlock.

The Far-Distant Oxus. London, Cape, 1937; New York, Mcmillan, 1938.
Escape to Persia. London, Cape, 1938; New York, Macmillan, 1939.
Oxus in Summer. London, Cape, 1939; New York, Macmillan, 1940.

Norman Hunter (1899–1995). British.

Norman Hunter wrote several adventures about the eccentric King and Queen of Incrediblania, but it is his fifteen books about the zany inventor Professor Branestawm, that have ensured his literary immortality. Professor Branestawm is a most learned gentleman, a fact substantiated by his remarkably high 'philosopher's' forehead. This noble pate is also needed to make room for all the different pairs of glasses he wears (a different pair for reading, for writing, for out of doors, for looking over the top and for searching for the other pairs when they are mislaid). He is, like all true geniuses, chronically absent-minded and keeps losing a book called, 'The Life and Likings of a Lobster'. The frontispiece of *Stories of Professor Branestawm* (1939), which was rather surprisingly first issued as a paperback, is by the illustrious W. Heath Robinson and shows the creative academic at his most destructive:

> The Professor wasn't much good at riding bicycles and he ran into three carts, seven lampposts, a pond, and several policemen before he got to the library at North Pagwell, which was next on the list.
>
> And when he did get to the library he couldn't stop, and went whizzing straight inside, scattering all sorts of studious looking people about all over the floor.

W. Heath Robinson also illustrated *The Incredible Adventures of Professor Branestawm* (1933).

Jingle Tales, illustrated by Gordon Robinson. London, Warne, 1930.
The Bad Barons of Crashbania, illustrated by Eve Garnett. Oxford, Blackwell, 1932.
The Incredible Adventures of Professor Branestawm, illustrated by W. Heath Robinson. London, Lane, 1933.

'He went whizzing straight inside'—*Page 24*

Professor Branestawm's Treasure Hunt and Other Incredible Adventures, illustrated by James Arnold. London, Lane, 1937.

Larky Legends, illustrated by James Arnold. London, Lane, 1938; abridged edition, as

The Dribblesome Teapots and Other Incredible Stories, London, Bodley Head, 1969.

Stories of Professor Branestawm, illustrated by W. Heath Robinson. Leeds, Arnold, 1939.

W(illiam) E(arl) Johns (1893–1968). British.
a.k.a. William Earle.
a.k.a. Captain W.E. Johns.

W.E. Johns made an indelible mark on children's fiction by creating three legendary figures of adventure stories: Biggles, Gimlet and Worrals. Johns served in the Royal Flying Corps from 1917 until 1929, and it was to these experiences he turned when he created an aeronautical hero in 1932 for his *Popular Flying*, the aviation magazine he edited. The adventures of Major James Bigglesworth, D.S.O., M.C. proved so popular that seventeen stories appeared in book form at the end of this year under the title *The Camels are Coming*. Controversy has surrounded the first edition of this book, with some sources alleging that it was written under the pseudonym William Earle. However, the only name on the dust wrapper is that of W.E. Johns, and the title-page mentions the alias only as an afterthought. This was done because Johns wrote his fiction stories for *Popular Flying* as Earle, and presumably the readers wanted to be reassured that their favourite author was responsible for the entire collection as well. Nevertheless, Johns never wrote a 'Biggles' book under anything except his own name. The second volume, a novel rather than a collection of short stories, *The Cruise of the Condor* (1933), pits the slim, clean shaven, upright, boyish faced, steady, grey eyed air ace against a band of treasure seeking gangsters in post-war South America. Howard Leigh's lavishly coloured illustration for this book's dust wrapper shows the amphibian 'The Condor' coming into land on the smooth water of a South American lake,

watched with some interest by a pair of natives. The early 'Biggles' books are rare in dust wrapper and therefore highly sought after by collectors. There were ninety-seven 'Biggles' books in all, the last thrilling adventure of Biggles, Algy and Ginger not being published until 1970.

A lesser known series character is "Steeley", the aristocratic air ace Deeley Montfort Delaroy, who after the First World War, uses his flying skills to be a successful air smuggler and later an unofficial police agent. Unlike Biggles, Steeley is not a conventional, clean cut hero, but introverted and sometimes morally ambiguous. He is joined in his adventures by his old comrades Eric "Tubby" Wilde and Brian Ballantyne. The "Steeley" books were actually written for an adult audience, but are equally suitable for teenagers.

The Camels Are Coming, illustrated by Howard Leigh. London, John Hamilton, 1932.

The Cruise of the Condor: A Biggles Story, illustrated by Howard Leigh. London, John Hamilton, 1933.

The Spy Flyers, illustrated by Howard Leigh. London, John Hamilton, 1933.

Biggles of the Camel Squadron, illustrated by Howard Leigh. London, John Hamilton, 1934.

Biggles Flies Again. London, John Hamilton, 1934.

Biggles Learns to Fly. London, Boys' Friend Library, 1935.

Biggles Flies East, illustrated by Howard Leigh and Alfred Sindall. London, Oxford University Press, 1935.

Biggles Hits the Trail, illustrated by Howard Leigh and Alfred Sindall. London, Oxford University Press, 1935.

Biggles in France. London, Boys' Friend Library, 1935.

The Black Peril: A Biggles Story, illustrated by Howard Leigh. London, John Hamilton, 1935; as *Biggles Flies East* (not same as 1935 book), London, Boys' Friend Library, 1938.

Biggles in Africa, illustrated by Howard Leigh and Alfred Sindall. London, Oxford University Press, 1936.

Biggles & Co., illustrated by Howard Leigh
and Alfred Sindall. London, Oxford
University Press, 1936.
Sky High: A "Steeley" Adventure, London,
Newnes, 1936.
Steeley Flies Again, London, Newnes, 1936.
Murder by Air: A "Steeley" Adventure.
London, Newnes, 1937.
Biggles—Air Commodore, illustrated by
Howard Leigh and Alfred Sindall.
London, Oxford University Press, 1937.
Biggles Flies West, illustrated by Howard
Leigh and Alfred Sindall. London, Oxford
University Press, 1937.
Biggles Flies South, illustrated by Howard
Leigh and Jack Nicolle. London, Oxford
University Press, 1938.
Biggles Goes to War, illustrated by Howard
Leigh and Martin Tyas. London, Oxford
University Press, 1938.
Champion of the Main, illustrated by H.
Gooderman. London, Oxford University
Press, 1938.
*Murder at Castle Deeping: A "Steeley"
Adventure.* London, John Hamilton, 1938.
Wings of Romance: A "Steeley" Adventure.
London, Newnes, 1938.
Biggles Flies North, illustrated by Howard
Leigh and Will Narraway. London,
Oxford University Press, 1939.

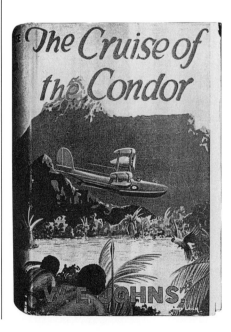

Biggles in Spain, illustrated by Howard Leigh
and J. Abbey. London, Oxford University
Press, 1939.
The Rescue Flight: A Biggles Story, illustrated
by Howard Leigh and Alfred Sindall.
London, Oxford University Press, 1939.

Erich Kästner (1899–1974). German.

Eric Kästner wrote several popular stories for
German youngsters, but only one of his books
achieved international fame. *Emil and the
Detectives* (1931) tells the perennially
irresistible tale of children getting the better of
scoundrelly grown-ups. Emil Tischbein is
robbed of money belonging to his mother on
his first solo railway journey *en route* to
relatives in Berlin. A gang of boys his own age
helps him to chase and catch the thief. The
book's cover contains Walter Trier's full-
length portrait of Emil in profile with his
hands thrust deep into the pockets of his
Sunday best blue suit.

Emil And The Detectives, illustrated by Walter
Trier. London, Cape, 1931.
Annaluise And Anton, illustrated by Walter
Trier. London, Cape, 1932.
The 35th Of May, illustrated by Walter Trier.
London, Cape, 1933.
The Flying Classroom, Illustrated by Walter
Trier. London, Cape, 1934.
Emil And The Three Twins, illustrated by
Walter Trier. London, Cape, 1935.

Rudyard Kipling (1865–1936). British.

Ham and the Porcupine. New York,
Doubleday, 1935.

Robert Lawson (1892–1957). American.

For main author article see 1940 to 1950.

Illustrated by the author.

Ben and Me. Boston, Little Brown, 1939.

Munro Leaf (1905–76). American.
a.k.a. John Calvert.
a.k.a Mun.

Munro Leaf's didactic all-American tales have now faded into obscurity. However, the work that is most against type is the one that has retained its popularity. *The Story of Ferdinand* (1936) is a droll piece about a peace-loving calf which finds itself accidentally selected to fight against a famous matador in a Madrid bullring. Any potential unpleasantness is avoided by the young bull's determined pacifism when he is required to perform.

Lo, The Poor Indian (as Mun), illustrated by the author. New York, Leaf Mahony Seidel and Stokes, 1934.
Robert Francis Weatherbee, illustrated by the author. New York, Stokes, 1935; London, Chatto & Windus, 1936.
The Story of Ferdinand, illustrated by Robert Lawson. New York, Viking Press, 1936; London, Hamish Hamilton, 1937.
Noodle, illustrated by Ludwig Bemelmans. New York, Stokes, 1937; London, Hamish Hamilton, 1938.
Wee Gillis, illustrated by Robert Lawson. New York, Viking Press, and London, Hamish Hamilton, 1938.

Amy Le Feuvre (d. 1929). British.
a.k.a. Mary Thurston Dodge

Under A Cloud. London, Ward Lock, 1930.
Rosebuds: Choice and Original Short Stories. London, Pickering and Inglis, 1931.
A Strange Courtship. London, Ward Lock, 1931.

Robert Leighton (1859–1934). British.

A Jewel of the Seas. London, J.F. Shaw, 1930.
The Red Shadow and other tales. London, Collins, 1930.
Under the Foeman's Flag. London, Pilgrim Press, 1930.

Elizabeth Foreman Lewis (1892–1958). American.

Elizabeth Foreman Lewis wrote passionately about China. She lived in the country for several years whilst working for the Methodist Women's Foreign Missionary Society and witnessed a time of great social upheaval. Her children's books tell of individuals and a whole people struggling through a slough of despond, but always striving for a better way of life. Her sympathetic portrayal of Chinese youngsters trying to make sense of life, when traditional values were being swept away in the wake of the Civil War and contact with the West, made her books popular in both America and Europe. Such a book was *Young Fu of the Upper Yangtze* (1932), for which she won the Newbery Medal for 1933.

Young Fu of the Upper Yangtze, illustrated by Kurt Wiese. Philadelphia, Winston, 1932; London, Harrap, 1934.
Ho-ming, Girl of New China, illustrated by Kurt Wiese. Philadelphia, Winston, 1934; London, Harrap, 1935.
China Quest, illustrated by Kurt Wiese. Philadelphia, Winston, 1936; London, Harrap, 1938.

Hilda Lewis (1896–1974). British.

Hilda Lewis only wrote four children's books. However, the first, and best, of these, *The Ship That Flew* (1939), is enough to make anyone wish for more. Peter Grant buys what he believes to be a model boat in a mysterious little shop. The boat grows suddenly and is revealed to be the legendary magic flying ship of the Norse god, Frey. Peter and his siblings use the ship to travel to Ancient Egypt, to the land of the Vikings and to Sherwood Forest at the time of Robin Hood. As they are whisked through time, the children enjoy some hair-raising adventures and learn the importance of believing in magic. Nora Lavrin's dust-wrapper design in red, white and blue depicts the Ship That Flew bobbing about off the pier at Radcliff-on-Sea.

The Ship That Flew, illustrated by Nora Lavrin. London, Oxford University Press, 1939; New York, Criterion, 1958.

Norman Lindsay (1879–1969). Australian.

Illustrated by the author.

The Flyaway Highway. Sydney, Angus and Robertson, 1936.

Hugh Lofting (1886–1947). British.

Illustrated by the author unless otherwise stated.

The Twilight of Magic, illustrated by Lois Lenski. New York, Stokes, 1930; London, Cape, 1931.
Gub Gub's Book: An Encyclopedia of Food. New York, Stokes, and London, Cape, 1932.
Doctor Dolittle's Return. New York, Stokes, and London, Cape, 1933.
Tommy, Tilly and Mrs. Tubbs. New York, Stokes, 1936; London, Cape, 1937.

Patricia Lynch (1898–1972). Irish.

The Cobbler's Apprentice, illustrated by M.R. Lamb. London, Shaylor, 1930.

The Turf-Cutter's Donkey, illustrated by Jack B. Yeats. London, Dent, 1934; New York, Dutton, 1935.
The Turf-Cutter's Donkey Goes Visiting, illustrated by George Attendorf. London, Dent, 1935; as *The Donkey Goes Visiting*, New York, Dutton, 1936.
King of the Tinkers, illustrated by Katherine C. Lloyd. London, Dent, and New York, Dutton, 1938.
The Turf-Cutter's Donkey Kicks Up His Heels, illustrated by Eileen Coghlan. New York, Dutton, 1939; London, Dent, 1952.
The Grey Goose of Kilnevin, illustrated by John Keating. London, Dent, 1939; New York, Dutton, 1940.

Ruth Manning-Sanders (1888–1988). British.

Ruth Manning-Sanders was fascinated by the folk history of Britain and of Cornwall in particular. She composed such volumes as *Peter and the Piskies: Cornish Folk and Fairy Tales* (1958), as well as sixteen fiction books for children. Manning-Sanders worked her love for West Country lore and the vaguely supernatural into *Mystery at Penmarth* (1940), a light-hearted story of knavery in a

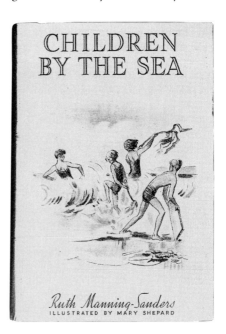

contemporary Cornish village, and *The Smugglers* (1962), which details the conflict between a band of daring rogues and hostile revenue men. *Children of the Sea* (1938) is a bright and breezy piece, as Mary Shepard's joyous dust wrapper design, primarily in cream and blue, signifies. The illustration shows Rebecca and her twin brother, Jimmy, frolicking in the sea with their cousins Bang and Sally. Rebecca and Jimmy had come to Cornwall for an enjoyable and relaxing summer holiday, but soon find themselves caught up in a web of intrigue.

Children by the Sea, illustrated by Mary Shepard. London, Collins, 1938; as *Adventure May Be Anywhere*, New York, Stokes, 1939.
Elephant. New York, Stokes, 1938; London, Collins, 1940.

Bessie Marchant (1862–1941). British.

Laurel the Leader, illustrated by Francis E. Hiley. London, Blackie, 1930.
Cuckoo of the Log Raft. London, Newnes, 1931.
Two on Their Own, illustrated by F.E. Hiley. London, Blackie, 1931.
The Homesteader Girl, illustrated by V. Cooley. London, Nelson, 1932.
Jane Fills the Breach, illustrated by F.E. Hiley. London, Blackie, 1932.
Silla the Seventh. London, Newnes, 1932.
Deborah's Find, illustrated by Henry Coller. London, Blackie, 1933.
The Courage of Katrine. London, Warne, 1934.
Erica's Ranch, illustrated by H. Coller. London, Blackie, 1934.
Lesbia's Little Blunder. London, Warne, 1934.
Hosea's Girl. London, Hutchinson, 1934.
Anna of Tenterford, illustrated by F.E. Hiley. London, Blackie, 1935.
Felicity's Fortune. London, Blackie, 1936.
Nancy Afloat. London, Nelson, 1936.
A Daughter of the Desert. London, Blackie, 1937.
Miss Wilmer's Gang, illustrated by J.A. May. London, Blackie, 1938.
Waifs of Woollamoo. London, Warne, 1938.

A Girl Undaunted; or, The Honey Queen, illustrated by J.A. May. London, Blackie, 1939.

John Masefield (1878–1967). British.

John Masefield's *The Box of Delights* (1935) is a timeless portrayal of the struggle between good and evil. It is Masefield's most famous work of children's literature, but is in fact the sequel to an earlier book, *The Midnight Folk* (1927). Young Kay Harper is entrusted with the Box of Delights. This enables him to enter a magical new world. Here Kay is confronted with hostile forces searching for treasure and the elixir of life. The white wrapper is bordered with red and blue lines, and small line drawings coloured in red and blue. These depict the fascinating characters and creatures Kay encounters through the Box of Delights. There are, amongst others, dancing and pistol-toting mice, Roman gladiators, a policeman and a Punch and Judy show.

The Bird of Dawning; or, The Fortune of the Sea. London, Heinemann, and New York, Macmillan, 1933.
The Box of Delights; or, When the Wolves Were Running. London, Heinemann, and New York, Macmillan, 1935.

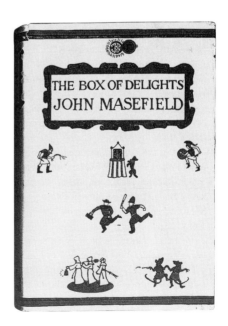

Dead Ned: The Autobiography of a Corpse.
London, Heinemann, and New York,
Macmillan, 1938.
Live and Kicking Ned. London, Heinemann,
and New York, Macmillan, 1939.

Stephen W(arren) Meader (1892–1977).
American.

Stephen W. Meader's forty-three children's
books, written over half a century, chart the
growth and development of the United States
and the playing out and occasional jading of the
'American dream'. Meader created scores of
juvenile heroes who, like the author's teenage
readers, have to work through the diverse
emotional challenges that confront them. It is
the author's ability to stir the feelings that has
been credited as his principal achievement.
However, his seemingly effortless formulation
of realistic and evocative settings is equally
impressive. Whether they be trekking
Westward with the very first colonisers of
America, or suffering in the American Civil or
Korean Wars, Meader's young characters and
their dilemmas are instantly recognisable to
readers of all ages and times.

Red Horse Hill, illustrated by Lee Townsend.
New York, Harcourt Brace, 1930.
Away to Sea, illustrated by Clinton Balmer.
New York, Harcourt Brace, 1931.
King of the Hills, illustrated by Lee Townsend.
New York, Harcourt Brace, 1933.
Lumberjack, illustrated by Henry Pitz. New
York, Harcourt Brace, 1934; London
Bell, 1955.
The Will to Win and Other Stories, illustrated
by John Gincano. New York, Harcourt
Brace, 1936.
Who Rides in the Dark?, illustrated by James
MacDonald. New York, Harcourt Brace,
1937; Oxford, Blackwell, 1938.
T-Model Tommy, illustrated by Edward
Shenton. New York, Harcourt Brace,
1938.
Boy with a Pack, illustrated by Edward Shenton.
New York, Harcourt Brace, 1939.
Bat, The Story of a Bull Terrier, illustrated by
Edward Shenton. New York, Harcourt
Brace, 1939.

Florence Crannell Means (1891–1980).
American.

Florence Crannell Means wrote
sympathetically about America's ethnic
minorities. At a time when the country was
strictly segregated and stereotypical caricatures
of coloured people were in vogue, Means'
Red Indians (or Native Americans, as they
like to be known) are more *Dances With
Wolves* than Little Plum. Her unconventional
attitude stemmed from an upbringing in a
Baptist Manse, where the integration of
people of all creeds and colours was
encouraged. Means' stories do not offer a
sentimentalised and sanitised portrayal of her
subjects, but one that revealed Indians,
negroes and others in a realistic fashion that
stressed their equality with the white man.
Means took great care before putting pen to
paper. For instance, she spent some time in
the Hopi reservation, gathering information
about Indian life at first hand, before writing
Whispering Girl (1941).

A Candle in the Mist, illustrated by
Marguerite de Angeli. Boston, Houghton
Mifflin, 1931.
Ranch and Ring, illustrated by Henry Peck.
Boston, Houghton Mifflin, 1932.
Dusky Day, illustrated by Manning Lee.
Boston, Houghton Mifflin, 1933.
A Bowlful of Stars, illustrated by Henry Pitz.
Boston, Houghton Mifflin, 1934.
Rainbow Bridge, illustrated by Eleanor
Lattimore. New York, Friendship Press,
1934.
Penny for Luck, illustrated by Paul Quinn.
Boston, Houghton Mifflin, 1935.
Tangled Waters, illustrated by Herbert Morton
Stoops. Boston, Houghton Mifflin, 1936.
The Singing Wood, illustrated by Manning
Lee. Boston, Houghton Mifflin, 1937.
Shuttered Windows, illustrated by Armstrong
Sperry. Boston, Houghton Mifflin, 1938.
Adella Mary in Old New Mexico, illustrated by
Herbert Morton Stoops. Boston,
Houghton Mifflin, 1939.

Cornelia Meigs (1884–1973). American.
a.k.a. Adair Aldon.

The Willow Whistle, illustrated by E. Boyd
   Smith. New York, Macmillan, 1931.
Swift Rivers, illustrated by Forrest Orr.
   Boston, Little Brown, 1932.
Wind in the Chimney, illustrated by Louise
   Mansfield. New York, Macmillan, 1934.
The Covered Bridge, illustrated by Marguerite
   de Angeli. New York, Macmillan, 1936.
The Scarlet Oak, illustrated by Elizabeth
   Orton Jones. New York, Macmillan,
   1938; Birmingham, Cambridge, 1939.

Naomi Mitchison (b. 1897). British.

Immense historical knowledge and a flair for
uncomplicated narrative made Naomi
Mitchison one of the most popular exponents
of tales of yesteryear for young people. Her
books provide a vivid picture of the past, and
are extremely effective when dealing with
everyday matters, as well as weightier
concerns, such as important battles and the
deeds of mighty monarchs. *The Hostages*
(1930) is a collection of nine rousing
adventure stories set between the fourth
century BC and the eleventh century AD. It

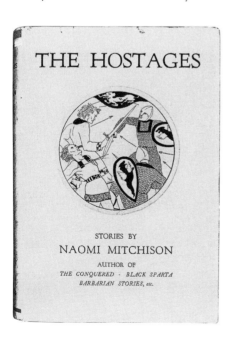

traces the development (if that is the correct
word to use of an art that became increasingly
barbaric) of warfare during this period. Logi
Southby's circular collage in orange and black
on a cream wrapper sets the scene in dramatic
fashion. It depicts Normans and Saxons
fighting to the death with swords and bows
and arrows.

*The Hostages and Other Stories for Boys and
   Girls*, illustrated by Logi Southby.
   London, Cape, 1930; New York,
   Harcourt Brace, 1931.
Boys and Girls and Gods. London, Watts, 1931.

L(ucy) M(aud) Montgomery (1874–1942).
Canadian.

A Tangled Web. New York, Stokes, 1931; as
   Aunt Becky Began It, London, Hodder &
   Stoughton, 1931.
Pat of Silver Bush. New York, Stokes, and
   London, Hodder & Stoughton, 1933.
Mistress Pat: A Novel of Silver Bush. New
   York, Stokes, and London, Harrap, 1935.
Anne of Windy Poplars. New York, Stokes,
   1936; as *Anne of Windy Willows*, London,
   Harrap, 1936.
Jane of Lantern Hill. Toronto, McClelland and
   Stewart, New York, Stokes, and London,
   Harrap, 1937.
Anne of Ingleside. New York, Stokes, and
   London, Harrap, 1939.

Rutherford Montgomery (1894–1985).
American.
a.k.a. Al Avery.
a.k.a. Everitt Proctor

In the latter part of his career, Rutherford
Montgomery wrote for the Walt Disney
studio, and his brand of all-American schmaltz
was ideally suited to the company's style. His is
a world where sunsets are always wonderfully
golden, the grass always lusciously green and
the animal characters inevitably more attractive
than their human counterparts. Montgomery
wrote eighty books in praise of youth, outdoor
living and cute and clever beasts, including the
popular 'Gold Stallion' series.

Troopers Three, illustrated by Zhenya Gay.
New York, Doubleday, 1932.

Broken Fang, illustrated by Lynn Bogue Hunt.
Chicago, Donohue, 1935.

Carcajou, illustrated by L.D. Cram. Caldwell,
Idaho, Caxton, 1936; Bristol,
Arrowsmith, 1937.

Yellow Eyes, illustrated by L.D. Cram.
Caldwell, Idaho, Caxton, 1937; London,
Blackie, 1939.

Gray Wolf, illustrated by Jacob Bates Abbott.
Boston, Houghton Mifflin, 1938;
London, Hutchinson, 1939.

Timberline Tales, illustrated by Jacob Bates
Abbott. Philadelphia, McKay, 1939;
London, Hutchinson, 1951.

The Trail of the Buffalo, illustrated by Kurt
Wiese. Boston, Houghton Mifflin, 1939.

Orphans of the Wind, illustrated by Janet
Dean. Bristol, Arrowsmith, 1939.

Dorothea Moore (1881–1933). British.

Judy, Patrol Leader [Lends a Hand]. London,
Collins, 2 vols., 1930–32.

Nicky of Nine Schools. London, Oxford
University Press, 1932.

Sara to the Rescue. London, Nisbet, 1932.

At Friendship's Call. London, Oxford
University Press, 1932.

Dick of the Day-Girls. London, Nisbet, 1933.

Queens for Choice. London, Oxford
University Press, 1934.

Babs Goes to Court. London, Sheldon Press,
1936.

The Crooked Headstone. London, Pearson,
1939.

Ursula Moray Williams (b. 1911). British.

Ursula Moray Williams wrote quaint tales for
young children. Although not unpalatably
moralistic, her stories contain a clear sense of
right and wrong. *The Twins and Their Ponies*
(1936) is a refreshing antidote to the umpteen
conventional pony books of this and the
following decade. It tells its youthful readers
not to be despondent if their wishes remain
unfulfilled in a material sense, but instead to
employ their imaginations. Twins Bubble and

Squeak, unable to have the real horses they
desire, enjoy hours of inventive fun with the
hobby horses their mother has made for them.
Moray Williams's own dust wrapper design
depicts the sisters bringing their horses to
water, and apparently making them drink as
well!

Jean-Pierre, illustrated by the author. London,
A. & C. Black, 1931.

The Pettabomination, illustrated by the author.
London, Archer, 1933.

Kelpie, The Gipsies' Pony, illustrated by the
author and Barbara Moray Williams.
London, Harrap, 1934; Philadelphia,
Lippincott, 1935.

Anders and Marta, illustrated by the author.
London, Harrap, 1935.

Adventures of Anne, illustrated by the author.
London, Harrap, 1935.

The Twins and Their Ponies, illustrated by the
author. London, Harrap, 1936.

Sandy-on-the-Shore, illustrated by the author.
London, Harrap, 1936.

Tales for the Sixes and Sevens, illustrated by the
author. London, Harrap, 1936.

Dumpling, illustrated by the author. London,
Harrap, 1937.

Elaine of La Signe, illustrated by the author
and Barbara Moray Williams. London,
Harrap, 1937; as *Elaine of the Mountains*,
Philadelphia, Lippincott, 1939.

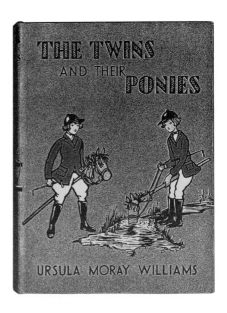

Adventures of Boss and Dingbat, photographs
by Peter John. London, Harrap, 1937.
Adventures of the Little Wooden Horse,
illustrated by Joyce Lankester Brisley.
London, Harrap, 1938; Philadelphia,
Lippincott, 1939.
Adventures of Puffin, illustrated by Mary
Shillabeer. London, Harrap, 1939.
Peter and the Wanderlust, illustrated by Jack
Matthew. London, Harrap, 1939;
Philadelphia, Lippincott, 1940.

Violet Needham (1876–1967). British.

Violet Needham's thrilling romances are in a
different league to the other children's books
of this period. They are classy adventures on a
grand scale, with royal heroes and magnificent
settings. Although she later wrote four slightly
offbeat contemporary stories based in
England, it is for her eight 'Ruritanian' books
that Needham is justly best known. Ruritania
and its environs are modelled on the Balkan
principalities of the early decades of the
century, with their child monarchs, glamour
and intrigue. *The Black Riders* (1939)
introduces the reader to a world that
sometimes resembles that of a dark fairy tale.
The story was originally composed for
Needham's nephews some twenty years
before eventual publication, and by the
beginning of the Second World War some
people found Needham's style old fashioned.
This does not prevent *The Black Riders* being a
ripping and popular yarn. It features
Needham's most constant hero, Dick
Fauconbois, who is a twelve-year-old
schoolboy in the first tale and has to summon
up all the enterprise he can to survive into his
twenties and the final book, *The Red Rose of
Ruvina* (1957), so beset is he by constant
danger. Needham's other principal series
character is Etonian Alexander Valesciano,
who, much to his horror, discovers himself to
be the heir to the kingdom of Flavonia in *The
Emerald Crown* (1940). This happens to be the
only book in the series not to feature
Fauconbois. The books concentrate on the
dual struggles for power and survival and how,
in a tempestuous environment, the two are
rarely compatible. The Black Riders of the

The
Black Riders

A boy's exciting adventures
by VIOLET NEEDHAM
Illustrated by Anne Bullen

first book's title are a crack cavalry unit who,
along with the powerful Count Jasper,
Governor of the Citadel, hold sway in a
Ruritanian state. Fauconbois has to cross their
path before his adventure's done. Anne Bullen
(who was well-known for her pictures of
horses) depicts the Black Riders in full charge
on the book's dust wrapper.

'Magnificent men they were, in black
uniforms, riding magnificent black horses; not
a speck of colour anywhere about them, black
tunics and breeches … only the silver of bit
and stirrup shone like silver.'

The Black Riders, illustrated by Anne Bullen.
London, Collins, 1939.

Elsie J. Oxenham (1880–1960). British.
Pseudonym for Elsie Jeanette Dunkerley.
a.k.a. Elsie Oxenham.
a.k.a. Elsie Jeanette Oxenham.

Although she produced only about half the
number of books in this decade as she had done
in the twenties, Elsie J. Oxenham was still a
mighty force in the field of girls' school stories.
Nina K. Brisley's rather lovely painting for the
overwhelmingly green and cream wrapper of
Dorothy's Dilemma (1930) has Dorothy Bayne

ELSIE J. OXENHAM

of White House School showing Miss Dickinson, her teacher, the beauty of the dew pond. In return, she receives understanding advice to cope with her dilemma.

The Abbey Girls at Home, illustrated by I. Burns. London, Collins, 1930.

The Abbey Girls Play Up. London, Collins, 1930.

Dorothy's Dilemma, illustrated by Nina K. Brisley. Edinburgh, Chambers, 1930.

The Abbey Girls on Trial. London, Collins, 1931.

Deb of Sea House, illustrated by Nina K. Brisley. Edinburgh, Chambers, 1931.

Biddy's Secret. Edinburgh, Chambers, 1932.

The Camp Mystery. London, Collins, 1932.

The Reformation of Jinty. Edinburgh, Chambers, 1933.

Rosamund's Victory. London, Harrap, 1933.

The Call of the Abbey School. London, Collins, 1934.

Jinty's Patrol. London, Newnes, 1934.

Maidlin to the Rescue, illustrated by R. Cloke. Edinburgh, Chambers, 1934.

Joy's New Adventure. Edinburgh, Chambers, 1935.

Peggy and the Brotherhood. London, Religious Tract Society, 1936.

Rosamund's Tuck-Shop. London, Religious Tract Society, 1937.

Sylvia of Sarn. London and New York, Warne, 1937.

Damaris at Dorothy's. London, Sheldon Press, 1937.

Maidlin Bears the Torch. London, Religious Tract Society, 1937.

Schooldays at the Abbey. London, Collins, 1938.

Rosamund's Castle. London, Religious Tract Society, 1938.

Secrets of the Abbey, illustrated by Heade. London, Collins, 1939.

M(argot) Pardoe (b. 1902). British.

M. Pardoe will always be associated with a boy called Bunkle. This is actually Billy de Salis (nicknamed 'Bunkle' by his older sister and brother due to his tendency to spout 'a lot of bunk'). Bunkle and his siblings undergo a series of adventures, initially in wartime Europe. They, apparently unlike some child heroes, are susceptible to the aging process and bodily functions. The dozen 'Bunkle' books are in many ways jolly escapism, with the children foiling the best laid plans of Nazi spies, Communist kidnappers and other scurrilous rogues. However, there is an underlying current of real danger and permanent social change that endows the books with some emotional depth. *Four Plus Bunkle* (1939) starts the series as it carries on. The plot is rather far-fetched, involving the conveyance of secret documents to the British Secret Service, but this is offset by the characters' warmth and good humour. J.D. Evans' dust-wrapper drawing shows the de Salis family at breakfast. The meal is suddenly disturbed by the butler who bears a letter for the head of the family.

The Far Island, illustrated by R.M. Turvey. London, Routledge, 1936.

Four Plus Bunkle, illustrated by J.D. Evans. London, Routledge, 1939.

Mervyn Peake (1911–68). British.

Illustrated by the author.

Captain Slaughterboard Drops Anchor, London,
Country Life, 1939; New York,
Macmillan, 1967.

Beatrix Potter (1866–1943). British.
a.k.a. Beatrix Heelis.

Illustrated by the author.

The Tale of Little Pig Robinson. Philadelphia,
McKay, and London, Warne, 1930.
Sister Anne, illustrated by Katharine Sturges.
Philadelphia, McKay, 1932.

Evadne Price (1896–1985). British.
Pseudonym for Helen Zenna Smith.

Frank R. Grey is the illustrator closest
associated with the 'Jane' stories of Evadne
Price. Although he provided later editions of
all the books with illustrations, *Jane the Fourth*
(1937) was the earliest book in the series for
which he drew for the first edition. The dust
wrapper for *Jane the Sleuth* (1939) shows off
Grey's slightly zany, cartoon-like style to good
effect. Jane Turpin, Pug Washington and
Chaw Smith are in the guise of Brindley
Belton and his two Brilliant Assistants, a
celebrated trio famous for 'solving every
baffling mystery throughout five continents
after Scotland Yard had given up in despair.'
The three are shown on the trail of their latest
suspect: 'But for the gardener at the Laurels
threatening to turn the hose on them they
might have solved the mystery there and
then.'

Meet Jane. London, Marriott, 1930.
Enter – Jane. London, Newnes, 1932.
Jane the Fourth, illustrated by Frank R. Grey.
London, Hale, 1937.
Jane the Sleuth, illustrated by Frank R. Grey.
London, Hale, 1939.
Jane the Unlucky, illustrated by Frank R.
Grey. London, Hale, 1939.
Jane the Popular, illustrated by Frank R. Grey.
London, Hale, 1939.

Gwynedd Rae (1892–1977). British.

At a glance, anyone surveying a bibliography
that contains over a dozen such titles as *Mostly
Mary* (1930) and *Mary Plain on Holiday* (1937)
would probably initially guess that the
principal character was a mischievous, fun-
loving moppet. This is not far from the truth,
but in fact Gwynedd Rae's 'Mary Plain' series
has an ursine heroine, Mary Plain, who used
to live in the bear pits at Berne before she
came to England with her friend the Owl
Man. Unlike another Bear of Very Little
Brain, Mary Plain's adventures have never
gained a huge following. However, this
anthropomorphic small bear and her antics
provide enjoyable and diverting entertainment
for the young.

Mostly Mary, illustrated by Harry Rountree.
London, Mathews and Marrot, 1930;
New York, Morrow, 1931.
All Mary, illustrated by Harry Rountree.
London, Mathews and Marrot, 1931.
Mary Plain in Town, illustrated by Irene
Williamson. London, Cobden Sanderson,
1935.
Mary Plain on Holiday. London, Cobden
Sanderson, 1937.

Arthur Ransome (1884–1967). British.

Arthur Ransome was a well-respected journalist long before his first children's novel was published, and his eye-witness account of the Russian revolution is a remarkable historical document. However, Ransome always yearned to write for the young, and his immense natural talent, coupled with the passion for sailing he had cultivated during his childhood holidays in the Lake District, resulted in one of the most enduringly popular series of children's outdoor adventure books. The 'Swallows and Amazons' sequence of stories runs to a dozen volumes. Ransome did not restrict his sailing yarns to his beloved Lake District, but also set them in the Norfolk Broads, the Essex Marshes and even the South Seas. Here the children encounter the Chinese pirate Missee Lee, who turns out to be a Latin mistress who can threaten walking the plank as the ultimate sanction against slacking in class. *Swallows and Amazons* (1930) introduced the reader to the nautically enthused youngsters who were to dominate the series, and who captained and manned the two vessels, the *Swallow*, a sailing boat, and the *Amazon*, a centre-board dinghy. The former craft was peopled by the Walker children, John, the ship's master, Susan, the first mate, Titty, able-seaman, and Roger, ship's boy, whilst Peggy and Nancy Blackett controlled the *Amazon*. The camp on Wild Cat Island is disputed by the two parties, but a truce and eventual friendship comes into being. Ransome was always keen that the illustrations in his books should have a simplicity about them that would not betray the fact that they were drawn by an adult hand. He soon took on the task of illustrator himself, but the decorations for the first edition of *Swallows and Amazons* are in keeping with the later style. There are no illustrations in the text itself, but some wonderful work on the dust wrapper, end papers, frontispiece and title page by Stephen Spurrier (not Helen Carter as other publications would have it). The book has turquoise cloth, with the spine and front cover lettered in gilt.

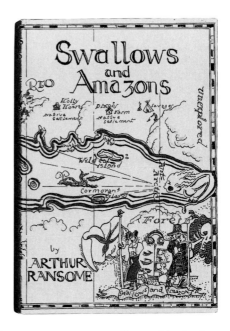

Swallows and Amazons, illustrated by Stephen Spurrier. London, Cape, 1930. Philadelphia, Lippincott, 1931.

Swallowdale, illustrated by Clifford Webb. London, Cape, 1931; Philadelphia, Lippincott, 1932.

Peter Duck, illustrated by the author. London, Cape, 1932; Philadelphia, Lippincott, 1933.

Winter Holiday, illustrated by the author. London, Cape, 1933; Philadelphia, Lippincott, 1934.

Coot Club, illustrated by the author and Helene Carter. London, Cape, 1934; Philadelphia, Lippincott, 1935.

Pigeon Post, illustrated by the author. London, Cape, 1936; Philadelphia, Lippincott, 1937.

We Didn't Mean to Go to Sea, illustrated by the author. London, Cape, 1937; New York, Macmillan, 1938.

Secret Water, illustrated by the author. London, Cape, 1939; New York, Macmillan, 1940.

Charles G(eorge) D(ouglas) Roberts (1860–1943). Canadian.

Eyes of the Wilderness, illustrated by Dorothy Burroughes. New York, Macmillan, and London, Dent, 1933.

Further Animal Stories. London, Dent, 1935.

Ruth Sawyer (1880–1970). American.

Toño Antonio, illustrated by F. Luis Mora.
New York, Viking Press, 1934.
Roller Skates, illustrated by Valenti Angelo.
New York, Viking Press, 1936; London,
Bodley Head, 1964.

Helen Sewell (1896–1957). American.

The later career of Helen Sewell was largely
taken up by assignments to illustrate other
authors' work. She also wrote and illustrated
nine picture books herself. These could not be
described as loquacious. Indeed some contain
virtually no text whatsoever. This hardly
matters, as Sewell's delightful drawings do the
talking for her. *Peggy and the Pony* (1937)
follows the fortunes of little Peggy Doe as she
gamely visits France and then her Aunt Daisy
in England whilst searching for the perfect
pony. As the dust wrapper shows, the girl
eventually gets her horse. The book has red
cloth with the title and a small design in blue
on the front cover.

Illustrated by the author.

A Head for Happy. New York, Macmillan,
1931.
Blue Barns. New York, Macmillan, 1933;
London, Woodfield, 1955.
Ming and Mehitable. New York, Macmillan,
1936.

Peggy and the Pony. New York and London,
Oxford University Press, 1937.

C(icely) Fox Smith (1882–1954). British.

C. Fox Smith's books possess a strong sense of
British heritage and culture. Her half dozen
children's novels were composed after nearly
forty years of writing about rural customs and
the sea for an adult audience. It is hardly
surprising that these themes make up a
substantial amount of her corpus of juvenilia.
The Ship Aground (1940) is an exciting
seafaring story with a historical setting. It
involves mystery, piracy and buried treasure.

Three Girls in a Boat, with Madge Smith.
London, Oxford University Press, 1938.

Caroline Dale Snedeker (1871–1956).
American.

The Forgotten Daughter, illustrated by Dorothy
P. Lathrop. New York, Doubleday, 1933.
Uncharted Ways, illustrated by Manning Lee.
New York, Doubleday, 1935.

Phil(ip) Stong (1899–1957). American.

Phil Stong's career writing for children started
with a bang and ended, as most acknowledge,
with a whimper. *Honk, The Moose* (1935) is
the very lively story of a friendly but famished
moose, who is welcomed in from the cold by
some kindly children, stays for Christmas, but
then refuses to leave. The ensuing
complications and attempts to evict the animal
provoke much hilarity. Unfortunately, Stong's
later work did not live up to this encouraging
start, and is now largely forgotten.

Farm Boy. New York, Doubleday, 1934.
Honk, The Moose. New York, Dodd Mead,
1935; London, Harrap, 1936.
No-Sitch, The Hound. New York, Dodd
Mead, 1936; London, Harrap, 1937.
High Water. New York, Dodd Mead, 1937.
Edgar, The 7:58, illustrated by Lois Lenski.
New York, Farrar and Rinehart, 1938.
Young Settler. New York, Dodd Mead, 1938.

Cowhand Goes to Town. New York, Dodd Mead, 1939.

The Hired Man's Elephant, illustrated by Doris Lee. New York, Dodd Mead, 1939.

Herbert Strang. Pseudonym for George Herbert Ely (1866–1958), British, and C. James L'Estrange (1867–1947). British.

Ships and Their Story: Scouting Stories. London, Oxford University Press, 1931.

Dickon of the Chase: A Story of Tudor Times, illustrated by Terence Cuneo. London, Oxford University Press, 1931.

A Servant of John Company, illustrated by Alfred Sindall, Terence Cuneo, Henry Evidon and D. Stacey. London, Oxford University Press, 1932.

Noel Streatfeild (1895–1986). British.

Noel Streatfeild was well fitted to put on her famous *Ballet Shoes* (1936). She had spent ten years on the stage herself and was able to write from first-hand experience about the highs and lows of show business. The story tells the fortunes of three adopted 'sisters', Pauline, Petrova and Posy Fossil, as they train for the stage at Madame Fidolia's Academy of Dancing after a downturn in the family's fortune. Each girl discovers, sometimes painfully, whether she has a natural talent for ballet. The book has green cloth and silver lettering on the spine. The dazzling silver dust wrapper has black and green letters and an illustration by Ruth Gervis, Streatfeild's sister, showing one of the trainee ballerinas in action. Streatfeild followed up the success of *Ballet Shoes*, which was an adaptation of an earlier adult novel, *The Whichcarts* (1931), with another story of young hopefuls, *Tennis Shoes* (1937). The heroine of this book, Nicky, is unglamorous and rather 'difficult', the antithesis to her rival, golden girl Susan. Interestingly, it is Nicky who triumphs and becomes a tennis star, reflecting Streatfeild's interest in the underdog. Streatfeild's books were well-received and she became the unofficial doyen of the children's book world in later years, but she was unable to replicate the triumph of her first two books.

Ballet Shoes, illustrated by Ruth Gervis. London, Dent, 1936; New York, Random House, 1937.

Tennis Shoes, illustrated by D.L.Mays. London, Dent, 1937; New York, Random House, 1938.

The Circus Is Coming, illustrated by Steven Spurrier. London, Dent, 1938; as *Circus Shoes*, New York, Random House, 1939.

Dennis the Dragon, illustrated by Ruth Gervis. London, Dent, 1939.

L(eonard) A(lfred) G(eorge) Strong (1896–1958). British.

L.A.G. Strong's *King Richard's Land* (1933) is a historical drama charting the tragic story of the Peasant's Revolt of the latter part of the fourteenth century. C. Walter Hodges' fine portrait for the dust wrapper is of the young King Richard II, who eventually dealt so ruthlessly with the revolting peasants.

The Old Argo, illustrated by Ruth Cobb. Oxford, Blackwell, 1931.

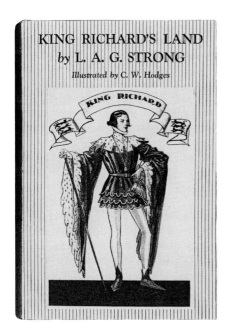

King Richard's Land, illustrated by C. Walter Hodges. London, Dent, 1933; New York, Knopf, 1934.

Fortnight South of Skye, illustrated by Laurence Dunn. Oxford, Blackwell, 1934; New York, Loring and Mussey, 1935.

The Westward Rock, illustrated by L.R. Brightwell. Oxford, Blackwell, 1934.

Mr. Sheridan's Umbrella, illustrated by C. Walter Hodges. London and New York, Nelson, 1935.

The Fifth of November, illustrated by Jack Matthew. London, Dent, 1937.

Odd Man In, illustrated by P. Lefroy. London, Pitman, 1938.

Ethel Talbot. British.

Billy of the Wolf Cubs and Other "Good Turn" Tales. London, Epworth Press, 1930.

Jean's Two Schools, illustrated by E. Brier. London, Nelson, 1930.

Meggy at St. Monica's. London, Ward Lock, 1930.

Nancy, New Girl, and The Girl Who Was Different. London, Warne, 1930.

The Mystery of the Manor. London, Sheldon Press, 1930.

Little Books (How Golly Grew Good. The Story of Little Bo-Peep. The Story of Mother Hubbard and the Silver Sixpence, The Adventure of Mary Contrary, The Adventures of Noah and Poll in Fairyland, The Ark Animal Scouts). London, Religious Tract Society, 6 vols., 1931.

Brownies All! London, Warne, 1931.

The Foolish Phillimores. London, Nelson, 1931.

"Good Turn Tales" for Wolf Cubs. London, Epworth Press, 1931.

Anne of Queen Anne's. London, Warne, 1932.

The Brownie Pack and Other Good Turn Tales. London, Epworth Press, 1932.

Dearly Bought. London, Leng, 1932.

A Girl Die-Hard. London, Thomson, 1932.

Phoebe of the Fourth, illustrated by E. Brier. London, Nelson, 1932.

Red Caps at School. London, Sheldon Press, 1932.

Anne-on-Her-Own. London, Ward Lock, 1933.

Fairy Tales for Brownie Folk. London, Epworth Press, 1933.

Paul and Pam: The Twins' Holiday Adventure. London, Warne, 1933.

Surprise Island. London, Blackie, 1933.

The Upper Hand. London, Leng, 1933.

Betty and the Brownies. London, Warne, 1934.

The Middletons Make Good. London, Nelson, 1934.

Mascot of the School. London, Hutchinson, 1934.

Brownie Island. London, Warne, 1935.

Fifty-Two Thrilling Stories for Girls, illustrated by Glossop. London, Hutchinson, 1935.

The Girls of the Big House. London, Nelson, 1935.

Pioneer Pat. London, Ward Lock, 1935.

Pluck at St. Cyprian's. London, Pilgrim Press, 1935.

Schoolgirl by Chance. London, Hutchinson, 1935.

Sea Rangers All. London, Warne, 1935.

Old House. London, Nelson, 1936.

Sea Rangers' Holiday. London, Warne, 1937.

Diana the Daring. London, Ward Lock, 1938.

Guide's Luck. London, Pearson, 1938.

Nesta on Her Own, illustrated by J.R. Burgess. London, Nelson, 1938.

Rangers and Strangers and Other Stories. London, Nelson, 1938.

Sadie Sees It Through. London, Ward Lock, 1939.

Terry's Only Term, illustrated by F.G. Moorson. London, Blackie, 1939.

Barbara Euphan Todd (1897–1976). British.

a.k.a. Euphan.

Barbara Euphan Todd created the likeable Scarecrow of Scatterbrook, Worzel Gummidge, in 1936.

> Worzel Gummidge's face is carved from a turnip and one of his eyebrows is much longer than the other, and grows quite high at hay harvest. His arms and legs are made from broomsticks, and his stuffing is straw. He has green sprouting hair. He generally wears a bowler hat, a blue shirt, black trousers, tarred string braces and bottle-straw boots, but he is fond of dressing up in other people's clothes.

It is this last characteristic that gets Gummidge into trouble in *More About Worzel Gummidge* (1938). He steals Lady Piddingfold's clothes and pretends to be her at the local bazaar. This leads to a whole series of adventures on a train and in the circus, culminating in a well-deserved breakfast with the other scarecrows on the village rubbish heap. Altogether there are ten entertaining books about the adventures of Worzel Gummidge.

Happy Cottage, with Marjory Royce. London, Collins, 1930.

South Country Secrets (as Euphan), with Klaxon (pseudonym for John Graham Bower). London, Burns Oates and Washbourne, 1935.

The Touchstone (as Euphan), with Klaxon (pseudonym for John Graham Bower). London, Burns Oates and Washbourne, 1936.

Worzel Gummidge; or, The Scarecrow of Scatterbrook, illustrated by Elizabeth Alldridge. London, Burns Oates, 1936.

Worzel Gummidge Again, illustrated by Elizabeth Alldridge. London, Burns Oates, 1937.

The Mystery Train, illustrated by Alison Fuller. London, University of London Press, 1937.

The Splendid Picnic, illustrated by Frank Rogers. London, University of London Press, 1937.

More about Worzel Gummidge, illustrated by Elizabeth Alldridge. London, Burns Oates and Washbourne, 1938.

Mr. Dock's Garden, illustrated by Ruth Westcott. Leeds, Arnold, 1939.

Gertrude the Greedy Goose, illustrated by Benjamin Rabier. London, Muller, 1939.

J(ohn) R(onald) R(euel) Tolkien (1892–1973). British.

> In a hole in the ground there lived a hobbit. Not a nasty, dirty, wet hole, filled with the ends of worms and an oozy smell, nor yet a dry, bare, sandy hole with nothing in it to sit down on or to eat: it was a hobbit-hole, and that means comfort.

So begins one of the most admired and popular children's books of all time. J.R.R. Tolkien's

The Hobbit (1937) tells of how Bilbo Baggins is whisked away by the wizard Gandalf and a dozen dwarves (Tolkien's spelling). He endures encounters with trolls, goblins, and giant spiders, so that he can snatch some treasure from under the nose of the watchful dragon, Smaug. The tone is generally cozy, but there are darker undertones to the last section of the story that preempt Tolkien's epic, *The Lord of the Rings* (1954–55). This revolves around the potentially world-changing significance of Bilbo's acquisition of a magic ring from the villainous Gollum. *The Hobbit*, however, is most memorable for the creation of Tolkien's diminutive and reluctantly heroic inhabitants of The Shire (representing Middle England):

> They [Hobbits] are inclined to be fat; … they dress in bright colours; … wear no shoes, because their feet grow natural leathery soles and thick warm brown hair; … have … good natured faces, and laugh deep fruity laughs (especially after dinner, which they have twice a day when they can get it).

The first edition of *The Hobbit* contained eight black and white illustrations by Tolkien

himself and a wraparound dust wrapper design, also by the author, in black, green and white, showing dragons flying over the western peaks of Wilderland. The frontispiece picture of Hobbiton was in black and white, whilst in every other edition it is in colour. Tolkien's brave new world (although in part concocted as early as the First World War) paved the way for many more fantasy tales for children, at a time when fairy stories were distinctly démodé, including the Narnia fables of his friend and fellow Oxonian, C.S. Lewis.

The Hobbit; or, There and Back Again, illustrated by the author. London, Allen and Unwin, 1937; Boston, Houghton Mifflin, 1938.

Mary Tourtel (1874–1948). British.

Illustrated by the author.

Daily Express Children's Annual. London, Lane Publications, 5 vols., 1930–34.
Rupert and the Little Prince. London, Sampson Low, 1930.
Rupert and King Pippin. London, Sampson Low, 1930.
Rupert and the Wilful Princess. London, Sampson Low, 1930.
Rupert's Mysterious Flight. London, Sampson Low, 1930.
Rupert in Trouble Again; Rupert and the Fancy Dress Party. London, Sampson Low, 1930.
Rupert and the Wooden Soldiers; Rupert's Christmas Adventure. London, Sampson Low, 1930.
Rupert and the Old Man of the Sea. London, Sampson Low, 1931.
Rupert and Algy at Hawthorne Farm. London, Sampson Low, 1931.
Monster Rupert. London, Sampson Low, 7 vols., 1931–50.
Rupert and the Magic Whistle. London, Sampson Low, 1931.
Rupert Gets Stolen. London, Sampson Low, 1931.
Rupert and the Wonderful Boots. London, Sampson Low, 1931.

Rupert and the Christmas Tree Fairies; Rupert and Bill Badger's Picnic Party. London, Sampson Low, 1931.

Rupert and His Pet Monkey Again; Beppo Back with Rupert. London, Sampson Low, 1932.

Rupert's Latest Adventure. London, Sampson Low, 1932.

Rupert and Prince Humpty-Dumpty. London, Sampson Low, 1932.

Rupert's Holiday Adventure; Rupert's Message to Father Christmas; Rupert's New Year's Eve Party. London, Sampson Low, 1932.

Rupert's Christmas Tree; Rupert's Picnic Party. London, Sampson Low, 1932.

Rupert. The Witch, and Tabitha. London, Sampson Low, 1933.

Rupert Goes Hiking. London, Sampson Low, 1933.

Rupert and Willy Wispe. London, Sampson Low, 1933.

Rupert, Margot and the Bandits. London, Sampson Low, 1933.

Rupert and Bill Keep Shop; Rupert's Christmas Thrills. London, Sampson Low, 1933.

Rupert and Algernon; Rupert and the White Dove. London, Sampson Low, 1934.

Rupert and Dapple. London, Sampson Low, 1934.

Rupert and Bill's Aeroplane Adventure. London, Sampson Low, 1934.

Rupert and the Magician's Umbrella. London, Sampson Low, 1934.

Rupert and Bill and the Pirates. London, Sampson Low, 1935.

Rupert at the Seaside; Rupert and Bingo. London, Sampson Low, 1935.

Rupert Gets Captured; Rupert and the Snow Babe's Christmas. London, Sampson Low, 1935.

Rupert, The Manikin and the Black Night. London, Sampson Low, 1935.

Rupert and the Greedy Princess. London, Sampson Low, 1935.

Rupert and Bill's Seaside Holiday; Rupert and the Twin's Birthday Cake. London, Sampson Low, 1936.

Rupert and Edward and the Circus. London, Sampson Low, 1936.

The Rupert Story Book. London, Sampson Low, 1938.

Rupert Little Bear: More Stories. London, Sampson Low, 1939.

Katharine Tozer (b. 1905). British.

Katharine Tozer's popularity in the picture book market is undoubtedly due to the character, warmth and detail of her own illustrations that grace almost every page of her stories. She produced seven books about the colourful escapades of a toy elephant, Mumfie, and his friend, Scarecrow. During the course of the books, Mumfie finds himself in peril at sea, floating skyward on a cloud and ascending a mountain to the lair of a fierce ogre. Although Mumfie has been criticised in some quarters for 'racial harassment' of a golliwog in the nursery, children have always warmed to this little elephant and his good-hearted adventures. The eye-catching pink, white and blue wrapper for *Here Comes Mumfie* (1936) shows the toy elephant running in his jolly sailor suit. The same scene is depicted on the book's boards.

Illustrated by the author.

The Wanderings of Mumfie. London, Murray, 1935.

Here Comes Mumfie. London, Murray, 1936.

Mumfie the Admiral. London, Murray, 1937.

Mumfie's Magic Box. London, Murray, 1938.

Mumfie's Uncle Samuel. London, Murray, 1939.

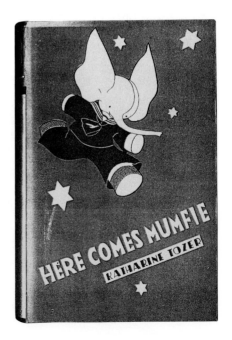

P(amela) L(yndon) Travers (1899–1996). British.

The world was introduced to the taciturn, vain, practical, forbidding and yet endearing nanny of P.L. Travers' imagination in *Mary Poppins* (1934). There is much more to Mary Poppins than first meets the eye. She is swept into the Banks family's life by a gust of the east wind, swiftly takes charge, slides *up* the banister and proceeds to unpack her seemingly bottomless carpet bag. From then on norms are subverted and magic intrudes into the Banks' comfortable domestic arrangements, but Mary Poppins through everything is the very personification of good order. Travers wrote eight 'Mary Poppins' titles between 1934 and 1988 and the whimsical nature of the books reflects the author's life-long interest in mysticism. Travers wrote other stories besides the 'Poppins' series, most notably *I Go by Sea, I Go by Land* (1941), the diary of a girl who is evacuated to America during the Second World War. The dust-wrapper design in grey and yellow for *Mary Poppins* is by Mary Shepard (daughter of E.H.). It shows Mary Poppins grasping her familiar parrot-headed umbrella and attended by a worried-looking Mr Banks and his four

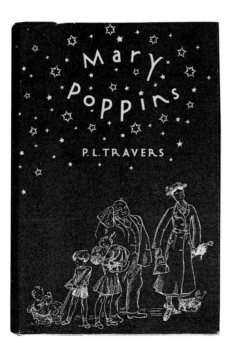

children, Jane, Michael, and the twins John and Barbara.

Mary Poppins, illustrated by Mary Shepard. London, Howe, and New York, Reynal, 1934.
Mary Poppins Comes Back, illustrated by Mary Shepard. London, Dickson and Thompson, and New York, Reynal, 1935.

Geoffrey Trease (1909–98). British.

For main author article see 1940 to 1950.

Bows Against the Barons, illustrated by Michael Boland. London, Lawrence and New York, International, 1934.
Comrades for the Charter, illustrated by Michael Boland. London, Lawrence, 1934.
The Call to Arms. London, Lawrence, 1935.
Red Comet, illustrated by Fred Ellis. Moscow, Co-operative Publishing Society of Foreign Workers 1936; London, Lawrence and Wishart, 1937.
Missing from Home, illustrated by Scott. London, Lawrence and Wishart, 1936.
The Christmas Holiday Mystery, illustrated by Alfred Sindall. London, A. & C. Black, 1937; as *The Lakeland Mystery*, 1942.
Mystery on the Moors, illustrated by Alfred Sindall. London, A. & C. Black, 1937.
Detectives of the Dales, illustrated by A.C.H. Gorham. London, A. & C. Black, 1938.
In the Land of the Mogul, illustrated by J.C.B. Knight. Oxford, Blackwell, 1938.
North Sea Spy. London, Fore, 1939.

Alison Uttley (1884–1976). British.

How Little Grey Rabbit Got Back Her Tail, illustrated by Margaret Tempest. London, Heinemann, 1930.
The Great Adventure of Hare, illustrated by Margaret Tempest. London, Heinemann, 1931.
Moonshine and Magic, illustrated by Will Townsend. London, Faber, 1932.
The Story of Fuzzypeg the Hedgehog, illustrated by Margaret Tempest. London, Heinemann, 1932.

Squirrel Goes Skating, illustrated by Margaret
Tempest. London, Collins, 1934.
Wise Owl's Story, illustrated by Margaret
Tempest. London, Collins, 1935.
The Adventures of Peter and Judy in Bunnyland,
illustrated by L. Young. London, Collins,
1935.
Candlelight Tales, illustrated by Elinor
Bellingham-Smith. London, Faber, 1936.
Little Grey Rabbit's Party, illustrated by
Margaret Tempest. London, Collins,
1936.
The Knot Squirrel Tied, illustrated by Margaret
Tempest. London, Collins, 1937.
The Adventures of No Ordinary Rabbit,
illustrated by Alec Buckels. London,
Faber, 1937.
Mustard, Pepper, and Salt, illustrated by Gwen
Raverat. London, Faber, 1938.
Fuzzypeg Goes to School, illustrated by
Margaret Tempest. London, Collins,
1938.
A Traveller in Time. London, Faber, 1939;
New York, Putnam, 1940.
Tales of the Four Pigs and Brock the Badger,
illustrated by Alec Buckels. London,
Faber, 1939.
Little Grey Rabbit's Christmas, illustrated by
Margaret Tempest. London, Collins,
1939.

Elfrida Vipont (1902–92). British.
a.k.a. Charles Vipont.

Many of Elfrida Vipont's soul-searching family
sagas written in the 1940s, 1950s and 1960s
reflect the author's deep interest in music and
Quakerism, but *Blow the Man Down* (1939) is
a very early and quite different sort of book. It
is a swashbuckling adventure for boys and so,
understandably, was written under the
pseudonym of Charles Vipont. The dust
wrapper by Norman Hepple depicts sailors
aboard Admiral Blake's frigate as they prepare
to fire on a Spanish Galleon. Young Richard
Croly, a victim of the press-gang, finds himself
among them at this crucial moment in the
vessel's history.

Blow the Man Down (as Charles Vipont),
illustrated by Norman Hepple. London,

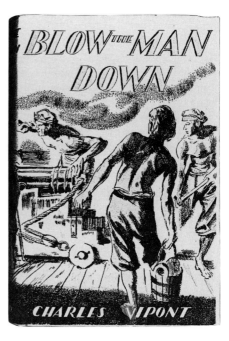

Oxford University Press, 1939;
Philadelphia, Lippincott, 1952.

Percy F(rancis) Westerman (1876–1959).
British.
a.k.a. P.F. Westerman.
a.k.a. P. Westerman.

Captain Sang. London, Blackie, 1930.
Leslie Dexter Cadet, illustrated by Norman
Hepple. London, Blackie, 1930.
A Mystery of the Broads, illustrated by E.A.
Cox. London, Blackie, 1930.
The Secret of the Plateau, illustrated by W.E.
Wigfull. London, Blackie, 1931.
The Senior Cadet, illustrated by Rowland
Hilder. London, Blackie, 1931.
In Defiance of the Ban, illustrated by E.S.
Hodgson. London, Blackie, 1931.
All Hands to the Boats!, illustrated by
Rowland Hilder. London, Blackie,
1932.
The Amir's Ruby, illustrated by W.E. Wigfull.
London, Blackie, 1932.
Captain Fosdyke's Gold, illustrated by E.S.
Hodgson. London, Blackie, 1932.
King for a Month, illustrated by Comerford
Watson. London, Blackie, 1933.

Rocks Ahead!, illustrated by D.L. Mays. London, Blackie, 1933.

The White Arab, illustrated by Henry Coller. London, Blackie, 1933.

The Disappearing Dhow, illustrated by D.L. Mays. London, Blackie, 1933.

Chasing the "Pleiad", illustrated by W. Edward Wigfull. London, Blackie, 1933.

Tales of the Sea, with others, illustrated by Terence Cuneo. London, Tuck, 1933.

The Westow Talisman, illustrated by W.E. Wigfull. London, Blackie, 1934.

Andy-All-Alone, illustrated by D.L. Mays. London, Blackie, 1934.

The Black Hawk, illustrated by Rowland Hilder. London, Blackie, 1934.

Standish of the Air Police, illustrated by W. Edward Wigfull. London, Blackie, 1935.

The Red Pirate, illustrated by Rowland Hilder. London, Blackie, 1935.

Sleuths of the Air, illustrated by Comerford Watson. London, Blackie, 1935.

On Board the "Golden Effort". London, Blackie, 1935.

The Call of the Sea, illustrated by D.L. Mays. London, Blackie, 1935.

Captain Flick, illustrated by E.S. Hodgson. London, Blackie, 1936.

Tireless Wings, illustrated by Comerford Watson. London, Blackie, 1936.

His First Ship. London, Blackie, 1936.

Midshipman Raxworthy. London, Blackie, 1936.

Ringed by Fire. London, Blackie, 1936.

Winged Might. London, Blackie, 1937.

Under Fire in Spain, illustrated by Ernest Prater. London, Blackie, 1937.

The Last of the Buccaneers. London, Blackie, 1937.

Haunted Harbour, illustrated by John de Walton. London, Blackie, 1937.

His Unfinished Voyage, illustrated by D.L. Mays. London, Blackie, 1937.

Cadet Alan Carr, illustrated by D.L. Mays. London, Blackie, 1938.

Midshipman Webb's Treasure, illustrated by D.L. Mays. London, Blackie, 1938.

Standish Gets His Man, illustrated by W.E. Wigfull. London, Blackie, 1938.

Standish Loses His Man, illustrated by W.E. Wigfull. London, Blackie, 1939.

In Eastern Seas. London, Blackie, 1939.

The Bulldog Breed, illustrated by E. Boye Uden. London, Blackie, 1939.

T(erence) H(anbury) White (1906–64). British.

T.H. White is best known for his books on life and adventures in Arthurian England, for him a chivalrous Mediaeval Never-Never-Land. The first, best and most famous of these is *The Sword in the Stone* (1938). It tells of how young Wart comes to pull a sword out of a stone; a deed that will change life forever for the future King Arthur. Wart is taken under the wing of the wizard Merlyn and learns that there is more to the world than first meets the eye. As is appropriate for a courtly tale, the book's black and white dust wrapper is emblazoned with the shields of various knights. The book has black cloth, with white lettering on the spine.

The Sword in the Stone, illustrated by the author. London, Collins, 1938; New York, Putnam, 1939; revised edition, in *The Once and Future King*, 1958.

The Witch in the Wood, illustrated by the author. New York, Putnam, 1939; London, Collins, 1940.

Laura Ingalls Wilder (1867–1957). American.

Laura Ingalls Wilder was one of the greatest exponents of children's fiction in the history of American literature. The use of the word 'fiction' in conjunction with this author is mildly misleading. For she wrote at length and in detail about her own childhood and young adulthood in the pioneer mid-west. Wilder's skill as a writer was such that she could describe situations exciting and commonplace in a straightforward but effective way that never resorted to self-absorbed reminiscence. Thus the narrative is brisk and compelling. The small family unit, buffeted by tempests, plagues and a constant Indian threat, is made up of redoutable Pa, calm and homely Ma, golden Mary, who is later struck blind by scarlet fever, baby Carrie and Laura herself. In Wilder's most famous book, *Little House on the Prairie* (1935), Pa feels that the family's privacy is being encroached upon by the presence of other settlers. Pa consequently decides that they will leave their cabin in the Wisconsin woods, and the book charts their traversing of the Mississippi and their push westwards in search of a new home. This is built but, as malaria and redskins prepare to strike, the family's problems have only just begun. The later books relate Laura's early days as a schoolteacher and her meeting with Almanzo Wilder, the man she eventually marries. Each of the books is a wonderful read, and a testament to the pluck of the early settlers of America.

Little House in the Big Woods, illustrated by Helen Sewell. New York, Harper, 1932; London, Methuen, 1956.
Farmer Boy, illustrated by Helen Sewell. New York, Harper, 1933; London, Lutterworth Press, 1965.
Little House on the Prairie, illustrated by Helen Sewell. New York, Harper, 1935; London, Methuen, 1957.
On the Banks of Plum Creek, illustrated by

Helen Sewell and Mildred Boyle. New York, Harper, 1937; London, Methuen, 1958.
By the Shores of Silver Lake, illustrated by Helen Sewell and Mildred Boyle. New York, Harper, 1939; London, Lutterworth Press, 1961.

Henry Williamson (1895–1977). British.

Salar the Salmon. London, Faber, 1935; Boston, Little Brown, 1936.

May Wynne (1875–1949). British.
Pseudonym for Mabel Winifred Knowles.

Enter – Jennie Wren (1933) is an example of May Wynne's girls' school stories. These often had unusual or exotic settings, and although the Highlands of Scotland is hardly a drastically unconventional location, some of the book's contents are extraordinary. Sutcliffe's design for the jacket captures the moment when Edna, Greta and June catch sight of what they believe to be the ghost of Hugh o' the Red Dale. Hugh was a feared Scottish freedom fighter who perished whilst fleeing from Redcoats, who were pursuing Bonnie Prince Charlie in 1745. The glimpse has a strange effect on the schoolgirls:

> Suddenly the three had stiffened, heads turned in one direction, a queer chill clutching them.

A Term to Remember. London, Aldine, 1930.
Two Girls in the Hawk's Den, illustrated by R.B. Ogle. London, Pearson, 1930.
Bobbety the Brownie. London, Warne, 1930.
The Masked Rider, illustrated by Peggy Beck. Chicago, Laidlaw, 1931.
Patient Pat Joins the Circus, illustrated by Bess Goe Willis. Philadelphia, Altemus, 1931.
Peter Rabbit and the Big Black Crows, illustrated by Bess Goe Willis. Philadelphia, Altemus, 1931.
Juliet of the Mill. London, Ward Lock, 1931.
Girls of the Pansy Patrol. London, Aldine, 1931.

Patsy from the Wilds. London, Warne, 1931.

Belle and Her Dragons. London, Jarrolds, 1931.

The Secret of Marigold Marnell. London, Religious Tract Society, 1931.

The Old Brigade. London, Religious Tract Society, 1932.

Who Was Wendy? London, Newnes, 1932.

The Heart of Glenayrt. London, Nelson, 1932.

The School Mystery. London, Readers' Library, 1933.

The Camping of the Marigolds. London, Marshall Morgan and Scott, 1933.

The Greater Covenant. London, Marshall Morgan and Scott, 1933.

Pixie's Mysterious Mission. London, Newnes, 1933.

Enter Jenny Wren, illustrated by Norman Sutcliffe. London, Ward Lock, 1933.

Comrades to Robin Hood. London, Religious Tract Society, 1934.

Malys Rockell. London, Ward Lock, 1934.

The Smugglers of Penreen. London, Religious Tract Society, 1934.

The Mysterious Island. London, Mellifont Press, 1935.

Their Girl Chum. London, Religious Tract Society, 1935.

Under Cap'n Drake. London, Religious Tract Society, 1935.

Up to Val. London, Newnes, 1935.

"Peter," The New Girl. London, Queensway Press, 1936.

The Daring of Star. London, Religious Tract Society, 1936.

Bunny and the Aunt. London, Religious Tract Society, 1936.

The Haunted Ranch. London, Dean, 1936.

Thirteen for Luck, illustrated by Norman Sutcliffe. London, Ward Lock, 1936.

Vivette on Trial. London, Queensway Press, 1936.

The Secret of Brick House. London, Ward Lock, 1937.

Two Maids of Rosemarkie. London, Epworth Press, 1937.

The Luck of Penrayne. London, Religious Tract Society, 1937.

Audrey on Approval. London, Ward Lock, 1937.

The Girl Sandy. London, Ward Lock, 1938.

The Lend-a-Hand Holiday. London, Epworth Press, 1938.

Heather the Second. London, Nelson, 1938.

The Term of Many Adventures. London, Nelson, 1939.

The Unexpected Adventure. London, Ward Lock, 1939.

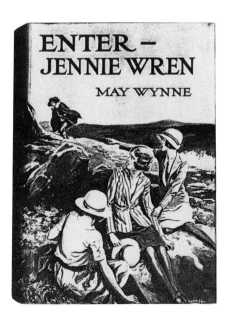

1940–1950

Ruth Ainsworth
C.W. Anderson
Edward Ardizzone
Richard Armstrong
Ruth Arthur
M.E. Atkinson
Harold Avery
The Rev. W. Awdry
'BB'
Margaret J. Baker
Cicely Mary Barker
S.G. Hulme Beaman
Alfred Bestall
Val Biro
Enid Blyton/Mary Pollock
Helen Dore Boylston
Christianna Brand
Angela Brazil
Elinor M. Brent-Dyer/ E.M. Brent-
    Dyer
Capt. F.S. Brereton/ Lt. Col. F.S.
    Brereton/Lt. Col. F.S. Brereton,
    CBE
Molly Brett
Joyce Lankester Brisley
Dorita Fairlie Bruce
Anthony Buckeridge
Virginia Lee Burton
Arthur Catherall/A.R. Channel
Christine Chaundler
Joseph E. Chipperfield
Catherine Christian/Catherine Mary
    Christian
Richard Church
Mavis Thorpe Clark
Beverly Cleary
Dorothy Clewes
Elizabeth Coatsworth
Padraic Colum
Mrs H. C. Cradock
Richmal Crompton
Primrose Cumming
Roald Dahl
Maureen Daly

Peter Dawlish/Lennox Kerr
C. Day Lewis
Marguerite de Angeli
Jean de Brunhoff
Olive Dehn
Meindert De Jong
Elizabeth Borton de Trevino
V.H. Drummond
William Pène du Bois
Monica Edwards
Elizabeth Enright
Walter Farley
Kathleen Fidler
Charles J. Finger
Dorothy Canfield Fisher/Dorothy
    Canfield
Marjorie Flack
Esther Forbes
Antonia Forest
Roy Fuller
Rose Fyleman
Wanda Gág
Eve Garnett
Doris Gates
Charles Gilson/C.L. Gilson/Captain
    Charles Gilson/Major Charles Gilson
Rumer Godden
Elizabeth Goudge
Eleanor Graham
Kenneth Grahame
Hardie Gramatky
Graham Greene
Roderick Haig-Brown/R.L. Haig-
    Brown
Kathleen Hale
Cynthia Harnett
Mary K. Harris
Robert A. Heinlein
Racey Helps
Marguerite Henry
Constance Heward
Lorna Hill
C. Walter Hodges
Edith Howes

Richard Hughes
Katharine Hull & Pamela Whitlock
Tove Jansson
W.E Johns/William Earle/Captain W.E. Johns
Erich Kästner
James W. Kenyon
Eric Knight
Frank Knight
Elizabeth Kyle
Robert Lawson
Munro Leaf/John Calvert/Mun
C.S. Lewis
Elizabeth Foreman Lewis
Eric Linklater
Hugh Lofting
Patricia Lynch
Robert McCloskey
Angus MacVicar
Ruth Manning-Sanders
Bessie Marchant
Stephen W. Meader
Florence Crannell Means
Cornelia Meigs/Adair Aldon
Annette Mills
Naomi Mitchison
Rutherford Montgomery/Al Avery/Everitt Proctor
Ursula Moray Williams
Bill Naughton
Violet Needham
Mary Norton
Mary O'Hara
Elsie J. Oxenham/Elsie Oxenham/Elsie Jeanette Oxenham
M. Pardoe
Richard Parker
Mervyn Peake
Beatrix Potter/Beatrix Heelis
Rhoda Power
Evadne Price

Willard Price
Christine Pullein-Thompson
Diana Pullein-Thompson
Josephine Pullein-Thompson
Virginia Pye
Gwynedd Rae
Arthur Ransome
Frank Richards/Hilda Richards/Martin Clifford
Charles G.D. Roberts
Diana Ross
Philip Rush
Malcolm Saville
Ruth Sawyer
Ian Serraillier
David Severn
Helen Sewell
C. Fox Smith
Caroline Dale Snedeker
Phil Stong
Noel Streatfeild
L.A.G Strong
Donald Suddaby/Alan Griff
Ethel Talbot
Barbara Euphan Todd/Euphan
H.E. Todd
J.R.R. Tolkien
Mary Tourtel
Katharine Tozer
P.L. Travers
Geoffrey Trease
Alison Uttley
Elfrida Vipont/Charles Vipont
Percy F. Westerman/P.F. Westerman/P. Westerman
E.B. White
T.H. White
Laura Ingalls Wilder
Henry Williamson
May Wynne

Ruth Ainsworth (b. 1908). British.

Richard's First Term, illustrated by Winifred M. Ackroyd. London, Epworth Press, 1940.
Five and a Dog, illustrated by Winifred M. Ackroyd and Peggy Rushton. London, Epworth Press, 1949.

C(larence) W(illiam) Anderson (1891–1971). American.

Illustrated by the author.

Salute. New York, Macmillan, 1940.
High Courage. New York, Macmillan, 1941.
Bobcat. New York, Macmillan, 1949.
Blaze Finds the Trail. New York, Macmillan, 1950.

Edward Ardizzone (1900–79). British.

The first edition of Edward Ardizzone's *Nicholas and the Fast Moving Diesel* (1947) is a large-sized book. It is dedicated 'To Nicholas from his father'. The dust-wrapper design in Edward Ardizzone's distinctive style, is of Nicholas and his dog Jock stopping the diesel express to prevent it crashing into another train.

> Nicholas jumped out of the cab, ran to the end of the train, stood between the lines, pulled off his red coat and waved and waved while Jock stood beside him and barked as loudly as he could.
> The diesel came rushing towards them …

Tim to the Rescue (1949) continues the nautical adventures of Ardizzone's young hero who first appeared in 1936 but was issued in a slightly smaller format. Tim is presented on the wrapper, clinging to the rigging of a boat in the teeth of as howling a gale as ever swept the Atlantic. He looked around: 'there was no boat, no Ginger, and no cat.'

Ilustrated by the author.

Nicholas and the Fast-Moving Diesel. London, Eyre & Spottiswoode, 1947; New York, Walck, 1959.
Paul, The Hero of the Fire. London, Penguin, 1948; Boston, Houghton Mifflin, 1949; revised edition, London, Constable, 1962; New York, Walck, 1963.
Tim to the Rescue. London and New York, Oxford University Press, 1949.

Richard Armstrong (1903–86). British.

It was his own great experience in engineering and the Merchant Navy that provided Richard Armstrong with the material for his rousing stories. Armstrong's view of life in the factory and at sea is in no way touched by romanticism. His young heroes require real grit, skill and good fortune to survive. Sometimes, and this is truly rare in children's fiction, they are lacking in luck, and perish. *The Mystery of Obadiah* (1943) is his earliest work, and less harrowing than later adventures, but it does contain the recurrent theme of the real danger overtly inquisitive little boys can place themselves in. Marjorie Sankey's wrapper has Mathias Stringer, Norman Robson and Dick Musgrove hiding behind a bush in the Northumbrian fells. They

THE MYSTERY OF
OBADIAH

RICHARD ARMSTRONG

watch the mysterious Obadiah, whom they suspect is a burglar, make his way up the hill.

The Mystery of Obadiah, illustrated by Marjorie Sankey. London, Dent, 1943.
Sabotage at the Forge, illustrated by L.P. Lupton. London, Dent, 1946.
Sea Change, illustrated by M. Leszczynski. London, Dent, 1948.

Ruth Arthur (1905–79). British.

The Crooked Brownie at the Seaside, illustrated by R.M. Turvey. London, Harrap, 1942.
Cowslip Mollie, illustrated by Helen Haywood. London, Hutchinson, 1949.

M(ary) E(velyn) Atkinson (1899–1974). British.

Going Gangster, illustrated by Harold Jones. London, Lane, 1940.
Crusoe Island, illustrated by Harold Jones. London, Lane, 1941.
Challenge to Adventure, illustrated by Stuart Tresilian. London, Lane, 1942.
The Monster of Widgeon Weir, illustrated by Stuart Tresilian. London, Lane, 1943.

The Nest of the Scarecrow, illustrated by Stuart Tresilian. London, Lane, 1944.
Problem Party, illustrated by Stuart Tresilian. London, Lane, 1945.
Chimney Cottage, illustrated by Dorothy Craigie. London, Lane, 1947.
The House on the Moor, illustrated by Charlotte Hough. London, Lane, 1948.
The Thirteenth Adventure, illustrated by Charlotte Hough. London, Lane, 1949.
Steeple Folly, illustrated by Charlotte Hough. London, Lane, 1950.

Harold Avery (1867–1943). British.

The Girl at the Helm. London, Nelson, 1941.

The Rev. W(ilbert) Awdry (1911–97). British.

The Rev. W. Awdry created an almost timeless world in which steam engines have definite and diverse personalities, and where humans, with the exception of the omnipotent Fat Controller, are incidental and characterless figures. Awdry's tales of Thomas, the Tank Engine, and his associates on the railway were originally composed for the clergyman's sickly son. Although containing a degree of fantasy, especially regarding the engines' individuality, Awdry ensured that the books portrayed details of life on the railway accurately and that all the dramatic incidents in the stories were based on ones in real life. They also contained, naturally enough considering the author's vocation, morals for the young readers. For instance, in *The Three Railway Engines* (1945), Edward, the Blue Engine, can only pull a long train with the help of Henry, the Green Engine, who had previously been decommissioned because of his lack of cooperation. Consequently, Henry learns that pride must have its fall and Edward that a job is done best if it is done in harmonious collaboration with a friend,

> 'Peep, peep', said Edward, 'I'm ready'
> 'Peep, peep, peep', said Henry, 'so am I' …

The Three Railway Engines
by The Rev. W. Awdry

'Pull hard we'll do it', they puffed together.

The heavy coaches jerked and began to move,

slowly at first, then faster and faster.

'We've done it together! We've done it together!'

This scene is captured by C. Reginald Dalby on the book's yellow-bordered dust wrapper. The conceited and intimidating Gordon sits on a nearby line with a burst safety valve.

The Three Railway Engines, illustrated by C.
   Reginald Dalby. Leicester, Ward, 1945.
Thomas, The Tank Engine, illustrated by C.
   Reginald Dalby. Leicester, Ward, 1946.
James, The Red Engine, illustrated by C.
   Reginald Dalby. Leicester, Ward, 1948.
Tank Engine Thomas Again, illustrated by C.
   Reginald Dalby. Leicester, Ward, 1949.
Troublesome Engines, illustrated by C.
   Reginald Dalby. Leicester, Ward, 1950.

'BB' (1905–90). British. Pseudonym for D(enys) J(ames) Watkins-Pitchford.

The Little Grey Men (1942), written and illustrated by D.J. Watkins-Pitchford, is a captivating story. The dust wrapper illustration depicts Sneezewort, Baldmoney and Dodder, three gnomes who live in a hollow oak by the banks of Folly Brook in Warwickshire. They are about to embark on an epic trip up the Folly in search of their lost friend, Cloudberry, who had set off to trace its source. *Down the Bright Stream* (1948) is a sequel and in it the English countryside is again tellingly described.

Ilustrated by the author.

The Little Grey Men. London, Eyre &
   Spottiswoode, 1942; New York, Scribner,
   1949.
Brendon Chase. London, Hollis and
   Carter, 1944; New York, Scribner,
   1945.
Down the Bright Stream. London, Eyre &
   Spottiswoode, 1948.

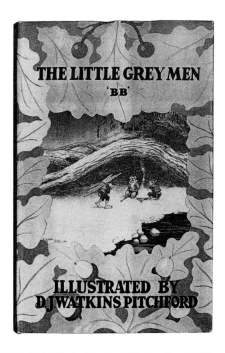

BB's Fairy Book: Meeting Hill. London, Hollis and Carter, 1948.

Margaret J(oyce) Baker (b. 1918). British.

It is Margeret J. Baker's passion for animals that propels her narratives. Children find affection and self-confidence through interaction with members of different species. However, the writer's natural warmth, good humour and storytelling ability prevent her stories descending to the level of kitsch. *"Nonsense!", Said the Tortoise* (1949) is the first of five books about Homer, the talking tortoise. Leo Bates's dust wrapper illustration shows Homer, followed by his owner, Lettice Brown, winning the pets' race. Lettice's sister, Dulcibella, in pig-tales, leads the celebrations for the famous victory.

"Nonsense!" Said the Tortoise, illustrated by Leo Bates. Leicester, Brockhampton Press, 1949; as *Homer the Tortoise,* New York, McGraw Hill, 1950.

Four Farthings and a Thimble, illustrated by Decie Merwin. New York, Longman, 1950; London, Lane, 1952.

Cicely Mary Barker (1895–1973). British.

Illustrated by the author.

Groundsel and Necklaces. London, Blackie, 1946; as *The Fairy's Gift,* Blackie, and New York, Hippocrene, 1977.

S(ydney) G(eorge) Hulme Beaman (1886–1932). British.

Illustrated by the author unless otherwise stated.

Dirty Work at the Dog and Whistle, illustrated by Ernest Noble. London, Lapworth, 1942.

Tea for Two, illustrated by Ernest Noble. London, Lapworth, 1942.

The Brave Deed of Ernest the Policeman, illustrated by Ernest Noble. London, Lapworth, 1942.

Pistols for Two, illustrated by Ernest Noble. London, Lapworth, 1942.

Mr. Noah's Holiday, illustrated by Ernest Noble. London, Lapworth, 1942.

The Adventures of Larry the Lamb (Frightfulness in the Theatre Royal, Dreadful Doings in Ark Street, Golf (Toytown Rules), Mr. Growser

Moves), illustrated by Ernest Noble. London, Lapworth, 4 vols., 1943.

Larry the Lamb. London, Collins, 1946.

The Extraordinary Affair of Ernest the Policeman, illustrated by Ernest Noble. London, Lapworth, 1947.

A Portrait of the Mayor, illustrated by Ernest Noble. London, Lapworth, 1947.

Alfred Bestall (1892–1986). British.

Illustrated by the author.

Daily Express Rupert Annuals, London, *Daily Express*, 10 vol., 1940–50.

Rupert Adventure Series, London, *Daily Express*, 1948–50.

Val Biro (b. 1921). British.

Val Biro supplied artwork for more than four hundred books by other authors (for instance, Richard Parker's *A Camel from the Desert* [1947], illustrated in this decade). Although outside the compass of the present study, he also wrote and illustrated a marvellous series of books about the adventures of Gumdrop, a vintage car based on the author's own Austin Heavy Twelve-Four, the Clifton model. In *Bumpy's Holiday*, Bumpy, a black baby elephant visits a fun fair and has a ride on a toy train. Both the train and Bumpy feature on the book's cover against a blue background.

Illustrated by the author.

Bumpy's Holiday. London, Sylvan Press, 1943; New York, Transatlantic Arts, 1945.

Enid Blyton (1897–1968). British.
a.k.a. Mary Pollock

During this decade Enid Blyton started many different series of books, perhaps the most popular being 'The Famous Five', featuring Julian (twelve years old), Dick (eleven), Georgina (eleven), Anne (ten) and Timothy the dog. This quintet feature in twenty one books written between 1942 to 1963 which have been perennial favourites with children

ever since. In the first book of the series, *Five on a Treasure Island* (1942), Julian, Dick and Anne go and stay with their Uncle Quentin and Aunt Fanny at Kirrin Cottage. Georgina is their daughter, but hates being a girl and insists she is called George, as if she were a boy. Timothy is 'a big brown mongrel dog with an absurdly long tail and a big wide mouth that really seemed to grin!' He is Georgina's 'very greatest friend'. During the holiday they visit

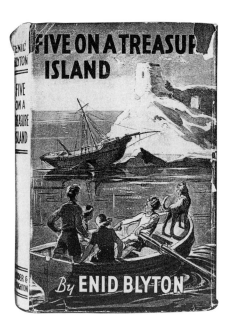

Kirrin Island, with its ruined castle, and swim around a sunken wreck. For the dust wrapper Eileen A. Soper paints the scene after the storm, of the wreck 'piled high on some sharp rocks'. Inside a box from the wreck, a map of the castle dungeons is discovered with 'Ingots!' marked on it, sending the Famous Five on further exploits.

In *Five Go Off in a Caravan* (1946), they all become involved with a travelling circus. The dust wrapper, which was again painted by Eileen A. Soper, shows Anne stepping out of the horse-drawn caravan, wearing a blue and white dress, carrying glasses of ginger beer on a tray. Julian, who is sitting on the ground, and Dick are both looking at Georgina as she points out a small spire of smoke across Merran Lake.

Collectors of first editions should note that the dust wrappers for the first eight Famous Five titles have white spines lettered with the author, title and publisher.

The Mystery of the Spiteful Letters (1946), is the fourth of fifteen books in the 'Mysteries' series. They feature the Five Find-Outers: Laurence Daykin (Larry), the leader, and his sister Margaret Daykin (Daisy), Philip Hilton (Pip) and his young sister Elizabeth (Bets), plus Frederick Algernon Trotteville (Fatty). They are assisted by Buster, a Scottie dog, who acts as their bloodhound. The dust wrapper illustration is by J. Abbey and depicts Fatty, disguised as a telegraph boy, as he delivers a parcel to Nosey and his wife. He asks Nosey to sign for it since he suspects him of sending spiteful letters to local inhabitants. Unfortunately for Fatty, Nosey proves to be illiterate.

All the eight books in the 'Adventure' series are illustrated by Stuart Tresilian. They record the adventures of two sets of brothers and sisters, Philip and Dinah Mannering and Jack and Lucy-Ann Trent. Jack's talking scarlet-and-grey parrot, Kiki, who has a big crest on her head, has an important role to play in many of the stories as does Bill Cunningham, a friend of the four children. The vivid composition of the dust wrapper of *The Island of Adventure* (1944) is of Philip and Dinah on the Isle of Gloom discovering 'a large hole, about six feet round … with a ladder going down,' which leads to some old disused copper-mines.

Enid Blyton created two series of girls' school stories: Malory Towers and St Clare's. Darrell Rivers is the main character in the six Malory Towers stories and becomes head girl in the last book of the series. Darrell Rivers,

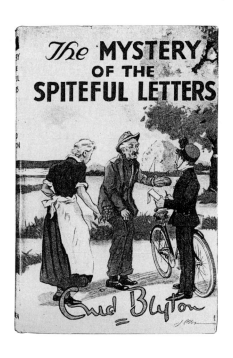

Alicia Johns and Betty Hill are all first-formers in *First Term at Malory Towers* (1946), and Stanley Lloyd draws them swimming in the sea near their Cornish boarding school. The stars of the six St Clare's School stories are twins Pat and Isabel O'Sullivan, with a supporting cast of Janet, Hilary, Kathleen, Bobby and Prudence, who all 'sit in class under Mam'zelle's stern eye'.

There are twenty-four numbered Noddy books. Number one, *Noddy Goes To Toyland*, was published in 1949 with the same red-boarded design on the dust wrapper and front cover of the book and was illustrated by Harmsen Van Beek. Noddy and his friend Big Ears first meet when they collide in the woods when Big Ears the brownie was hurrying along on his red bicycle. '"You're not a pixie or a brownie or a goblin, are you?" asked Big Ears. "I'm a little nodding man", said the small fellow.' He had been made by Old Man Carver who used blue beads for bright eyes and cat's fur for hair. Big Ears names him Noddy after the action of his head and gives him a ride to catch the Toy Land train to Toy Town where Big Ears buys Noddy's famous outfit at the market. Towards the end of the book Noddy says, 'I'll have heaps of adventures … Oh heaps and heaps.' He does, and his adventures have so far enthralled over

four decades of young children who discover many of Toy Town's different characters, such as Mr Plod, Miss Fluffy Cat, Mr Wobbly-Man, Tessie Bear, Bert Monkey, Sam and Sally Skittle, Bumpy Dog, Mr & Mrs Tubby Bear, Mr & Mrs Noah, George and Gilbert Golly and Katie Kitten.

The 'Secret Seven' are Janet, Pam, Barbara, Colin, Jack, George and Peter, and this much liked series consists of fifteen different titles. The artist George Brook designed the wrapper for *The Secret Seven* (1949), picturing Janet, with the dog Scamper at her feet, opening the door of a shed to George and Peter after they have given the password 'Wenceslas'. The shed is used for meetings of the 'Secret Seven'.

The six books in the 'Barney' series have always been popular. All are exciting mysteries about Barney, a circus boy, and his little monkey Miranda, as well as Roger and Diana and their irrepressible cousin Snubby who has a dog, a spaniel called Loony. The dust-wrapper design for the first book of the series, *The Rockingdown Mystery* (1949), was painted by Gilbert Dunlop. Miranda, Roger, Snubby and Loony are in a cellar 'They all knelt down in the corner and examined the iron ring set in the wall.'

Brockhampton Press published twenty-three 'Mary Mouse' strip books, approximately 14.5cms x 7 cms, with pictorial covers but no dust wrappers. These stories have a strong appeal for young children. The yellow, red, black and white front cover of *Mary Mouse and the Doll's House* (1942), shows Mary Mouse pushing Roundy in his pram, being followed by Pip, Daddy Doll, Mummy Doll and Melia.

This was a very prolific decade for Enid Blyton. Besides writing many titles for her popular series, she continued to write over one hundred and fifty other books ranging from volumes for the very young through to works for teenagers.

It was during this period that Enid Blyton wrote six books under the pseudonym Mary Pollock. Kidillin is a Scottish village and for the dust wrapper of *The Children of Kidillin* (1940), E. Wilson shows the four cousins, Sandy, Jeanie, Tom and Sheila, plus the two Scottie dogs, Mack and Paddy, sharing a picnic. 'The children looked at the little steamer slipping slowly along, and hoped it would not be sunk' by submarines.

The Children of Cherry Tree Farm, illustrated by Harry Rountree. London, Country Life, 1940.

The Little Tree-House, Being the Adventures of Josie, Click, and Bun, illustrated by Dorothy M. Wheeler. London, Newnes, 1940; as Josie, Click, and Bun and the Little Tree House, 1951.

Mr. Meddle's Mischief, illustrated by Joyce Mercer and Rosalind M. Turvey. London, Newnes, 1940.

The Naughtiest Girl in the School, illustrated by W. Lindsay Cable. London, Newnes, 1940.

The Secret of Spiggy Holes, illustrated by E.H. Davie. Oxford, Blackwell, 1940.

Twenty-Minute Tales, illustrated by May Smith. London, Methuen, 1940.

Tales of Betsy-May, illustrated by Joan Gale Thomas. London, Methuen, 1940.

The Treasure Hunters, illustrated by E. Wilson and Joyce Davies. London, Newnes, 1940.

The Children of Kidillin (as Mary Pollock), illustrated by E. Wilson. London, Newnes, 1940.

Three Boys and a Circus (as Mary Pollock), illustrated by E. Wilson. London, Newnes, 1940.

The Adventures of Mr Pink-Whistle, illustrated by Dorothy M. Wheeler, London, Newnes, 1941.

The Adventurous Four, illustrated by E.H. Davie. London, Newnes, 1941.

Five O'Clock Tales, illustrated by Dorothy M. Wheeler. London, Methuen, 1941.

The Further Adventures of Josie, Click, and Bun, illustrated by Dorothy M. Wheeler. London, Newnes, 1941.

The Secret Mountain, illustrated by Harry Rountree. Oxford, Blackwell, 1941.

The Twins at St. Clare's, illustrated by W. Lindsay Cable. London, Methuen, 1941.

The Children of Willow Farm, illustrated by Harry Rountree. London, Country Life, 1942.

Circus Days Again, illustrated by E.H. Davie. London, Newnes, 1942.

Happy Story Book. London, Hodder & Stoughton, 1942.

Enid Blyton's Little Books (Brer Rabbit, Bedtime Stories, Jolly Tales, Ho-Ho and Too Smart, Tales of the Toys, Happy Stories), illustrated by Alfred Kerr. London, Evans, 6 vols, 1942.

Five on a Treasure Island, illustrated by Eileen A. Soper. London, Hodder & Stoughton, 1942; New York, Crowell, 1950.

Hello, Mr. Twiddle, illustrated by Hilda McGavin. London, Newnes, 1942.

I'll Tell You a Story, illustrated by Eileen A. Soper. London, Macmillan, 1942.

John Jolly at Christmas Time [by the Sea, on the Farm, at the Circus]. London, Evans, 4 vols, 1942–45.

Mary Mouse and the Doll's House. Leicester, Brockhampton Press, 1942.

The Naughtiest Girl Again, illustrated by W. Lindsay Cable. London, Newnes, 1942.

The O'Sullivan Twins, illustrated by W. Lindsay Cable. London, Methuen, 1942.

Shadow, The Sheep-Dog, illustrated by Lucy Gee. London, Newnes, 1942.

Six O'Clock Tales: Thirty-Three Short Stories for Children, illustrated by Dorothy M. Wheeler. London, Methuen, 1942.

Bimbo and Topsy, illustrated by Lucy Gee. London, Newnes, 1943.

Come to the Circus, illustrated by Eileen A. Soper. Leicester, Brockhampton Press, 1943.

Dame Slap and Her School, illustrated by Dorothy M. Wheeler. London, Newnes, 1943.

I'll Tell You Another Story, illustrated by Eileen A. Soper. London, Macmillan, 1943.

Mischief at St. Rollo's, (as Mary Pollock). London, Newnes, 1943.

More Adventures on Willow Farm, illustrated by Eileen A. Soper. London, Country Life, 1943.

The Secret of Cliff Castle, (as Mary Pollock). London, Newnes, 1943.

Five Go Adventuring Again, illustrated by Eileen A. Soper. London, Hodder & Stoughton, 1943; New York, Crowell, 1951.

The Magic Faraway Tree, illustrated by Dorothy M. Wheeler. London, Newnes, 1943.

Merry Story Book, illustrated by Eileen A. Soper. London, Hodder & Stoughton, 1943.

More Adventures of Mary Mouse, illustrated by Olive F. Openshaw. Leicester, Brockhampton Press, 1943.

The Mystery of the Burnt Cottage, illustrated by J. Abbey. London, Methuen, 1943; Los Angeles, McNaughton, 1946.

The Secret of Killimooin, illustrated by Eileen A. Soper. Oxford, Blackwell, 1943.

Seven O'Clock Tales: Thirty Short Stories for Children, illustrated by Dorothy M. Wheeler. London, Methuen, 1943.

Summer Term at St. Clare's, illustrated by W. Lindsay Cable. London, Methuen, 1943.

The Adventures of Scamp (as Mary Pollock). London, Newnes, 1943.

Smuggler Ben (as Mary Pollock). London, Newnes, 1943.

The Toys Come to Life, illustrated by Eileen A. Soper. Leicester, Brockhampton Press, 1943.

Polly Piglet, illustrated by Eileen A. Soper. Leicester, Brockhampton Press, 1943.

At Appletree Farm, illustrated by Eileen A. Soper. Leicester, Brockhampton Press, 1944.

Billy and Betty at the Seaside, illustrated by E.O. Dundee, Valentine, 1944.

The Dog That Went to Fairyland, illustrated by Eileen A. Soper. Leicester, Brockhampton Press, 1944.

Claudine at St. Clare's, illustrated by W. Lindsay Cable. London, Methuen, 1944.

Jolly Little Jumbo, illustrated by Eileen A. Soper. Leicester, Brockhampton Press, 1944.

Little Mary Mouse Again, illustrated by Olive F. Openshaw. Leicester, Brockhampton Press, 1944.

The Boy Next Door, illustrated by Alfred Bestall. London, Newnes, 1944.

Eight O'Clock Tales, illustrated by Dorothy M. Wheeler. London, Methuen, 1944.

Five Run Away Together, illustrated by Eileen A. Soper. London, Hodder & Stoughton, 1944; Chicago, Reilly and Lee, 1960.

The Island of Adventure, illustrated by Stuart Tresilian. London, Macmillan, 1944; as *Mystery Island*, New York, Macmillan, 1945.

Jolly Story Book, illustrated by Eileen A. Soper. London, Hodder & Stoughton, 1944.

A Book of Naughty Children, illustrated by Eileen A. Soper. London, Methuen, 1944.

The Mystery of the Disappearing Cat, illustrated by J. Abbey. London, Methuen, 1944; Los Angeles, McNaughton, 1948.

Rainy Day Stories, illustrated by Nora S. Unwin. London, Evans, 1944.

The Second Form at St. Clare's, illustrated by W. Lindsay Cable. London, Methuen, 1944.

Tales of Toyland, illustrated by Hilda McGavin. London, Newnes, 1944.

The Three Golliwogs, illustrated by Joyce A. Johnson. London, Newnes, 1944.

The Blue Story Book, illustrated by Eileen A. Soper. London, Methuen, 1945.

The Caravan Family, illustrated by William Fyffe. London, Lutterworth Press, 1945.

The Conjuring Wizard and Other Stories, illustrated by Eileen A. Soper. London, Macmillan, 1945.

The Family at Red Roofs, illustrated by W. Spence. London, Lutterworth Press, 1945.

Fifth Formers at St. Clare's, illustrated by W. Lindsay Cable. London, Methuen, 1945.

Five Go to Smuggler's Top, illustrated by Eileen A. Soper. London, Hodder & Stoughton, 1945; Chicago, Reilly and Lee, 1960.

Hallo, Little Mary Mouse, illustrated by Olive F. Openshaw. Leicester, Brockhampton Press, 1945.

Hollow Tree House, illustrated by Elizabeth Wall. London, Lutterworth Press, 1945.

The Mystery of the Secret Room, illustrated by J. Abbey. London, Methuen, 1945.

The Naughtiest Girl is a Monitor, illustrated by Kenneth Lovell. London, Newnes, 1945.

Round the Clock Stories, illustrated by Nora S. Unwin. London, National Magazine Company, 1945.

The Runaway Kitten, illustrated by Eileen A. Soper. Leicester, Brockhampton Press, 1945.

Sunny Story Book. London, Hodder & Stoughton, 1945.

The Teddy Bear's Party, illustrated by Eileen A. Soper. Leicester, Brockhampton Press, 1945.

The Twins Go to Nursery-Rhyme Land, illustrated by Eileen A. Soper. Leicester, Brockhampton Press, 1945.

Amelia Jane Again, illustrated by Sylvia I. Venus. London, Newnes, 1946.

The Bad Little Monkey, illustrated by Eileen A. Soper. Leicester, Brockhampton Press, 1946.

The Castle of Adventure, illustrated by Stuart Tresilian. London, Macmillan, and New York, Macmillan, 1946.

The Children at Happy House, illustrated by Kathleen Gell. Oxford, Blackwell, 1946.

Chimney Corner Stories, illustrated by Pat Harrison. London, National Magazine Company, 1946.

First Term at Malory Towers, illustrated by Stanley Lloyd. London, Methuen, 1946.

Five Go Off in a Caravan, illustrated by Eileen A. Soper. London, Hodder & Stoughton, 1946.

The Folk of the Faraway Tree, illustrated by Dorothy M. Wheeler. London, Newnes, 1946.

Gay Story Book, illustrated by Eileen A. Soper. London, Hodder & Stoughton, 1946.

Josie, Click, and Bun Again, illustrated by Dorothy M. Wheeler, London, Newnes, 1946.

The Little White Duck and Other Stories, illustrated by Eileen A. Soper. London, Macmillan, 1946.

Mary Mouse and Her Family, illustrated by Olive F. Openshaw. Leicester, Brockhampton Press, 1946.

The Mystery of the Spiteful Letters, illustrated by J. Abbey. London, Methuen, 1946.

The Put-em-Rights, illustrated by Elizabeth Wall. London, Lutterworth Press, 1946.

The Red Story Book, illustrated by Eileen A. Soper. London, Methuen, 1946.

The Surprising Caravan, illustrated by Eileen A. Soper. Leicester, Brockhampton Press, 1946.

Tales of Green Hedges, illustrated by Gwen White. London, National Magazine Company, 1946.

The Brown Family, illustrated by E. and R. Buhler. London, News Chronicle, 1946.

The Train That Lost Its Way, illustrated by Eileen A. Soper. Leicester, Brockhampton Press, 1946.

The Adventurous Four Again, illustrated by Jessie Land. London, Newnes, 1947.

At Seaside Cottage, illustrated by Eileen A. Soper. Leicester, Brockhampton Press, 1947.

Five on Kirrin Island Again, illustrated by Eileen A. Soper. London, Hodder & Stoughton, 1947.

The Green Story Book, illustrated by Eileen A. Soper. London, Methuen, 1947.

The Happy House Children Again, illustrated by Kathleen Gell. Oxford, Blackwell, 1947.

Here Comes Mary Mouse Again, illustrated by Olive F. Openshaw. Leicester, Brockhampton Press, 1947.

Little Green Duck and Other Stories, illustrated by Eileen A. Soper. Leicester, Brockhampton Press, 1947.

The House at the Corner, illustrated by Elsie Walker. London, Lutterworth Press, 1947.

Lucky Story Book, illustrated by Eileen A. Soper. London, Hodder & Stoughton, 1947.

The Mystery of the Missing Necklace, illustrated by J. Abbey. London, Methuen, 1947.

The Second Form at Malory Towers, illustrated by Stanley Lloyd. London, Methuen, 1947.

Rambles with Uncle Nat, illustrated by Nora S. Unwin. London, National Magazine Company, 1947.

A Second Book of Naughty Children: Twenty-Four Short Stories, illustrated by Kathleen Gell. London, Methuen, 1947.

The Smith Family 1–3 (At Home, At the Zoo, At the Circus). Leeds, E.J. Arnold, 3 vols, 1947.

The Valley of Adventure, illustrated by Stuart Tresilian. London, Macmillan, and New York, Macmillan, 1947.

The Very Clever Rabbit, illustrated by Eileen A. Soper. Leicester, Brockhampton, 1947.

The Adventures of Pip, illustrated by Raymond Sheppard. London, Sampson Low, 1948.

The Boy with the Loaves and Fishes, illustrated by Elsie Walker. London, Lutterworth Press, 1948.

Come to the Circus, illustrated by Joyce M. Johnson (different book from the 1944 title). London, Newnes, 1948.

Five Go Off to Camp, illustrated by Eileen A. Soper. London, Hodder & Stoughton, 1948; as *Five on the Track of a Spook Train*, New York, Atheneum, 1972.

How Do You Do, Mary Mouse, illustrated by Olive F. Openshaw. Leicester, Brockhampton Press, 1948.

More Adventures of Pip, illustrated by Raymond Sheppard. London, Sampson Low, 1948.

Just Time for a Story, illustrated by Grace Lodge. London, Macmillan, 1948; New York, St. Martin's Press, 1952.

Let's Have a Story, illustrated by George Bowe. London, Pitkin, 1948.

The Little Girl at Capernaum, illustrated by Elsie Walker. London, Lutterworth Press, 1948.

Mister Icy-Cold, illustrated by Will Nickless. Oxford, Blackwell, 1948.

More about Josie, Click, and Bun, illustrated by Dorothy M. Wheeler. London, Newnes, 1948.

The Mystery of the Hidden House, illustrated by J. Abbey. London, Methuen, 1948.

Nature Tales, illustrated by Cuthill. London, Johnston, 1948.

Now for a Story, illustrated by Frank Varty. Newcastle-upon-Tyne, Harold Hill, 1948.

The Red-Spotted Handkerchief and Other Stories, illustrated by Kathleen Gell. Leicester, Brockhampton Press, 1948.

The Sea of Adventure, illustrated by Stuart Tresilian. London, Macmillan, and New York, Macmillan, 1948.

The Secret of the Old Mill, illustrated by Eileen A. Soper. Leicester, Brockhampton Press, 1948.

Six Cousins at Mistletoe Farm, illustrated by Peter Beigel. London, Evans, 1948.

Tales after Tea. London, T. Werner Laurie, 1948.

Tales of the Twins, illustrated by Eileen A. Soper. Leicester, Brockhampton Press, 1948.

The "Saucy Jane" Family, illustrated by Ruth Gervis. London, Lutterworth Press, 1948.

They Ran Away Together, illustrated by Jeanne Farrar. Leicester, Brockhampton Press, 1948.

Third Year at Malory Towers, illustrated by Stanley Lloyd. London, Methuen, 1948.

We Want a Story, illustrated by George Bowe. London, Pitkin, 1948.

Enid Blyton's Bluebell Story Book, illustrated by Helen Jacobs, Kathleen Gell, Norman Meredith, Hilda Boswell. London, Gifford, 1949.

A Cat in Fairyland and Other Stories, illustrated by E.H. Davie and M. Thorp. London, Pitkin, 1949.

The Dear Old Snow Man, illustrated by Eileen A. Soper. Leicester, Brockhampton Press, 1949.

Don't Be Silly, Mr Twiddle, illustrated by Hilda McGavin. London, Newnes, 1949.

The Enchanted Sea and Other Stories, illustrated by E.H. Davie. London, Pitkin, 1949.

Bumpy and His Bus, illustrated by Dorothy M. Wheeler. London, Newnes, 1949.

The Circus Book. London, Latimer House, 1949.

Good Morning Book, illustrated by Don and Ann Goring. London, National Magazine Company, 1949.

Five Get into Trouble, illustrated by Eileen A. Soper. London, Hodder & Stoughton, 1949; as *Five Caught in a Treacherous Plot*, New York, Atheneum, 1972.

Jinky's Joke and Other Stories, illustrated by Kathleen Gell, Leicester, Brockhampton Press, 1949.

Noddy Goes to Toyland, illustrated by Harmsen Van Beek. London, Sampson Low, 1949.

Mr. Tumpy and His Caravan, illustrated by Dorothy M. Wheeler. London, Sidgwick & Jackson, 1949; Los Angeles, McNaughton, 1951.

The Mountain of Adventure, illustrated by Stuart Tresilian. London, Macmillan, and New York, Macmillan, 1949.

The Rockingdown Mystery, illustrated by Gilbert Dunlop. London, Collins, 1949.

The Secret Seven, illustrated by George Brook. Leicester, Brockhampton Press, 1949; as *The Secret Seven and the Mystery of the Empty House*, Chicago, Children's Press, 1972.

A Story Party at Green Hedges, illustrated by Grace Lodge. London, Hodder & Stoughton, 1949.

Enid Blyton's Daffodil Story Book. London, Gifford, 1949.

Tales after Supper. London, T. Werner Laurie, 1949.

Those Dreadful Children, illustrated by Grace Lodge. London, Lutterworth Press, 1949.

Humpty Dumpty and Belinda, illustrated by Sally Gee. London, Collins, 1949.

The Mystery of the Pantomine Cat, illustrated by J. Abbey. London, Methuen, 1949.

Oh, What a Lovely Time, illustrated by Jeanne Farrar. Leicester, Brockhampton Press, 1949.

The Strange Umbrella and Other Stories, illustrated by E.H. Davie and M. Thorp. London, Pitkin, 1949.

Enid Blyton's Tiny Tales, illustrated by Eileen A. Soper. Worcester, Littlebury, 1949.

The Upper Fourth at Malory Towers, illustrated by Stanley Lloyd. London, Methuen,1949.

Chuff the Chimney Sweep and Other Stories. London, Pitkin, 1949.

Rubbalong Tales, illustrated by Norman Meredith. London, Macmillan, 1949.

The Astonishing Ladder and Other Stories, illustrated by Eileen A. Soper. London, Macmillan, 1950.

Enid Blyton's Poppy Story Book. London, Gifford, 1950.

Five Fall into Adventure, illustrated by Eileen A. Soper. London, Hodder & Stoughton, 1950; New York, Atheneum, 1972.

Hurrah for Little Noddy, illustrated by Harmsen Van Beek. London, Sampson Low, 1950.

In the Fifth at Malory Towers, illustrated by Stanley Lloyd. London, Methuen, 1950.

The Magic Knitting Needles and Other Stories, illustrated by Eileen A. Soper. London, Macmillan, 1950.

Mister Meddle's Muddles, illustrated by Rosalind M. Turvey and Joyce Mercer. London, Newnes, 1950.

Mr. Pink-Whistle Interferes, illustrated by Dorothy M. Wheeler. London, Newnes, 1950.

The Mystery of the Invisible Thief, illustrated by Treyer Evans. London, Methuen, 1950.

The Pole Star Family, illustrated by Ruth Gervis. London, Lutterworth Press, 1950.

The Rilloby Fair Mystery, illustrated by Gilbert Dunlop. London, Collins, 1950.

The Seaside Family, illustrated by Ruth Gervis. London, Lutterworth Press, 1950.

The Secret Seven Adventure, illustrated by George Brook. Leicester, Brockhampton Press, 1950; as *The Secret Seven and the Circus Adventure*, Chicago, Children's Press, 1972.

The Ship of Adventure, illustrated by Stuart Tresilian. London, Macmillan, and New York, Macmillan, 1950.

Six Cousins Again, illustrated by Maurice Tulloch. London, Evans, 1950.

Tales about Toys, illustrated by Jeanne Farrar. Leicester, Brockhampton Press, 1950.

The Three Naughty Children and Other Stories, illustrated by Eileen A. Soper. London, Macmillan, 1950.

Tricky the Goblin and Other Stories, illustrated by Eileen A. Soper. London, Macmillan, 1950.

We Do Love Mary Mouse, illustrated by Olive F. Openshaw, Leicester, Brockhampton Press, 1950.

Welcome Mary Mouse, illustrated by Olive F. Openshaw. Leicester, Brockhampton press, 1950.

What an Adventure, illustrated by Eileen A. Soper. Leicester, Brockhampton Press, 1950.

The Wishing Chair Again, illustrated by Hilda McGavin. London, Newnes, 1950.

The Yellow Story Book, illustrated by Kathleen Gell. London, Methuen, 1950.

Helen Dore Boylston (1895–1984). American.

Sue Barton, Superintendent of Nurses, illustrated by Forrest Orr. Boston, Little Brown, 1940; London, Lane, 1942.

Carol Goes Backstage, illustrated by Frederick Wallace. Boston, Little Brown, 1941; as *Carol Goes on the Stage*, London, Lane, 1943.

Carol Plays Summer Stock, illustrated by Major Felten. Boston, Little Brown, 1942; as *Carol in Repertory*, London, Lane, 1944.

Carol on Broadway, illustrated by Major Felten. Boston, Little Brown, 1944; as *Carol Comes to Broadway*, London, Lane, 1945.

Carol on Tour, illustrated by Major Felten. Boston, Little Brown, 1946; London, Lane, 1948.

Sue Barton, Neighborhood Nurse. Boston, Little Brown, 1949; London, Lane, 1950.

Christianna Brand (1907–88). British.

Christianna Brand is best-known for her ingenious detective fiction stories. However, she also wrote four books for children. These include the 'Nurse Matilda' trilogy about a fearsome nanny, who in appearance seems a closer relative to Barrie's Nana than Mary Poppins. Even with her overbearing personality, Nurse Matilda has difficulty keeping the wickedly mischievous Brown children in order.

Danger Unlimited. New York, Dodd Mead, 1948; as *Welcome to Danger*, illustrated by William Stobbs. London, Foley House Press, 1950.

Angela Brazil (1869–1947). British.

The New School at Scawdale, illustrated by M. Mackinlay. London, Blackie, 1940.
Five Jolly Schoolgirls. London, Blackie, 1941.
The Mystery of the Moated Grange, illustrated by W. Lindsay Cable. London, Blackie, 1942.
The Secret of the Border Castle, illustrated by Charles Willis. London, Blackie, 1943.
The School in the Forest, illustrated by J. Dewar Mills. London, Blackie, 1944.
Three Terms at Uplands, illustrated by D.L. Mays. London, Blackie, 1945.
The School on the Loch, illustrated by W. Lindsay Cable. London, Blackie, 1946.

Elinor M(ay) Brent-Dyer (1894–1969). British.
a.k.a. E.M. Brent-Dyer.

Besides her long series of 'Châlet School' books, Elinor Brent-Dyer produced another important series, the 'La Rochelle' books, of which there are seven titles. The first three books written by Elinor Brent-Dyer belong to this series. There is a link between the two series as some of the female offsprings of the 'La Rochelle' girls feature in various 'Châlet School' stories. *The Highland Twins at the Châlet School* (1942) is the sixteenth title in the series. The attractive dust-wrapper design by

Nina K. Brisley depicts a smartly dressed Joey Maynard (formerly Joey Bettany) greeting the twins Fiona and Flora McDonald, who have travelled in full Highland dress on their train journey.

The Châlet School in Exile, illustrated by Nina K. Brisley. Edinburgh, Chambers, 1940.
The Châlet School Goes to It, illustrated by Nina K. Brisley. Edinburgh, Chambers, 1941.
The Highland Twins at the Châlet School, illustrated by Nina K. Brisley. Edinburgh, Chambers, 1942.
The Little Missus, illustrated by Mackay, Edinburgh, Chambers, 1942.
Lavender Laughs in the Châlet School, illustrated by Nina K. Brisley. Edinburgh, Chambers, 1943.
Gay from China at the Châlet School, illustrated by Nina K. Brisley. Edinburgh, Chambers, 1944.
Jo to the Rescue, illustrated by Nina K. Brisley. Edinburgh, Chambers, 1945.
The Lost Staircase, illustrated by Nina K. Brisley. Edinburgh, Chambers, 1946.
Lorna at Wynyards, illustrated by Victor J. Bertoglio. London, Lutterworth Press, 1947.
Stepsisters for Lorna, illustrated by John Bruce. London, Temple, 1948.

Three Go to the Châlet School. Edinburgh, Chambers, 1949.

Peggy of the Châlet School, illustrated by Nina K. Brisley. Edinburgh, Chambers, 1950.

The Châlet School and the Island. Edinburgh, Chambers, 1950.

Fardingdales. London, Latimer, 1950.

Captain F(rederick) S(adleir) Brereton
(1872–1957). British.
a.k.a. Lt. Col. F.S. Brereton.
a.k.a. Lt. Col. F.S. Brereton, CBE

Trapped in the Jungle!, illustrated by Vernon Soper. London, Hollis and Carter, 1945.

Molly Brett (1902–90). British.

Illustrated by the author.

Drummer Boy Duckling. London, Partridge, 1945.

Follow Me Round the Farm. London, Raphael Tuck, 1947.

Puppy School-Days. Leicester, Brockhampton Press, 1948.

Mr Turkey Runs Away. Leicester, Brockhampton Press, 1948.

Master Bunny the Baker's Boy. Leicester, Brockhampton Press, 1950.

Joyce Lankester Brisley (1896–1978). British.

Illustrated by the author.

The Adventures of Purl and Plain. London, Harrap, 1941.

Milly-Molly-Mandy Again. London, Harrap, 1948; New York, McKay, 1977.

Dorita Fairlie Bruce (1885–1970). British.

Dorita Fairlie Bruce is most famous for her 'Dimsie' and 'Nancy' series of schoolgirl yarns. Besides her four historical novels, Dorita Fairlie Bruce also wrote three other series with school locations, the 'Springdale' (six books), 'Sally' (three books) and 'School on the Moor' (three

books). *The School in the Woods* (1940) is the second of the 'School on the Moor' series and is an incredibly scarce book in its original dust wrapper painted by G.M. Anson. In the eerie nighttime scene portrayed on the wrapper, Toby Barrett, a sixth former at Thatches School, has caught sight of a dark figure moving swiftly and stealthily in the woods.

The School in the Woods, illustrated by G.M. Anson. London, Oxford University Press, 1940.

Dimsie Carries On, illustrated by W. Bryce Hamilton. London, Oxford University Press, 1942.

Toby at Tibbs Cross, illustrated by Margaret Horder. London, Oxford University Press, 1943.

Nancy Calls the Tune, illustrated by Margaret Horder. London, Oxford University Press, 1944.

A Laverock Lilting, illustrated by Margaret Horder. London, Oxford University Press, 1945.

Wild Goose Quest. London, Lutterworth Press, 1945.

The Serendipity Shop, illustrated by Margaret Horder. London, Oxford University Press, 1947.

Triffeny, illustrated by Margaret Horder. London, Oxford University Press, 1950.

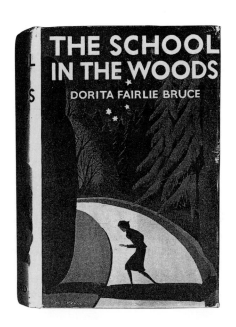

Anthony Buckeridge (b. 1912). British.

Anthony Buckeridge first told the 'Jennings' stories, set at Linbury Court School, Sussex, to his pupils at the preparatory school where he taught. A number were submitted to the BBC and were broadcast on *Children's Hour* to great acclaim during 1948. Two years later, the initial story, *Jennings Goes to School*, was published in book form, the first of twenty-five volumes published between 1950 and 1994. During that time, John Christopher Timothy Jennings, who never progresses beyond eleven years of age, having reached his eleventh birthday in the first chapter of *Jennings and Darbishire* (1952), manages to wreak much well-meaning mayhem, and finds himself in countless scrapes, often caused by his latest super-wizzo-sonic scheme. His partner in chaos is the bespectacled Charles Edwin Jeremy Darbishire, a more retiring soul, who is often left asking, 'Why do these gruesome hoo-hahs always have to pick on us to happen to?' Bearing the brunt of Jennings and Darbishire's 'bat-witted wheezes' are placid Mr Carter (nicknamed Benedick in the first book beacuse he entones 'Benedicata' after every meal) and the hot-tempered and bellowing Mr Wilkins ('Doh! I-I-Corwumph!'. 'If there's any more trouble … I'll … I'll … Well, there'd better not *be* any more trouble').

The books are characterised by the boys' wide use of slang, much of which, although invented by Buckeridge, has since entered the English language more widely ('Fossilised fish hooks!', 'You addle-pated clodpoll!', 'Crystallised cheesecakes!'). Whether Buckeridge is describing a Test Match between a 'World Cricket XI' and an 'Outer Space XI', the latest school craze, a disastrous day out or a contribution to a House match, heroic or hopeless, the stories are priceless entertainment. The first chapter of *Jennings Goes to School*, 'Jennings Learns the Ropes', introduces the main characters and sets the scene. The marvellous 'wraparound' dust wrapper by S. van Abbé also helps in creating an atmosphere for the reader before the book is even opened. The picture reflects the hustle and bustle that accompanies the beginning of every academic year:

> Twelve times Mr Carter shook hands; twelve times he was pleased to say that his health was excellent, and twelve times he informed the earnest inquirer that he had spent a pleasant holiday. He moved on, his right hand somewhat stickier than before.

Also shown is Mr Martin Winthrop Barlow

Pemberton-Oakes (MA, Oxon.), Linbury Court's headmaster, who is giving a tour of the school to the Reverend Percival Darbishire, who seems bemused by the whole experience. The younger Darbishire, 'a small-scale model of his father', has had his attention caught by Jennings, who gives his future best friend a cheery 'thumbs up'.

Jennings Goes to School, illustrated by S. van Abbé. London, Collins, 1950.

Virginia Lee Burton (1909–68). American.

Virginia Lee Burton was an expert exponent of picture books. She only produced six over a period of fifteen years, but they have all become American classics of this type of literature. Burton perceived herself as almost solely an artist and only fitted words to match her illustrations when the pictures were complete. *Choo Choo: Story of a Little Engine who Ran Away* (1937) is the exhilarating tale of a mischievous truant train. *Mike Mulligan and the Steam Shovel* (1939) is a more complicated story of a man and his vapour-powered spade, Mary Ann, as they race to dig a new basement for the local civic centre. At the beginning of *The Little House* (1942), the hero stands in the countryside, surrounded by trees and fields, and with birds, flowers and a few children for company. The lights of the big city twinkle in the distance and the little house wonders what it would be like there. It finds out too clearly because steam shovels arrive and the little house is soon surrounded by tall skyscrapers. Trapped in a large city, the little house longs to escape back to the country. The question is, can this wish be fulfilled?

Illustrated by the author.

Calico the Wonder Horse; or, The Saga of Stewy Stinker. Boston, Houghton Mifflin, 1941; London, Faber, 1942.
The Little House. Boston, Houghton Mifflin, 1942; London, Faber, 1946.
Katy and the Big Snow. Boston, Houghton Mifflin, 1943; London, Faber, 1947.

Arthur Catherall (1906–80). British. **a.k.a. A.R. Channel.**

Keepers of the Khyber. London, Nelson, 1940.
Lost with All Hands. London, Nelson, 1940.
Raid on Heligoland. London, Collins, 1940.
The Flying Submarine. London, Collins, 1942.
The River of Burning Sand. London, Collins, 1947.
The Bull Patrol. London, Lutterworth Press, 1949.
Riders of the Black Camel. Bath, Venturebooks, 1949.
Cock o'the Town, illustrated by Kenneth Brookes. London, Boy Scouts Association, 1950.

Christine Chaundler (1887–1972). British.

The Odd Ones, illustrated by Harry Rountree. London, Country Life, 1941.
Winkie Wee and the Silver Sixpence. London, Museum Press, 1947.
Winkie-Wee's Spring Cleaning. London, Museum Press, 1947.
Prize for Gardening, illustrated by L.M. Dufty. London, Nelson, 1948.
More Stories for the Children's Hour, illustrated by Cyril Fosser. London, Hale, 1949.

Joseph E(ugene) Chipperfield (1912–76). British.

Storm of Dancerwood, illustrated by C. Gifford Ambler. London, Hutchinson, 1948; New York, Longman, 1949.
Greatheart, The Salvation Hunter: The Epic of a Shepherd Dog, illustrated by C. Gifford Ambler. London, Hutchinson, 1950; New York, Roy 1953.

Catherine Christian (b. 1901). British. **a.k.a. Catherine Mary Christian.**

At a time when far-fetched adventures were the staple diet for readers of 'girls' fiction', Catherine Christian was producing Guide Stories of remarkable realism. This was largely due to Christian's extensive first-hand knowledge of the Girl Guide Association. She was editor of the Association's own periodical, *The Guide*, during the Second World War. Christian also had a keen interest in the Ancient World, reflected in *The Legions Go North* (1935) and *The Silver Unicorn* (1946). The latter is a tale of adventure and intrigue at Rome in AD 180. The jacket illustration by E.E. shows the hero, Hilarion (on the right of the picture) fighting Artimedorous in the gladiatorial arena before the new emperor, Commodus.

Diana Takes A Chance, illustrated by A.A. Nash. London, Blackie, 1940.

The Pharaoh's Secret. London, Religious Tract Society, Lutterworth Press, 1940.

Harriet: The Return of Rip Van Winkle. London, Pearson, 1941.

Harriet Takes the Field. London, Pearson, 1942.

The "Kingfishers" See it Through. London, Blackie, 1942.

The School at Emery's End. London, Pearson, 1944.

The Seventh Magpie, illustrated by E. Spring-Smith. London, Blackie, 1946.

The Silver Unicorn, London, Hutchinson, 1946.

Phyllida's Fortune. London, Newnes, 1947.

Sally Joins the Patrol. London, Blackie, 1948.

Richard Church (1893–1972). British.

Richard Church, like Walter de la Mare, C. Day Lewis and John Masefield before him, was a notable poet and literary critic, who also wrote some children's fiction. Church's stories contain an emotional depth that reflects his diverse intellectual interests. Consequently, such titles as *A Squirrel Called Rufus* (1941), *Dog Toby* (1953) and *The White Doe* (1968) are not straightforward or cute 'animal stories', but, respectively, an allegorical account of the Allies' struggle in the Second World War, a tale of the tragic and contrived separation of nations and individuals and a debate about hunting and human nature. *The Cave* (1950) is apparently a conventional adventure about five boys, John Walters, George Reynolds, Lightning Soames, Alan Hobbs and Meaty Saunders, exploring some limestone caves. However, it is also a complex study of a power struggle within the group, and a review of the qualities necessary to be a good leader. Clarke Hutton's atmospheric dust wrapper design, which nicely reflects the story's physical and emotional claustrophobia, finds the 'Tomahawk Club', as the five call themselves, crowding round a skull that is lying in the sand. The boys assume it is a relic of primitive man, and George proceeds to sketch it.

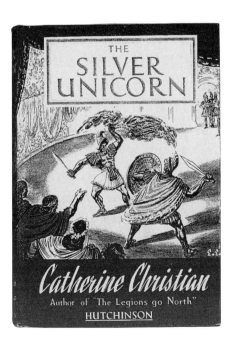

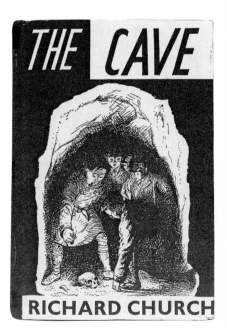

A Squirrel Called Rufus, illustrated by John
Skeaping. London, Dent, 1941;
Philadelphia, Winston, 1946.
The Cave, illustrated by Clarke Hutton.
London, Dent, 1950; as *Five Boys in a
Cave*, New York, Day, 1951.

Mavis Thorpe Clark (b. 1912?). Australian.

Mavis Thorpe Clark wrote about her
Australian homeland with an enthusiasm that
permeates her text. In an age when eco-
friendliness was not even a concept in many
quarters, Clark stressed the importance of
maintaining her country's beautiful lansdscape
for future generations. Her books are played
out before spectacular scenery, always lovingly
described, but there is much more to her
books than a series of breath-taking
descriptive passages. Although a thing of
beauty is a joy for ever, Clark's characters
often have to battle against nature to ensure
survival in the lonely surroundings of the
outback.

Dark Pool Island. Melbourne, Oxford
University Press, 1949.
The Twins from Timber Creek. Melbourne,
Oxford University Press, 1949.
Home Again at Timber Creek. Melbourne,
Oxford University Press, 1950.

Beverly Cleary (b. 1916). American.

Henry Huggins (1950) was the first of Beverly
Cleary's eight books about eight-year-old
Henry and his friends, who live in Klickitat
Street in Portland, Oregon. The books are a
good humoured, if slightly formulaic, study of
growing up in America during the early part
of this century. The scrapes young Henry
manages to get himself into, and then extricate
himself from, are commonplace ones, which
would be familiar to the youngsters at whom
the stories are aimed.

Henry Huggins, illustrated by Louis Darling.
New York, Morrow, 1950.

Dorothy Clewes (b. 1907). British.

Dorothy Clewes wrote for a variety of age
groups, including teenagers for whom she
composed suitably angst-ridden material. Her
early career was dominated by works aimed at
a younger audience. A series of holiday
mysteries featuring child sleuths was a
moderate success, and she wrote four books
about Henry Hare. *Henry Hare's Boxing Match*
(1950) tells of a celebrated prize fight at the
Brown Burrows Flower Show. Henry's
opponent in this match was supposed to be
Wellington Weasel. Unfortunately, Wellington
is kidnapped by villainous Red Fox. The fox's
aim, when, disguised as Wellington, he enters
the fray, is to win the fight, and then to eat
Henry Hare for supper! He is foiled in this aim
largely by the tightness of the jacket he stole
from the weasel. In the crowd is P.C.
Prickletop, who soon steps in to call time and
ensure that Red Fox is not only knocked out
but also locked away. Each of the 'Henry
Hare' books is illustrated by Patricia W.
Turner.

*The Cottage [Stream, Treasure, Fair] in the Wild
Wood*, illustrated by Irene Hawkins.
London, Faber, 4 vols, 1945–49.

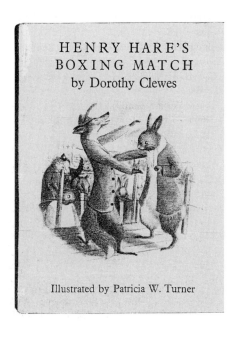

HENRY HARE'S
BOXING MATCH
by Dorothy Clewes

Illustrated by Patricia W. Turner

The Wild Wood (includes *The Cottage in the Wild Wood* and *The Stream in the Wild Wood*), illustrated by Irene Hawkins. New York, Coward McCann, 1948.

Henry Hare's Boxing Match, illustrated by Patricia W. Turner. London, Chatto & Windus, and New York, Coward McCann, 1950.

Henry Hare's Earthquake, illustrated by Patricia W. Turner. London, Chatto & Windus, 1950; New York, Coward McCann, 1951.

Elizabeth Coatsworth (1893–1986). American.

The Littlest House, illustrated by Marguerite Davis. New York, Macmillan, 1940; Kingswood, Surrey, World's Work, 1958.

The Fair American, illustrated by Helen Sewell. New York, Macmillan, 1940; London, Blackie, 1970.

A Toast to the King, illustrated by Forrest Orr. New York, Coward McCann, 1940; London, Dent, 1941.

Tonio and the Stranger, illustrated by Winifred Bronson. New York, Grossett and Dunlap, 1941.

You Shall Have a Carriage, illustrated by Henry Pitz. New York, Macmillan, 1941.

Forgotten Island, illustrated by Grace Paull. New York, Grosset and Dunlap, 1942.

Houseboat Summer, illustrated by Marguerite Davis. New York, Macmillan, 1942.

The White Horse, illustrated by Helen Sewell. New York, Macmillan, 1942; as *The White Horse of Morocco*, London, Blackie, 1973.

Thief Island, illustrated by John Wonsetler. New York, Macmillan, 1943; Kingswood, Surrey, World's Work, 1960.

Twelve Months Make a Year, illustrated by Marguerite Davis. New York, Macmillan, 1943.

The Big Green Umbrella, illustrated by Helen Sewell. New York, Grosset and Dunlap, 1944.

Trudy and the Tree House, illustrated by Marguerite Davis. New York, Macmillan, 1944.

The Kitten Stand, illustrated by Kathleen Keeler. New York, Grosset and Dunlap, 1945.

The Wonderful Day, illustrated by Helen Sewell. New York, Macmillan, 1946; London, Blackie, 1973.

Plum Daffy Adventure, illustrated by Marguerite Davis. New York, Macmillan, 1947; Kingswood, Surrey, World's Work, 1965.

Up Hill and Down: Stories, illustrated by James Davis. New York, Knopf, 1947.

The House of the Swan, illustrated by Kathleen Voute. New York, Macmillan, 1948; Kingswood, Surrey, World's Work, 1959.

The Little Haymakers, illustrated by Grace Paull. New York, Macmillan, 1949.

The Captain's Daughter, illustrated by Ralph Ray. New York, Macmillan, 1950; London, Collier Macmillan, 1963.

Door to the North, illustrated by Frederick Chapman. Philadelphia, Winston, 1950; Kingswood, Surrey, World's Work, 1960.

Padraic Colum (1881–1972). Irish.

Where the Winds Never Blew and the Cocks Never Crew, illustrated by Richard Bennett. New York, Macmillan, 1940.

Mrs H(enry) C. Cradock. British.

Josephine Goes Travelling, illustrated by Honor C. Appleton. London, Blackie, 1940.

Teddy Bear's Farm, illustrated by Joyce L. Brisley. London, Harrap, 1941.

Richmal Crompton (1890–1969). British.

William and the Evacuees (1940), is one of the very rarest 'William' first editions and has been thought to exist no longer in dust wrapper by many collectors and dealers. The inspiration for Thomas Henry's dust wrapper design comes from the first story in the collection, which also gives the book its title. William is leading a band of local children, including Arabella Simpkins, 'a red-haired long-nosed girl'. Ella Poppleham, 'a morose-looking child, with a shock of black hair and a squint', Maisie Fellowes, 'who bore a striking resemblance to Queen Victoria in her old age', and Carolina Jones, 'with carefully tended ringlets and film star eyelashes', to Bolsover Lodge. Jealous of the attention paid to evacuees from London, the group pose as wartime refugees in the hope of receiving generous hospitality. This they obtain, but, unfortunately for William, all good things come to an end.

All illustrated by Thomas Henry with the exception of *Jimmy*.

William and the Evacuees. London, Newnes, 1940; as *William the Film Star*, 1956.
William Does His Bit. London, Newnes, 1941.
William Carries On. London, Newnes, 1942.
William and the Brains Trust. London, Newnes, 1945; abridged edition, as *William the Hero*, London, Collins, 1972.
Just William's Luck. London, Newnes, 1948.
Jimmy, illustrated by Lunt Roberts. London, Newnes, 1949.
William the Bold. London, Newnes, 1950.

Primrose Cumming (b. 1915). British.

The Chestnut Filly. London, Blackie, and New York, Mill, 1940.
Silver Eagle Carries On, illustrated by Cecil Trew. London, A. & C. Black, 1940.
Owls Castle Farm, illustrated by Veronica Baker. London, A. & C. Black, 1942.
The Great Horses, illustrated by Lionel Edwards. London, Dent, 1946.
Trouble at Trimbles, illustrated by Geoffrey Whittam. London, Country Life, 1949.

Roald Dahl (1916–93). British.

Roald Dahl is now the widest-read children's author in Britain and the worldwide success of his darkly humorous stories, with their bizarre situations and grotesque characters, is phenomenal. The Dahl canon is often considered to have started with *James and the Giant Peach* (1961), but a little-known and out-of-print work, *The Gremlins*, was published as early as 1943. It was written whilst Dahl was Assistant Attaché at the British Embassy in Washington, and in part reflects the author's experiences as a fighter pilot in the Royal Air Force. The Gremlins, 'little men scarcely more than six inches high, with large round faces and a little pair

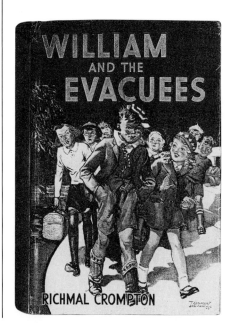

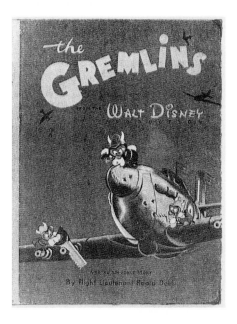

of horns growing out of their heads', are the blight of the RAF. They drill holes in spitfires to look like bullet holes, and thereby bring the aeroplanes down to earth with a bump! This rare, large-sized book was illustrated by the Walt Disney studio, whose projected film of the story never came to fruition.

The Gremlins, illustrated by Walt Disney Studio. New York, Random House, 1943; London, Collins, 1944.

Maureen Daly (b. 1921). American.

Maureen Daly's *Seventeenth Summer* (1942) has been an enduringly popular novel with teenagers. This success is largely due to the fact that the author was herself a teenager at the time of writing. Consequently, the book's characters are not unrealistically glamorous young things, but troubled, unconfident and not necessarily beautiful individuals. They are real people who find themselves in real situations, and have to find their feet socially and emotionally. The happy ending is perhaps a concession to the genre, but it is an undeniable confidence-booster for ugly ducklings everywhere.

Seventeenth Summer. New York, Dodd Mead, 1942; London, Hollis and Carter, 1947.

Peter Dawlish (1899–1963). British. Pseudonym for **James Lennox Kerr. a.k.a. Lennox Kerr.**

Peg-Leg and the Invaders, illustrated by Jack Matthew. London, Oxford University Press, 1940.
Peg-Leg Sweeps the Sea, illustrated by Leonard Boden. London, Oxford University Press, 1940.
Dauntless Finds Her Crew, illustrated by P.A. Jobson. London, Oxford University Press, 1947.
The First Tripper, illustrated by P.A. Jobson. London, Oxford University Press, 1947.
Dauntless Sails Again, illustrated by P.A. Jobson. London, Oxford University Press, 1948.

Dauntless and the Mary Baines, illustrated by P.A. Jobson. London, Oxford University Press, 1949.
North Sea Adventure, illustrated by P.A. Jobson. London, Oxford University Press, 1949.
Dauntless Takes Recruits, illustrated by P.A. Jobson. London, Oxford University Press, 1950.

C(ecil) Day Lewis (1904–72). British.

The Otterbury Incident (1948) was C. Day Lewis' second and last story for youngsters. The book's quality and success ensured that, even with such a slight output, Day Lewis would always be considered a leading children's author. The novel's idea is not original. Readers had delighted in tales of children outwitting adult crooks at least as early as Sherlock Holmes' 'Baker Street Irregulars', and *Emil and the Detectives* (1930) had been a more recent success. Nevertheless, the jovial cockiness of the young narrator, George, is infectious. Soon the reader is inextricably involved in the post-war suburban landscape of Otterbury, still marred by the scars of war, and the child gangs who secure it as 'their territory'. This is much to the chagrin of the underworld types who wish to make the most of the disorderd confusion of the time. The tensions between the two sides reach a climax when a villainous band kidnaps Ted Marshall. The action-packed dust-wrapper scene, in the distinctive hand of Edward Ardizzone, who also provided many internal illustrations, shows the decisive 'Battle in Skinner's Yard'. As one can see, the boys seem to have the upper hand, as the fate of one of the rogues makes clear,

> The Wart gave a high whimpering scream. He released Ted and hurled himself through the main door out into the yard, where four boys at once wrapped themselves round his legs, dragged him to the ground, and in a minute had him trussed up with a scout rope.

The violent scene is depicted in shades of pink, grey and yellow.

The Otterbury Incident, illustrated by Edward Ardizzone. London, Putnam, 1948; New York, Viking Press, 1949.

Marguerite de Angeli (1889–1987). American.

Illustrated by the author.

A Summer Day with Ted and Nina. New York, Doubleday, 1940.
Thee Hannah! New York, Doubleday, 1940; Kingswood, Surrey, World's Work, 1962.
Ellin's Amerika. New York, Doubleday, 1941; Kingswood, Surrey, World's Work, 1964.
Up the Hill. New York, Doubleday, 1942.
Yonie Wondernose. New York, Doubleday, 1944.
Turkey for Christmas. Philadelphia, Westminster Press, 1944.
Bright April. New York, Doubleday, 1946.
Jared's Island. New York, Doubleday, 1947.
The Door in the Wall. New York, Doubleday, 1949; Kingswood, Surrey, World's Work, 1959.

Jean de Brunhoff (1899–1937). French.

Illustrated by the author.

Babar And Father Christmas. New York, Random House, 1940; London, Methuen, 1940.

Olive Dehn (b. 1914). British.

Come In, illustrated by Kathleen Gell. Oxford, Shakespeare Head Press, 1946.

Meindert De Jong (1906–91). American.

Wheels over the Bridge, illustrated by Aldren Watson. New York, Harper, 1941.
Bells of the Harbor, illustrated by Kurt Wiese. New York, Harper, 1941.
The Cat That Walked a Week, illustrated by Tessie Robinson. New York, Harper, 1943; London, Lutterworth Press, 1965.
The Little Stray Dog, illustrated by Edward Shenton. New York, Harper, 1943.
Billy and the Unhappy Bull, illustrated by Marc Simont. New York, Harper, 1946; London, Lutterworth Press, 1966.
Good Luck Duck, illustrated by Marc Simont. New York, Harper, and London, Hamish Hamilton, 1950.
Tower by the Sea, illustrated by Barbara Comfort. New York, Harper, and London, Hamish Hamilton, 1950.

Elizabeth Borton de Trevino (b. 1904). American.

About Bellamy, illustrated by Jessie Robinson. New York, Harper, 1940.

V(iolet) H(ilda) Drummond (b. 1911). British.

Illustrated by the author.

Mrs. Easter's Parasol. London, Faber, 1944.
Miss Anna Truly. London, Faber, 1945; Boston, Houghton Mifflin, 1949.
Lady Talavera. London, Faber, 1946.

Tidgie's Innings. London, Faber, 1947.
The Charming Taxi-cab. London, Faber, 1947.
The Mountain That Laughed. London, Grey
    Walls Press, 1947.
The Flying Postman. London, Penguin, 1948;
    Boston, Houghton Mifflin, 1949.

William Pène du Bois (1916–93).
American.

Illustrated by the author.

The Great Geppy. New York, Viking Press,
    1940; London, Hale, 1942.
The Flying Locomotive. New York, Viking
    Press, 1941; London, Museum Press, 1946.
The Twenty-One Balloons. New York, Viking
    Press, 1947; London, Hale, 1950.
Peter Graves. New York, Viking Press,
    1950; Kingswood, Surrey, World's
    Work, 1974.

Monica Edwards (b. 1912). British.

Monica Edwards was one of several country
ladies who began to write 'pony stories'
during this decade. The human participants in
her books are, unusually, bestowed with as
much character as the various wonder horses.
Edwards wrote two series of books, which
appeared concurrently, one about 'Romney
Marsh' and the other set at 'Punchbowl Farm',
both based on her own rural experiences.
Besides revelling in their wonderful
surroundings and enjoying some thrilling
adventures, the children in the books are faced
with the frequently distressing consequences
of mishaps concerning animals in their
community. Edwards was learning her trade
with *Wish for a Pony* (1947). It is the story of
Tamzin, who has dreamt constantly of owning
a pony of her own during a long summer of
caring for other people's steeds. Cascade, a
white Arab, is the fine beast whose portrait
Anne Bullen has painted for the dust wrapper
and who makes Tamzin's dream come true.

Wish for a Pony, illustrated by Anne Bullen.
    London, Collins, 1947.
No Mistaking Corker, illustrated by Anne
    Bullen. London, Collins, 1947.

The Summer of the Great Secret, illustrated by
    Anne Bullen. London, Collins, 1948.
The Midnight Horse, illustrated by Anne
    Bullen. London, Collins, 1949; New
    York, Vanguard Press, 1950.
The White Riders, illustrated by Geoffrey
    Whittam. London, Collins, 1950.
Black Hunting Whip, illustrated by Geoffrey
    Whittam. London, Collins, 1950.

Elizabeth Enright (1909–68). American.

Illustrated by the author.

The Sea Is All Around. New York, Farrar &
    Rinehart, 1940; London, Heinemann,
    1959.
The Saturdays. New York, Farrar & Rinehart,
    1941; London, Heinemann, 1955.
The Four-Story Mistake. New York, Farrar &
    Rinehart, 1942; London, Heinemann,
    1955.
Then There Were Five. New York, Farrar &
    Rinehart, 1944; London, Heinemann,
    1956.

Walter Farley (1922–89). American.

The central figure, commanding the reader's attention, should, by rights, be the hero of any adventure book. The same is true of Walter Farley's books, and it does not matter that the hero happens to be a horse. The series that began with *The Black Stallion* (1941) and extended over a period of forty years was a tremendous success. Both the horse and his trainer are male, and this challenged the widely-held assumption that animal stories are exclusively for girls. *The Black Stallion* sets the breathless pace that was to be the series' trademark, and this is reflected in Keith Ward's dramatic dust wrapper design. Alec Ramsey is thrown from the deck of the doomed ship, 'Drake', as the Black Stallion 'snorted and plunged straight for the rail.' Alec grabs the rope trailing from the bridle, and is towed for hours through the sea to dry land.

The Black Stallion, illustrated by Keith Ward. New York, Random House, 1941; London, Lunn, 1947.
Larry and the Undersea Raider, illustrated by P.K. Jackson. New York, Random House, 1942; London, Muller, 1944.

The Black Stallion Returns, illustrated by Harold Eldridge. New York, Random House, 1945; London, Lunn, 1947.
Son of the Black Stallion, illustrated by Milton Menasco. New York, Random House, 1947; London, Collins, 1950.
The Island Stallion, illustrated by Keith Ward. New York, Random House, 1948; London, Hodder & Stoughton, 1973.
The Black Stallion and Satan, illustrated by Milton Menasco. New York, Random House, 1949.
The Blood Bay Colt, illustrated by Milton Menasco. New York, Random House, 1950.

Kathleen Fidler (1899–1980). British.

Kathleen Fidler contributed family adventure stories, historical dramas and animal books with equal skill to the field of children's fiction. Indeed, the only type of book for older children she did not embrace was the school story. *The Borrowed Garden* (1944) is one of Fidler's books about the Brydon family. These stories, based on her own family experiences, were originally written for radio and consequently contain sharp dialogue of an unusually high standard. The Brydon children are sent to stay at a cottage with just a cobbled yard at Milchester, when their mother has to return to a London hospital to work as a doctor during the war. Roger loves gardening and 'borrows' a strip of a neighbour's garden to 'dig for victory'. In the course of his labours, Roger uncovers a treasure trove. This last detail reflects Fidler's deep interest in archaeology, a field which she thought was neglected by children's writers. The attractive 'wraparound' dust wrapper design, showing Roger busy at work on his strip of land, is by Alfred Bestall, in a rare moment away from illustrating the adventures of Rupert Bear.

The Borrowed Garden, illustrated by Alfred Bestall. London, Lutterworth Press, 1944.
St. Jonathan's in the Country: A Sequel to "The Borrowed Garden", illustrated by Charles Koolman. London, Lutterworth Press, 1945.

Fingal's Ghost. London, John Crowther, 1945.

The Brydons at Smuggler's Creek, illustrated by H. Tilden Reeves. London, Lutterworth Press, 1946.

The White Cockade Passes. London, Lutterworth Press, 1947.

The Mysterious Mr. Simister. London, Lutterworth Press, 1947.

More Adventures of the Brydons, illustrated by Victor Bertoglio. London, Lutterworth Press, 1947.

The Brydons Go Camping, illustrated by A.H. Watson. London, Lutterworth Press, 1948.

Mr Simister Appears Again, illustrated by Margaret Horder. London Lutterworth Press, 1948.

Mr. Simister Is Unlucky, illustrated by Margaret Horder. London, Lutterworth Press, 1949.

The Brydons Do Battle, illustrated by A.H. Watson. London, Lutterworth Press, 1949.

The Brydons in Summer, illustrated by A.H. Watson. London, Lutterworth Press, 1949.

Guest Castle. London, Lutterworth Press, 1949.

I Rode with the Covenanters, illustrated by E. Boye Uden. London, Lutterworth Press, 1950.

The Brydons Look for Trouble, illustrated by T.R. Freeman. London, Lutterworth Press, 1950.

The Brydons in a Pickle, illustrated by T.R. Freeman. London, Lutterworth Press, 1950.

Surprises for the Brydons, illustrated by T.R. Freeman. London, Lutterworth Press, 1950.

Charles J(oseph) Finger (1869–1941). American.

The Yankee Captain in Patagonia, illustrated by Henry Pitz. New York, Grosset and Dunlap, 1941.

High Water in Arkansas, illustrated by Henry Pitz. New York, Grosset and Dunlap, 1943.

Dorothy Canfield Fisher (1879–1958). American.
a.k.a. Dorothy Canfield.

Tell Me a Story: A Book of Stories to Tell to Children, illustrated by Tibor Gergely. Lincoln, Nebraska, University Publishing Company, 1940.

Nothing Ever Happens and How It Does, with Sarah N. Cleghorn, illustrated by Esther Bristol. Boston, Beacon Press, 1940.

Something Old, Something New: Stories of People Who Are American, illustrated by Mary D. Shipman. Chicago, Scott Foresman, 1949.

Marjorie Flack (1897–1958). American.

Illustrated by the author unless otherwise stated.

Pedro, with Karl Larsson, illustrated by Larsson. New York, Macmillan, 1940.

The New Pet. New York, Doubleday, 1943; London, Lane, 1956.

I See a Kitty, illustrated by Hilma Larsson. New York, Doubleday, 1943.

The Boats on the River, illustrated by Jay Hyde Barnum. New York, Viking Press, 1946.

Esther Forbes (1891–1967). American.

Esther Forbes only wrote one children's book, but, probably due to its nationalistic bent, it is read in many an American High School. *Johnny Tremain* (1943) is a highly researched tale of the American revolution. T. Ritchie's illustration for the dust jacket shows Johnny Tremain, who is involved with the Boston 'patriots', looking out of a window. He is watching the Red Coats lined up by Boston Harbour in 1773, prior to the Boston Tea Party.

Johnny Tremain, illustrated by Lynd Ward.
    Boston, Houghton Mifflin, 1943;
    London, Chatto & Windus, 1944.

Antonia Forest. British.

Antonia Forest's tales set at Kingscote school are widely considered to be some of the best girls' school stories ever written. Forest's skill as a storyteller is immense. Her narrative is always gripping, but never resorts to improbabilities for dramatic effect. Indeed, ready indentification with the characters and the situations in which they find themselves is the key to Forest's success. All six Marlow girls

may have fair hair and blue eyes, but their characters are so different that the reader is almost sure to associate themselves with one of them. Karen (Kay) is the oldest sister and head girl at Kingscote. Clever and sometimes apparently snooty, Kay is a sensitive girl whose lofty position only rarely allows her to show her feelings. Rowan is hearty and good at games, Ann the efficient Girl Guide Patrol Leader and Virginia (Ginty or Gin) untidy and slightly 'wild' , but a very good sport indeed. However, the books concentrate mainly on the progress of the twelve-year-old twins, Nicola (Nick) and Lawrence (Lawrie), who start Kingscote in *Autumn Term* (1948). Nicola is vivacious and more prone to find herself in trouble, whilst Lawrie is seemingly more staid, but comes alive on the stage, and becomes the school's best actress. *Autumn Term* tells of the trials and tribulations of the twins' first term at Kingscote, and their prominent part in a production of *The Prince and the Pauper*. There are, of course, hurdles to get over: the disappointment of being put in the least academic class, the vindictiveness of an older girl, nasty Lois Sanger, and the wrath of 'Ironsides', humourless battleaxe Miss Cromwell. Marjorie Owens' dust wrapper illustration shows the twins talking with their

friend Thalia (Tim) Keith, the niece of the boarding school's headmistress and budding impresario. Forest also wrote stories about the holiday adventures of the Marlow sisters (and their brothers Giles and Peter), which, by endowing them with a definite life outside school walls and hours, gave her characters some extra depth.

Autumn Term, illustrated by Marjorie Owens. London, Faber, 1948.

Roy Fuller (1912–91). British.

Roy Fuller wrote only sporadically for young people, and even his most famous work, *With My Little Eye* (1948), was published as an adult crime novel in America. Frederick French, the son of a County Court judge, is on holiday from school, and sees a man shot dead during a trial in his father's court. A hunchback runs from the courtroom and Frederick, assuming the rôle of amateur sleuth, is soon on the murderer's trail. The striking jacket design is by the masterful Ronald Searle, and depicts Frederick following the fleeing hunchback.

Savage Gold, illustrated by Robert Medley. London, Lehmann, 1946.
With My Little Eye, illustrated by Alan Lindsay. London, Lehmann, 1948; New York, Macmillan, 1957.

Rose Fyleman (1877–1957). British.

Timothy's Conjuror, illustrated by Mary Clark. London, Methuen, 1942.
The Timothy Boy Trust, illustrated by Marjorie Wratten. London, Methuen, 1944.
Hob and Bob: A Tale of Two Goblins, illustrated by Charles Stewart. London, Hollis and Carter, 1944.
Adventures with Benghazi, illustrated by Peggy Fortnum. London, Eyre & Spottiswoode, 1946.
The Smith Family 4–6 (At the Seaside, In the Country, In Town). Leeds, E.J. Arnold, 3 vols, 1947.
Rose Fyleman's Nursery Stories, illustrated by Rosemary Brown. London, Evans, 1949.

Wanda Gág (1893–1946). American.

Illustrated by the author.

Storybook. New York, Coward McCann, 1940.
Nothing at All. New York, Coward McCann, 1941; London, Faber, 1942.

Eve Garnett (1900–91). British.

Ilustrated by the author.

In and Out and Roundabout: Stories of a Little Town. London, Muller, 1948.

Doris Gates (1901–87). American.

Doris Gates, who is little known in Britain, wrote stories on such diverse subjects as the relationship between horse and rider, classical mythology and home life on Texan ranches. In all her books she used settings not as a mere backdrop to her narrative but as a symbol of her characters' frame of mind. In *Blue Willow*

(1940) the trek Janey Larkin makes with her family from Texas to California mirrors her journey from childhood to maturity.

Blue Willow, illustrated by Paul Lantz. New York, Viking Press, 1940; London, Muller, 1942.

Sensible Kate, illustrated by Marjorie Torrey. New York, Viking Press, 1943; London, Muller, 1947.

Trouble for Jerry, illustrated by Marjorie Torrey. New York, Viking Press, 1944; London, Muller, 1954.

North Fork. New York, Viking Press, 1945; London, Muller, 1950.

My Brother Mike. New York, Viking Press, 1948.

River Ranch, illustrated by Jacob Landau. New York, Viking Press, 1949.

Charles Gilson (1878–1943). British.
a.k.a. C(harles) L(ouis) Gilson.
a.k.a. Captain Charles Gilson.
a.k.a. Major Charles Gilson.

Major Charles Gilson's *Robin of Sherwood* (1940) is an exciting retelling of the famous folk tales about the Mediaeval outlaw. Robin flees to Sherwood Forest after his father's murder and there, along with his trusty band of freedom fighters, scores notable successes against the tyrannical regime. He is aided in his task by the giant with a heart of gold, Little John, the corpulent Friar Tuck, the jolly minstrel Alan-a-dale and the beautiful Maid Marian. Heade's marvellous dust-wrapper portrait of Robin with his trusty longbow seems to have been inspired by Errol Flynn's dashing portrayal of the lead rôle in the 1938 film, *The Adventures of Robin Hood*.

Out of the Nazi Clutch, illustrated by L.D. Black. London, Blackie, 1940.

Robin of Sherwood, illustrated by Heade. London, Collins, 1940.

Christopher Faithful. London, Warne, 1941.

Sons of the Sword: A tale of the Sino-Japanese War. London, Oxford University Press, 1941.

Through the German Hordes. London, Blackie, 1941.

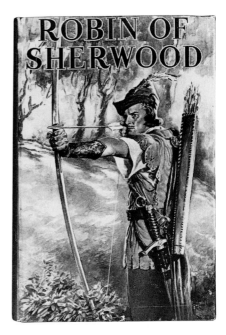

Libyan Patrol. London, Blackie, 1942.

The Yellow Mask. London, Warne, 1942.

The Battle of the Nile. London, Oxford University Press, 1943.

Dangerous Mission, illustrated by H. de Walton. London, Blackie, 1943.

The Secret Agent. London, Warne, 1946.

Rumer Godden (b. 1907). British.

Rumer Godden's nursery stories are a microcosm of life in the wider world. Godden may write ostensibly about dolls and other toys, but the experiences of these playthings are very similar to those likely to be met by the author's young readers. For instance, when noble-hearted Tottie Plantaganet, a farthing doll, eventually gets the better of the deeply unpleasant china doll Marchpane in *The Dolls' House* (1947), it is likely to warm the heart of any child who has suffered from bullying.

The Dolls' House, illustrated by Dana Saintsbury. London, Michael Joseph, 1947; New York, Viking Press, 1948.

Elizabeth Goudge (1900–84). British.

Elizabeth Goudge has been occasionally criticised for the heavily moralistic and sentimental nature of her writing, but no one could deny that her work is highly spirited and inventive. She writes about religion and the country life with passion , and is not afraid to sprinkle her stories with fairy dust to give them a magical dimension. Goudge is especially good at character, even bit players and animals have well-developed person-alities, and at exploring complex human emotions. *Smoky-House* (1940) is about the Treguddick family and their Devonshire inn. The children of the family enjoy some thrilling escapades when they become involved with some smugglers. Among the figures on C. Walter Hodges's dust wrapper are Mathilda the donkey and the family dogs, Spot and Sausage, who become involved in the children's adventures.

Smoky-House, illustrated by C. Walter Hodges. London, Duckworth, and New York, Coward McCann, 1940.
The Well of the Star. New York, Coward McCann, 1941.
Henrietta's House, illustrated by Lorna R. Steele. London, University of London Press – Hodder and Stoughton, 1942; as

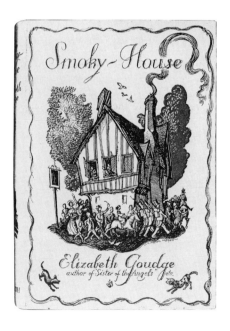

The Blue Hills, New York, Coward McCann, 1942.
The Little White Horse, illustrated by C. Walter Hodges. London, University of London Press, 1946; New York, Coward McCann, 1947.
Make-Believe, illustrated by C. Walter Hodges. London, Duckworth, 1949; Boston, Bentley, 1953.

Eleanor Graham (1896–1984). British.

Head o'Mey, illustrated by Arnold Bond. London, Benn, 1947.

Kenneth Grahame (1859–1932). British.

First Whisper of "The Wind in the Willows", edited by Elspeth Grahame. London, Methuen, 1944; Philadelphia, Lippincott, 1945.

Hardie Gramatky (1907–79). American.

Illustrated by the author.

Hercules: The Story of an Old-Fashioned Fire Engine. New York, Putnam, 1940; Kingswood, Surrey, World's Work, 1960.
Loopy. New York, Putnam, 1941; London, Dent, 1947.
Creeper's Jeep. New York, Putnam, 1948; Kingswood, Surrey, World's Work, 1960.

Graham Greene (1904–93). British.

Although Graham Greene achieved international fame through such novels as *Brighton Rock* (1938) and *Our Man In Havana* (1958), he also wrote four delightful children's books. The first of these, *The Little Train* (1946), was published anonymously. All had lively illustrations by Dorothy Craigie. *The Little Fire Engine* (1950) tells the story of Stan Tholley, fireman of Little Snoring, whose horse-driven fire engine is put out of business by the brand new motorised engine at a local town. A lonely and frustrating retirement for

man and engine seems in prospect, until Farmer Coote's barn catches fire one night. The motorised vehicle is unable to respond to the call, and so Sam and his Little Fire Engine leap into action once more, as the dust-wrapper illustration shows. Sam regains both his job and his position as a highly respected member of the local community.

The Little Train (written anonymously), illustrated by Dorothy Craigie. London, Eyre & Spottiswoode, 1946.
The Little Fire Engine, illustrated by Dorothy Craigie. London, Parrish, 1950.

Roderick Haig-Brown (1908–76). Canadian.
a.k.a. R.L. Haig-Brown.

Starbuck Valley Winter, illustrated by Charles De Feo. New York, Morrow, 1943; London, Collins, 1944.
Saltwater Summer. Toronto, Collins, and New York, Morrow, 1948; London, Collins, 1949.

Kathleen Hale (b. 1898). British.

Illustrated by the author.

Orlando's Evening Out. London, Penguin, 1941.
Orlando's Home Life. London, Penguin, 1942.
Orlando, The Marmalade Cat, Buys a Farm. London, Country Life, 1942.
Henrietta, The Faithful Hen. London and New York, Transatlantic Arts, 1943.
Orlando, The Marmalade Cat: His Silver Wedding. London, Country Life, 1944.
Orlando, The Marmalade Cat, Becomes a Doctor. London, Country Life, 1944.
Orlando's Invisible Pyjamas, London, Transatlantic Arts, 1947.
Orlando, The Marmalade Cat, Keeps a Dog. New York, Country Life, 1949.
Orlando, The Judge. London, Murray, 1950.
Orlando's Country Life: A Peep-Show Book. London, Chatto & Windus, 1950.

Cynthia Harnett (1893–1981). British.

To Be a Farmer's Boy, with G. Vernon Stokes, illustrated by the authors, London, Blackie, 1940.
Mudlarks, with G. Vernon Stokes, illustrated by the authors. London, Collins, 1941.
Mountaineers, with G. Vernon Stokes, illustrated by the authors. London, Collins, 1941.
Ducks and Drakes, with G. Vernon Stokes, illustrated by the authors. London, Collins, 1942.

Bob-Tail Pup, with G. Vernon Stokes, illustrated by the authors. London, Collins, 1944.

Sand Hoppers, with G. Vernon Stokes, illustrated by the authors. London, Collins, 1946.

Two and a Bit, with G. Vernon Stokes, illustrated by the authors. London, Collins, 1948.

Follow My Leader, with G. Vernon Stokes, illustrated by the authors. London, Collins, 1949.

The Great House, illustrated by the author. London, Methuen, 1949; Cleveland, World, 1968.

Pets Limited, with G. Vernon Stokes, illustrated by the authors. London, Collins, 1950.

Mary K(athleen) Harris (1905–66). British.

Perhaps despairing at the lightweight nature of many contemporary girls' school stories, Mary K. Harris tackles some mighty themes in her work. She writes about relations between classes and races in an unpatronising manner and to an unprecedented extent. For instance, the schoolgirl heroine of *Gretel at St Bride's* (1941) is an Austrian Jew fleeing from the

murderous might of Nazi Germany. She finds herself, haunted by ghastly memories and feelings, in the midst of a horde of 'jolly hockey sticks' schoolgirls. The narrow outlook of the English girls makes them seem incredibly shallow in comparison with Gretel the refugee. Drake Bookshaw's picture for the wrapper shows Gretel, who is sitting on the London bound train at Brideston with her friend Jane, surprised by the entrance of Dr Godfrey.

Gretel at St. Bride's, illustrated by Drake Brookshaw. London, Nelson, 1941.

The Wolf, illustrated by Kathleen Cooper. London, Sheed & Ward, 1946.

The Niche over the Door. London, Sheed & Ward, 1948.

Robert A(nson) Heinlein (1907–88). American.

Robert A. Heinlein wrote well-paced science fiction novels. They were the first of their kind, featuring and aimed at young people. Heinlein's dialogue is snappy, and the amount of genuine scientific information illuminating rather than cumbersome. *Rocket Ship Galileo* (1947) establishes the formula. Some young boys blast off into orbit in a home-made space rocket. They land on the moon and (at this point the story steps beyond the simply fantastic and moves into the surreal) thwart a plan for world domination by some clandestine Nazis.

Rocket Ship Galileo, illustrated by Thomas Voter. New York, Scribner, 1947; London, New English Library, 1971.

Space Cadet, illustrated by Clifford Geary. New York, Scribner, 1948; London, Gollancz, 1966.

Red Planet, illustrated by Clifford Geary. New York, Scribner, 1949; London, Gollancz, 1963.

Farmer In The Sky, illustrated by Clifford Geary. New York, Scribner, 1950; London, Gollancz, 1962.

Racey Helps (1913–71). British.

Illustrated by the author.

Racey Helps lovingly illustrated many picture books for young children. Helps's stories, like his pictures, are full of life, and feature scores of funny, friendly animal characters. He only began writing in his middle thirties, after some years in the antiquarian book trade, but his cosy creature tales were an immediate success. *The Upside-Down Medicine* (1946) was his first book. Shown on the see-saw on the book's cover are Barnaby Littlemouse, in his blue jacket, and Nubby Tope, the mole. They watch their friend, Torty, performing a hand-stand between them. The bottle leaning against the log contains the 'upside-down medicine', which turns people on their head to cure them of various maladies. Another beneficiary of this treatment is Tuppetty Nippet, the squirrel, who feels poorly after consuming an excessive number of nuts. Racey Helps's work has charmed several generations, and many examples of his artwork have been reproduced on greeting cards.

The Upside-Down Medicine. London, Collins, 1946.
Footprints in the Snow. London, Collins, 1946.
Barnaby Camps Out. London, Collins, 1947.
My Friend Wilberforce. London, Collins, 1947.
Barnaby in Search of a House. London, Collins, 1948.
Littlemouse Crusoe. London, Collins, 1948.
Tippetty's Treasure. London, Collins, 1949.
Nobody Loves Me: The Tale of a Dutch Doll. London, Collins, 1950.

Marguerite Henry (b. 1902). American.

Marguerite Henry's horse stories are leaders in the genre. The books combine carefully researched historical backgrounds with a thorough knowledge of specific horse breeds and a flair for exciting, imaginative narrative. Characters of both horses and humans are convincingly defined. Children may be drawn to Henry's books initially as pony stories but they will absorb a great deal of American history as they read and will come to appreciate the contribution that horses have made to the development and expansion of the West.

Auno and Tauno: A Story of Finland, illustrated by Gladys Blackwood. Chicago, Whitman, 1940.
Dilly Dally Sally, illustrated by Gladys Blackwood. Akron, Ohio, Saalfied, 1940.
Geraldine Belinda, illustrated by Gladys Blackwood. New York, Platt and Munk, 1942.
Their First Igloo on Baffin Island, with Barbara True, illustrated by Gladys Blackwood. Chicago, Whitman, 1943; London, Gifford, 1945.
A Boy and a Dog, illustrated by Diana Thorne and Ottilie Foy. Chicago, Wilcox and Follett, 1944.
Justin Morgan Had a Horse (stories), illustrated by Wesley Dennis. Chicago, Wilcox and Follett, 1945.
The Little Fellow, illustrated by Diana Thorne. Philadelphia, Winston, 1945.
Misty of Chincoteague, illustrated by Wesley Dennis. Chicago, Rand McNally, 1947; London, Collins, 1961.
Always Reddy, illustrated by Wesley Dennis. New York, McGraw Hill, 1947.
King of the Wind, illustrated by Wesley Dennis. Chicago, Rand McNally, 1948 London, Constable, 1957.
Little-or-Nothing from Nottingham, illustrated by Wesley Dennis. New York, McGraw Hill, 1949.
Sea Star: Orphan of Chincoteague, illustrated by Wesley Dennis. Chicago, Rand McNally, 1949; London, Collins, 1968.
Born to Trot, illustrated by Wesley Dennis. Chicago, Rand McNally, 1950.

Constance Heward (1884–1968). British.

Ameliaranne Keeps School, illustrated by S.B. Pearse. London, Harrap, and Philadelphia, McKay, 1940.
Ameliaranne Goes Touring, illustrated by S.B. Pearse. London, Harrap, and New York, McKay, 1941.
Chappie, illustrated by M.K. Mountain. London, Warne, 1945.
Dick in Command. Leeds, Arnold, 1950.
Bobby Budge from Nowhere. Leeds, Arnold, 1950.

Lorna Hill (b. 1902). British.

Lorna Hill wrote conventional 'pony stories', often set in her native Northumberland, and also tales about a young ballerina's fortunes at the Sadler's Wells Ballet School. The latter, which began with *A Dream of Sadler's Wells* (1950), was in part based upon her daughter's experiences whilst training at the Wells, and has helped to feed the fantasies of countless would-be dancers. *Marjorie & Co* (1948) is an archetypal 'pony story'. It is the first in a series of books about 'The Clan', Guy Charlton (elected leader), Toby Martin, Esmé Martin,

Pansy (Pan) Pierce and Marjorie Manners, who enjoy diverse adventures on their trusty and beloved steeds. Gilbert Dunlop's wrapper shows Marjorie, 'who never arrived decently', on her pony, Black Magic.

Marjorie & Co., illustrated by Gilbert Dunlop. London, Art and Educational, 1948.
Stolen Holiday, illustrated by Gilbert Dunlop. London, Art and Educational, 1948.
Border Peel, illustrated by Esmé Verity. London, Art and Educational, 1950.
A Dream of Sadler's Wells, illustrated by Eve Guthrie. London, Evans, 1950; New York, Holt, 1955.

C(yril) Walter Hodges (b. 1909). British.

In C. Walter Hodges's *The Flying House* (1947), Nicky and his sister Linda go to stay with eccentric Uncle Ben, a retired lighthouse-keeper, and sensible Aunt Daisy. Uncle Ben dabbles with experiments, but one day he loses the key to the gas and the balloon in his workshop expands to an enormous size, with surprising results:

> The house was floating in mid air! A long way down they could see the

little square of stone toadstools on which it had stood and the greenhouse and the toolshed and the vegetable garden. But it was all moving away from them.

The house and its occupants enjoy all kinds of adventures until, after crash-landing in the jungle, the children find their father who has been building a railway.

Illustrated by the author.

The Flying House: A Story of High Adventure. London, Benn, 1947; as *Sky High: The Story of a House that Flew.* New York, Coward McCann, 1947.

Edith Howes (1874–1954). New Zealander.

Riverside Family, illustrated by McGregor Williams. Auckland, Collins, 1944.

Richard Hughes (1900–76). British.

Don't Blame Me! (1940), a collection of thirteen short stories, shows off Richard

Hughes' ingenious, if slightly off-beat, humour to good effect. The dust wrapper illustration by Fritz Eichenberg details a scene from 'The Jungle School'. Miss Crocodile, who has established an academy for the young of the jungle, announces that it is dinner time. Unfortunately for her charges, it is they who are on the menu.

Don't Blame Me! and Other Stories, illustrated by Fritz Eichenberg. London, Chatto & Windus, and New York, Harper, 1940.

Katharine Hull (1921–77) and **Pamela Whitlock** (1920–82). British.

Illustrated by Pamela Whitlock.

Crowns. London, Cape, 1947.

Tove Jansson (b. 1914). Finnish.

Tove Jansson's books are lavishly illustrated by her remarkable drawings. The world was introduced to the Moomin family in *Finn Family Moomintroll* whose English translation was published in 1950. The book was published in America as *The Happy Moomins* (1951). The story begins with snow falling in the Valley of the Moomins and the Moomin family settle down for their long winter's sleep after a supper of pine needles. 'It's important to have your tummy full of pine needles if you intend to sleep all the winter.' When they awaken, the following spring, Moomintroll and his friends Snufkin and Sniff have many odd adventures, such as finding the Hobgoblin's Hat, the discovery of Hattifattner's Island, the hunt for the Mameluke and finding a mysterious suitcase. Moominpappa, Moominmamma, the rest of the family and friends feature in seven more Moominbooks.

Finn Family Moomintroll, illustrated by the author. London, Benn, 1950; as *The Happy Moomins*, New York, Henry Z. Walck, 1951.

W(illiam) E(arl) Johns (1893–1968).
British.
a.k.a. William Earle.
a.k.a. Captain W.E. Johns.

The dust wrapper painted by the artist Howard Leigh, for the first edition of *Biggles in the Baltic* (1940), is a very scarce item and hence this Capt. W.E. Johns title would, if put up for sale, command a high price. The book is set at the outbreak of the Second World War and Major Bigglesworth's (Biggles) first commission is to form a Royal Air Force unit for special duty in the Baltic. The unit is to operate from a secret base prepared sometime previously by the Admiralty on a small island bought by the British Government. *Biggles in the Orient* (1945), is another typical adventure for Squadron Leader Bigglesworth., Algy Lacey, 'Ginger' Hebblethwaite and the rest of Number 666 (Fighter) Squadron, R.A.F. Their mission is to discover how the Japanese are bringing down an increasing number of R.A.F. planes and not apparently through obvious enemy action. The story stresses the virtue of 'loyalty; loyalty to the service, to the team, and above all, to their leader'.

It was during this decade that the thoughtful, courageous, brunette, air-ace Flight Officer Joan Worralson (Worrals) and her frivolous, attractive, blonde friend, Betty Lovell (Frecks) made their debut. They went on to feature in eleven books, several set in war torn Europe. The books, emphasising the admirable qualities of friendship, cooperation and reliability, were very popular with girls. A full length portrait of Worrals, by A.R., is presented on the dust wrapper of *Worrals of the W.A.A.F.* (1941), showing her dressed in her full pilot ensemble, standing on the wing of her plane, leaning against the cockpit.

Captain W.E. Johns also created a third series of ten books about a special detachment of Combined Operations (Commandos). Captain Lorrington 'Gimlet' King, D.S.O., M.C., is the leader of these commandos, which became known as King's 'Kittens', due to the fact that the shoulder cypher chosen for No.9 Commando was a wildcat. Corporal Albert Edward 'Copper' Collson, an ex-London policeman, Private 'Trapper' Troublay, a French Canadian and Nigel Norman Peters (Cub) are all part of the detachment. Some of their various escapades involve fighting Nazis, destroying a motor-car factory in German occupied Paris, looking for werewolves and travelling to Siam.

Biggles in the Baltic, illustrated by Howard Leigh and Alfred Sindall. London, Oxford University Press, 1940.

Biggles in the South Seas, illustrated by Norman Howard. London, Oxford University Press, 1940.

Biggles – Secret Agent, illustrated by Howard Leigh and Alfred Sindall. London, Oxford University Press, 1940.

Worrals of the W.A.A.F., illustrated by A.R. London, Lutterworth Press, 1941.

Spitfire Parade: Stories of Biggles in War-Time, illustrated by Ratcliffe Wilson. London, Oxford University Press, 1941.

Biggles Sees It Through, illustrated by Howard Leigh and Alfred Sindall. London, Oxford University Press, 1941.

Biggles Defies the Swastika, illustrated by Howard Leigh and Alfred Sindall. London, Oxford University Press, 1941.

Biggles in the Jungle, illustrated by Terence Cuneo. London, Oxford University Press, 1942.

Sinister Service, illustrated by Stuart Tresilian. London, Oxford University Press, 1942.

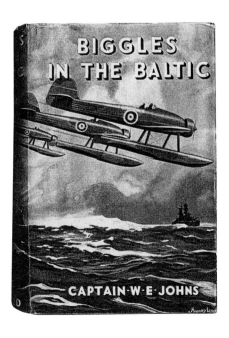

Biggles Sweeps the Desert, illustrated by Leslie Stead. London, Hodder and Stoughton, 1942.

Worrals Flies Again, illustrated by Leslie Stead. London, Hodder and Stoughton, 1942.

Worrals Carries On, illustrated by Mays. London, Lutterworth Press, 1942.

Worrals on the War-Path, illustrated by Leslie Stead. London, Hodder and Stoughton, 1943.

Biggles – Charter Pilot, illustrated by Mendoza. London, Oxford University press, 1943.

Biggles "Fails to Return", illustrated by Leslie Stead. London, Hodder and Stoughton, 1943.

Biggles in Borneo, illustrated by Stuart Tresilian. London, Oxford University Press, 1943.

King of the Commandos, illustrated by Leslie Stead. London, University of London Press, 1943.

Gimlet Goes Again, illustrated by Leslie Stead. London, University of London Press, 1944.

Worrals Goes East, illustrated by Leslie Stead. London, Hodder and Stoughton, 1944.

Biggles in the Orient, illustrated by Leslie Stead. London, Hodder and Stoughton, 1944.

Worrals of the Islands: A Story of the War in the Pacific, illustrated by Leslie Stead. London, Hodder and Stoughton, 1945.

Biggles Delivers the Goods, illustrated by Leslie Stead. London, Hodder and Stoughton, 1946.

Gimlet Comes Home, illustrated by Leslie Stead. London, University of London Press, 1946.

Sergeant Bigglesworth C.I.D., illustrated by Leslie Stead. London, Hodder and Stoughton, 1947.

Comrades In Arms, illustrated by Leslie Stead. London, Hodder and Stoughton, 1947.

Gimlet Mops Up, illustrated by Leslie Stead. Leicester, Brockhampton Press, 1947.

Worrals in the Wilds, illustrated by Leslie Stead. London, Hodder and Stoughton, 1947.

Biggles Hunts Big Game, illustrated by Leslie Stead. London, Hodder and Stoughton, 1948.

Biggles' Second Case, illustrated by Leslie Stead. London, Hodder and Stoughton, 1948.

Gimlet's Oriental Quest, illustrated by Leslie Stead. Leicester, Brockhampton Press, 1948.

The Rustlers of Rattlesnake Valley, illustrated by Drake Brookshaw. London, Nelson, 1948.

Worrals Down Under, illustrated by Leslie Stead. London, Lutterworth Press, 1948.

Biggles Breaks the Silence, illustrated by Leslie Stead. Leicester, London, Hodder and Stoughton, 1949.

Biggles Takes a Holiday, illustrated by Leslie Stead. London, Hodder and Stoughton, 1949.

Gimlet Lends a Hand, illustrated by Leslie Stead. Brockhampton Press, 1949.

Worrals Goes Afoot, illustrated by Leslie Stead. London, Lutterworth Press, 1949.

Worrals in the Wastelands, illustrated by Leslie Stead. London, Lutterworth, 1949.

Worrals Investigates, illustrated by Eade. London, Lutterworth Press, 1950.

Biggles Gets His Men, illustrated by Leslie Stead. London, Hodder and Stoughton, 1950.

Gimlet Bores In, illustrated by Leslie Stead, Leicester, Brockhampton Press, 1950.

Erich Kästner (1899–1974). German.

Lottie And Lisa, illustrated by Walter Trier. London, Cape, 1950.

James W(illiam) Kenyon (b. 1910). British.

James W. Kenyon's stories often had a conventional setting or theme, but also contained a more surprising subplot. For instance, he wrote several adventures about sporting superman Peter Trant, but, as the title *Peter Trant, Cricketer-Detective* (1944) suggests, Trant was no muscle-bound air head, but a keenly intelligent amateur sleuth. *Mystery At Brinsford* (1946) begins as a conventional school story, but soon gains murkier depths. Even the new Classics master at Brinsford Grammar School, Wiltshire, turns out to be not what he seems (some of

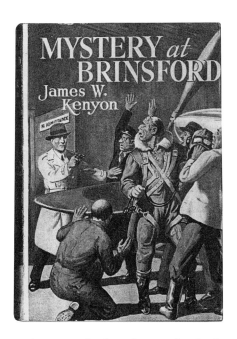

the boys guess this from the mere fact that he is interesting!). R.T. Cooper's dust-wrapper design shows Dr Smailes, a Nazi collaborator, who is preparing to fly out to bomb London from his secret base near the school. In the nick of time, he and his comrades are surprised by the British Secret Service Agent, Captain Gray.

"On My Right", illustrated by S. Drigin. London, Nelson, 1940.
Racing Wheels. London, Nelson, 1941.
Peter Trant, Cricketer-Detective, illustrated by J. Abbey. London, Methuen, 1944.
Alan of the Athletic, illustrated by J. Abbey. London, Methuen, 1945.
The Fighting Avenger. London, Mellifont Press, 1945.
'Beau' Nash: Heavyweight Champion. London, Mellifont Press, 1946.
Mystery At Brinsford, illustrated by R.T. Cooper. London, Nelson, 1946.
Peter Trant: Heavyweight Champion, illustrated by J. Abbey. London, Methuen, 1946.
Lightweight Honours, illustrated by J. Phillips Paterson. London, Nelson, 1947.
Peter Trant: Speed King. London, Methuen, 1949.

Eric Knight (1897–1943). British.

Eric Knight only wrote one book for children, but it has achieved such classic status that Knight is considered to be in the top league of children's writers. *Lassie Come-Home* (1940) is one of the most exciting and thoughtful animal stories ever written, all the better for its lack of sentimentality when portraying the relationship between man and dog. Lassie has to be sold to the Duke of Rudling's family when her owners find themselves hard up. However, she treks hundreds of miles to return from Scotland to her home in Greenall Bridge, Yorkshire. The portrait of a perky Lassie on the dust wrapper is by the well-known animal artist, Marguerite Kirmse.

Lassie Come-Home, illustrated by Marguerite Kirmse. Philadelphia, Winston, 1940; London, Cassell, 1942.

Frank Knight (b. 1905). British.

Frank Knight was a first class writer of naval and historical novels. Knight made good use of his time in the Merchant Navy during the inter-war years, and also of the stories he had been told as a lad by old sea dogs, whose memories stretched back to the early part of the nineteenth century. Knight's first books were intended to give the young a taste of what life in the Navy was really like. Later, he wrote stories of seafaring in the previous three centuries, as well as four contemporary novels set in Chichester Harbour.

The Albatross Comes Home, illustrated by A.R. Morley. London, Hollis and Carter, 1949.
Four in the Half-Deck, illustrated by S. Drigin. London, Nelson, 1950.
The Island of the Radiant Pearls, illustrated by Stephen Russ. London, Hollis and Carter, 1950.

Elizabeth Kyle (d. 1982). British. Pseudonym for Agnes Mary Robertson Dunlop.

Scotland, with its colourful landscape, history and people, provided Elizabeth Kyle with the material for nearly two dozen children's novels. None of her stories are spectacularly inventive, but each gives an interesting insight into the way of life of both ordinary folk and royalty. *Holly Hotel* (1945) is the story of what happens when the occupants of Holly House require an extra source of income, and transform their home into a hotel. Nora Lavrin's jacket illustration shows Jane and Julian Rocke walking up the hotel's driveway to check in. They are accompanied by Mollie Maitland, whose eccentric advertisement for Holly House the Rockes had seen on arrival in Doone. In addition to her fiction, Kyle also wrote a successful series of factual studies about the early lives of illustrious women in history.

Visitors from England, illustrated by A. Mason Trotter. London, Davies, 1941.
Vanishing Island, illustrated by A. Mason Trotter. London, Davies, 1942; as *Disappearing Island*, Boston, Houghton Mifflin, 1944.
Behind the Waterfall, illustrated by A. Mason Trotter. London, Davies, 1943.
The Seven Sapphires, illustrated by Nora Lavrin. London, Davies, 1944; New York, Nelson, 1957.
Holly Hotel, illustrated by Nora Lavrin. London, Davies, 1945; Boston, Houghton Mifflin, 1947.
Lost Karin, illustrated by Nora Lavrin. London, Davies, 1947; Boston, Houghton Mifflin, 1948.
The Mirrors of Castle Doone, illustrated by Nora Lavrin. London, Davies, 1947; Boston, Houghton Mifflin, 1949.
West Wind, illustrated by Francis Gower. London, Davies, 1948; Boston, Houghton Mifflin, 1950.
The House on the Hill, illustrated by Francis Gower. London, Davies, 1949.
The Provost's Jewel, illustrated by Joy Colesworthy. London, Davies, 1950; Boston, Houghton Mifflin, 1951.

Robert Lawson (1892–1957). American.

Robert Lawson was a celebrated artist in America before he began writing and illustrating his folksy little tales about animals who speak with American accents. All the animal inhabitants of *Rabbit Hill* (1944) are terribly excited by the prospect of 'New Folks coming to the Big House'. The key question is whether these 'new folks' are going to grow rich crops to feed the animals' insatiable

HOLLY HOTEL

ELISABETH KYLE

Munro Leaf (1905–76). American.
a.k.a. John Calvert.
a.k.a. Mun.

John Henry Davis, illustrated by the author.
New York, Stokes, 1940.
The Story of Simpson and Sampson, illustrated
by Robert Lawson. New York, Viking
Press, 1941; London, Warne, 1944.
Gordon the Goat, illustrated by the author.
Philadelphia, Lippincott, 1944; London,
Warne, 1947.
Gwendolyn the Goose (as John Calvert),
illustrated by Garrett Price. New York,
Random House, 1946.
Boo, Who Used to Be Scared of the Dark,
illustrated by Frances Hunter. New York,
Random House, 1948; as *Boo, The Boy
Who Didn't Like the Dark*, London,
Publicity Products, 1954.
Sam and the Superdroop, illustrated by the
author. New York, Viking Press, 1948.

C(live) S(taples) Lewis (1898–1963).
British.

C.S. Lewis's seven 'Narnia' stories are
amongst the most popular children's books
ever written. Lewis, like his Oxford chum

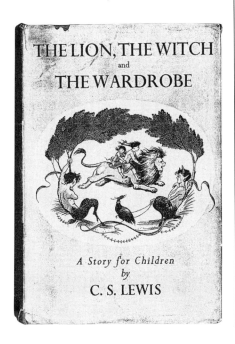

appetites, or hunt, shoot and poison the fluffy
creatures. Lawson's jacket depicts Little
Georgie slightly incongruously leaping over
the Big House. Georgie is joined in his
adventures by William Field Mouse, Porkey
the Woodskunk and Phewie the Skunk, who
all live on the hill.

Illustrated by the author.

They Were Strong and Good. New York,
Viking Press, 1940.
I Discover Columbus. Boston, Little Brown,
1941; London, Harrap, 1943.
Rabbit Hill. New York, Viking Press, 1944;
London, Harrap, 1947.
Mr. Wilmer. Boston, Little Brown, 1945;
London, Muller, 1946.
Mr. Twigg's Mistake. Boston, Little Brown,
1947.
Robbut: A Tale of Tails. New York, Viking
Press, 1948; London, Heinemann,
1949.
The Fabulous Flight. Boston, Little Brown,
1949.
Smeller Martin. New York, Viking Press,
1950.

J.R.R. Tolkien, creates a whole new world in which his characters, many of whom are weird and wonderful creatures, play out their lives in a beautiful, if frequently unsettled, landscape. Unlike Tolkien's Middle-Earth, Narnia is visited by humans from Earth and Lewis' stories also contain a large element of allegory, reflecting the author's deep interest in christianity. The saga begins when Lucy Pevensie steps through a wardrobe and finds herself 'standing in the middle of a wood at night-time with snow under her feet and snowflakes falling through the air.' In this manner the reader is introduced to Narnia in *The Lion, The Witch and the Wardrobe* (1950). Lucy meets the faun, Mr Tumnus, but is not believed by her siblings, Peter, Edmund and Susan, when she returns through the wardrobe. However, all four children are soon in Narnia and battling against the evil machinations of the White Witch. In the background is the lion Aslan, who is viewed as a Messiah-like figure by the inhabitants of Narnia. The battle between good and evil is fought on a spiritual, as well as a physical, plain, and this was to be the course of the following six books also. The book was illustrated by Pauline Baynes in delightful fashion. She was also responsible for the now amazingly rare grey dust wrapper. This depicts Aslan, with Susan and Lucy on his back, watched by a pair of fauns.

The Lion, The Witch, and the Wardrobe, illustrated by Pauline Baynes. London, Bles, and New York, Macmillan, 1950.

Elizabeth Foreman Lewis (1892–1958). American.

When the Typhoon Blows, illustrated by Kurt Wiese, Philadelphia. Winston, 1942; London, Harrap, 1944.

Eric Linklater (1899–1974). British.

The Wind on the Moon (1944), the first of only two books Eric Linklater wrote with children in mind, is a fantasy that is in turn comic and tragic. Humans are enabled to be transformed into whatever animals they wish, and much fun is had as a result. However, in a development appropriate to a tale spun in the war years, the dark cloud of tyranny and death soon overwhelms the characters' lives.

The Wind on the Moon, illustrated by Nicolas Bentley. London and New York, Macmillan, 1944.
The Pirates in the Deep Green Sea, illustrated by William Reeves. London and New York, Macmillan, 1949.

Hugh Lofting (1886–1947). British.

Illustrated by the author.

Doctor Dolittle and the Secret Lake. Philadelphia, Lippincott, 1948; London, Cape, 1949.
Doctor Dolittle and the Green Canary. Philadelphia, Lippincott, 1950; London, Cape, 1951.

Patricia Lynch (1898–1972). Irish.

Patricia Lynch's *Fiddler's Quest* (1941), follows the adventures of Ethne Cadogan, who is stranded in Dublin whilst on the way to stay with her grandfather. She is taken in by the

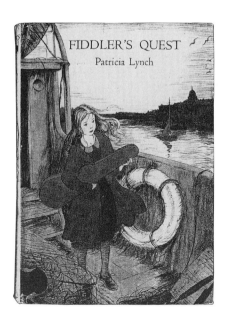

Rafferty family, who live on the quays, and supports herself by playing the fiddle. The book, rather controversially, tackles the delicate question of Irish Nationalism in addition to being a conventional quest story. The dust wrapper is by the talented Isobel Morton-Sale, whose delicate painting shows Ethne carrying her instrument on a boat overlooking the Dublin waterfront. The girl makes her way further westward and finally meets her elusive grandfather.

Fiddler's Quest, illustrated by Isobel Morton-Sale. London, Dent, 1941; New York, Dutton, 1943.
Long Ears: The Story of a Little Grey Donkey, illustrated by Joan Kiddell-Monroe. London, Dent, 1943.
Strangers at the Fair and Other Stories, illustrated by Eileen Coghlan. Dublin, Browne and Nolan, 1945; London, Penguin, 1949.
Lisheen at the Valley Farm and Other Stories, with Helen Staunton and Teresa Deevy. Dublin, Gayfield Press, 1945.
Brogeen of the Stepping Stones, illustrated by Alfred Kerr. London, Kerr Cross, 1947.
The Mad O'Haras, illustrated by Elizabeth Rivers. London, Dent, 1948; as *Grania of Castle O'Hara*, Boston, Page, 1952.

Robert McCloskey (b. 1914). American.

Robert McCloskey wrote a couple of books about children growing up in twenties midwest America, but is best known for his excellent picture books. *Make Way for Ducklings* (1941) won the Caldecott Medal for being 'the most distinguished American picture book for children'. The book contains many engaging sepia drawings by the author. Mr and Mrs Mallard agree to build a nest on a quiet island in the Charles River. Eight fuzzy ducklings hatch, are taught to swim and dive, to walk in a line and to come when called. The whole family eventually processes down Mount Vernon Street, along Charles Street and across Beacon Street to the public gardens, where they know they will be fed peanuts.

Illustrated by the author.

Lentil. New York, Viking Press, 1940.
Make Way for Ducklings. New York, Viking Press, 1941; Oxford, Blackwell, 1944.
Homer Price, New York, Viking Press, 1943; London, Penguin, 1976.
Blueberries for Sal. New York, Viking Press, 1948; London, Angus and Robertson, 1967.

Angus MacVicar (b. 1908). British.

Angus MacVicar wrote many well-paced, action-packed adventure stories, including a large number set in outer space. His earlier stories are more down-to-earth, but sometimes contain exotic settings. The heroes of *The Crocodile Men* (1948), for instance, trek to the depths of Madagascar in search of lost gold. Haworth's dust-wrapper picture shows John Nicholson, on the right, and Professor Daudet paddling into the cave of the Crocodile Men to recover Trabonjy's treasure.

The Crocodile Men. London, Art and Educational, 1948.
The Black Wherry. London, Foley House Press, 1948.
Faraway Island, illustrated by Denis Alford. London, Foley House Press, 1949.

King Abbie's Adventure, illustrated by James Clark. London, Burke, 1950.
Stubby Sees It Through, illustrated by Lunt Roberts. London, Burke, 1950.

Ruth Manning-Sanders (1888–1988). British.

Mystery at Penmarth, illustrated by Anne Bullen. London, Collins, 1940; New York, McBride, 1941.
Circus Book, illustrated by Patric O'Keefe. London, Collins, 1947; as *The Circus*, New York, Chanticleer Press, 1948.

Bessie Marchant (1862–1941). British.

Marta the Mainstay, illustrated by J.A. May. London, Blackie, 1940.
Two of a Kind. London, Blackie, 1941.
The Triumphs of Three, illustrated by W. Bryce Hamilton. London, Blackie, 1942.

Stephen W(arren) Meader (1892–1977). American.

Clear for Action!, illustrated by Frank Beaudouin. New York, Harcourt Brace, 1940.
Blueberry Mountain, illustrated by Edward Shenton. New York, Harcourt Brace, 1941; London, Bell, 1960.
Shadow in the Pines, illustrated by Edward Shenton. New York, Harcourt Brace, 1942.
The Sea Snake, illustrated by Edward Shenton. New York, Harcourt Brace, 1943.
The Long Trains Roll, illustrated by Edward Shenton. New York, Harcourt Brace, 1944.
Skippy's Family, illustrated by Elizabeth Korn. New York, Harcourt Brace, 1945.
Jonathan Goes West, illustrated by Edward Shenton. New York, Harcourt Brace, 1946.
Behind the Ranges, illustrated by Edward Shenton. New York, Harcourt Brace, 1947.
River of the Wolves, illustrated by Edward Shenton. New York, Harcourt Brace, 1948.
Cedar's Boy, illustrated by Lee Townsend. New York, Harcourt Brace, 1949.
Whaler round the Horn, illustrated by Edward Shenton. New York, Harcourt Brace, 1950; London, Museum Press, 1953.

Florence Crannell Means (1891–1980). American.

Across the Fruited Plain, illustrated by Janet Smalley. New York, Friendship Press, 1940.
At the End of Nowhere, illustrated by David Hendrickson. Boston, Houghton Mifflin, 1940.
Children of the Promise, illustrated by Janet Smalley. New York, Friendship Press, 1941.
Whispering Girl, illustrated by Oscar Howard. Boston, Houghton Mifflin, 1941.
Shadow over Wide Ruin, illustrated by Lorence Bjorklund. Boston, Houghton Mifflin, 1942.

Teresita of the Valley, illustrated by Nicholas Panesis. Boston, Hougton Mifflin, 1943.

Peter of the Mesa, illustrated by Janet Smalley. New York, Friendship Press, 1944.

The Moved-Outers, illustrated by Helen Blair. Boston, Houghton Mifflin, 1945.

Great Day in the Morning, illustrated by Helen Blair. Boston, Houghton Mifflin, 1946.

Assorted Sisters, illustrated by Helen Blair. Boston, Houghton Mifflin, 1947.

The House under the Hill, illustrated by Helen Blair. Boston, Houghton Mifflin, 1949.

The Silver Fleece, with Carl Means, illustrated by Edwin Schmidt. Philadelphia, Winston, 1950.

Cornelia Meigs (1884–1973). American. **a.k.a. Adair Aldon.**

Call of the Mountain, illustrated by James Daugherty. Boston, Little Brown, 1940.

Mother Makes Christmas, illustrated by Lois Lenski. New York, Grosset and Dunlap, 1940.

Vanished Island, illustrated by Dorothy Bayley. New York, Macmillan, 1941.

Mounted Messenger, illustrated by John Wonsetler. New York, Macmillan, 1943.

The Two Arrows. New York, Macmillan, 1949.

Annette Mills (1894–1955). British.

Annette Mills was a puppeteer and television presenter of great skill, as well as an entertaining storyteller. Although anyone who saw her live on television must now be middle-aged, Mills is still best known for her immensely popular programme, *Muffin the Mule*. Mills transferred this success into print. She wrote nine adventures about Muffin and his animal chums, including Peregrine the Penguin and Oswald the Ostrich. It was part of this lady's charm that, in a spirit of true self-effacement, the mule on strings was the star of the show. This modesty, and Muffin's massive contemporary popularity, is in evidence in *More about Muffin* (1950).

By ones and twos and dozens and hundreds, the children followed Muffin across Hampstead Heath, because they all recognised Muffin the Mule and wanted his autograph. Soon there was such an enormous crowd that mounted policemen had to be sent for to clear the way for Muffin.

This is not to say that Mills did not make the most of her illustrious family connections. *Muffin the Mule* (1949) has an introduction by the author's film star brother, John Mills, and the actor's two daughters, themselves future actresses, Juliet and Hayley, were officially 'Friends of Muffin' and used to promote the books. To complete the family enterprise, Molly Blake, the author's daughter, designed the dust wrappers and the decorated end papers for the first six 'Muffin' books. She also provided dozens of delightful internal illustrations in both colour and black and white. The dust jacket for *Muffin the Mule* shows Muffin speeding through the air on a giant, magic flying carrot. The Mule is depicted in a more contemplative fashion on the predominantly yellow wrapper of *More About Muffin*, reading the very book he is on the cover of!

Muffin the Mule, illustrated by Molly Blake. London, University of London Press, 1949.

More About Muffin, illustrated by Molly Blake, London, University of London Press, 1950.

Naomi Mitchison (b. 1897). British.

The Big House. London, Faber, 1950.

Rutherford Montgomery (1894–1985). American.
a.k.a. Al Avery.
a.k.a. Everitt Proctor.

Midnight, illustrated by Jacob Bates Abbott. New York, Holt, 1940; London, Hutchinson, 1944.

Stan Ball of the Rangers, illustrated by Jacob Bates Abbott. Philadelphia, McKay, 1941.

Ice Blink, illustrated by Rudolph Freund. New York, Holt, 1941; London, Hutchinson, 1949.

A Yankee Flier with the R.A.F. [in the Far East, in North Africa, in the South Pacific, in Italy, over Berlin, in Normandy, on a Rescue Mission, under Secret Orders] (as Al Avery), illustrated by Paul Laune and Clayton Knight. New York, Grosset and Dunlap, 9 vols, 1941–46.

Thumbs Up!, illustrated by E. Franklin Wittmack. Philadelphia, McKay, 1942; London, Hutchinson, 1943.

Hurricane Yank, illustrated by James Shimer. Philadelphia, McKay, 1942; London, Hutchinson, 1943.

Ghost Town Adventure, illustrated by Russell Sherman. New York, Holt, 1942.

Husky, Co-Pilot of the Pilgrim, illustrated by Jacob Landau. New York, Holt, 1942; London, Ward Lock, 1949.

Spike Kelly of the Commandos, illustrated by J.R. White. Racine, Wisconsin, Whitman, 1942.

Out of the Sun, illustrated by Clayton Knight. Philadelphia, McKay, 1943; London, Wells Gardner Darton, 1947.

War Wings, illustrated by Clayton Knight. Philadelphia, McKay, 1943; London, Wells Gardner Darton, 1948.

Trappers' Trail, illustrated by Harold Cressingham. New York, Holt, 1943; London, Hutchinson, 1948.

Warhawk Patrol, illustrated by Clayton Knight. Philadelphia, McKay, 1944; London, Wells Gardner Darton, 1948.

Big Brownie, illustrated by Jacob Landau. New York, Holt, 1944; London, Hutchinson, 1947.

The Last Cruise of the "Jeanette" (as Everitt Proctor). Philadelphia, Westminster Press, 1944.

Thar She Blows (as Everitt Proctor). Philadelphia, Westminster Press, 1945; London, Pictorial Art, 1947.

Sea Raiders Ho!, illustrated by E. Franklin Wittmack. Philadelphia, McKay, 1945; London, Wells Gardner Darton, 1947.

Thunderboats Ho!, illustrated by E. Franklin Wittmack. Philadelphia, McKay, 1945; London, Wells Gardner Darton, 1948.

Rough Riders Ho!, illustrated by E. Franklin Wittmack, Philadelphia, McKay, 1946.

Blue Streak and Doctor Medusa, illustrated by Francis Kirn. Racine, Wisconsin, Whitman, 1946.

The Mystery of the Turquoise Frog, illustrated by Millard McGee. New York, Messner, 1946; London, Hutchinson, 1951.

Men Against Ice (as Everitt Proctor), illustrated by Isa Barnett. Philadelphia, Westminster Press, 1946.

Kildee House, illustrated by Barbara Cooney. New York, Doubleday, 1949; London, Faber, 1953.

Ursula Moray Williams (b. 1911). British.

Pretenders' Island, illustrated by Joyce Lankester Brisley, London, Harrap, 1940; New York, Knopf, 1942.

A Castle for John-Peter, illustrated by Eileen A. Soper. London, Harrap, 1941.

Gobbolino the Witch's Cat, illustrated by the author. London, Harrap, 1942.

The Good Little Christmas Tree, illustrated by the author. London, Harrap, 1943.

The Three Toymakers, illustrated by the author. London, Harrap, 1945.

The House of Happiness, illustrated by the author. London, Harrap, 1946.

Malkin's Mountain, illustrated by the author. London, Harrap, 1948.

The Story of Laughing Dandino, illustrated by the author. London, Harrap, 1948.

Bill Naughton (1910–92). British.

Bill Naughton's childhood experiences on the streets of a Lancashire town resulted in some of the century's liveliest writing about the working class. Naughton immortalised a world, now long gone, where children could play outside until late and fun-loving male gangs roamed the streets, causing well-meaning, non-violent, mayhem. *Pony Boy* (1946) is set in the East End, but the chipper characters and chirpy dialogue, in this tale of Corky and Ginger's misadventures, are notably influenced by Naughton's intimate knowledge of street life. The book's dust wrapper shows a typical moment of pandemonium, as the boys' horse and cart careers wildly past Eros in Piccadilly Circus, scattering crockery everywhere.

Pony Boy, illustrated by George Buday. London, Pilot Press, 1946.

Violet Needham (1876–1967). British.

The Emerald Crown, illustrated by Anne Bullen. London, Collins, 1940.

The Stormy Petrel, illustrated by Joyce Bruce. London, Collins, 1942.

The Horn of Merlyns, illustrated by Joyce Bruce. London, Collins, 1943.

The Woods of Windri, illustrated by Joyce Bruce. London, Collins, 1944.

The House of the Paladin, illustrated by Joyce Bruce. London, Collins, 1945.

The Changeling of Monte Lucio, illustrated by Joyce Bruce. London, Collins, 1946.

The Bell of the Four Evangelists, illustrated by Joyce Bruce. London, Collins, 1947.

The Boy in Red, illustrated by Joyce Bruce. London, Collins, 1948.

The Betrayer, illustrated by Joyce Bruce. London, Collins, 1950.

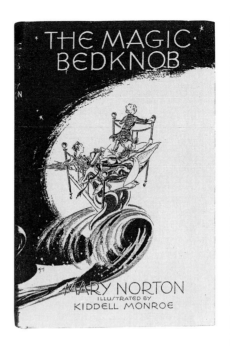

Mary Norton (1903–92). British.

Mary Norton wrote two popular and excellent fantasy series for children. Her most famous books are about the Borrowers, a dwindling race of little people who live, if they can, beneath the earth, and survive by 'borrowing' things from humans. Doughty Pod, domestic Homily and their daughter, the irrepressible Arrietty, are constantly forced to seek a new home, as humans encroach upon their lives and habitations. Norton also wrote the three 'Bedknob and Broomstick' books about magic in wartime Britain. In the first volume, *The Magic Bedknob* (1945), Charles, Paul and Carey, three evacuees from London, come to stay with Miss Price in her cottage. The children inadvertently discover that Miss Price is a white witch. In order to ensure their silence, she allows them to use a magic bedknob which, when attached to a bed, will allow them to travel wherever they want. Joan Kiddell Monroe's dust-wrapper illustration shows Miss Price and her three charges on a flight to adventure.

The Magic BedKnob; or, How to Become a Witch in Ten Easy Lessons, illustrated by Waldo Peirce. New York, Hyperion Press, 1943 as *The Magic Bed-Knob*, illustrated by Joan Kiddell-Monroe. London, Dent, 1945.

Bonfires and Broomsticks, illustrated by Mary Adshead. London, Dent, 1947.

Mary O'Hara (1885–1980). American.

Mary O'Hara's three novels about ranch life are unusally realistic portrayals of domestic and rural life. Based on O'Hara's childhood experiences, the books follow the fortunes of the McLaughlin family over a course of seven years, and particularly young Rob's training of his colt Flicka and Flicka's first foal. The drawing on the yellow dust wrapper of *My Friend Flicka* (1941) is by C.E. Tunnicliffe and shows Flicka under the trees in Calf Pasture. Rob's father Ken has recently brought him there to recover after a near fatal accident.

My Friend Flicka. Philadelphia, Lippincott, 1941; illustrated by C.E. Tunnicliffe, London, Eyre & Spottiswoode, 1943.

Thunderhead. Philadelphia, Lippincott, 1943; London, Eyre & Spottiswoode, 1945.

Green Grass of Wyoming. Philadelphia, Lippincott, 1946; London, Eyre & Spottiswoode, 1947.

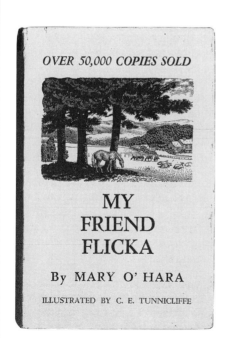

OVER 50,000 COPIES SOLD

MY FRIEND FLICKA

By MARY O'HARA

ILLUSTRATED BY C. E. TUNNICLIFFE

Elsie J. Oxenham (1880–1960). British. Pseudonym for Elsie Jeanette Dunkerley.
a.k.a. Elsie Oxenham.
a.k.a. Elsie Jeanette Oxenham.

Stowaways in the Abbey, illustrated by Heade. London, Collins, 1940.

Damaris Dances, illustrated by Margaret Horder. London, Oxford University Press, 1940.

Patch and a Pawn. London and New York, Warne, 1940.

Adventure for Two, illustrated by Margaret Horder. London, Oxford University Press, 1941.

Jandy Mac Comes Back, illustrated by Heade. London, Collins, 1941.

Pernel Wins, illustrated by Margaret Horder. London, Muller, 1942.

Maid of the Abbey, illustrated by Heade. London, Collins, 1943.

Elsa Puts Things Right, illustrated by Margaret Horder. London, Muller, 1944.

Two Joans at the Abbey, illustrated by Margaret Horder. London, Collins, 1945.

Daring Doranne. London, Muller, 1945.

An Abbey Champion, illustrated by Margaret Horder. London, Muller, 1946.

Robins in the Abbey, illustrated by Margaret Horder. London, Collins, 1947.

The Secrets of Vairy, illustrated by Margaret Horder. London, Muller, 1947.

Margery Meets the Roses. London, Lutterworth Press, 1947.

A Fiddler for the Abbey, illustrated by Margaret Horder. London, Muller, 1948.

Guardians of the Abbey, illustrated by Margaret Horder. London, Muller, 1950.

Schoolgirl Jen at the Abbey. London, Collins, 1950.

M(argot) Pardoe (b. 1902). British.

Bunkle Began It [Butts In, Bought It, Breaks Away, and Belinda, Baffles Them, Went for Six, Gets Busy], illustrated by Julie Neild. London, Routledge, 8 vols., 1942–51.

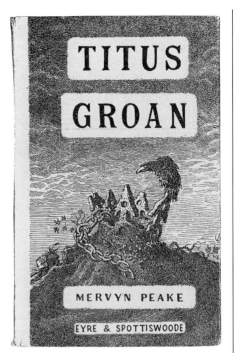

Richard Parker (1915–90). British.

Richard Parker, in the latter part of his career, wrote some tough stories for teenagers. However, his early books, written when a primary school teacher, have a zany originality that is most refreshing. The main characters in *A Camel from the Desert* (1947) are all animals who have escaped from a zoo. The lion decides that the camel needs a wife, so the animals set off in Ron's aeroplane to Egypt to find 'a camel from the desert'. Val Biro's wrapper shows the prospective bride posing for the photographer.

Escape from the Zoo, illustrated by Val Biro. London, Sylvan Press, 1945.
A Camel from the Desert, illustrated by Val Biro. London, Sylvan Press, 1947.

Mervyn Peake (1911–68). British.

Mervyn Peake created a dark, claustrophobic 'Gothic' world, which owed something to Nordic epic. His 'Titus' trilogy is a work of nightmarish intensity, set in and around the castle of Gormenghast,

> This tower, patched unevenly with black ivy, arose like a mutilated finger from among the fists of knuckled masonry and pointed blasphemously at heaven.

Violence, madness and even uneasy comedy contribute towards the creation of a unique and fantastic, but also worryingly familiar, backdrop before which the seventy-seventh Lord Groan of Gormenghast plays out his troubled existence. Titus is only two years old when he succeeds to the title at the end of *Titus Groan* (1946), after the gruesome death of his father. The young Titus is said to be,

> Suckled on shadows; weaned, as it were, on webs of ritual: for his ears, echoes, for his eyes, a labyrinth of stone.

In *Gormenghast* (1950), Titus finds himself constantly battling for his life and sanity in his oppressive and crumbling family pile. However, when he exiles himself from 'home' in *Titus Alone* (1959) he discovers that the outside world contains even greater dangers.

Peake's own atmospheric design for the grey wrapper of *Titus Groan* has a vulture

213

perched on a huge crown on top of a hill. The crown is symbolically shackled to the hill.

Illustrated by the author.

Titus Groan, London, Eyre & Spottiswoode, 1946; New York, Reynal & Hitchcock, 1946.
Letters From A Lost Uncle From Polar Regions, London, Eyre & Spottiswoode, 1948.
Gormenghast, London, Eyre & Spottiswoode, 1950; New York, Weybright & Talley, 1967.

Beatrix Potter (1866–1943). British. **a.k.a. Beatrix Heelis.**

Illustrated by the author.

Wag-by-Wall. London, Warne, and Boston, Horn Book, 1944.

Rhoda Power (1890–1957). British.

Ten Minute Tales and Dialogue Stories, illustrated by Gwen White. London, Evans, 1943.
Here and There Stories, illustrated by Phyllis Bray. London, Evans, 1945.

Evadne Price (1896–1985). British. Pseudonym for Helen Zenna Smith.

Jane the Patient, illustrated by Frank R. Grey. London, Hale, 1940.
Jane Gets Busy, illustrated by Frank R. Grey. London, Hale, 1940.
Jane at War, illustrated by Frank R. Grey, London, Hale, 1947.

Willard Price (1887–1983). American.

Willard Price was the doyen of modern American adventure stories. An explorer himself, he enjoyed a rip roaring life to rival that of any of his fictional heroes. His 'Adventure' books have proved perennially popular on both sides of the Atlantic. The Hunt brothers, sensible Hal and rash Roger, sons of an eminent zoologist, trek to all corners of the globe in search of animals and adventure.

Amazon Adventure, illustrated by Georg Hartmann. New York, Day, 1949; London, Cape, 1951.

Christine Pullein-Thompson (b. 1926). British.

Christine Pullein-Thompson, along with her twin, Diana, and other sibling, Josephine, was part of the family that has dominated the 'pony book' world in the second half of this century. The books, sniffed at for their slightness by some adults, have always proved immensely popular with the people who count: the young readers. They evoke perfectly the 'horse world', a fiercely competitive place where youngsters' personal faults are mitigated by their adoration of ponies. *It Began with Picotee* (1946) was a joint work by each of the young sisters and, even at this early stage, the narration of the highs and lows of horsemanship are deftly expressed. Although not as polished as their later work, the book possesses a rare immediacy, freshness and enthusiasm. The reason for this, and the particular popularity of the early writings of all three Pullein-Thompsons, is the extreme youth of the sisters at the time of publication. Unlike many authors who are writing in retrospect, the Pullein-Thompson's were still keen young pony enthusiasts when they were writing their story. This ardour is infectious. Appropriately, Rosemary Robertson's jacket illustration depicts three young girls and their steeds in profile. Christine, besides her many pony books, wrote non-pony stories for younger children.

It Began with Picotee, with Diana and Josephine Pullein-Thompson, illustrated by Rosemary Robinson. London, A. & C. Black, 1946.
We Rode to the Sea, illustrated by Mil Brown. London, Collins, 1948.
We Hunted Hounds, illustrated by Marcia Lane Foster. London, Collins, 1949.

Diana Pullein-Thompson (b. 1926). British.

Diana Pullein-Thompson is regarded by many as the finest writer of the Pullein-Thompson triumvirate. Her first solo work, *I Wanted a Pony* (1946), is still her most popular. It follows the usual pony book formula – the narrator can only look on as her wealthier friends and relatives enjoy riding, until her fortune changes – but is told with great zest and humour. The dust wrapper illustration by Anne Bullen shows Augusta Thornedyke riding Daybreak, the horse she was given, much to her delight, for preventing a farm from burning down. Like both her sisters, Diana Pullein-Thompson produced some worthy successors to Anna Sewell's *Black Beauty* (1877).

It Began with Picotee, with Christine and Josephine Pullein-Thompson, illustrated by Rosemary Robinson. London, A. & C. Black, 1946.
I Wanted a Pony, illustrated by Anne Bullen. London, Collins, 1946.
Three Ponies and Shannan, illustrated by Anne Bullen. London, Collins, 1947.
The Pennyfields, illustrated by Richard Kennedy, London, Collins, 1949.

A Pony to School, illustrated by Anne Bullen. London, Collins, 1950.

Josephine Pullein-Thompson (b. 1924). British.

Josephine Pullein-Thompson wrote to satisfy her pony readers' desire to read about the exploits of various fictional horses, but she also took great care to pass on useful information to her readers in the hope of making them better horsewomen. As well as imparting knowledge, she also created attractive characters and wrote snappy dialogue. All these elements make her required reading for the pony lover. Josephine Pullein-Thompson also wrote three murder mysteries, which showed off her narrative skill, as well as her passion for hunting and other traditional British rural activities.

It Began with Picotee, with Christine and Diana Pullein-Thompson, illustrated by Rosemary Robinson. London, A. & C. Black, 1946.
Six Ponies, illustrated by Anne Bullen. London, Collins, 1946.
I Had Two Ponies, illustrated by Anne Bullen. London, Collins, 1947.
Plenty of Ponies, illustrated by Anne Bullen. London, Collins, 1949.
Pony Club Team, illustrated by Sheila Rose. London, Collins, 1950.

Virginia Pye (b. 1901). British.

Virginia Pye's family adventure stories were a breath of fresh air during the dark war years and the difficult period afterwards. Pye's lively dialogue, characterisation of an unsubmissive girl, Johanna Allard, and creation of some hair-raising incidents made her somewhat ahead of her time. Her stories revolve around the Price family, Susan, Tom and Alan, who constantly find themselves involved in exciting escapades during the school holidays. Interestingly, these three siblings and their tomboy friend fell into their first adventure two years before Enid Blyton's comparable Famous Five initially appeared. *Half Term*

Mary Plain to the Rescue, illustrated by Irene
Williamson. London, Routledge, 1950.

Arthur Ransome (1884–1967). British.

The Big Six, illustrated by the author.
London, Cape, 1940; New York,
Macmillan, 1941.
Missee Lee, illustrated by the author. London,
Cape, 1941; New York, Macmillan, 1942.
*The Picts and the Martyrs; or, Not Welcome at
All*, illustrated by the author. London,
Cape, and New York, Macmillan, 1943.
Great Northern? London, Cape, 1947; New
York, Macmillan, 1948.

Frank Richards (1876–1961). British.
Pseudonym for Charles Harold St. John
Hamilton.
a.k.a. Hilda Richards.
a.k.a. Martin Clifford.

Holiday (1943) finds the Price clan in
Somerset, where they become involved with
mysterious events on the moors. Richard
Kennedy's wrapper shows images from the
holiday, including milking a cow, a comic
misadventure with a saucepan and a sinister
smoking pistol.

Red-Letter Holiday, illustrated by Gwen
Raverat. London, Faber, 1940.
Snow Bird. London, Faber, 1941.
Primrose Polly. London, Faber, 1942.
Half-term Holiday, illustrated by Richard
Kennedy. London, Faber, 1943.
The Prices Return. London, Faber, 1946.
The Stolen Jewels. London, Faber, 1948.

Gwynedd Rae (1892–1977). British.

Mary Plain in Trouble. London, Routledge,
1940.
Mary Plain in War-Time. London, Routledge,
1942; as *Mary Plain Lends a Paw*, 1949.
Mary Plain Big Adventure. London,
Routledge, 1944.
Mary Plain Home Again. London, Routledge,
1949.

When Frank Richards created Billy Bunter in
the early part of this century he devised not
merely a character but a national institution.
For William George Bunter, the most famous
schoolboy of all time, with his tuck poaching
and guzzling, sly deceit, whoppings and
characteristic vocabulary ('Yarooh!', 'I say, you
fellows', 'Beast!'), is one of the most
memorable figures in the corpus of English
literature. Richards began writing about Billy
Bunter's school, Greyfriars, when the boy's
paper *The Magnet* first appeared in 1908.
Readers soon became acquainted with the
Famous Five (not to be confused with Enid
Blyton's quintet), Harry Wharton the Remove
captain, cheery Bob Cherry, gruff
Yorkshireman Johnny Bull, amiable Frank
Nugent and the exotic Hurree Jamset Ram
Singh, the Nabob of Bhanipur, for whom all
things are 'terrific'. These enthusiastic and
athletic chaps have endless tea parties, sporting
occasions and trips out encroached upon by the
unwelcome presence of Bunter, the Owl of the
Remove. Holding sway in the Remove
classroom is gimlet-eyed Mr Quelch, a
'Rhadamanthus and Aeacus' with 'the stony
stare of the Gorgon'. A whole host of
supporting figures, including fearless and

thickheaded Horace Coker of the Fifth and lackadaisical Lord Mauleveror, helped Richards create a gallery of characters more memorable than that of any author since Dickens. *The Magnet* was a victim of paper rationing in 1940, but Bunter & Co. were given a new lease of life when the publisher Charles Skilton commissioned Richards to write a new series of stories to be published in book form. *Billy Bunter of Greyfriars School* appeared in 1947 and was a great success, introducing Bunter to a new generation of readers. This and the next fifteen volumes were illustrated by R.J. Macdonald but from *Backing up Billy Bunter* (1955) till the thirty-eighth and final book, all the artwork was by C.H. Chapman, whose name had been so closely associated with the original *Magnet* stories. Richards was especially famous for evoking the joviality that traditionally accompanies the Yuletide period, although he was equally good at conjuring up lazy summer days. *Billy Bunter's Christmas Party* (1949) tells what occurs when Billy Bunter 'stands' a Christmas celebration for the Famous Five and Squiff, an Australian junior, at his uncle's country pile, Tankerton Hall. However, all is not what it seems. Not only is the Hall a hotel, where Bunter's 'guests' are expected to 'cough up', but there is the ghost of Tankerton

Hall to deal with. It is the visage of this spectre that disturbs Bunter, who 'now filled an armchair, as amply as turkey, Christmas pudding and mince pies filled Bunter', during the scene depicted on the book's dust wrapper. Squiff goes to the window and there finds 'an old, old face – white as the snow that ridged the sill, half-hidden by a white beard and shaggy white eyebrows and tangled white hair that seemed to float in the wind. The face of an old, old man, a face of death that stared in from the December darkness.' As well as the Greyfriars yarns, one 'Bessie Bunter' book, *Bessie Bunter of Cliff House School* (1949), was published, tracing the misadventures of Billy's equally gluttonous sister. A wider success were the 'Tom Merry' books about the St. Jim's characters Richards (as Martin Clifford) had established in *The Gem*. As Billy Bunter dominates one series, so Arthur Augustus D'Arcy, the bemonocled 'swell of St. Jim's' ('Yaas, wathah', 'Bai Jove!'), is the character who demands most attention in these books. In *The Secret of the Study* (1949), regarded by many as the most sublimely funny school story of all time, D'Arcy finds himself under suspicion for the pilfering of a pound note. Gussy, although ostentatiously innocent, manages to dig himself deeper into trouble in characteristically comic fashion.

Schoolboy series (*The Secret of the School, The Black Sheep of Sparshott*), *First Man In, Looking after Lamb, The Hero of Sparshott, Pluck Will Tell*). London, Merrett, 6 vols., 1946.

Billy Bunter of Greyfriars School, illustrated by R.J. Macdonald. London, Skilton, 1947.

Mascot Schoolboy series (*Top Study at Topham, Bunny Binks on the War-Path, The Dandy of Topham, Sent to Coventry*). London, John Matthew, 4 vols., 1947.

Billy Bunter's Barring-Out, illustrated by R.J. Macdonald. London, Skilton, 1948.

Billy Bunter's Banknote, illustrated by R.J. Macdonald, London, Skilton, 1948.

Billy Bunter in Brazil, illustrated by R.J. Macdonald. London, Skilton, 1949.

Billy Bunter's Christmas Party, illustrated by R.J. Macdonald. London, Skilton, 1949.

Bessie Bunter of Cliff House School (as Hilda Richards), illustrated by R.J. Macdonald. London, Skilton, 1949.

Tom Merry and Co. of St. Jim's (as Martin
Clifford), illustrated by R.J Macdonald.
London, Mandeville, 1949.

The Secret of the Study (as Martin Clifford),
illustrated by R.J. Macdonald. London,
Mandeville, 1949.

Billy Bunter among the Cannibals, illustrated by
R.J. Macdonald. London, Skilton, 1950.

Billy Bunter's Benefit, illustrated by R.J.
Macdonald. London, Skilton, 1950.

Jack of All Trade, illustrated by J. Abbey.
London, Mandeville, 1950.

Rallying Round Gussy (as Martin Clifford),
illustrated by J. Abbey. London,
Mandeville, 1950.

Charles G(eorge) D(ouglas) Roberts
(1860–1943). Canadian.

Thirteen Bears, edited by Ethel Hume
Bennett, illustrated by John A. Hall.
Toronto, Ryerson Press, 1947.

Forest Folk, edited by Ethel Hume Bennett,
illustrated by John A. Hall. Toronto,
Ryerson Press, 1949.

Diana Ross (b. 1910). British.

Diana Ross delighted readers with her gentle
fantasies about everyday objects that do
remarkable things. Her Little Red Engine
puffed his way through his first adventure
some years before Awdry's Thomas
appeared, and all her stories possess a rare
streak of originality. Ross illustrated a
number of her books under the pseudonym
Gri. *Whoo, Whoo, The Wind Blew* (1946)
takes a simple concept and transforms it into
a delightfully whacky story. Whoo Whoo the
wind, whose power is shown on Leslie
Wood's wrapper, visits the homes of an
alderman, a pretty little girl, a tough boy, a
fat old dowager and a corporation dustman.
As a memento of his visit, Whoo Whoo
picks up an item of clothing from each
home.

The Story of the Beetle Who Lived Alone,
illustrated by Margaret Kaye. London,
Faber, 1941.

Uncle Anty's Album, with Antony Denney.
London, Faber, 1942.

The Golden Hen and Other Stories, illustrated
by Gri. London, Faber, 1942.

The Little Red Engine Gets a Name, illustrated by George Lewitt-Him. London, Faber, 1942.

The Wild Cherry, illustrated by Gri. London, Faber, 1943.

Nursery Tales, illustrated by Nancy Innes. London, Faber, 1944.

The Story of the Little Red Engine, illustrated by Leslie Wood. London, Faber, 1945.

The Story of Louisa, illustrated by Margaret Kaye. London, Penguin, 1945.

The Little Red Engine Goes to Market, illustrated by Leslie Wood. London, Faber,1946.

Whoo, Whoo, The Wind Blew, illustrated by Leslie Wood. London, Faber, 1946.

Philip Rush (b. 1908). British.

Philip Rush preserved the grand tradition of the historical novel for children at a time when it was in danger of extinction. Unlike some of the earlier purveyors of this type of fiction, Rush's intention was to instruct the young about life in the past, not indoctrinate them with a moral code. Consequently, war is not glamorised, and the suffering and want of many in the past is elucidated. Rush was

nevertheless a masterful storyteller, who delivers the sort of action-packed narrative the young reader demands. An exciting sea battle between an English ship and a Spanish galleon in the Gulf of Panama is the subject of Richard Ogle's colourful 'wraparound' dust wrapper for *He Sailed with Dampier* (1947). William Dampier, later a well-known explorer, is caught up in the battle in a long boat, and is shown firing at the Spanish admiral's vessel.

He Sailed with Dampier, illustrated by Richard Ogle. London, Boardman, 1947.

Malcolm Saville (1901–82). British.

Malcolm Saville wrote eight series of books for children of all ages, but by far the most enduring of them has been the 'Lone Pine' series. These twenty books, published between 1943 and 1978, chart the exploits of the Lone Pine Club, a group of children who make up a clandestine society at the foot of a solitary pine tree on the side of the Long Mynd in Shropshire. The original club consists of David, Richard, and Mary Morton, Petronella (Peter) Stirling and Tom Ingles. In *Mystery at Witchend* (1943) they thwart the villainous scheme of some covert Nazi spies. As the club is constantly invigorated by new adventures, so the stories retain vitality by a steady flow of fresh blood into the group. Mercurial Jenny Harman and donnish John Warrender were characters who entered the fray at a later date, but who were immediately popular with readers. Besides his well-paced and exciting plots, Saville is also famous for his descriptive passages. Indeed, he wrote several factual volumes on the English countryside, and this deep knowledge and love of the landscape pervades his fiction. The 'Lone Piners' enjoy adventures in all four corners of the country. Consequently, most readers would be able to recognise, and even visit, the setting of at least one of the stories. Bertram Prance's dust wrapper illustration for *Seven White Gates* (1944) shows members of the Lone Pine Club in a typically perilous position. Tom and Petronella swing precariously on the iron cable car above Black

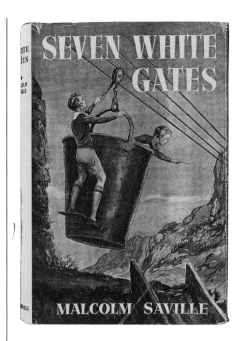

Dingle in Shropshire, whilst on the path towards solving the mystery of the Seven White Gates.

Mystery at Witchend, illustrated by G.E. Breary. London, Newnes, 1943; as *Spy in the Hills*, New York, Farrar and Rinehart, 1945.

Seven White Gates, illustrated by Bertram Prance. London, Newnes, 1944.

The Gay Dolphin Adventure, illustrated by Bertram Prance. London, Newnes, 1945.

Trouble at Townsend, illustrated by Lunt Roberts. London, Transatlantic Arts, 1945.

The Secret of Grey Walls, illustrated by Bertram Prance. London, Newnes, 1947.

The Riddle of the Painted Box, illustrated by Lunt Roberts. London, Transatlantic Arts, 1947.

Redshank's Warning, illustrated by Lunt Roberts. London, Lutterworth Press, 1948.

Two Fair Plaits, illustrated by Lunt Roberts. London, Lutterworth Press, 1948.

Lone Pine Five, illustrated by Bertram Prance. London, Newnes, 1949.

Strangers at Snowfell, illustrated by Wynne. London, Lutterworth Press, 1949.

The Master of Maryknoll, illustrated by Alice Bush. London, Evans, 1950.

The Sign of the Alpine Rose, illustrated by Wynne. London, Lutterworth press, 1950.

The Flying Fish Adventure, illustrated by Lunt Roberts. London, Murray, 1950.

Ruth Sawyer (1880–1970). American.

The Year of Jubilo, illustrated by Edward Shenton. New York, Viking Press, 1940; as *Lucinda's Year of Jubilo*, London, Bodley Head, 1965.

The Least One, illustrated by Leo Politi. New York, Viking Press, 1941.

The Christmas Anna Angel, illustrated by Kate Seredy. New York, Viking Press, 1944; London, Cassell, 1948.

Old Con and Patrick, illustrated by Cathal O'Toole. New York, Viking Press, 1946.

The Little Red Horse, illustrated by Jay Hyde Barnum. New York, Viking Press, 1950.

Ian Serraillier (b. 1912). British.

Ian Serraillier's main work as a writer was as a reteller of old tales, whether they be set in Ancient Greece, Dark Age Scandinavia or Mediaeval Sherwood Forest. However, he also wrote eight thrillers, which, in the main,

involve perilous adventures in war torn Europe. *Flight to Adventure* (1947) follows the fortunes of young David, after he and his Uncle Bill have to make a forced landing in an Alpine valley. C. Walter Hodges's dust wrapper artwork captures the moment when the pair begin their descent, after a problem arises with the petrol flow in their aeroplane. This setback leads to a whole series of Swiss adventures for David and the new friends he makes *en route*.

They Raced for Treasure, illustrated by C. Walter Hodges. London, Cape, 1946.
Flight to Adventure, illustrated by C. Walter Hodges. London, Cape, 1947.
Captain Bounsaboard and the Pirates, illustrated by Michael Bartlett and Arline Braybrooke. London, Cape, 1949.
There's No Escape, illustrated by C. Walter Hodges. London, Cape, 1950; New York, Scholastic, 1973.

David Severn (b. 1918). British.
Pseudonym for David Storr Unwin.

David Severn's later stories often involved magic and the supernatural, and found the heroes in weird and wonderful places and predicaments. However, his early books, for which he is best known, are conventional family adventure stories. They contain well-knit plots, dynamic dialogue and some loving descriptions of the English countryside and rural lore. In *Rick Afire!* (1942), the Longmore and Sanville children are staying at White House Farm, when all sorts of mysterious things start happening locally. Joan Kiddell-Monroe's marvellously evocative dust-wrapper design shows Derek and Diana Longmore, accompanied by twins Pamela and Brian Sanville, running down the lane to see the rick fire.

Rick Afire!, illustrated by Joan Kiddell-Monroe. London, Lane, 1942.
A Cabin for Crusoe, illustrated by Joan Kiddell-Monroe. London, Lane, 1943; Boston, Houghton Mifflin, 1946.
Waggon for Five, illustrated by Joan Kiddell-Monroe. London, Lane, 1944; Boston, Houghton Mifflin, 1947.
Hermit in the Hills, illustrated by Joan Kiddell-Monroe. London, Lane, 1945.
Forest Holiday, illustrated by Joan Kiddell-Monroe. London, Lane, 1946.
Ponies and Poachers, illustrated by Joan Kiddell-Monroe. London, Lane, 1947.
Bill Badger and the Pine Martens [Bathing Pool, Buried Treasure], illustrated by Geoffrey Higham. London, Lane, 3 vols., 1947–50.
Wily Fox and the Baby Show [Christmas Party, Missing Fire-works], illustrated by Geoffrey Higham. London, Lane, 3 vols., 1947–50.
The Cruise of the "Maiden Castle", illustrated by Joan Kiddell-Monroe. London, Lane, 1948; New York, Macmillan, 1949.
Treasure for Three, illustrated by Joan Kiddell-Monroe. London, Lane, 1949; New York, Macmillan, 1950.
Dream Gold, illustrated by A.K. Lee. London, Lane, 1949; New York, Viking Press, 1952.

Helen Sewell (1896–1957). American.

Illustrated by the author.

Jimmy and Jemima. New York, Macmillan, 1940.

Peggy and the Pup. New York and London, Oxford University Press, 1941.

Birthdays for Robin. New York, Macmillan, 1943; London, Hale, 1947.

Belinda the Mouse. New York and London, Oxford University Press, 1944.

Three Tall Tales, with Elena Eleska. New York, Macmillan, 1947.

C(icely) Fox Smith (1882–1954). British.

The Ship Aground, illustrated by C. Walter Hodges. London and New York, Oxford University Press, 1940.

Painted Ports, illustrated by C. Walter Hodges. London and New York, Oxford University Press, 1948.

Caroline Dale Snedeker (1871–1956). American.

The White Isle, illustrated by Fritz Kredel. New York, Doubleday, 1940.

Luke's Quest, illustrated by Nora S. Unwin. New York, Doubleday, 1947.

Phil(ip) Stong (1899–1957). American.

Captain Kidd's Cow. New York, Dodd Mead, 1941.

Way Down Cellar. New York, Dodd Mead, 1942.

Missouri Canary. New York, Dodd Mead, 1943.

Censored, The Goat. New York, Dodd Mead, 1945.

Positive Pete! New York. Dodd Mead, 1947.

The Prince and the Porker. New York, Dodd Mead, 1950.

Noel Streatfeild (1895–1986). British.

The House in Cornwall, illustrated by D.L. Mays. London, Dent, 1940; as *The Secret of the Lodge*, New York, Random House, 1940.

The Children of Primrose Lane, illustrated by Marcia Lane Foster. London, Dent, 1941; as *The Stranger in Primrose Lane*, New York, Random House, 1941.

Harlequinade, illustrated by Clarke Hutton. London, Chatto & Windus, 1943.

Curtain Up, illustrated by D.L. Mays. London, Dent, 1944; as *Theater Shoes; or, Other People's Shoes*, New York, Random House, 1945.

Party Frock, illustrated by Anna Zinkeisen. London, Collins, 1946; as *Party Shoes*, New York, Random House, 1947.

The Painted Garden, illustrated by Ley Kenyon. London, Collins, 1949; as *Movie Shoes*, New York, Random House, 1949.

Osbert, illustrated by Susanne Suba. Chicago, Rand McNally, 1950.

L(eonard) A(lfred) G(eorge) Strong (1896–1958). British.

They Went to the Island, illustrated by Rowland Hilder. London, Dent, 1940.

Wrong Foot Foremost, illustrated by E.P.L. London, Pitman,1940.

House in Disorder, illustrated by C. Morse. London, Lutterworth Press, 1941.

Sink or Swim. London, Lutterworth Press, 1945.

Donald Suddaby (1900–64). British. **a.k.a. Alan Griff.**

Donald Suddaby's *New Tales of Robin Hood* (1950) was the first of a number of swashbuckling yarns that this author wrote about the outlaw of Sherwood Forest. These stories contain an admirable amount of excitement for the young reader, but are very different from the fantasy and science fiction tales that made up the bulk of Suddaby's output. In later years he had his heroes blasting off to all parts of the solar system. In *Lost Men In the Grass* (1940), Suddaby shrinks his protagonists to the size of insects and then pits them against other inhabitants of the garden.

Lost Men in the Grass (as Alan Griff), illustrated by Eric Newton. London, Oxford University Press, 1940.

Masterless Swords: Variations on a Theme.
London, Laurie, 1947.
New Tales of Robin Hood, illustrated by T.
Heath Robinson. London, Blackie, 1950.
The Star Raiders, illustrated by Carl Haworth.
London, Oxford University Press, 1950.

Ethel Talbot. British.

The Warringtons in War-Time, illustrated by
E.E. Brier. London, Nelson, 1940.
Gerda Gets There. London, Ward Lock,
1940.
Jane Steps Out. London, Ward Lock, 1948.

Barbara Euphan Todd (1897–1976).
British.
a.k.a. Euphan.

The House That Ran Behind, with Esther
Boumphrey. London, Muller, 1943.
*Worzel Gummidge, The Scarecrow of
Scatterbrook Farm* (from *Worzel
Gummidge; or, The Scarecrow of
Scatterbrook* and *Worzel Gummidge Again*),
illustrated by Ursula Koering. New
York, Putnam, 1947.
Worzel Gummidge and Saucy Nancy, illustrated
by Will Nickless. London, Hollis and
Carter, 1947.
Worzel Gummidge Takes a Holiday, illustrated
by Will Nickless. London, Hollis and
Carter, 1949.
Aloysius Let Loose (as Euphan) with Klaxon
(pseudonym for John Graham Bower),
illustrated by A.E. Batchelor. London,
Collins, 1950.

H(erbert) E(atton) Todd (1908–88).
British.

H.E. Todd created an immensely popular
character in Bobby Brewster, a young lad with
whom many children are able to relate. Bobby
manages to cause humorous havoc in the most
everyday situations. However, even the most
ridiculous happenings have a ring of truth
about them. The very first book in the series,
Bobby Brewster and the Winkers' Club (1949), is

perhaps the most far-fetched, but reflects the
boundless imagination of the three-year-old
child. Bobby learns to wink and so becomes a
member of the Winkers' Club. Bryan Ward's
illustration for the brown and yellow wrapper
shows Bobby with the animal members of the
club, with whom he becomes friendly.

Bobby Brewster and the Winkers' Club,
illustrated by Bryan Ward. Leicester,
Ward, 1949.

J(ohn) R(onald) R(euel) Tolkien
(1892–1973). British.

J.R.R. Tolkien's *Farmer Giles of Ham* (1949),
published in a decade that was largely taken up
by the author's composition of *The Lord of the
Rings* (1954–55), is a slight but diverting
piece. It tells the quaint story of Farmer Giles's
defiance of the treasure-obsessed 'great
worm', Chrysophylax ('Guardian of gold' in
Greek). Pauline Baynes's delightful dust-
wrapper illustration, although having no
direct connection with the story of the heroic
dragon-fighting farmer, reflects the book's
fantastic and chivalric tone.

Farmer Giles of Ham, illustrated by Pauline
Baynes. London, Allen and Unwin, 1949;
Boston, Houghton Mifflin, 1950.

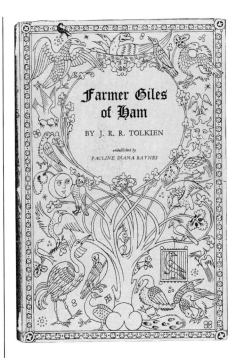

Mary Tourtel (1874–1948). British.

Illustrated by the author.

Rupert Again. London, Sampson Low, 1940.

Katherine Tozer (b. 1905). British.

Illustrated by the author.

Noah: The Story of Another Ark. London, Murray, 1940.
Adventures of Alfie. London, Murray, 1941.
Mumfie Marches On. London, Murray, 1942.
Mumfie's Picture Book, edited by Eiluned Lewis. London, Murray, 1947.

P(amela) L(yndon) Travers (1899–1996). British.

Happy Ever After, illustrated by Mary Shepard. Privately printed, 1940.
I Go by Sea, I Go by Land, illustrated by Gertrude Hermes. London, Davies, and New York, Harper, 1941.
Mary Poppins Opens the Door, illustrated by

Mary Shepard and Agnes Sims. New York, Reynal, 1943; London, Davies, 1944.

Geoffrey Trease (1909–98). British.

Geoffrey Trease has been the leading exponent of historical fiction for children during the last sixty years. His stories combine a remarkable degree of historical veracity, packaged in such a way as never to allow tedium, with an often breathtaking pace of narrative and a generous amount of thrills and spills. For instance, the first four chapters of *The Hills of Varna* (1948) send Alan Drayton away from the Cambridge of 1509, after a violent brawl in an inn and a meeting with Erasmus, across Europe to the house of Aldus Manutius, the renowned printer, in Venice and into the hands of the villainous Duke of Molfetta and his dagger-toting confederates. Alan is searching for the sole manuscript of a Greek play, long thought lost to the world. Uncovering a new work is every palaeographer's dream: 'There is always the chance that some of them may be found even now, hidden away and neglected in some corner – that of Sophocles' hundred lost plays

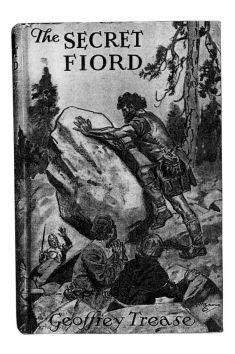

we may yet find some to add to the mere seven we know.' Unfortunately for Alan, the Duke is determined to get his hands on the manuscript at all costs, and Alan is dogged by his associates during his journey over the Adriatic to Turkey. *The Secret Fiord* (1949), a tale of adventure in Norway, is a very different book, but just as exciting. The dustwrapper illustration is by the redoubtable H.M. Brock and shows the crucial scene in which Eric, Roger and Jillian (not pictured) escape the clutches of the murderous Müllar and his men. They are saved by the timely intervention of the fearsome Troll King (actually Roger and Jillian's father).

Cue for Treason, illustrated by Beatrice Goldsmith. Oxford, Blackwell, 1940; New York, Vanguard Press, 1941.

The Running of the Deer, illustrated by W. Lindsay Cable. London, Harrap, 1941.

The Grey Adventurer, illustrated by Beatrice Goldsmith. Oxford, Blackwell, 1942.

Black Night, Red Morning, illustrated by Donia Nachsen. Oxford, Blackwell, 1944.

Army Without Banners. London, Fore, 1945.

Trumpets in the West, illustrated by Alan Blyth. Oxford, Blackwell, and New York, Harcourt Brace, 1947.

Silver Guard, illustrated by Alan Blyth. Oxford, Blackwell, 1948.

The Hills of Varna, illustrated by Treyer Evans. London, Macmillan, 1948; as *Shadow of the Hawk*, New York, Harcourt Brace, 1949.

The Mystery of Moorside Farm, illustrated by Alan Blyth. Oxford, Blackwell, 1949.

No Boats on Bannermere, illustrated by Richard Kennedy. London, Heinemann, 1949; New York, Norton, 1965.

The Secret Fiord, illustrated by H.M. Brock, London, Macmillan, 1949; New York, Harcourt Brace, 1950.

Under Black Banner, illustrated by Richard Kennedy. London, Heinemann, 1950.

Alison Uttley (1884–1976). British.

Although Little Grey Rabbit was Alison Uttley's most enduring character, she also scored a significant success with the 'Sam Pig'

series in the early 1940s. Stout-hearted Sam Pig falls into all sorts of crack(l)ing adventures in the thirteen collections of short stories about his escapades, many of which reached a wider audience through serialisation on BBC's *Children's Hour*. Sam and his siblings, Ann, Bill and Tom, live in a cosy cottage in the midst of idyllic countryside, and are looked after by Brock, a superficially grumpy badger who actually possesses a heart of gold.

The dust wrapper illustration for *Sam Pig Goes to Market* (1941) is by A.E. Kennedy and is taken from the second story in the collection, 'Whistle for the Wind'. Whilst spring-cleaning the cottage, Sam Pig finds the wind's whistle. Later, when lost, Sam remembers his find:

> 'I will blow just a tiny wee blast' said Sam, and he put the whistle to his lips and blew very gently. Although he scarcely breathed into it, the whistle seemed to spring to life. A shrill note came from it, changing to a higher sound, wailing and calling, reaching down to the limits of earth and up to the stars.

The West Wind arrives, and soon puts Sam Pig back on the right tracks.

Moldy Warp, The Mole, illustrated by Margaret Tempest. London, Collins, 1940.

The Adventures of Sam Pig, illustrated by Francis Gower. London, Faber, 1940.

Sam Pig Goes to Market, illustrated by A.E. Kennedy. London, Faber, 1941.

Six Tales of Brock the Badger, illustrated by Alec Buckels and Francis Gower. London, Faber, 1941.

Six Tales of Sam Pig, illustrated by Alec Buckels and Francis Gower. London, Faber, 1941.

Six Tales of the Four Pigs, illustrated by Alec Buckels. London, Faber, 1941.

Ten Tales of Tim Rabbit, illustrated by Alec Buckels and Francis Gower. London, Faber, 1941.

Hare Joins the Home Guard, illustrated by Margaret Tempest. London, Collins, 1942.

ALISON UTTLEY

Little Grey Rabbit's Washing-Day, illustrated by Margaret Tempest. London, Collins, 1942.

Nine Starlight Tales, illustrated by Irene Hawkins. London, Faber, 1942.

Sam Pig and Sally, illustrated by A.E. Kennedy. London, Faber, 1942.

Cuckoo Cherry-Tree, illustrated by Irene Hawkins. London, Faber, 1943.

Sam Pig at the Circus, illustrated by A.E. Kennedy. London, Faber, 1943.

Water-Rat's Picnic, illustrated by Margaret Tempest. London, Collins, 1943.

Little Grey Rabbit's Birthday, illustrated by Margaret Tempest. London, Collins, 1944.

The Spice Woman's Basket and Other Tales, illustrated by Irene Hawkins. London, Faber, 1944.

Mrs. Nimble and Mr. Bumble. illustrated by Horace Knowles. London, James, 1944.

Some Moonshine Tales, illustrated by Sarah Nechamkin. London, Faber, 1945.

The Adventures of Tim Rabbit, illustrated by A.E. Kennedy. London, Faber, 1945.

The Weather Cock and Other Stories, illustrated by Nancy Innes. London, Faber, 1945.

The Speckledy Hen, illustrated by Margaret Tempest. London, Faber, 1946.

Little Grey Rabbit and the Weasels, illustrated by Margaret Tempest. London, Collins, 1947.

Grey Rabbit and the Wandering Hedgehog, illustrated by Margaret Tempest. London, Collins, 1948.

John Barleycorn: Twelve Tales of Fairy and Magic, illustrated by Philip Hepworth. London, Faber, 1948.

Sam Pig in Trouble, illustrated by A.E. Kennedy. London, Faber, 1948.

The Cobbler's Shop and Other Tales, illustrated by Irene Hawkins. London, Faber, 1950.

Macduff, illustrated by A.E. Kennedy. London, Faber, 1950.

Little Grey Rabbit Makes Lace, illustrated by Margaret Tempest. London, Collins, 1950.

Snug and Serena Meet a Queen, illustrated by Katherine Wigglesworth. London, Heinemann, 1950.

Snug and Serena Pick Cowslips, illustrated by Katherine Wigglesworth. London, Heinemann, 1950.

Elfrida Vipont (1902–92). British. **a.k.a. Charles Vipont.**

Elfrida Vipont's most famous book, *The Lark in the Morn* (1948), tells of how young Kit Haverard, who comes from a well-known musical Quaker family, discovers, against expectations, that she too has a great natural gift for music. "'She never told me she could sing," growled Sir Geoffrey. "Whoever heard of a Quaker who could sing, anyhow?'" Kit is taught by gentle Papa Andreas how best to convey a song's immense emotion and after her performance at the Leavers' Concert for Heryot School, 'The applause thundered out, and the visitors clapped and cheered.' *The Lark on the Wing* (1950) continues Kit's story as she decides to build a singing career. These delightful and thought-provoking books have been a perennial favourite with the young girls at whom they were aimed.

The Lark in the Morn, illustrated by T.R. Freeman. London, Oxford University Press, 1948; Indianapolis, Bobbs Merrill, 1951.

The Lark on the Wing, illustrated by T.R. Freeman. London, Oxford University Press, 1950; Indianapolis, Bobbs Merrill, 1951.

Percy F(rancis) Westerman (1876–1959). British.
a.k.a. P.F. Westerman.
a.k.a. P. Westerman.

At Grips with the Swastika, illustrated by Leo Bates. London, Blackie, 1940.
Eagles' Talons, illustrated by M. Mackinlay. London, Blackie, 1940.
In Dangerous Waters, illustrated by D.L. Mays. London, Blackie, 1940.
Standish Pulls it Off, illustrated by W. Edward Wigfull. London, Blackie, 1940.
When the Allies Swept the Seas, illustrated by J.C.B. Knight. London, Blackie, 1940.
The War – And Alan Carr, illustrated by E. Boye Uden. London, Blackie, 1940.
War Cargo. London, Blackie, 1941.
Sea Scouts at Dunkirk. London, Blackie, 1941.
Standish Holds On. London, Blackie, 1941.
Fighting for Freedom. London, Blackie, 1941.
Alan Carr in the Near East. London, Blackie, 1942.
Destroyer's Luck. London, Blackie, 1942.
On Guard for England, illustrated by J.C.B. Knight. London, Blackie, 1942.
Secret Flight. London, Blackie, 1942.
With the Commandoes, illustrated by S. van Abbé. London, Blackie, 1943.
Sub-Lieutenant John Cloche, illustrated by H. Pym. London, Blackie, 1943.
Alan Carr in Command, illustrated by Terence Cuneo. London, Blackie, 1943.
Alan Carr in the Arctic, illustrated by E. Boye Uden. London, Blackie, 1943.
Combined Operations, illustrated by S. van Abbé. London, Blackie, 1944.
Engage the Enemy Closely, illustrated by Terence Cuneo. London, Blackie, 1944.
Secret Convoy, illustrated by Terence Cuneo. London, Blackie, 1944.
One of the Many, illustrated by Ellis Silas. London, Blackie, 1945.
Operations Successfully Executed, illustrated by S. Drigin. London, Blackie, 1945.

By Luck and Pluck, illustrated by Terence Cuneo. London, Blackie, 1946.
Return to Base, illustrated by Leslie Wilcox. London, Blackie, 1946.
Squadron Leader, illustrated by Terence Cuneo. London, Blackie, 1946.
Unfettered Night, illustrated by S. Jezzard. London, Blackie, 1947.
Trapped in the Jungle, illustrated by A.S. Forrest. London, Blackie, 1947.
The Phantom Submarine, illustrated by J.C.B. Knight. London, Blackie, 1947.
The "Golden Gleaner", illustrated by M. Mackinlay. London, Blackie, 1948.
First Over, illustrated by Ellis Silas. London, Blackie, 1948.
Mystery of the Key, illustrated by Ellis Silas. London, Blackie, 1948.
Missing, Believed Lost, illustrated by Will Nickless. London, Blackie, 1949.
Contraband, illustrated by A. Barclay. London, Blackie, 1949.
Beyond the Burma Road, illustrated by Victor Bertoglio. London, Blackie, 1949.
Sabarinda Island, illustrated by A. Barclay. London, Blackie, 1950.
Mystery of Nix Hall, illustrated by D.C. Eyles. London, Blackie, 1950.
By Sea and Air, illustrated by Day. London, Blackie, 1950.
Desolation Island, illustrated by W. Gale. London, Blackie, 1950.

E(lwyn) B(rooks) White (1899–1985). American.

Stuart Little (1945), E.B. White's first book, is a strange, almost perverse, piece about a couple who beget a mouse-like creature rather than a human child. Stuart, as the beast is known, makes the most of his two-inch height to collect jewellery from otherwise unassailable places and falls in love with a bird. The greater part of the book is taken up with Stuart's unsuccessful search for his bird. White's most famous book, *Charlotte's Web* (1952), is the equally bizarre story of a pig, Wilbur, who has his fateful visit to the abattoir delayed by the trusty spider, Charlotte.

Stuart Little, illustrated by Garth Williams. New York, Harper, 1945; London, Hamish Hamilton, 1946.

T(erence) H(anbury) White (1906–64). British.

The Ill-Made Knight, illustrated by the author. New York, Putnam, 1940; London, Collins, 1941.
Mistress Masham's Repose, illustrated by Fritz Eichenberg. New York, Putnam, 1946; London, Cape, 1947.
The Elephant and the Kangaroo, illustrated by the author. New York, Putnam and London, Cape, 1948.

Laura Ingalls Wilder (1867–1957). American.

The Long Winter, illustrated by Helen Sewell and Mildred Boyle. New York, Harper, 1940; London, Lutterworth Press, 1962.
Little Town on the Prairie, illustrated by Helen Sewell and Mildred Boyle. New York, Harper, 1941; London, Lutterworth Press, 1963.
These Happy Golden Years, illustrated by Helen Sewell and Mildred Boyle. New York, Harper, 1943; London, Lutterworth Press, 1964.

Henry Williamson (1895–1977). British.

Scribbling Lark. London, Faber, 1949.

May Wynne (1875–1949). British. Pseudonym for Mabel Winifred Knowles.

The Coming of Verity, illustrated by J. Dewar Mills. London, Ward Lock, 1940.
Sadie Comes to School. London, Epworth Press, 1942; as *Sally Comes to School*, London, Ward Lock, 1949.
Little Brown Tala. London, Mellifont Press, 1944.
Brown Tala Finds Little Tulsi. London, Mellifont Press, 1945.
Little Brown Tala Stories, illustrated by Stanley Jackson. London, Harrap, 1947.
Patch the Piebald. Croydon, Surrey, Blue Book, 1947.
Playing the Game. Croydon, Surrey, Blue Book, 1947.
Snow Fairies. London, Mellifont Press, 1947.
Ginger Ellen, illustrated by Doreen Debenham. London, Nelson, 1947.
The Great Adventure. London, Ward Lock, 1948.
The Furry Fairies. London, Mellifont Press, 1949.